Other Kaplan Books on Business School Admissions

Business School Admissions Adviser
GRE & GMAT Math Workbook
MBA Part Time: An Insider's Guide
Yale Daily News *Guide to Fellowships and Grants*

GMAT*

Fifth Edition

By the Staff of Kaplan, Inc.

Simon & Schuster

NEW YORK · LONDON · SINGAPORE · SYDNEY · TORONTO

*GMAT is a registered trademark of the Graduate Management Admission Council, which is not affiliated with this product.

Kaplan Publishing
Published by Simon & Schuster
1230 Avenue of the Americas
New York, NY 10020

Contributing Editor: Albert Chen and Chip Hurlburt
Project Editor: Larissa Shmailo
Cover Design: Cheung Tai
Interior Page Production: Hugh Haggerty
Production Editor: Maude Spekes
Production Manager: Michael Shevlin
Editorial Coordinator: Dea Alessandro
Executive Editor: Del Franz

Special thanks to: Aaron Bacall, Bently Boyd, Dave Chipps, Laurel Douglas, Megan Duffy, Sara Pearl, Julie Schmidt, and Jeff White.

Manufactured in the United States of America
Published simultaneously in Canada

March 2001

10 9 8 7 6 5 4 3 2

ISSN: 1090-9019
ISBN: 0-7432-0528-6

Table of Contents

About the Authors..ix

Mapping Your Strategy...xi

A Special Note for International Students xiii

Part One: The GMAT
Chapter 1: Introduction to the GMAT...3
Chapter 2: Verbal Section Overview...15
Chapter 3: Critical Reasoning 19
Chapter 4: Sentence Correction...51
Chapter 5: Reading Comprehension...81
Chapter 6: Quantitative Section Overview...103
Chapter 7: Problem Solving..107
Chapter 8: Data Sufficiency..131
Chapter 9: Word Problems...163
Chapter 10: GMAT Math Reference..179
Chapter 11: Analytical Writing Assessment..207

Part Two: Taking Control of the Test
Chapter 12: Test Mentality...223
Chapter 13: Tips for the Final Week...229

Part Three: The Practice Test
The Practice Test for the GMAT..235
Practice Test Answer Key...274
Compute Your GMAT Practice Test Score 275

Part Four: Practice Test Explanations
Quantitative Section Explanations 281
Verbal Section Explanations 295

Part Five: Getting Into Business School
Chapter 14: Where to Apply 313
Chapter 15: When to Apply..323
Chapter 16: How to Apply..325

CD-ROM Installation and Technical Support...349

Dear Student:

For more than 60 years, Kaplan has been helping students meet their academic and admissions goals. More than three million students have passed through our doors, and as their evaluations of our courses have repeatedly shown, one thing stands out that sets Kaplan apart from the rest: our teachers.

We have long known that our outstanding teaching staff is Kaplan's most important asset. Throughout the years we have committed ourselves to finding expert, enthusiastic, and engaging teachers for every Kaplan course. That's why we interview only those candidates who scored high on the test they are to teach and from this pool select only the most promising candidates: individuals who are enthusiastic about helping students reach their goals. All prospective teachers complete an intensive Kaplan training, and from ongoing observations, evaluations, and reviews of student feedback, they get even better as they teach.

The knowledge and experience that our teachers have acquired from working with students like you—about standardized tests, study habits, test panic, and more—is something we'd like to share outside of the classroom. We're pleased to incorporate the wisdom, tips, and inspiration of Kaplan's teachers in this test-prep guide so that you may benefit from the best we have to offer. I hope you find their expertise useful in your quest for academic success. If you decide you'd also like to work with our first-rate instructors in person, give us a call at (800) KAP-TEST.

Sincerely,

Jonathan Grayer
President and CEO, Kaplan, Inc.

About the Authors

Eric Goodman has been teaching the Kaplan GMAT, GRE, and LSAT courses for over a decade and also works for Kaplan as a product consultant. When not teaching or writing for Kaplan, Eric works as a composer and musician in New York City.

Ingrid Multhopp is Senior Curriculum Manager for Kaplan's Graduate Programs, where she has worked extensively on Kaplan's GMAT, GRE, and LSAT courses, researching changes to the tests and developing effective and innovative test-taking strategies. Before writing curriculum for Kaplan, she spent nine years teaching thousands of students how to score high on the GMAT and get into the business schools of their choice. She has taken the GMAT many times and always scored in the ninety-ninth percentile. She graduated from the University of Chicago with a B.A. in English Language and Literature.

David Stuart, a Senior Instructional Designer for Kaplan, graduated from the University of Adelaide with a B.S. in geophysics. He worked as an exploration seismologist and wellsite geologist in oil fields worldwide. Since joining Kaplan he has focused his energies on analyzing the GMAT, GRE, and SAT, and on designing the best curriculum to tackle these tests. He has developed techniques so effective that they have forced the test makers to withdraw some question types entirely.

Bob Verini is currently Director of Academic Excellence for the western United States and a national training associate for Kaplan, Inc. Since joining Kaplan in 1980, Bob has taught thousands of students how to ace the GMAT. He also trains new Kaplan instructors nationally, works in course development, and serves as academic counselor in Kaplan's one-on-one Admissions Consulting program. He holds a B.A. from SUNY/Albany and an M.F.A. from Indiana University. In his spare time, Bob is a writer, actor, and director, with several films and extensive stage experience to his credit. He is also one of the biggest money winners in the history of the game show *Jeopardy*™ and was a winner of the 1987 Tournament of Champions.

Mapping Your Strategy: A Study Plan for the GMAT

This book and the CD-ROM that accompanies it contain the best preparation you can get for the computer adaptive GMAT. No other test-preparation company knows the GMAT like Kaplan. The cutting-edge strategies contained in this book and on the CD-ROM will help you maximize your performance on the GMAT.

For technical information on how to use the CD-ROM, turn to the back of this book. What follows is a suggested study plan for how to get the most out of the content of this GMAT multimedia package.

Step One: Familiarize Yourself with the GMAT

Kaplan's live GMAT course has been the industry standard for decades. We've distilled the main techniques and approaches from our course for this book and CD-ROM. We'll introduce you to the mysteries of the GMAT and show you how to make the computer-adaptive test format work for you. You'll also find important points regarding the GMAT and invaluable Kaplan teacher advice in easy-to-read sidebars throughout the book.

Step Two: Practice Each Type of Question

We'll give you specific methods and strategies for every kind of question you're likely to see on the GMAT: Critical Reasoning, Sentence Correction, Reading Comprehension, Problem Solving, and Data Sufficiency. We also have tips to help you with the essay portion of the GMAT, the Analytical Writing Assessment.

Step Three: Assess Your Strengths and Weaknesses

To find out where you need to concentrate your study efforts, take the Diagnostic Test on the CD-ROM. The Practice Test included in this book has scoring information, so you can get even more feedback on how you're doing.

Step Four: Review to Shore Up Weak Points

The book and the CD-ROM make it easy to review math content, grammar topics, and any other test subject you need more help with. Use the reference material in the book and on the CD-ROM to sharpen your skills.

Step Five: Take a Simulated GMAT on CD-ROM—and Take It Again

Use this simulated GMAT as a test run for the real thing. Like the actual GMAT, Kaplan's practice GMAT selects questions based on your performance, drawing from a large pool of items. You can take Kaplan's practice GMAT up to a dozen times without seeing a question repeated. So you have plenty of chances to practice taking the GMAT.

Step Six: Take Control of the Test

Performing your best on the GMAT means developing "test mentality." You need to be cool, calm, and collected in order to put all you've learned into practice when it counts. Read the "Test Mentality" and "Tips for the Final Week" chapters of this book to make sure you're in top shape on Test Day.

Special Bonus: The "Getting into Business School" Section

Sure, your GMAT performance is a very important criterion in your application, so the bulk of this book is devoted to test prep. But business schools base their admissions decisions on far more than just the GMAT. So, to give you the very best odds, we provide expert advice to lead you through the parts of the application process before and beyond the GMAT. This section will give you an overview of the entire application process. We'll outline a plan to make your application as strong as it can be. We've also included checklists and schedules to keep you on track.

A Special Note for International Students

The M.B.A. (Master of Business Administration) has become a degree of choice for businesspersons around the globe. Variations of U.S.-style M.B.A. programs exist in Asia, Europe, and the Americas. In recent years, hundreds of thousands of international students have studied business and management in the United States.

As the United States increases its participation in the global economy, U.S. business schools are reaching out to attract exceptional international candidates into their graduate programs. However, competition for admission to prestigious programs is heavy and international students need to plan carefully if they wish to enter a top U.S. graduate management program.

If you are not from the United States, but are considering attending a graduate management program at a university in the United States, here is what you'll need to get started.

- If English is not your first language, start there. You will probably need to take the Test of English as a Foreign Language (TOEFL) or show some other evidence that your proficient in English prior to gaining admission to a graduate program in business. Some graduate business schools now require a minimum TOEFL score of 550 (213 on the computer-based TOEFL), while others will require a minimum of 600 (250 on the computer-based TOEFL). The ability to communicate in English, both verbally and in writing, is extremely important to your success in an American M.B.A. program.

- You may also need to take the GMAT (Graduate Management Admissions Test). Some graduate business programs may require you to take the GRE (Graduate Record Examination) as well.

- Since admission to many graduate business programs is quite competitive, you may wish to select three or four programs you would like to attend and complete applications for each program.

- Select a program that meets your current or future employment needs, rather than simply a program with a big name. For example, if you hope to work in the hotel and tourism industry, make sure the program you choose specializes in that distinct area.

- You need to begin the application process at least a year in advance.

Be aware that many programs only offer August or September start dates. Find out application deadlines and plan accordingly.

• Finally, you will need to obtain an 1-20 Certificate of Eligibility from the school you plan to attend if you intend to apply for an F-1 Student Visa to study in the United States.

Kaplan International Programs

If you need more help with the complex process of business school admissions, assistance preparing for the TOEFL or GMAT, or help improving your English skills in general, you may be interested in Kaplan's programs for international students.

Kaplan International Programs were designed to help students and professionals from outside the United States meet their educational and career goals. At locations throughout the United States, international students take advantage of Kaplan's programs to help them improve their academic and conversational English skills, raise their scores on the TOEFL, GMAT, and other standardized exams, and gain admission to the schools of their choice. Our staff and instructors give international students the individualized instruction they need to succeed. Here is a brief description of some of Kaplan's programs for International Students:

General Intensive English
Kaplan's General Intensive English classes are designed to help you improve your skills in all areas of English and to increase your fluency in spoken and written English. Classes are available for beginning to advanced students, and the average class size is 12 students.

English for TOEFL and University Preparation
This course provides you with the skills you need to improve your TOEFL score and succeed in an American university or graduate program. It includes advanced reading, writing, listening, grammar and conversational English, plus university admissions counseling. You will also receive training for the TOEFL using Kaplan's exclusive computer-based practice materials.

English and GMAT
This course includes a combination of English instruction and GMAT test preparation. Our English and GMAT course is for students who need to boost their English skills while preparing for the GMAT and graduate business school.

GMAT Test Preparation Course

The Graduate Management Admissions Test (GMAT) is required for admission to many graduate programs in business in the United States. Hundreds of thousands of American students have taken this course to prepare for the GMAT. This course includes the skills you need to succeed on each section of the GMAT, as well as access to Kaplan's exclusive computer-based practice materials.

Other Kaplan Programs

Since 1938, more than 3 million students have come to Kaplan to advance their studies, prepare for entry to American universities, and further their careers. In addition to the above programs, Kaplan offers courses to prepare for the SAT, GRE, LSAT, MCAT, DAT, USMLE, NCLEX, and other standardized exams at locations throughout the United States.

Applying to Kaplan International Programs

To get more information, or to apply for admission to any of Kaplan's programs for international students and professionals, contact us at:

Kaplan International Programs
370 Seventh Avenue
New York, NY 10001 USA
Telephone: (212) 492-5990
Fax: (917) 339-7505
E-mail: world@kaplan.com
Web: www.kaptest.com

- Kaplan is authorized under federal law to enroll nonimmigrant alien students.
- Kaplan is authorized to issue Form IAP-66 needed for a J-1 (Exchange Visitor) visa.
- Kaplan is accredited by ACCET (Accrediting Council for Continuing Education and Training).
- Test names are registered trademarks of their respective owners.

Part One

The GMAT

CHAPTER ONE

Introduction to the GMAT

HIGHLIGHTS

- Find out what's on the GMAT
- Learn how the GMAT's format works and how it's scored
- Navigate the GMAT: Computer basics
- Pros and cons of the computer-adaptive test

Let's start with the basics: The GMAT is, among other things, an endurance test. The GMAT consists of 150 minutes of multiple-choice testing, plus two 30-minute Analytical Writing Assessment sections. Add in the administrative details, plus two 5-minute breaks, and you can count on being in the test center for about four hours.

It's a grueling experience, to say the least. And if you don't approach it with confidence and rigor, you'll quickly lose your composure. That's why it's so important that you take control of the test, just as you take control of the rest of your application process.

What's on the GMAT?

The GMAT begins with two Analytical Writing Assessment sections. For each of these sections, you have 30 minutes to type an essay into the computer using a simple word-processing program. The test may start with either the "Analysis of an Issue" topic or the "Analysis of an Argument" topic.

Teacher Tip

One thing that I always tell my students is that the GMAT is ultimately a test of confidence. Because it is adaptive, it is designed to be as hard as possible as soon as possible. Those who aren't prepared for it keep waiting for the easy questions that never come, and are thoroughly discouraged by the time the test is complete. Look forward to the hardest questions GMAT can throw at you, because it means that you are doing well on the test.
—Jason Anderson
  Chicago, IL

Note

Many people could ace the GMAT if they had unlimited time. But they don't. To succeed on the GMAT, you've got to think smart and fast.

After the essay sections, there are two 75-minute multiple-choice sections—one Quantitative and one Verbal. The Quantitative section contains 37 math questions in two formats: Problem Solving and Data Sufficiency, which are mixed together throughout the section. The Verbal section contains 41 questions in three formats: Reading Comprehension, Sentence Correction, and Critical Reasoning, which are also mixed throughout the section. Within each section, question types appear in random order, so you never know what's coming next.

This is how the sections break down:

Analytical Writing Assessment	Analytical Writing Assessment
"Analysis of an Issue" Topic	"Analysis of an Argument" Topic
1 essay 30 minutes	1 essay 30 minutes

Quantitative Section	Verbal Section
• Data Sufficiency • Problem Solving	• Reading Comp • Sentence Correction • Critical Reasoning
37 questions 75 minutes	41 questions 75 minutes

Some important things to note:
- You'll get a five-minute break after the second essay section and another break between the two multiple-choice sections.

- So-called experimental questions will be scattered through the test. They will look just like the other multiple-choice questions, but won't contribute to your score.

We'll talk more about each of the question types in later chapters. The big thing to take note of right now: You'll be answering roughly 78 multiple-choice questions in two and a half hours. That's just a little less than two minutes for each question, not counting the time required to read passages. Clearly, you're going to have to move fast. But you can't let yourself get careless. Taking control of the GMAT means increasing the speed of your work without sacrificing accuracy!

Your GMAT Scores

You'll receive four scores for the GMAT:

- Overall scaled score, ranging from 200 to 800
- Quantitative scaled subscore, ranging from 0 to 60
- Verbal scaled subscore, ranging from 0 to 60
- Analytical Writing Assessment score, ranging from 0 to 6 (this score is separate from your overall quantitative and verbal score)

Because the test is graded on a preset curve, the scaled score will correspond to a certain percentile, which will also be given on your score report. An overall score of 590, for instance, corresponds to the 80th percentile, meaning that 80 percent of test takers scored at or below this level. The percentile figure is important because it allows admissions officers at business schools to quickly get a sense of where you fall in the pool of applicants.

SOME SAMPLE PERCENTILES

Percentile	Approximate Score (Range 200–800)
99th percentile	750
95th percentile	700
90th percentile	670
80th percentile	620
75th percentile	600
50th percentile	530

Although many factors play a role in admissions decisions, the GMAT score is usually an important one. And, generally speaking, being average just won't cut it. Although the median GMAT score is somewhere around 500, you need a score of at least 600 to be considered competitive by the top B-schools. According to the latest Kaplan/*Newsweek* careers guide, the average GMAT scores at the best business schools in the country—such as Stanford, Sloan (MIT), Kellogg (Northwestern), and Wharton (Penn)—are above 670. That translates to a percentile figure of 90 and up!

Fortunately, there are strategies that can give you an advantage on the computer-adaptive GMAT. You can learn to exploit the way that the computer-adaptive test (CAT) generates a score. We'll explain how in the next section.

Definition

The percentile figure tells you what percent of test takers scored at or below your level. In other words, a percentile figure of 80 means that 80 percent did as well or worse than you did and that only 20 percent did better.

Note

The average GMAT scores of the entering classes at top U.S. business schools are in the 650 and over range.

Source: *Newsweek/ Kaplan's Careers 2000*

How Does the Computer-Adaptive Test Format Work?

The computer-adaptive format takes some getting used to—in fact, it's pretty weird at first. Here's how it works. You will see only one question at a time. Instead of having a predetermined mixture of basic, medium, and hard questions, the computer will select questions for you based on how well you are doing.

The first question will be of medium difficulty. If you get it right, the second question will be selected from a large pool of questions that are a little harder; if you get the first question wrong, the second will be a little more basic.

If you keep getting questions right, the test will get harder and harder; if you slip and make some mistakes, the test will adjust and start giving you easier problems, but if you answer them correctly, it will go back to the hard ones. Ideally, the test gives you enough questions to ensure that scores are not based on luck. If you get one hard question right, you might just have been lucky, but if you get ten hard questions right, then luck has little to do with it. So the test is self-adjusting and self-correcting.

Because of this format, the computer-adaptive GMAT is structurally very different from a paper-based test. After the first problem, every problem that you see is based on how you answered the prior problem. That means you cannot return to a question once you've answered it, because that would throw off the sequence. Once you answer a question, it's part of your score, for better or worse. That means you can't skip around within a section and do questions in the order that you like.

Another major consequence of the GMAT format is that hard problems count more than easy ones. It has to be this way, because the very purpose of this adaptive format is to find out at what level you reliably get about half the questions right; that's your scoring level.

Imagine two students—one who does ten basic questions, half of which she gets right and half of which she gets wrong, and one who does ten very difficult questions, half of which she gets right and half of which she gets wrong. The same number of questions have been answered correctly in each case, but this does not reflect an equal ability on the part of the two students. In fact, the student who answered five out of ten very difficult questions incorrectly could still get a very high score on the GMAT. But in order to get to these hard questions, she first had to get medium-difficulty questions right.

What this means for you is that no matter how much more comfortable you might be sticking to the basic questions, you definitely want to get to the hard questions if you can, because that means your score will be higher.

Section Management Techniques

In the chapters that follow, we'll cover techniques for answering various types of questions that you can expect to see on the GMAT. But you'll also need strategies for managing a section as a whole. Here are some strategies for attacking a section of the GMAT.

Be Systematic

Because it's so important to get to the hard questions as early as possible, work systematically at the beginning of a GMAT section. Use scratch paper to organize your thinking. If you eliminate choices, cross them off and guess intelligently. The first 10–15 questions of a section are crucial in determining your ability estimate, so invest the necessary time to try to answer these questions correctly. You must, however, leave enough time to mark an answer for every question in the section. You will be penalized for questions you don't reach.

Draw a Grid

If crossing off answer choices on paper tests really helps to clarify your thinking (using a process of elimination), you may want to consider making a grid on your scratch paper before you begin the GMAT. Use it to mark off answer choices that you have eliminated, as shown below. That way you can tell at a glance which answer choices are still in the running. If you end up using it often, it'll be worth the 10 seconds it takes to draw a simple grid, like this one:

A	✗	✗		✗		✗			✗		✗		
B		✗	✗	✗			✗	✗	✗	✗		✗	
C					✗			✗					✗
D	✗		✗		✗		✗		✗		✗		
E	✗	✗		✗			✗		✗				

Kaplan Rules

If you need to, make a grid to keep track of the answer choices you've eliminated.

Note

On some tough, time-consuming questions, you just have to take your best guess and move on. Remember, there's no point of honor at stake here, but there are GMAT points on the line.

Teacher Tip

When taking a computerized adaptive test, you have to overcome your reluctance to guess. Most people don't like to guess, but if you don't guess strategically as you go along, you'll have to guess randomly at the end.
—Kurt Keefner
  Bethesda, MD

Pace Yourself

Of course, the last thing you want to happen is to have time called before you've done half the questions. It's essential, therefore, that you pace yourself, keeping in mind the general guidelines for how long to spend on any individual question or passage.

No one is saying that you should spend, for instance, exactly 90 seconds on every Critical Reasoning question. But you should have a sense of how long you have to do each question, so you know when you're exceeding the limit and should start to move faster. You'll develop this sense if you time yourself while working on practice GMAT questions.

Stop the Clock

The timer in the corner can work to your advantage, but if you find yourself looking at it so frequently that it becomes a distraction, you should turn it off for 10 or 15 minutes and try to refocus your attention on the test, even if you lose track of time somewhat. The GMAT rewards focus and accuracy much more than it does speed.

Don't Waste Time on Questions You Can't Do

We know that foregoing a possibly tough question is easier said than done; we all have the natural instinct to plow through test sections, answering every question as it appears. But it just doesn't pay off on the GMAT. If you dig in your heels on a tough question, refusing to move on until you've cracked it, you're letting your test macho get in the way of your test score. Like life itself, a test section is too short to waste on lost causes.

Remain Calm

It's imperative that you remain calm and composed while working through a section. You can't allow yourself to be rattled by one hard question or Reading Comp passage to the degree that it throws off your performance on the rest of the Verbal section. Expect to find some difficult questions, but remember, you won't be the only one encountering difficult problems. The test is designed to challenge everyone who takes it. Having trouble with a difficult question isn't going to ruin your score, but getting upset about it and letting it throw you off track will. When you understand that part of the test maker's goal is to reward those who keep their composure, you'll recognize the importance of not panicking when you run into challenging material.

Analytical Writing Assessment— GMAT Style

The GMAT begins with two 30-minute essay topics. You not only have to analyze the given topic and plan your attack, but you must also type your essays into a simple word processing program. If you aren't comfortable with complex word processing programs, don't worry. The only commands you'll use are *cut, paste,* and *undo.* There's nothing fancy here, not even a spell-check. If you're worried about having to type your essays, you should spend some time practicing typing and getting comfortable with a keyboard between now and the day of the test. A slow typing speed could lower your score.

Your essays will be graded by a human grader as well as a computerized essay grader, called the e-rater. But don't be thrown by this high-tech twist. The e-rater was designed to make the same judgments that a good human grader would make. Even though you don't have to reinvent your writing style to suit the e-rater, there are some steps you can take to improve your chances of getting a good score for the e-rater.

- Good organization always counted, and now it's more important than ever. Outline your essay before you begin to write.
- Keep in mind that the length of your essay is not a factor; the computer doesn't count the number of words in your response.
- Use transitional phrases like *first, therefore, because,* and *for example* so that the computer can recognize the structured argument your essay contains.
- Avoid spelling and grammar errors. Although the e-rater doesn't grade spelling per se, if it can't tell what word you were trying to use or thinks you used the wrong words, it could give you a lower score.

Strategically, assuming your typing skills are adequate, you don't have to do much of anything differently on the computer-adaptive test than you would when writing an essay on paper. You can write an outline on your scratch paper. You should spend about five minutes developing, 20 minutes composing, and the last five minutes proofreading each essay. For more tips on dealing with the GMAT AWA, take a look at chapter 11.

Navigating the GMAT: Computer Basics

Let's preview the primary computer functions that you will use to move around on the GMAT. ETS calls them "testing tools," but they're basically just boxes that you can click with your mouse. The screen on the following page is typical for an adaptive test.

Kaplan Rules

Developing a systematic, organized way to use your scratch paper will help you save time and eliminate mistakes.

You can't skip questions on the GMAT CAT; you have to answer every question you get. But you do get more time per question on the CAT.

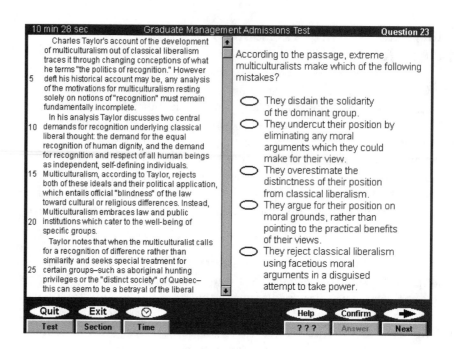

Here's what the various buttons do.

The Time *Button*
Clicking on this button turns the time display at the top of the screen on and off. When you have five minutes left in a section, the clock flashes and the display changes from Hours/Minutes to Hours/Minutes/Seconds.

The Exit *Button*
This allows you to exit the section before the time is up. If you budget your time wisely you should never have to use this button—time will run out just as you are finishing the section.

The Help *Button*
This one leads to directions and other stuff from the tutorial. You should know all this already, and besides, the test clock won't pause just because you click on Help.

The Quit *Button*
Hitting this button ends the test.

The Next *Button*
Hit this when you want to move on to the next question. After you press Next, you must hit Confirm.

The Confirm *Button*
This button tells the computer you are happy with your answer and are

really ready to move to the next question. You cannot proceed until you have hit this button.

The Scroll Bar
Similar to the scroll bar on a Windows-style computer display, the scroll bar is a thin, vertical column with up and down arrows at the top and bottom. Clicking on the arrows moves you up or down the page you're reading.

Pros and Cons of the Computer-Adaptive Format

There are both good and annoying things about the GMAT's computer-adaptive format. The following are a few things you should be thankful for/watch out for as you prepare to try your luck on the test.

Eight Good Things about the Computer-Adaptive Test

- There is a little timer at the top of the computer screen to help you pace yourself (you can hide it if it distracts you).

- There will be only a few other test takers in the room with you—it won't be like taking it in one of those massive lecture halls with distractions everywhere.

- You get a pause of five minutes between each section. The pause is optional, but you should always use it to relax and stretch.

- The computer-adaptive test is much more convenient for your schedule than the pencil-and-paper exam was. It's offered at more than 175 centers three to six days a week (depending on the center) all year long.

- Registering to take the computer-adaptive test is very easy, and sometimes you can sign up only days before the test. However, depending upon the time of the year and the availability of testing centers in your area, you may have to register several weeks in advance for a desired test date.

- The computer-adaptive test gives you more time to spend on each question than you got on the paper-based test.

- You can see your scores before you decide which schools you want to send them to.

- Perhaps the computer-adaptive test's best feature is that it gives you your scores immediately and will send them to schools just 10 to 15 days later.

> **Note**
>
> One advantage of the GMAT CAT is that it gives you the chance to work methodically on one question at a time, with no other questions there to distract you.

Seven Annoying Things about the Computer-Adaptive Test

- You cannot skip around on this test; you must answer the questions one at a time in the order the computer gives them to you.

- If you realize later that you answered a question incorrectly, you can't go back and change your answer.

- If the person next to you is noisy or distracting, the proctor cannot move you or the person, since your test is on the computer.

- You can't cross off an answer choice and never look at it again, so you have to be disciplined about not reconsidering choices you've already eliminated.

- You have to scroll through Reading Comprehension passages, which means you won't be able to see the whole thing on the screen at once.

- You can't write on your computer screen the way you can on the paper test (though some have tried), so you have to use scratch paper they give you, which will be inconveniently located away from the computer screen.

- Lastly, many people find that computer screens tire them and cause eyestrain—especially after four hours.

The following chapters of this book provide an overview of the different sections you'll encounter on the GMAT exam. But before you move on to them, take note of the GMAT Registration Checklist opposite. This checklist will serve as a useful resource for you when it's time to sign up for the test.

GMAT Registration Checklist

- To get registration materials, write to GMAT, Educational Testing Service, P.O. Box 6103, Princeton, NJ 08541-6103 or e-mail gmat@ets.org. You can also fax to (609) 883-4349 or call ETS at (800) GMAT-NOW or (609) 771-7330. The TTY number is (800) 529-3590.

- The *GMAT Information Bulletin* has details about registering for the test. It is available from ETS by mail or downloadable from the ETS Website. You can also find this bulletin at most Kaplan centers and at colleges and universities.

- Check ETS' Website at http://www.gmat.org for complete information about registering for the GMAT.

- Register early to secure the time you want at the test center of your choice. Many centers have long waits.

- Cost at press time: $190.00 (USD) worldwide.

- Check with ETS yourself for all the latest information on the GMAT! Every effort is made to keep the information in this book up to date, but changes may occur after the book is published.

CHAPTER TWO

Verbal Section Overview

HIGHLIGHTS ···

- Learn what's on the Verbal section and how to manage it
- Get to know the three Verbal question types
- Find out how to get your best score

···

A little more than half of the multiple-choice questions on the GMAT appear in the Verbal section. You'll have 75 minutes to answer 41 Verbal questions in three formats: Reading Comprehension, Sentence Correction, and Critical Reasoning. These three types of questions are mingled throughout the Verbal section, so you never know what's coming next. Here's what you can expect to see.

Verbal Question Type	Approximate Number of Questions
Critical Reasoning	12
Reading Comprehension	14
Sentence Correction	15
Total: 41 questions in 75 minutes	

In the next three chapters, we'll show you strategies for each of these question types. But first, let's look at some techniques for managing the whole section.

The Verbal Section at a Glance

- 41 questions
- 75 minutes
- Three formats:
  Critical Reasoning
  Reading Comprehension
  Sentence Correction

How the Verbal Section of the GMAT Is Scored

The Verbal section of the GMAT is quite different from the Verbal sections of most paper-and-pencil tests. The major difference between the test formats is that the GMAT "adapts" to your performance. Each test taker is given a different mix of questions depending on how well he or she is doing on the test. What this means is that the questions get harder or easier depending on whether you answer them correctly or not. Your GMAT score is not directly determined by *how many* questions you get right, but by *how hard* the questions you get right are.

When you start a section, the computer:
- Assumes you have an average score (500)
- Gives you a medium-difficulty question. About half of the people who take the test will get this question right, and half will get it wrong

What happens next depends on whether you answered the question correctly.

If you answer the question correctly:
- Your score goes up
- You are given a slightly harder question

If you answer the question incorrectly:
- Your score goes down
- You are given a slightly easier question

This pattern continues for the rest of the section. Every time you get a question right, the computer raises your score, then gives you a slightly harder question. Every time you get a question wrong, the computer lowers your score, then gives you a slightly easier question. In this way the computer tries to "home in" on your score.

Theoretically, as you get to the end of a section, you will reach a point where every time the computer raises the difficulty level of a question, you get it wrong, but every time it lowers the difficulty level of a question, you get it right. Your score at this point will supposedly be an accurate measure of your ability.

How to Manage the Verbal Section

The best way to attack the GMAT is to exploit the way it determines your score. Since early questions are worth more, spend more time on those questions. Since you can't skip any questions, you'll have to guess intelligently if you get stuck.

Having a systematic approach to each section will ensure that you spend your time as wisely as possible. The best way to approach the Verbal section on the GMAT is to think of it as being divided into two separate zones.

You should spend more time on the first 10–15 questions, double-checking your answers before you move on. These questions are crucial in determining your ability estimate, so invest the necessary time and try to answer these questions correctly.

Make sure, however, to pace yourself so that you have time to mark an answer for every question in the section, because you will be penalized for questions you don't reach. If you don't have time to give some thought to the answer to every question, guess if necessary during the final minutes allotted to you in order to get to the end of the section.

Guessing

Whether it is because you're running short of time or you've hit a question that totally flummoxes you, you will have to guess occasionally. But don't just guess at random. You should try to narrow down the answer choices before you guess. This will greatly improve your chances of guessing the right answer. When you guess, you should follow this plan:

1. Eliminate answer choices you know are wrong. Even if you don't know the right answer, you can often tell that some of the answer choices are wrong. For instance, on Sentence Correction questions, you can eliminate answer choices as soon as you find an error, thus reducing the number of choices to consider.

2. Avoid answer choices that make you suspicious. These are the answer choices that just "look wrong" or conform to a common wrong-answer type. For example, if an answer choice in a Reading Comprehension question mentions a term you don't remember reading, chances are it will be wrong. (The next three chapters will have more information about common wrong-answer types on the Verbal section.)

3. Choose one of the remaining answer choices.

> **Teacher Tip**
>
> Students have to become aware of all the common mistakes that can be made on a question. If they do this, they will be more careful not to make these errors.
> —Derek Veazey
> Fort Worth, TX

Avoid the Penalty

There is a penalty for not completing a section. Every question that you leave unanswered at the end of a section is twice as damaging to your score as an incorrect answer. For this reason it is very important that you answer all the questions. If you have only a minute or two to go, and you have several questions remaining, guess at random to get to the end of the section.

Treat Every Question as if It Were Scored

About one quarter of the questions on the test are experimental—questions that the test makers are checking out for possible use on future tests. These questions do not contribute to your score, and there is no way of identifying them. Treat every question as if it were scored.

Use Your Scratch Paper Strategically

One of the skills you will have to master for the GMAT is the systematic use of scratch paper. Since you can't write on the screen, you will need to transfer some information to your scratch paper to be able to solve many problems. Although this sounds simple, it takes practice; otherwise you may find yourself transferring reams of data, or not enough at all.

To practice using scratch paper efficiently, use scratch paper as you work through the questions in this book. Treat all testlike questions in this book as if they were on a computer screen. Make your notes on a separate piece of paper. Don't mark up questions in the book.

CHAPTER THREE

Critical Reasoning

HIGHLIGHTS

- Learn the Seven Basic Principles of Critical Reasoning
- Study the Kaplan Method for answering Critical Reasoning questions
- Focus on the most common types of Critical Reasoning questions and the targeted strategies for approaching each type
- Complete the Critical Reasoning Practice Quiz

The directions for Critical Reasoning questions are short and to the point. They look like this:

Directions: Select the best answer for each question.

The GMAT will give you about 12 Critical Reasoning questions. Here's an example of one.

> A study of twenty overweight men revealed that each man experienced significant weight loss after adding SlimDown, an artificial food supplement, to his daily diet. For three months, each man consumed one SlimDown portion every morning after exercising, and then followed his normal diet for the rest of the day. Clearly, anyone who consumes one portion of SlimDown every day for at least three months will lose weight and will look and feel his best.

Critical Reasoning Tally

Expect to see approximately 12 Critical Reasoning questions scattered throughout the Verbal section.

Which one of the following is an assumption on which the argument depends?

- (A) The men in the study will gain back the weight if they discontinue the SlimDown program.
- (B) No other dietary supplement will have the same effect on overweight men.
- (C) The daily exercise regimen was not responsible for the effects noted in the study.
- (D) Women won't experience similar weight reductions if they adhere to the SlimDown program for three months.
- (E) Overweight men will achieve only partial weight loss if they don't remain on the SlimDown program for a full three months.

On the GMAT, in business school, and in your career, you'll need the ability to see and understand complex reasoning. It's not enough to sense whether an argument is strong or weak; you'll need to analyze precisely *why* it is so. This presumes a fundamental skill that's called on by nearly every Critical Reasoning question—the ability to isolate and identify the various components of any given argument. And that brings us to the basic principles of Critical Reasoning on the GMAT.

The Seven Basic Principles of Critical Reasoning

Here are the basic things that you need to succeed on CR questions:

1. Understand the structure of arguments.

Success in Critical Reasoning depends on knowing the structure of arguments so that you can break an argument down into its core components. First of all, let's clarify what's meant by the word *argument*. We don't mean a conversation in which two or more people are shouting at one another. The word *argument* in Critical Reasoning means any piece of text where an author puts forth a set of ideas and/or a point of view, and attempts to support it.

Every GMAT Critical Reasoning argument is made up of two basic parts:

- The conclusion (the point that the author is trying to make)

- The evidence (the support that the author offers for the conclusion)

Success on this section hinges on your ability to identify these parts of the argument. There is no general rule about where conclusion and evidence appear in the argument—the conclusion could be the first sentence, followed by the evidence, or it could be the last sentence, with the evidence preceding it. Consider the stimulus (a passage is called a stimulus in ETS-speak):

The Brookdale Public Library will require extensive physical rehabilitation to meet the new building codes passed by the town council. For one thing, the electrical system is inadequate, causing the lights to flicker sporadically. Furthermore, there are too few emergency exits, and even those are poorly marked and sometimes locked.

Let's suppose that the author of this argument was allowed only one sentence to convey her meaning. Do you think that she would waste her lone opportunity on the statement: "The electrical system at the Brookdale Public Library is inadequate, causing the lights to flicker sporadically"? Would she walk away satisfied that she got her main point across? Probably not. Given a single opportunity, she would have to state the first sentence: "The Brookdale Public Library will require extensive physical rehabilitation . . . ." This is her *conclusion*. If you pressed her for her *reasons* for making this statement, she would then cite the electrical and structural problems with the building. This is the *evidence* for her conclusion.

But does that mean that an evidence statement like, "The electrical system at the Brookdale Public Library is inadequate" can't be a conclusion? No; we're saying that it's not the conclusion for *this particular argument*. Every idea, every new statement, must be evaluated in the context of the stimulus in which it appears. Let's see what a stimulus would look like in which the statement above serves as the conclusion:

> The electrical wiring at the Brookdale Public Library was installed over 40 years ago, and appears to be corroded in some places (*evidence*). An electrician, upon inspection of the system, found a few frayed wires as well as some blown fuses (*evidence*). Clearly, the electrical system at the Brookdale Public Library is inadequate (*conclusion*).

To succeed in Critical Reasoning, you have to be able to determine the precise function of every sentence in the stimulus. Use structural signals when attempting to isolate evidence and conclusion. Key words in the stimulus—such as *because, for, since*—usually indicate that evidence is about to follow, whereas such words as *therefore, hence, thus,* and *consequently* usually signal a conclusion.

The explanations to the Practice Test in the back of this book discuss the structure of many of the Critical Reasoning arguments on the test, so read these carefully to shore up your understanding of this crucial aspect of Critical Reasoning.

Kaplan Rules

Certain words and phrases can help you identify the conclusion and the evidence in a stimulus. Clues that signal evidence: *because, since, for, as a result of, due to.* Clues that signal the conclusion: *consequently, hence, therefore, thus, clearly, so, accordingly.*

2. Preview the question.

Looking over the question before reading the stimulus tells you what to focus on in your initial reading of the stimulus. In effect, it gives you a jump on the question. For example, let's say the question attached to the original library argument above asked the following:

> The author supports her point about the need for rehabilitation at the Brookdale Library by citing which of the following?

If you were to preview this question stem before reading the stimulus, you would know what to look for in advance—namely, evidence, the "support" provided for the conclusion. Similarly, if the question asked you to find an assumption on which the author is relying, this would tell you in advance that there was a crucial piece of the argument missing, and you could begin to think about it right off the bat.

Previewing the stem allows you to set the tone of your attack on each particular question, and thus saves you time in the long run. As you'll soon see, this technique will come in especially handy when we discuss methods for the various question types.

3. Paraphrase the author's point.

After you read the stimulus, you'll want to paraphrase the author's main argument, i.e., restate the author's ideas in your own words. Frequently, the authors in Critical Reasoning (and in Reading Comprehension, as we'll see) say pretty simple things in complex ways. But if you mentally translate the verbiage into a simpler form, you'll find the whole thing more manageable.

In the library argument, for instance, you probably don't want to deal with the full complexity of the author's stated conclusion:

> The Brookdale Public Library will require extensive physical rehabilitation to meet the new building codes just passed by the town council.

Instead, you probably want to carry a much simpler form of the point in your mind, something like:

> The library will need fixing up to meet new codes.

Often, by the time you begin reading through answer choices, you run the risk of losing sight of the gist of the stimulus. After all, you can concentrate on only a certain amount of information at one time. Restating the argument in your own words will not only help you get the author's point in the first place, but it'll also help you hold on to it until you've found the correct answer.

4. Judge the argument's persuasiveness.

You must read actively, not passively, on the GMAT. Active readers are always thinking critically, forming reactions as they go along. They constantly question whether the author's argument seems valid or dubious. On a section where many of the questions deal with finding flaws in the author's reasoning, it's imperative to read with a very critical eye.

For instance, how persuasive is the argument about the library? Well, it's pretty strong, because the evidence certainly seems to indicate that certain aspects of the library's structure need repair. But without more evidence about what the new building codes are like, we can't say for sure that the conclusion of this argument is valid. So this is a strong argument but not an airtight one.

Remember, part of what you're called on to do in this section is to evaluate arguments, so don't allow yourself to fall into the bad habits of the passive reader—reading solely for the purpose of getting through the stimulus. Those who read this way don't have a clue when it comes to answering the questions and invariably find themselves having to read the stimuli twice or even three times. Then they are caught short on time on the section. Read the stimuli right the first time—with a critical eye and an active mind.

5. Make sure you answer the question being asked.

One of the most disheartening experiences in Critical Reasoning is to understand the author's argument fully and then blow the point by supplying an answer to a question that wasn't asked. For example, when you're asked for an inference supported by the argument, it does you no good to jump on the choice that paraphrases the author's conclusion. Likewise, if you're asked for an assumption, don't be fooled into selecting a choice that looks vaguely like a summary of the author's evidence.

When asked why they chose a particular wrong choice, students sometimes respond by saying such things as: "Well, it's true, isn't it?" and "Look, it says so right there," pointing to the stimulus. Unfortunately, that's not good enough. The question stem doesn't ask: "Which one of the following looks vaguely familiar to you?" It asks for something very specific. It's your job to follow the test makers' line of reasoning to the credited response.

The classic example of this error occurs on "Strengthen/Weaken" questions. Whenever a question asks you to strengthen or weaken the argu-

Kaplan Rules

It's much easier to understand and remember an argument if you restate it simply, in your own words.

Kaplan Rules

You read the argument. You see a major weakness in it. You find an answer choice that points out this weakness. You choose that answer. And you miss the point. Why? Because the question stem asked for a statement that *strengthened* the argument, not one that weakened it. Don't let this happen to you. Always double-check the question stem.

ment, you can be sure that there'll be one, two, or sometimes even three choices that do the opposite of what's asked. Choosing such a wrong choice is less a matter of failing to understand the argument than of failing to remember the task at hand.

Also, be on the lookout for "reversers," words such as *not* and *except.* These little words are easy to miss, but they change entirely the kind of statement you're looking for among the choices.

6. Try to prephrase an answer.

This principle, which is really an extension of the last one, is crucial. You must try to approach the answer choices with at least a faint idea of what the answer should look like. This is not to say that you should ponder the question for minutes until you're able to write out your own answer—it's still a multiple-choice test, so the right answer is on the screen. Just try to get in the habit of instinctively framing an answer to each question in your own mind.

If you can come up with a hint as to a possible answer, scan the choices. Sure, the correct answer will be worded differently and will be more fleshed out than your little seed of an idea. But if it matches your thought, you'll know it in a second. And you'll find that there's no more satisfying feeling in Critical Reasoning than prephrasing correctly, and then finding the correct answer quickly and confidently.

For instance, let's say a question for the library argument went like this:

> The author's argument depends on which of the following assumptions about the new building codes?

Having thought about the stimulus argument, an answer to this question may have sprung immediately to mind—namely, the assumption that the new codes apply to existing buildings as well as to new buildings under construction. After all, the library will have to be rehabilitated to meet the new codes, according to the author. Clearly, the assumption is that the codes apply to existing buildings. And that's the kind of statement you would look for among the choices.

Don't be discouraged if you can't always prephrase an answer. Some questions just won't have an answer that jumps out at you. But if used correctly, prephrasing works on many questions. It will really boost your confidence and increase your speed on the section when you can come up with a glimmer of what the right answer should look like, and then have it jump right off the page at you.

Teacher Tip

With Critical Reasoning questions, don't get too philosophical. If there's one really strong answer, it's right—don't get bogged down in the "maybes."
—Ed Cotrell
  Houston, TX

7. Keep the scope of the argument in mind.

One of the most important Critical Reasoning skills, particularly when you're at the point of actually selecting one of the five choices, is the ability to focus on the scope of the argument. The majority of wrong choices on this section are wrong because they are "outside the scope." In everyday language, that simply means that these choices contain elements that don't match the author's ideas or that go beyond the context of the stimulus.

Some common examples of scope problems are choices that are too narrow, too broad, or literally have nothing to do with the author's points. Also, watch for and eliminate choices that are too extreme to match the argument's scope; they're usually signaled by such words as *all*, *always*, *never*, *none*, and so on. Choices that are more qualified are often correct for arguments that are moderate in tone and contain such words as *usually*, *sometimes*, *probably*, etcetera.

To illustrate the scope principle, let's look again at the question mentioned above:

> The author's argument depends on which of the following assumptions about the new building codes?

Let's say one of the choices read as follows:

> Ⓐ The new building codes are far too stringent.

Knowing the scope of the argument would help you to eliminate this choice very quickly. You know that this argument is just a claim about what the new codes will require: that the library be rehabilitated. It's not an argument about whether the requirements of the new codes are good, or justifiable, or ridiculously strict. That kind of value judgment is *outside the scope* of this argument.

Recognizing scope problems is a great way of eliminating dozens of wrong answers quickly. Make sure to pay special attention to the scope issues discussed in the Practice Test explanations.

Typical CR Question Types

Now that you're familiar with the basic principles of Critical Reasoning, let's look at the most common types of questions you'll be asked. As we said earlier, certain question types crop up again and again on the GMAT, and it pays to be familiar with them.

Kaplan Rules

A remarkable number of wrong answers in CR have scope problems. Always be on the lookout for choices that are too extreme, that contain value judgments irrelevant to the argument, or that don't match the stimulus in tone or subject matter.

Assumption Questions

An assumption bridges the gap between an argument's evidence and conclusion. It's a piece of support that isn't explicitly stated but that is required for the conclusion to remain valid. When a question asks you to find an author's assumption, it's asking you to find the statement without which the argument falls apart.

Denial Test

In order to test whether a statement is necessarily assumed by an author, we can employ the Denial Test. Here's how it works: Simply deny or negate the statement and see if the argument falls apart. If it does, that choice is a necessary assumption. If, on the other hand, the argument is unaffected, the choice is wrong. Consider, as an example, this simple stimulus:

> Allyson plays volleyball for Central High School.
> Therefore, Allyson must be over six feet tall.

You should recognize the second sentence as the conclusion and the first sentence as the evidence for it. But is the argument complete? Obviously not. The piece that's missing—the unstated link between the evidence and conclusion—is the assumption, and you could probably prephrase this one pretty easily:

> All volleyball players for Central High School are over six feet tall.

To test whether this really is an assumption necessary to the argument, let's apply the Denial Test, by negating it. What if it's not true that all volleyball players for Central High School are over six feet tall? Can we still logically conclude that Allyson must be taller than six feet? No, we can't. Sure, it's possible that she is, but it's also possible that she's not. By denying the statement, then, the argument falls to pieces; it's simply no longer valid. And that's our conclusive proof that the statement above is a necessary assumption of this argument.

Okay, we can use the Denial Test to check whether a statement is an assumption, but what if we don't have a clue what the assumption is? Is there any way to track it down? Sure enough, Kaplan has a powerful, if not foolproof, method for doing so: Compare the ideas in the evidence with those in the conclusion. If you find an idea—an important word—in the conclusion, but not in the evidence, then you've found an assumption. There must be an assumption about this new idea because new ideas can't occur in the conclusion. Every idea in the conclusion needs support—evidence. While it may still not be clear exactly what the assumption is, knowing something about it allows us to prephrase and eliminate choices.

As we've just seen, you can often prephrase the answer to an Assumption question. By previewing the question stem, you'll know what to look for. And stimuli for Assumption questions just "feel" as if they're missing something. Often, the answer will jump right out at you, as in this case. In more difficult Assumption questions, the answers may not be as obvious. But in either case, you can use the Denial Test to quickly check whichever choice seems correct.

Sample Stems

Here are some of the ways in which assumption questions are worded:

- Which one of the following is assumed by the author?

- Upon which one of the following assumptions does the author rely?

- The argument depends on the assumption that . . .

- Which one of the following, if added to the passage, will make the conclusion logical?

- The validity of the argument depends on which one of the following?

- The argument presupposes which one of the following?

Strengthen or Weaken Questions

Determining an argument's necessary assumption, as we've just seen, is required to answer Assumption questions. But it also is required for the GMAT's most common question type: Strengthen or Weaken the Argument questions.

One way to weaken an argument is to break down a central piece of evidence. Another way is to attack the validity of any assumptions the author may be making. The answer to many Weaken the Argument questions is the one that reveals an author's assumption to be unreasonable; conversely, the answer to many Strengthen the Argument questions provides additional support by affirming the truth of an assumption or by presenting more persuasive evidence.

Let's take the same stimulus we used before but look at it in the context of these other question types:

> Allyson plays volleyball for Central High School.
> Therefore, Allyson must be over six feet tall.

Remember the assumption holding this argument together? It was that all volleyball players for Central High School are over six feet tall. That's the assumption that makes or breaks the argument. So, if the question asked you to weaken the argument, you'd want to attack that assumption:

Assumption Questions at a Glance

- Assumption questions appear frequently on the GMAT.
- An assumption is evidence unstated in the stimulus.
- An assumption bridges the gap between evidence and conclusion.
- An assumption must be true in order for the conclusion to be valid.
- An assumption can be checked by applying the Denial Test.
- An assumption can be found by comparing the terms in the conclusion to those in the evidence.

Which one of the following, if true, would most weaken the argument?

Answer: Not all volleyball players at Central High School are over six feet tall.

Strengthen or Weaken Questions at a Glance

- They are the type of CR question that appears most frequently.
- They are usually related to assumptions. Strengtheners often shore up central assumption, and Weakeners often show central assumption to be unreasonable.
- They require that you evaluate each choice as to the effect it would have on the argument if true.
- They often have correct choices that don't prove or disprove the argument but simply tip the scale in the desired direction.

We've called into doubt the author's basic assumption, thus damaging the argument.

But what about strengthening the argument? Again, the key is the necessary assumption:

Which one of the following, if true, would most strengthen the argument?

Answer: All volleyball players at Central High School are over six feet tall.

Here, by confirming the author's assumption, we've in effect bolstered the argument.

Extra Tips
Strengthen or Weaken questions are very common on the GMAT. Here are a few concepts that apply to both Strengthen and Weaken questions.

- Weakening an argument is not the same thing as disproving the conclusion, and strengthening is not the same as proving the conclusion. A strengthener tips the scale towards believing in the validity of the conclusion; a weakener tips the scale in the other direction, towards doubting the conclusion.

- The wording of these question types always takes the form of, "Which one of the following, *if true*, would most [weaken or strengthen] the argument?" The "if true" part means that you have to accept the validity of the choice right off the bat, no matter how unlikely it may sound to you.

- Don't be careless. Wrong answer choices in these questions often have exactly the *opposite* of the desired effect. That is, if you're asked to strengthen a stimulus argument, it's quite likely that one or more of the wrong choices will contain information that actually weakens the argument. By the same token, Weaken questions usually contain a choice that strengthens the argument. So once again, pay close attention to what the question stem is asking.

Sample Stems
The stems associated with these two question types are usually self-explanatory. Here's a list of what you can expect to see on Test Day:

Weaken:

- Which one of the following, if true, would most weaken the argument above?
- Which one of the following, if true, would most seriously damage the argument above?
- Which one of the following, if true, casts the most doubt on the argument above?
- Which one of the following, if true, is the most serious criticism of the argument above?

Strengthen:

- Which one of the following, if true, would most strengthen the argument?
- Which one of the following, if true, would provide the most support for the conclusion in the argument above?
- The argument above would be more persuasive if which one of the following were found to be true?

It's also common that the question stem explicitly refers to part of the argument. You might, for example, see the following:

> Which of the following, if true, casts the most doubt on the author's conclusion that the Brookdale Public Library does not meet the requirements of the new building code?

This example illustrates another advantage of Basic Principle 2: Reading the question stem first. Here we would be told outright what the author's conclusion is, making the reading of the stimulus much easier to manage.

Inference Questions

The second most common question type you'll encounter on the Critical Reasoning section is the Inference question. The process of inferring is a matter of considering one or more statements as evidence and then drawing a conclusion from them.

Sometimes the inference is very close to the author's overall main point. Other times, it deals with a less central point. In Critical Reasoning, the difference between an inference and an assumption is that the conclusion's validity doesn't logically depend on an inference, as it does on a necessary assumption. A valid inference is merely something that *must be true* if the statements in the passage are true; it's an *extension* of the argument rather than a necessary *part* of it.

Kaplan Rules

A common CR trap is to have a statement that nicely weakens the argument hiding among the choices for a Strengthen question (or the reverse: a great strengthener statement in the choices for a Weaken question). Don't fall for this classic trap!

Teacher Tip

To strengthen an argument doesn't mean to prove it; it just means that you tighten the bond between the evidence and the conclusion that the author has drawn from it. Conversely, a weakened argument is one in which doubt has been cast that the evidence leads to the conclusion; the bond has been severed.
–Bob Verini
Los Angeles, CA

Inference Questions at a Glance

- Inference questions are the second most frequently appearing CR question type.
- The answer must be true if statements in the stimulus are true.
- They often stick close to the author's main point.
- The question stems vary considerably in appearance.
- They can be checked by applying the Denial Test.

Inference Rules

A good inference:

- Stays in line with the gist of the passage
- Stays in line with the author's tone
- Stays in line with the author's point of view
- Stays within the scope of the argument or the main idea
- Is neither denied by, nor irrelevant to, the argument or discussion
- Always makes more sense than its opposite

For instance, let's take a somewhat expanded version of the volleyball team argument:

> Allyson plays volleyball for Central High School, despite the team's rule against participation by nonstudents. Therefore, Allyson must be over six feet tall.
>
> Inference: Allyson is not a student at Central High School.

Clearly, if Allyson plays volleyball *despite* the team's rule against participation by nonstudents, she must not be a student. Otherwise, she wouldn't be playing *despite* the rule; she'd be playing *in accordance with* the rule. But note that this inference is not an essential assumption of the argument because the conclusion about Allyson's height doesn't depend on it.

So be careful; unlike an assumption, an inference need not have anything to do with the author's conclusion. It may simply be a piece of information derived from one or more pieces of evidence. Fortunately, the Denial Test works for inferences as well as for assumptions: A valid inference always makes more sense than its opposite. If you deny or negate an answer choice, and the denial has little or no effect on the argument, then chances are that choice cannot be inferred from the passage.

Sample Stems

Inference questions probably have the most varied wording of all the Critical Reasoning question stems. Some question stems denote inference fairly obviously. Others are more subtle, and still others may even look like other question types entirely. Here's a quick rundown of the various forms that Inference questions are likely to take on your test:

- Which one of the following is inferable from the argument above?
- Which one of the following is implied by the argument above?
- The author suggests that . . .
- If all the statements above are true, which one of the following must also be true on the basis of them?
- The author of the passage would most likely agree with which one of the following?
- The passage provides the most support for which of the following?
- Which one of the following is probably the conclusion toward which the author is moving?
- Which of the following, if true, would best explain . . .

The Kaplan Four-Step Method for Critical Reasoning

Now that you've learned the basic CR principles and have been exposed to the three common question types, it's time to learn how to orchestrate all of that knowledge into a systematic approach to Critical Reasoning questions. We've developed a four-step method that you can use to attack each and every CR question in the Verbal section.

1. Preview the question stem.

As we mentioned in the discussion of basic principles, previewing the stem is a great way to focus your reading of the stimulus, so that you know exactly what you're looking for.

2. Read the stimulus.

With the question stem in mind, read the stimulus, paraphrasing as you go. Remember to read actively and critically, pinpointing evidence and conclusion. Also get a sense for how strong or weak the argument is.

3. Try to prephrase an answer.

Sometimes, if you've read the stimulus critically enough, you'll know the answer without even looking at the choices. Other times, you'll have only a general idea of what the answer will say. Either way, it will be much easier to find the answer if you have a sense of what you're looking for among the choices.

4. Choose an answer.

If you were able to prephrase an answer, skim the choices for something that sounds like what you have in mind. Take this idea to the choices, aggressively. When you find one that mirrors your idea, treat the others with disdain. If you couldn't think of anything, read and evaluate each choice, throwing out the ones that are outside the scope of the argument. After settling on an answer, you may wish to briefly double-check the question stem to make sure that you're indeed answering the question that was asked.

Using the Kaplan Four-Step Method

Now let's try the Kaplan method on an entire Critical Reasoning item:

> A study of twenty overweight men revealed that each man experienced significant weight loss after adding SlimDown, an artificial food supplement, to his daily diet. For three months, each man consumed one SlimDown portion every morning after exercising, and then followed his normal diet for the rest of the day.

The Kaplan Four-Step Method for Critical Reasoning

1. Preview the question stem.
2. Read the stimulus.
3. Try to prephrase an answer.
4. Choose an answer.

Note

The Kaplan Four-Step Method is designed to give structure to your work on CR questions. But be flexible in using it. These are guidelines, not commandments.

Clearly, anyone who consumes one portion of SlimDown every day for at least three months will lose weight and will look and feel his best.

Which one of the following is an assumption on which the argument depends?

(A) The men in the study will gain back the weight if they discontinue the SlimDown program.

(B) No other dietary supplement will have the same effect on overweight men.

(C) The daily exercise regimen was not responsible for the effects noted in the study.

(D) Women won't experience similar weight reductions if they adhere to the SlimDown program for three months.

(E) Overweight men will achieve only partial weight loss if they don't remain on the SlimDown program for a full three months.

1. Preview the question stem.

We see, quite clearly, that we're dealing with an Assumption question. So, we can immediately adopt an "assumption mindset," which basically means that, before even reading the first word of the stimulus, we know the conclusion will be lacking an important piece of supporting evidence. We now turn to the stimulus, already on the lookout for this missing link.

2. Read the stimulus.

Sentence one introduces a study of twenty men using a food supplement product, resulting in weight loss for all twenty. Sentence two describes how they used it: once a day, for three months, after morning exercise. So far so good; it feels as if we're building up to something. The key word *clearly* usually indicates that some sort of conclusion follows, and in fact it does: The author concludes in sentence three that anyone who has one portion of the product daily for three months will lose weight, too.

You must read critically! Notice that the conclusion doesn't say that anyone who follows the *same routine* as the twenty men will have the same results; it says that anyone who simply *consumes the product* will have the same results. You should have begun to sense the inevitable lack of crucial information at this point. The evidence in sentence two describes a routine that includes taking the supplement after *daily exercise,* whereas the conclusion focuses primarily on the supplement and entirely ignores the part about the exercise. The conclusion, therefore, doesn't stem logically from the evidence in the first two sentences. This blends seamlessly into step three.

3. Prephrase an answer.

As expected, the argument is beginning to look as if it has a serious short-coming. Of course, we expected this because we previewed the question stem before reading the stimulus.

In really simplistic terms, the argument proceeds like so: "A bunch of guys did A and B for three months and had X result. If anyone does A for three months, that person will experience X result, too." Sound a little fishy? You bet. The author must be assuming that A (the product), not B (exercise), must be the cause that leads to the result. If not (here is the Denial Test), the conclusion makes no sense.

So, you might prephrase the answer like this: "Something about the exercise thing needs to be cleared up." That's it. Did you think your prephrasing had to be something fancy and glamorous? Well, it doesn't. All you need is an inkling of what the question is looking for, and in this case, it just seems that if we don't shore up the exercise issue, the argument will remain invalid and incomplete. So, with our vague idea of a possible assumption, we can turn to step four.

4. Choose an answer.

Because we were able to prephrase something, it's best to skim the choices looking for it. And, lo and behold, there's our idea, stated in choice (C). (C) clears up the exercise issue. Yes, this author must assume (C) to make the conclusion that eating SlimDown alone will cause people to lose weight.

At this point, if you're stuck for time, you simply choose (C) and move on. If you have more time, you may as well quickly check the remaining choices, to double-check that none of them fits the bill. Do so with an attitude. Be ready to dismiss the other choices unless they make a strong case for themselves. Since the difficulty in Critical Reasoning is often in the choices (rather than the stimulus), you can't let them make you indecisive.

Other Questions

Of course, once you grasp the structure of the argument and have located the author's central assumption, you should be able to answer any question the test makers throw at you. This one takes the form of an Assumption question. But it could just as easily have been phrased as a Weaken the Argument question:

> Which one of the following, if true, casts the most doubt on the argument above?

> Answer: Daily exercise contributed significantly to the weight loss experienced by the men in the study.

Now that you've got the basics of Critical Reasoning down, try the Practice Quiz on the next page.

Kaplan Rules

Your prephrasing of an answer need not be elaborate or terribly specific. Your goal is just to get an idea of what you're looking for, so the correct answer will jump out at you.

Critical Reasoning Practice Quiz

Directions: Select the best answer for each question. Darken the corresponding oval. (Answers and explanations can be found at the end of the quiz.)

Question 1

In Los Angeles, a political candidate who buys saturation radio advertising will get maximum name recognition.

The statement above logically conveys which of the following?

(A) Radio advertising is the most important factor in political campaigns in Los Angeles.

(B) Maximum name recognition in Los Angeles will help a candidate to win a higher percentage of votes cast in the city.

(C) Saturation radio advertising reaches every demographically distinct sector of the voting population in Los Angeles.

(D) For maximum name recognition a candidate need not spend on media channels other than radio advertising.

(E) A candidate's record of achievement in the Los Angeles area will do little to affect his or her name recognition there.

Question 2

In recent years, attacks by Dobermans on small children have risen dramatically. Last year saw 35 such attacks in the continental United States alone, an increase of almost 21 percent over the previous year's total. Clearly, then, it is unsafe to keep dogs as pets if one has small children in the house.

The argument above depends upon which of the following assumptions?

(A) No reasonable justification for these attacks by Dobermans on small children has been discovered.

(B) Other household pets, such as cats, don't display the same violent tendencies that dogs do.

(C) The number of attacks by Dobermans on small children will continue to rise in the coming years.

(D) A large percentage of the attacks by Dobermans on small children could have been prevented by proper training.

(E) The behavior towards small children exhibited by Dobermans is representative of dogs in general.

KAPLAN

Question 3

An investigation must be launched into the operations of the private group that is training recruits to fight against the Balaland Republic. The United States Neutrality Act plainly forbids United States citizens from engaging in military campaigns against any nation with which we are not at war. Since no war has been declared between the United States and the Balaland Republic, we should bring charges against these fanatics, who are in open defiance of the law.

Which of the following, if true, would most weaken the argument above?

(A) The Balaland Republic is currently engaged in a bloody and escalating civil war.

(B) Diplomatic relations between the United States and the Balaland Republic were severed last year.

(C) The recruits are being trained to fight only in the event the United States goes to war against the Balaland Republic.

(D) The training of recruits is funded not by United States citizens, but rather by a consortium of individuals from abroad.

(E) Charges cannot be brought against the private group that is training the recruits unless an investigation is first launched.

Question 4

Critics of strict "promotional gates" at the grade school level point to a recent study comparing students forced to repeat a grade with those promoted despite failing scores on an unscheduled, experimental competency test. Since there was no significant difference between the two groups' scores on a second test administered after completion of the next higher grade level, these critics argue that the retention policy has failed in its expressed purpose of improving students' basic skills.

Which of the following best expresses the argument made by critics of promotional gates?

(A) Anxiety over performance on standardized tests often hinders a student's ability to master challenging new material.

(B) A student's true intellectual development cannot be gauged by his score on a standardized competency test.

(C) The psychological damage a child suffers by repeating a grade outweighs the potential intellectual benefits of a second chance at learning.

(D) Strict requirements for promotion do not lead to harder work and greater mastery of fundamentals among students fearful of being held back.

(E) Socioeconomic factors as well as test scores influenced whether a given student in the study was promoted or forced to repeat a grade.

Question 5

Statistics show that more than half of the nation's murder victims knew their assailants; in fact, 24 percent last year were killed by relatives. Nor was death always completely unexpected. In one study, about half the murder victims in a particular city had called for police protection at least five times during the 24 months before they were murdered. Nonetheless, most people are more likely to fear being killed by a stranger in an unfamiliar situation than by a friend or relative at home.

Which of the following, if true, best explains the reaction of most people to the likelihood of being murdered?

- (A) Statistics are likely to be discounted no matter what the source, if their implication seems to run counter to common sense.
- (B) In the face of such upsetting problems as murder and assault, most people are more likely to react emotionally than rationally.
- (C) A study taken in only one city is not likely to have an effect on attitudes until similar studies have been undertaken at the national level and yielded similar results.
- (D) Most people do not consider themselves to be in the high-risk groups in which murder occurs frequently between relations, but do see themselves as at least minimally susceptible to random violence.
- (E) People who seek police protection from relatives and friends are often unwilling to press charges when the emotions of the moment have cooled.

Question 6

The extent to which a society is really free can be gauged by its attitude towards artistic expression. Freedom of expression can easily be violated in even the most outwardly democratic of societies. When a government arts council withholds funding from a dance performance that its members deem "obscene," the voices of a few bureaucrats have in fact censored the work of the choreographer, thereby committing the real obscenity of repression.

Which of the following, if true, would most seriously weaken the argument above?

- (A) Members of government arts councils are screened to ensure that their beliefs reflect those of the majority.
- (B) The term *obscenity* has several different definitions that should not be used interchangeably for rhetorical effect.
- (C) Failing to provide financial support for a performance is not the same as actively preventing or inhibiting it.
- (D) The council's decision could be reversed if the performance were altered to conform to public standards of appropriateness.
- (E) The definition of *obscenity* is something on which most members of a society can agree.

KAPLAN

Question 7

The local high school students have been clamoring for the freedom to design their own curricula. Allowing this would be as disastrous as allowing three-year-olds to choose their own diets. These students have neither the maturity nor the experience to equal that of the professional educators now doing the job.

Which of the following statements, if true, would most strengthen the above argument?

- (A) High school students have less formal education than those who currently design the curricula.
- (B) Three-year-olds do not, if left to their own devices, choose healthful diets.
- (C) The local high school students are less intelligent than the average teenager.
- (D) Individualized curricula are more beneficial to high school students than are the standard curricula, which are rigid and unresponsive to their particular strengths and weaknesses.
- (E) The ability to design good curricula develops only after years of familiarity with educational life.

Question 8

The rate of violent crime in this state is up 30 percent from last year. The fault lies entirely in our court system: Recently our judges' sentences have been so lenient that criminals can now do almost anything without fear of a long prison term.

The argument above would be weakened if it were true that

- (A) 85 percent of the other states in the nation have lower crime rates than does this state
- (B) white collar crime in this state has also increased by over 25 percent in the last year
- (C) 35 percent of the police in this state have been laid off in the last year due to budget cuts
- (D) polls show that 65 percent of the population in this state oppose capital punishment
- (E) the state has hired 25 new judges in the last year to compensate for deaths and retirements

Question 9

The education offered by junior colleges just after the Second World War had a tremendous practical effect on family-run businesses throughout the country. After learning new methods of marketing, finance, and accounting, the sons and daughters of merchants returned home, often to increase significantly the size of the family's enterprise or to maximize profits in other ways.

Which of the following statements is best supported by the information above?

- (A) The junior colleges principally emphasized methods of increasing the size of small businesses.
- (B) The business methods taught in the junior colleges were already widespread before the second World War.
- (C) The business curricula at junior colleges did not include theoretical principles of management.
- (D) Without the influence of junior colleges, many family-run businesses would have been abandoned as unprofitable.
- (E) Business methods in many postwar family-run businesses changed significantly as a result of the junior colleges.

Question 10

Techniques to increase productivity in the performance of discrete tasks, by requiring less human labor in each step of the production process, are widely utilized. Consultants on productivity enhancement point out, however, that although these techniques achieve their specific goal, they are not without drawbacks. They often instill enough resentment in the workforce eventually to lead to a slowdown in the production process as a whole.

Which of the following can be reasonably inferred from the statements above?

- (A) Productivity enhancement techniques do not attain their intended purpose and should not be employed in the workplace.
- (B) The fact that productivity enhancement techniques are so widely employed has led to a decline in the ability of American businesses to compete abroad.
- (C) If productivity enhancement consultants continue to utilize these techniques, complete work stoppages will eventually result.
- (D) Ironically, an increase in the productivity of discrete tasks may result in a decrease in the productivity of the whole production process.
- (E) Production managers are dissatisfied with the efforts that productivity enhancement consultants have made to increase productivity.

Question 11

Time and time again it has been shown that students who attend colleges with low faculty/student ratios get the most well-rounded education. As a result, when my children are ready for college, I'll be sure they attend a school with a very small student population.

Which of the following, if true, identifies the greatest flaw in the reasoning above?

(A) A low faculty/student ratio is the effect of a well-rounded education, not its source.

(B) Intelligence should be considered the result of childhood environment, not advanced education.

(C) A very small student population does not, by itself, ensure a low faculty/student ratio.

(D) Parental desires and preferences rarely determine a child's choice of a college or university.

(E) Students must take advantage of the low faculty/student ratio by intentionally choosing small classes.

Question 12

The increase in the number of newspaper articles exposed as fabrications serves to bolster the contention that publishers are more interested in boosting circulation than in printing the truth. Even minor publications have staffs to check such obvious fraud.

The argument above assumes that

(A) newspaper stories exposed as fabrications are a recent phenomenon

(B) everything a newspaper prints must be factually verifiable

(C) fact checking is more comprehensive for minor publications than for major ones

(D) only recently have newspapers admitted to publishing intentionally fraudulent stories

(E) the publishers of newspapers are the people who decide what to print in their newspapers

Question 13

Our architecture schools must be doing something wrong. Almost monthly we hear of domes and walkways collapsing in public places, causing great harm to human life. In their pursuit of some dubious aesthetic, architects design buildings that sway, crumble, and even shed windows into our cities' streets. This kind of incompetence will disappear only when the curricula of our architecture schools devote less time to so-called artistic considerations and more time to the basics of good design.

Which of the following, if true, would most seriously weaken the argument above?

(A) All architecture students are given training in basic physics and mechanics.

(B) Most of the problems with modern buildings stem from poor construction rather than poor design.

(C) Less than 50 percent of the curriculum at most architecture schools is devoted to aesthetics.

(D) Most buildings manage to stay in place well past their projected life expectancies.

(E) Architects study as long and as intensively as most other professionals.

Question 14

World War II had a profound effect on the growth of nascent businesses. The Acme Packaging Company netted only $10,000 in the year before the war. By 1948 it was earning almost ten times that figure.

The argument above depends upon which of the following assumptions?

(A) Acme's growth rate is representative of other nascent businesses.

(B) An annual profit of $10,000 is not especially high.

(C) Wars inevitably stimulate a nation's economy.

(D) Rapid growth for nascent businesses is especially desirable.

(E) Acme is not characterized by responsible, farsighted managers.

Question 15

This editorial cannot be a good argument because it is barely literate. Run-on sentences, slang, and perfectly dreadful grammar appear regularly throughout. Anything that poorly written cannot be making very much sense.

Which of the following identifies an assumption in the argument above?

(A) This editorial was written by someone other than the usual editor.

(B) Generally speaking, very few editorials are poor in style or grammar.

(C) The language of an argument is indicative of its validity.

(D) Generally speaking, the majority of editorials are poor in style and grammar.

(E) The author of the editorial purposely uses poor grammar to disguise what he knows is a bad argument.

Question 16

All German philosophers, except for Marx, are idealists.

From which of the following can the statement above be most properly inferred?

(A) Except for Marx, if someone is an idealist philosopher, then he or she is German.

(B) Marx is the only non-German philosopher who is an idealist.

(C) If a German is an idealist, then he or she is a philosopher, as long as he or she is not Marx.

(D) Marx is not an idealist German philosopher.

(E) Aside from the philosopher Marx, if someone is a German philosopher, then he or she is an idealist.

Question 17

Electrical engineers have developed an energy-efficient type of light bulb that can replace the traditional incandescent bulb. The new bulb, known as the electronic lamp, operates by using a high-frequency radio signal rather than the filament featured in incandescent bulbs. Although the electronic lamp currently costs 20 times as much as its traditional counterpart, its use will prove more cost effective in the long run. While a 100-watt incandescent bulb lasts six months if burned for four hours daily, a 25-watt electronic lamp used for the same amount of time each day lasts up to 14 years.

The argument above assumes that

(A) the typical household use of a light bulb is approximately four hours a day

(B) aside from its greater efficiency, the electronic lamp resembles the incandescent light bulb in most aspects

(C) the type of light cast by the electronic lamp is different from that cast by an incandescent bulb

(D) the price of electronic lamps will decrease as they are produced in increasingly greater quantities

(E) a 100-watt incandescent light bulb does not provide significantly more light than a 25-watt electronic lamp

Question 18

In interviews with jurors inquiring how they arrived at their verdicts, researchers found that 40 percent of the references jurors made were to factors that had not been included in courtroom testimony. To improve the jury system, the researchers suggested that judges give instructions to the jury at the beginning of a trial rather than at the end. They argued that this would permit jurors to concentrate on the most relevant evidence rather than filling in gaps with their own assumptions, which have little to do with the legality of a case.

The answer to which of the following questions is LEAST directly relevant to evaluating the researchers' suggestion above?

(A) Is it possible for a judge to instruct a jury at the end of a trial in such a way that jurors will disregard any irrelevant factors they had been using to weigh the evidence?

(B) Will a jury that hears a judge's instructions at the beginning of a trial be able to weigh the evidence accordingly once that evidence has actually been presented?

(C) Will having judges give instructions at the beginning of a trial rather than at the end significantly alter the customary procedures employed by the judicial system?

(D) When jurors are queried as to how they arrived at their verdicts, does their interpretation of their decision-making process include many references to factors that were not, in fact, influential?

(E) If jurors hear the judge's instructions at the beginning of a trial, what percentage of the factors that influence their decisions will be matters that were not presented in the evidence?

Question 19

Privatization of the large state enterprises that comprise the industrial sector in Russia is proceeding slowly, due to competing claims of ownership by various groups. Continued government subsidization of these enterprises creates large deficits that drive up the inflation rate and cause the ruble's value to decline. It is therefore unlikely that the government will make the ruble freely convertible to Western currencies until the question of ownership of state enterprises has been resolved.

If the author's prediction concerning the ruble is accurate, which of the following conclusions can most reliably be drawn?

(A) The industrial sector accounts for at least fifty percent of Russia's economic activity.

(B) Making the Russian ruble freely convertible to Western currencies will cause the ruble's value to decline.

(C) The Russian government can indefinitely withstand the expense of subsidiary state enterprises.

(D) The Russian government is among the groups claiming ownership of certain state enterprises.

(E) The Russian government is under pressure from the West to make the ruble freely convertible to Western currencies.

Question 20

Attempts to blame the mayor's policies for the growing inequality of wages are misguided. The sharp growth in the gap in earnings between college and high school graduates in this city during the past decade resulted from overall technological trends that favored the skills of more educated workers. Nor can the mayor's response to this problem be criticized, for it would hardly be reasonable to expect him to attempt to slow the forces of technology.

Which of the following, if true, casts the most serious doubt on the conclusion drawn in the last sentence above?

(A) The mayor could have initiated policies that would have made it easier for less-educated workers to receive the education necessary for better-paying jobs.

(B) Rather than cutting the education budget, the mayor could have increased the amount of staff and funding devoted to locating employment for graduating high school seniors.

(C) The mayor could have attempted to generate more demand for products from industries that paid high blue-collar wages.

(D) Instead of reducing the tax rate on the wealthiest earners, the mayor could have ensured that they shouldered a greater share of the total tax burden.

(E) The mayor could have attempted to protect the earnings of city workers by instigating policies designed to reduce competition from foreign industries.

Answer Key

1. D	6. C	11. C	16. E
2. E	7. E	12. E	17. E
3. C	8. C	13. B	18. C
4. D	9. E	14. A	19. B
5. D	10. D	15. C	20. A

Explanations

Question 1

An L.A. political candidate who buys saturation radio advertising will get maximum name recognition. In other words, such advertising is sufficient for maximum name recognition. If so, then it must be true that, as (D) says, a candidate can get such recognition without spending on other forms of media.

(A) suggests that radio advertising is the most important factor in L.A. political campaigns, but nothing like this was mentioned in the stimulus, so it's not inferable. Nor were we told the specific results of attaining maximum name recognition, so (B) is out. Similarly, we don't know precisely what is meant by "saturation radio advertising," so we can't infer anything as detailed as (C). Finally, although we know saturation radio advertising is sufficient for getting maximum name recognition, we can't infer that other things, such as the candidate's record mentioned in (E), have little effect on name recognition.

Question 2

The evidence discusses attacks by Dobermans, but the conclusion is that dogs—any dogs—are unsafe around little kids. This makes sense only if we assume (E): that Dobermans, in their behavior towards little kids, are generally representative of dogs. A good way of checking assumptions is to see what happens if we take their opposite: If the opposite of a statement weakens the argument, then that statement is assumed; if it doesn't, it's not. Here, if Dobermans' behavior towards small children isn't typical of dogs, the argument falls apart.

(A), whether the attacks were justified, is beside the point. Even if the kids were pulling the dogs' tails, the author's point that the dogs aren't safe still holds. Other pets are beyond the scope, so (B)'s out. As for (C), the argument doesn't deal with the future, so the author needn't assume anything about it. And it certainly wouldn't weaken the argument if, contrary to (D), many of the attacks could not have been prevented, so (D)'s not assumed.

Question 3

U.S. law forbids U.S. citizens from engaging in military campaigns against countries unless the United States is at war with those countries. Since no war has been declared between the United States and the Balaland Republic, the author concludes that the recruits being trained to fight against the Balaland Republic are defying U.S. law. But if, as (C) asserts, the recruits are being trained to fight only if a war is declared, then they're not in defiance of U.S. law. Being prepared for battle is different from actually engaging in it.

(A)'s no weakener; we can't assume that the country's escalating civil war justifies military action against it. In (B), severing diplomatic ties doesn't go far enough to show that training recruits is justifiable under U.S. law. As for (D), who funds the rebels was never mentioned by the author and is irrelevant. And as for (E), the author starts off calling for an investigation, so he doesn't assert that charges should be brought without launching an investigation first.

Question 4

Since the critics claim, based on the study's results, that the policy of leaving students back doesn't improve their skills, the best restatement of their view is (D). (A) fails for two reasons: one, the critics never hinted that test anxiety was the reason for poor performance, and two, (A) discusses "challenging new material," whereas the tests in question assessed students' basic skills. In (B), we're not interested in students' "true intellectual development"—again, it's their mastery of basic skills. Anyway, (B)'s criticism of standardized test scores tends to go against the critics' argument, which is based on those very scores. The psychological damage of being left back, raised in (C), is well beyond the scope; the critics never hinted at this. Finally, (E) fails because the critics never discussed socioeconomic factors at all—just test scores.

Question 5

Most murder victims were killed by people they knew, yet most people are more likely to fear being killed by a stranger. The best way to explain this

KAPLAN

apparent contradiction is (D): Most people don't believe they fall into the high-risk groups containing murderous friends and relations, but they do think they could be victims of random violence.

As for (A), did these people find it counterintuitive that most murder victims knew their killers? We don't know, so we can't assume they dismissed the statistics. (B)'s too vague to explain the discrepancy. In light of the statistics, people's fear of strangers seems irrational, but is it emotional? A more emotional response might be to become terrified of being killed by one's spouse or best friend. (C) fails because national statistics already exist, as the first sentence makes clear. Finally, (E) might explain why people who knew they might be killed ended up dead, but it doesn't resolve the discrepancy at hand.

Question 6

The author equates the withholding of government funding with censorship. (C), which denies that they're the same thing, destroys the argument. (A) is irrelevant. That the council's actions may reflect majority opinion wouldn't justify what the author considers censorship—her definition isn't dependent on what most people think. (B) complains that the term *obscenity* is used ambiguously, but it's the term *censorship* that's the problem here. (D) misses the whole point; in the author's view, denial of funding amounts to censorship, and (D) simply reaffirms this. And (E), like (A), points to majority opinion, but since the author never denies that most people can agree on what's obscene, this is beside the point.

Question 7

First, we need to understand the structure of the argument. Here the statement, "Allowing this would be as disastrous as . . . " clues us into the author's opinion. Assumption: One needs maturity and experience to design curricula. If the assumption were true, the argument would be strengthened. Check the answer choices, and look for one that affirms the assumption. (A) is just a restatement of the evidence; this choice adds no new information.

In (B) the argument made an analogy: "Allowing students to make their own curricula is a disastrous as letting three-year-olds choose their own diets." If an argument uses an analogy to make a point, it had better do so effectively. The better the analogy, the stronger the argument. This choice does strengthen the argument by showing the analogy to be true. But the question asks for the best strengthener and a more relevant strengthener may be present.

(C) is a classic faulty comparison choice; it is also out of scope. The author does not distinguish between local high school students and average teenagers. Moreover, the author focuses on experience and maturity, not intelligence.

(D) shifts the focus of the argument from "who should or should not design curricula" to "what kind of curricula is best." Notice the scope change in this choice. It is tempting, especially since it seems to bring up an intelligent point about tailoring to individuals. But this is a topic for an entirely different discussion.

The best strengthener is (E), citing the experience needed to design curricula.

Question 8

If we can show that something besides the court system may explain the increase in crime (if we can show a different cause for the same effect) we would weaken the argument. The author, after all, assumes that there is no other cause (a common GMAT assumption). Tackle the choices, looking for another cause besides the allegedly lenient court sentences. (A) is a classic faulty comparison. The argument does not compare one state to another. The argument's scope is the crime rate increase in this state only. In (B), the fact that white collar crime is also on the rise is more of a strengthener than a weakener—maybe it is the leniency in the courtroom that is responsible for an overall crime surge. (C) presents an alternative explanation for the increase in crime. Maybe it is not the judges at all but the fact that there are fewer cops on the street. As for (D), what if 65 percent of people in the state oppose capital punishment? What if 100 percent of people in this state oppose capital punishment? This provides little insight into why crime has gone up since last year. (E) tells us that numerous judges have been replaced in the last year. It is possible that the new judges are more lenient, but this would only strengthen the author's conclusion.

Question 9

This question asks, "Which of the following is best supported by the information above?" In other words, what can be inferred from the stated material? The author in this question discusses the impact of junior colleges on family-run businesses. Evidence: These colleges introduced people to new methods that were often successfully applied to family-run businesses. Conclusion: These colleges had a tremendous effect on family-run businesses.

A good inference will not go beyond this scope or read too much into particular detail. We go through the choices on Inference questions, because it's hard to predict what the correct answer will be.

In (A) the disqualifying word is *principally.* The information presented does not specify what the junior colleges emphasized. This choice reads too much into the fact that often family businesses increased in size because of the newly acquired knowledge. (B) is wrong because we really can't infer how popular or widespread these methods were before the war. For all we know these could have been revolutionary techniques or well-kept secrets. In (C), we know junior colleges taught new methods of marketing and finance and stuff like that; we do not know how much management theory was or was not presented. This choice relies on data we aren't given—a sure sign of an incorrect or unwarranted inference. In (D), all we are really told is that many family-run businesses became more profitable. It is possible that many family-run businesses could have been abandoned as unprofitable had it not been for the junior colleges, but nothing suggests that there necessarily would have been a significant number of business failures without colleges.

(E) is certainly true. Business methods did change because of the education. Notice how nonbiased this statement is, coming directly from the information given. Often people find the correct choice to be too obvious in Critical Reasoning questions; often it's just that straightforward.

Question 10

Keeping scope in mind, summarize or paraphrase the author's ideas. Here the author presents the consultants' ideas. Notice the paragraph uses words like *sometimes* and *slowdown.* The correct response should not go beyond such terminology. Consultants' conclusion: Techniques to increase productivity of discrete tasks have drawbacks, even though they accomplish their specific goals. Consultants' evidence: They often instill enough resentment to lead to a slowdown in the production process as a whole.

In (A), this statement is a sweeping generalization. It is too severe; do these techniques never work? Should they never be used? This is an unwarranted inference about productivity enhancement techniques. (B) is even farther out. Nowhere does the information imply that America is less competitive abroad than before. This is totally out of the blue. Since no geographic location is mentioned, for all we know, this data may have originated in Europe. (C) projects into the future, to an extreme result. All we are told is that sometimes (or even often) these techniques lead to a slowdown in the production process. This choice takes this much too far. (D) uses similar language (and tone) to the original paragraph and remains in scope without bringing in additional information. It is an accurate summary of the text.

You can almost disqualify (E) after the first few words. Although this choice picks up on the negative aspects of productivity enhancement, we really can infer nothing about production managers since they were never mentioned. In fact, many production managers may be ecstatic about the efforts that did pay off.

KAPLAN

Question 11

The evidence says that students who attend colleges with low faculty/student ratios get well-rounded educations, but the conclusion is that the author will send his kids to colleges with small student populations. Since colleges can have the second without necessarily having the first, (C) is correct.

(A) claims that the author confuses cause and effect, but how could getting a well-rounded education cause a low faculty/student ratio? Anyway, the real problem is the scope shift from faculty/student ratios to student populations. As for (B), the author never mentions intelligence at all. (D) fails because it doesn't point to a problem in the reasoning, just in implementing it. And (E) claims students must do something extra to take advantage of the low faculty/student ratio. Since the author never claimed the benefits would be conferred automatically, this isn't a flaw; more importantly, (E) misses the real flaw, which we find in (C).

Question 12

Evidence: more newspaper articles exposed as fabrications. Conclusion: Publishers want to increase circulation, not print the truth. This makes sense only if we assume (E), that publishers decide what to print. If (E) weren't true and this decision were up to someone else, the argument would fall apart.

Since the argument claims only an increase in made-up articles exposed, it's not necessary that they be a recent phenomenon, so (A)'s not assumed. (B) goes too far—it's not necessary that every article be factually verifiable in order for there to have been an increase in fabrications. As for (C), the author's claim that "even minor publications" have fact checkers is meant to emphasize that the publications know they're not printing the truth, not that minor ones are better at fact checking than major ones. And (D) brings up admission of guilt, which the author never mentions—the articles in question were exposed as frauds, not admitted to be frauds.

Question 13

Since the author concludes from evidence of collapsing buildings that architecture schools should spend more time teaching "the basics of good design," she obviously assumes that the buildings are falling down because of poor design rather than poor construction. (B) destroys the argument by demolishing this assumption.

The author claims A-schools don't focus enough on basic design, not basic physics and mechanics, so (A)'s no weakener. As for (C), the author never spells out how much of the curriculum should be spent on design, so more than half may not be enough for her. (D) distorts the argument—the author never claimed that most buildings are falling down, so the fact that most of them stay up doesn't matter. As for (E), other professionals are beyond the scope—the issue is how much A-schools focus on basic design rather than on more lofty artistic concerns.

Question 14

The author uses the single case of Acme to conclude that the war profoundly affected "nascent businesses." This assumes that Acme's growth rate is typical, or representative, of such businesses (A); otherwise, why hold it up as an example?

As for (B), the author needn't assume that $10,000 isn't much of a profit. Maybe he thinks it started out high and got even higher. (C), which brings up other wars, is beyond the scope—the argument concerns World War II, period. (D)'s tricky, but it's not assumed. Notice that the author claims only that World War II had a profound, not salutary, effect on nascent businesses, so we don't know just how he feels about rapid growth rates. As for (E), the author needn't assume Acme's managers had nothing to do with the company's success, just that the war also had an effect—and a marked one.

Question 15

The author's claim that the editorial's argument is no good because it's poorly written depends on the assumption that an argument's validity is related to its use of language. After all, if an argument's language didn't indicate its validity, the author's argument wouldn't make any sense at all.

(A)'s not assumed because the argument doesn't concern who's to blame for the bad editorial. (B) and (D) fail because the argument addresses this editorial only, so there's nothing assumed about what happens generally. And (E) goes too far: The author needn't assume that the writer deliberately wrote badly to hide a bad argument, just that, as (C) says, the poor writing indicates a poor argument.

Question 16

Read carefully! The question stem asks you to pick the choice from which the statement can be derived, and that's (E): If, as (E) says, anyone who is German is an idealist except for the philosopher Marx, then all Germans except for Marx are idealists. That being the case, it would certainly be true that, as the stimulus says, with the exception of Marx, all German philosophers—these folks being a subset of all Germans—are idealists. Now while (E)'s claim that all Germans are idealists may sound a bit absurd to you (perhaps you know some Germans who aren't idealists), we're concerned with strict logic here, not content.

(A) tells us that except for Marx, if someone's an idealist philosopher, then he or she is German, which is precisely the opposite of what we need: Knowing that all idealist philosophers (except Marx) are German doesn't prove that all German philosophers are idealists, because there could be other kinds of German philosophers. Since the stimulus statement tells us that Marx is a German philosopher who's not an idealist, (B), which contradicts this, is wrong. (C) lets us conclude that German idealists who aren't Marx are philosophers, but we need to conclude that German philosophers (except Marx) are idealists. As for (D), like the stimulus statement, it tells us that Marx isn't an idealist German philosopher, but we need a statement that ensures that every other German philosopher besides Marx is an idealist.

Question 17

Here we need to identify an assumption. The author attempts to demonstrate that the "electronic lamp" can replace the incandescent bulb (that's the conclusion) because although the electronic lamp now costs much more, it will prove more cost effective *in the long run* (that's a summary of the evidence). He backs up this claim with numbers: A 25-watt electronic lamp can last 28 times longer than a 100-watt incandescent bulb while costing only 20 times as much as the bulb (that's the hard evidence). There's one factor missing from the equation, though, and that's the amount of light the electronic lamp supplies. For the numbers given to support the author's conclusion, the electronic lamp and the normal bulb must each throw about the same amount of light. Otherwise, we might need 15 lamps for every bulb; and if this were the case, the argument would be dead wrong. Unless we assume, as (E) says, that the light produced by the lamp and the bulb is approximately equal, the evidence is meaningless.

(A) isn't assumed because the figure *four hours daily* doesn't have to represent typical household use; it need only provide a standard by which the lights can be compared. (B) is contradicted by the author. Since the electronic lamp operates by radio waves instead of a filament, it's clear that there are important structural aspects in which it differs from incandescent bulbs. (C) would actually make us doubt the reasonableness of the author's conclusion, so clearly it isn't assumed. If the electronic lamp is supposed to be a replacement for the incandescent bulb, its light should be similar to that produced by the bulb. (D) misconstrues why the electronic lamp is claimed to be cost effective in the long run—the point is that it lasts longer, not that it will become cheaper. The author is arguing that current electronic lamps are more cost effective, not that future lamps will be.

Question 18

In order to evaluate the suggestion in this question, we must know what problem the plan is intended to solve and how it is supposed to do so. That's the standard approach to Critical Reasoning arguments that put forth plans and proposals.

Simply put, after conducting interviews, researchers are alarmed at the extent to which jurors appear to base verdicts on factors outside testimony.

Researchers suggest that juries should get instructions at the beginning of a trial rather than at its end, so they can concentrate on relevant evidence. We want the question that is least helpful in evaluating this plan. Questions that are helpful in evaluating the plan will probably either test the researchers' understanding of the problem, or test the efficacy of their proposed solution. A good way to test the choices is to check whether "yes" and "no" answers to the question affect the plan's chances of success differently (where, of course, the question allows a "yes" or "no" answer). (C) fails the test. We're interested in whether the plan will be effective, or whether it's necessary, or whether there's a better approach. (C) asks only if implementing the suggestion will alter customary procedures. No matter what the answer to that question is, the researchers' suggestion is unaffected.

If the answer to (A) is yes, then the researchers' plan isn't even necessary—the present system will work if given a little refining. If the answer to (B) is "yes," then the researchers' suggestion is strengthened. If the answer is "no," then the suggestion is worthless. (D) strikes at the reason for developing the plan. If the answer is "yes," that jurors do report factors that weren't really influential to their decision making, then the plan may not be necessary. (E) asks if the plan will work; if jurors still consider many factors that have nothing to do with the evidence even when judges give their instructions ahead of time, then the plan will fail. If, on the other hand, jurors consider far fewer irrelevant factors, then the plan looks good.

Question 19

This question asks for the most reliable conclusion based on the author's prediction concerning the ruble. The author describes a chain of cause and effect and ends with a prediction: Competing claims of ownership are slowing efforts to privatize state enterprises; these enterprises must still be subsidized by the government; government subsidies lead to large deficits; deficits drive up the inflation rate; high inflation causes the ruble's value to decline. In a nutshell, the disagreement over ownership is causing the ruble to decline in value. The author's conclusion, which we're told to accept as accurate, is that until

the question of ownership has been resolved, the Russian government probably won't make the ruble freely convertible to Western currencies.

Be on the lookout for new ideas that occur in the conclusion. Here you should have thought, "What more is going on here? What else is the author assuming?" We want the connection the author sees between the competing claims for ownership and the conclusion's completely new idea of making the ruble freely convertible. Well, her point about the competing claims is that they cause the ruble's value to decline. So we should look for a choice that connects the action of making the ruble freely convertible to a decline in the ruble's value. (B) fits this scenario by concluding that making the ruble freely convertible to Western currency would also cause the ruble's value to decline, thereby (inferably) making matters worse. (B) explains quite nicely why the state's ownership of enterprises postpones the ruble's convertibility.

If you didn't see (B)'s place in the argument, you could have arrived at it anyway by eliminating the choices that couldn't be correct (a Kaplan method that works rather nicely here). (A) is unwarranted. Nothing in the argument justifies assigning a percentage to the industrial sector. (C) contradicts the spirit of the passage, which says that government subsidies are creating a strain, in the form of large deficits, on the economy. The statement that the government can withstand this strain is definitely farfetched. Contrary to (D), the argument doesn't state that the government is among the parties squabbling over ownership of state enterprises, but only that until the squabble is resolved the enterprises must remain in state hands. (E) would explain why the Russian government might want to make the ruble convertible in the first place, but one, there's no hint of it in the passage, and two, it doesn't jibe with the conclusion that the government will probably wait to make the ruble convertible.

Question 20

The Kaplan technique of prephrasing an answer works pretty well here. The author concludes that the mayor isn't responsible for the growing gap in earnings between high school and college graduates. Her evidence is one, that the growing need for technologically skilled workers is responsible, and two, that the mayor can't slow the force of technology. No, probably not, but he can take it upon himself to train the less skilled for better jobs. If that rebuttal occurred to you, you had no trouble finding (A). (A) argues that the mayor could have pursued policies that would have enabled the less educated to receive the education that would qualify them for well-paying jobs. If (A) is true, the author's argument is severely weakened.

(B) is off the mark. The problem addressed in the stimulus isn't the lack of employment for graduating high school students, it's the lack of employment that pays as well as high-skill employment. (C)'s proposal might help create more jobs that pay high blue-collar wages, but we don't know what "high" blue-collar wages are. They could still be far lower than the wages earned by people with college educations, in which case (C) wouldn't really address the inequality of wages. As for (D), the problem the mayor was supposed to solve was unequal wages, and it's not clear that taxing more heavily those with high wages constitutes a solution to that problem. Unskilled workers would still be stuck in low-paying jobs. (E) talks about protecting city workers' earnings, but this refers to all city workers. As such, (E)'s suggestion wouldn't improve the position of high school graduates compared to college graduates, which is what we want.

CHAPTER FOUR

Sentence Correction

HIGHLIGHTS

- Learn the Eight Basic Principles of Sentence Correction
- Study the Kaplan Method for answering Sentence Correction questions
- Review the common errors found in Sentence Correction problems
- Complete the Sentence Correction Drills and Sentence Correction Practice Quiz

The directions for these questions look like this:

Directions: The following questions consist of sentences that are either partly or entirely underlined. Below each sentence are five versions of the underlined portion of the sentence. Choice (A) duplicates the original version. The four other versions revise the underlined portion of the sentence. Read the sentence and the five choices carefully, and select the best version. If the original seems better than any of the revisions, select choice (A). If not, choose one of the revisions.

These questions test your recognition of correct grammatical usage and your sense of clear and economical writing style. Choose answers according to the norms of standard written English for grammar, word choice, and sentence construction. Your selected answer should express the intended meaning of the original sentence as clearly and precisely as possible, while avoiding ambiguous, awkward, or unnecessarily wordy constructions.

Sentence Correction Tally

Expect to see approximately 15 Sentence Correction questions on the Verbal section of the GMAT.

The GMAT Verbal section contains about 15 Sentence Correction questions, which are mixed in with Critical Reasoning and Reading Comprehension questions.

Sentence Correction questions cover a range of grammar and style errors, some of which are so obscure that even good writers commit them. That's the bad news. The good news is that you don't have to be a grammar expert to do well on this section. All you need is a mode of attack and some knowledge about what does—and does not—constitute good GMAT English.

GMAT Sentence Correction tests your command of "standard written English," the rather formal language that is used in textbooks and scholarly periodicals. It's the language that's used to convey complex information precisely, as opposed to the casual language that we use for everyday communication. As the Sentence Correction directions put it, it's a matter of "correctness of expression."

Another key element in GMAT English is style, or what the directions call "effectiveness of expression." GMAT English is "clear and exact, without awkwardness, ambiguity, or redundancy." (Note that the test makers don't call it "interesting." The test is set up to see whether you get worn down by difficult, often boring prose, or whether you rise above that to stay involved—and awake.)

Eliminating wrong answer choices and strategic guessing are keys to unlocking tougher Sentence Correction questions. Make an answer grid on your scratch paper to keep track of eliminated choices.

The Kaplan Three-Step Method for Sentence Corrections

1. Read the original sentence through carefully.
If you find an error in the sentence, cross out choice (A) immediately because you know it won't be the correct answer choice. Choice (A) will always repeat the wording of the original sentence.

2. Scan the answer choices for differences that may help you zero in on what types of errors are being tested.
If the answer choices present a variety of verb tenses or pronouns, for instance, you'll know where to focus your attention.

3. Eliminate a choice as soon as you find *one* error in it.
If you spot any error in an answer choice, eliminate that choice and move on to the next one. You should be able to eliminate enough answer choices to come up with the correct answer, or at least with a good percentage guess.

Sentence Correction at a Glance

- Read the entire original sentence once.
- Never read choice (A); it's the same as the underlined portion of the sentence.
- Don't worry about spelling, capitalization, or punctuation.
- Make an answer choice grid on your scratch paper to keep track of what you eliminate.

Using the Kaplan Three-Step Method

Now let's try the Kaplan Three-Step Method on the following Sentence Correction question.

> Several consumer protection agencies have filed suit, seeking to bar distributors from advertising treatments for baldness <u>that brings no discernible improvement and may even result in potential harm.</u>
>
> Ⓐ that brings no discernible improvement and may even result in potential harm
> Ⓑ that bring no discernible improvement and may even prove harmful
> Ⓒ bringing no discernible improvement and even being harmful
> Ⓓ that brings no discernible improvement and may even potentially result in harm being done
> Ⓔ that bring no discernible improvement, maybe even resulting in harm

The Kaplan Three-Step Method for Sentence Correction

1. Read the original sentence carefully.
2. Scan answer choices for errors.
3. Eliminate answer choices that contain errors.

1. Read the original sentence carefully.

You should immediately notice that the error lies in the second word of the underlined part, *brings*. What *brings* no discernible improvement? Treatments. But you can't say *treatments brings*. So cross out (A), which is (as always) the same as the original.

2. Scan the answer choices for differences.

The difference in verbs seems to be the issue. Some choices have *brings*, some have *bring*, and one has *bringing*. Which is correct here?

3. Eliminate answer choices that contain errors.

The beginning of each choice is a good place to start here, because there are three basic variations. You already know that *brings* is wrong, so you can eliminate (D) without reading any more of it. The answer, of course, turns out to be (B). *Bring* is the verb you need to agree with *treatments*.

Sentence Correction Tips

As you practice doing Sentence Correction problems, keep the following tips in mind:

- Always read the entire original sentence carefully. Don't try to save time by reading only the underlined portion and simply comparing it to the answer choices. You'll usually have to understand how the underlined portion of the sentence relates to the part that's not underlined. For instance, you may see a subject/verb agreement error in a sentence in which the verb is underlined, but the subject isn't.

> **Teacher Tip**
>
> Knowing what makes an answer wrong is just as important as knowing what makes an answer right. They're two sides of the same coin.
> —Marilyn Engle
> Encino, CA

- Never read choice (A), which always repeats the underlined portion of the original sentence. Immediately skip down to answer choice (B).

- The test makers never test spelling or capitalization. Certain answer choices differ in their punctuation, but it's never the punctuation itself that's being tested.

- Time is of the essence on Sentence Correction. Of course, the sentences vary in length and complexity, so you'll have to move considerably faster on the shorter ones in order to leave adequate time for the longer ones.

The Eight Basic Principles of Sentence Correction

1. Make sure you understand the directions.

There's no greater waste of your precious testing time than rereading the directions. Essentially, you're given a sentence in which some or all the words are underlined. The answer choices (B) through (E) present four other ways of expressing the underlined portion, and choice (A) repeats the original sentence's wording. You have to choose the best version of the sentence. So, if you think that the original sentence is fine and none of the rewrites is better, pick choice (A). If, however, you feel that the original sentence is awkward or contains a grammatical error, pick the answer that presents the best rewrite. That's all there is to it.

2. Verbs must agree with their subjects.

Make sure that singular subjects have singular verbs and that plural subjects have plural verbs. If you're a native speaker, you probably follow this simple grammatical rule so automatically that you may wonder why the GMAT tests it at all. But the test makers craftily separate subject and verb with lots of text, to make it harder to recognize whether the subject and verb agree. Also, it is often hard to tell whether the subject is singular or plural. As a result, Sentence Correction questions often feature separated subjects and verbs or subjects that aren't obviously singular or plural.

You should look out for:

- One or more long modifying phrases or clauses following the subject

- Phrases and clauses in commas between the subject and the verb

- Subjects joined by *either/or* and *neither/nor*

- Sentences in which the verb precedes the subject

- Collective nouns, such as *majority, system, audience,* and *committee*

Note

The GMAT tests only a limited number of grammar and style concepts. Once you learn what they are and practice recognizing errors, you'll be ready to tackle the Sentence Correction questions on the GMAT.

Subject-Verb Agreement Drill

Directions: Correct each of the following subject/verb errors. Write your corrections on the lines below the sentences.

1. The depletion of natural resources, in addition to the rapid increase in utilization of these resources, have encouraged many nations to conserve energy.

   _____

   _____

   _____

2. There is, without a doubt, many good reasons to exercise.

   _____

   _____

3. Among the many problems plaguing suburbanites is the ubiquity of shopping malls, the increasing cost of gasoline, and the unavailability of mortgages.

   _____

   _____

4. The neighbors told police investigators that neither Annette nor her brother are capable of telling the truth.

   _____

   _____

   _____

5. A majority of the voters want to unseat the incumbent.

   _____

Review

To determine whether a collective noun should have a singular or plural verb, ask yourself whether the *audience, committee,* or other collective noun is acting as a unit (in which case it takes a singular verb) or as separate individuals (in which case the noun takes a plural verb). Collective nouns will almost always be singular in Sentence Correction sentences.

Answers and Explanations

1. *Depletion* is the subject. Correct by changing *have* to *has*, or by changing *in addition to* to *and*.

2. There *are* many good reason*s*. (A good strategy is to temporarily ignore parts of the sentence that are set off by commas.)

3. If the sentence ended at *malls*, *is* would be correct. But because there is more than one problem plaguing suburbanites, *are* is the correct verb here.

4. "Neither Annette nor her brother *is* capable." (The verb agrees with whatever follows *nor*. So if it were "Neither Annette nor her friends," *are* would be called for.)

5. As a general rule, the number of the verb depends on the sense of the sentence. Because it is acting as an amorphous mass in this sentence, *majority* is singular: *The majority wants to unseat.*

3. A modifier should be as close as possible to the word or clause that it modifies.

A modifier is a word, phrase, or clause that describes another part of the sentence. You should place a modifier as close as possible to what it modifies. Modifiers often attach themselves to the closest word. They sometimes appear to modify words they actually don't. A long modifier that comes before the beginning of the main clause will seem to modify the subject. A long modifier that comes in the middle or end of the sentence will seem to describe the word immediately before it.

You should look out for:

*   Sentences beginning or ending with descriptive phrases
*   *That/which* clauses, especially ones that come at the end of sentences

Modification Drill

Directions: In each of the following sentences, what does each clause or phrase modify? What is it supposed to modify? Fix each error you find, using the lines below the sentences.

1. Upon landing at the airport, the hotel sent a limousine to pick us up.

    _____

    _____

2. Based on the most current data available, the company made plans to diversify its holdings.

    _____

    _____

Kaplan Rules

Check the words that immediately precede and follow each descriptive phrase or clause. Is the description logical?

3. Small and taciturn, Joan Didion's presence often goes unnoticed by those she will later write about.

_____

_____

4. I took several lessons to learn how to play tennis without getting the ball over the net even once.

_____

_____

5. The house overlooked the lake, which was set back from the shore.

_____

_____

Answers and Explanations

1. The sentence seems to be saying that the hotel landed at the airport. Your common sense will tell you that *upon landing at the airport* could modify only the unnamed *we*. You could say, "Upon landing at the airport, we were met by a limousine sent by the hotel."

2. As the sentence is written, the phrase *based on the most current data available* modifies the subject *company*. It sounds as though the company was based on current data. Obviously, though, what was based on the data were the plans, not the company. Thus, "Based on the most current data available, plans were made to diversify the company's holdings."

3. It's Joan Didion, not her presence, that's small and taciturn.

4. The way the sentence is written, it seems that the author wants to learn how to *not* hit the ball over the net. We need to revise the sentence to say something like this: "I took many tennis lessons without getting the ball over the net even once."

5. Misplacement produces an absurd image: a lake that's set back from its own shore. Of course, the *which* clause should follow *the house*. Then the sentence will read: *The house, which was set back from the shore, overlooked the lake.*

4. A pronoun must agree with its antecedent and refer to only one antecedent.

Luckily, the GMAT doesn't test every single kind of pronoun error. Errors fall into two general categories: *reference* and *agreement*. Correct pronoun *reference* means that any given pronoun must refer to, or stand for, one specific noun or pronoun in the sentence (its antecedent). For pronouns, as for verbs, *agreement* is mainly a question of number. A pronoun that refers to a singular noun must be in singular form; a pronoun that refers to a plural noun must be in plural form. As usual, the GMAT presents camouflaged examples of these two mistakes.

Look out for:

- Pronouns, especially *it* and *they*, that are often misused on the GMAT (and in everyday life)
- Pronouns that don't refer to specific nouns or pronouns
- Pronouns that don't agree in person or number with their antecedents

Pronoun Drill

Directions: Here are some common pronoun reference errors. Try to correct each one of them. Use the lines below the sentences for your corrections.

1. Beatrix Potter's stories depict animals in an unsentimental and humorous manner, and she illustrated them with delicate watercolor paintings.

   _____

   _____

2. There is no known cure for certain forms of hepatitis; they hope, though, that a cure will be found soon.

   _____

   _____

3. If the partners cannot resolve their differences, the courts may have to do it.

   _____

   _____

Review

Check each pronoun. Does it refer to a specific noun or pronoun? Does it agree in person or number with whatever it's supposed to refer to?

KAPLAN

4. In order to boost their name recognition, the Green Party sent canvassers to a busy shopping mall.

    _____

    _____

5. It is now recognized that the dangers of nuclear war are much graver than that of conventional warfare.

    _____

    _____

6. Not even your best friend can always be relied on to give one good advice.

    _____

    _____

Answers and Explanations

1. *She* could refer only to Beatrix Potter but notice that the proper noun *Beatrix Potter* doesn't exist in the sentence, only *Beatrix Potter's*. There's a second problem: The pronoun *them* seems to refer to animals, although it could logically refer only to *stories*. Here's a rewrite that solves all the problems: *Beatrix Potter not only wrote stories that depicted animals in an unsentimental and humorous manner, she also illustrated each story with delicate watercolor paintings.*

2. It's unclear what the word *they* refers to. The only plural noun is *forms*, but it can't be the *forms of hepatitis* that are hoping for a cure. It must be *scientists*, or some other group of people. You could say *scientists hope to find a cure soon* or *it is hoped that a cure will be found soon.*

3. *It* is the unclear noun here. There's no singular noun in the sentence for *it* to refer to. The main clause should read: *the courts may have to do so.*

4. A pronoun or possessive should match the actual form of the noun it refers to. Use *its* and not *their* in place of the Green Party, because *party*, like *majority*, is a singular noun that stands for a collective group.

5. *Dangers* is plural. The sentence should read *those of conventional warfare.*

6. The sentence can't say *your* best friend and give *one* good advice. It has to say either *your* and *you* or *one's* and *one.*

5. Verb tenses must reflect the sequence of events.

Different verb tenses indicate the order in which separate actions or events occur. Deciding which verb tense is appropriate in a given situation isn't just a matter of grammar, it's also a question of logic. Many GMAT sentences are long and complicated, involving or implying several different actions. The correct tenses make the sequence of events clear.

To determine whether the verbs in a sentence are in the proper tenses, pick one event as a standard and measure every other event against it. Ask yourself whether the other events are supposed to have happened *before* the standard event took place, *after* the standard event took place, or *during* the time that the standard event took place. Those aren't mutually exclusive options, by the way: English tenses allow for complex relationships, including the possibility of one action starting before a second action and continuing during that second action.

A frequent GMAT verb error is the inappropriate use of *-ing* forms: "I am going, I was going, I had been going," and so on. As far as the GMAT is concerned, there are only two basic reasons to use an *-ing* form: to emphasize the continuing nature of an action or to emphasize that two actions are occurring simultaneously. In other words, GMAT usually wants you to pick a simpler tense, one that doesn't use the *-ing* form, unless an action is continuing or happening during another action. A good way to remember this rule is to think of the word *during* and its *-ing* ending.

You should look out for:

- *-ing* forms
- The appearance of several verbs, indicating events that seem to have happened in sequence or at different times

Verb Tense Drill

Directions: Correct each of these sentences, using the lines below the sentences.

1. The criminal escaped from custody and is believed to flee the country.

   _____

   _____

2. Some archaeologists believe that the Minoans of 3,700 years ago had practiced a religion that involved human sacrifice.

_____

_____

_____

3. If the experiment works, it will be representing a quantum leap forward for pharmaceutical chemistry.

_____

_____

4. He had seen that movie recently, so he doesn't want to see it tonight.

_____

_____

5. When she retires, she will save enough money to allow her to live comfortably.

_____

_____

6. She already closed the door behind her when it occurred to her that she wasn't able to get back in later.

_____

_____

Answers and Explanations

1. *The criminal escaped* uses simple past tense. So, to reflect the logical sequence of events, the criminal *is believed to have fled the country.*

2. Use the past perfect verb, *had*, plus another verb to indicate a past action taking place before another past action: *He had quit smoking when he died.* There's no indication the Minoans practiced human sacrifice for a while and then did something else. So use the simple past *practiced* instead of *had practiced.*

3. The experiment won't *be representing a quantum leap*, it *will represent a quantum leap.* Avoid *to be* when you can. It often indicates wordiness in GMAT questions.

4. *Had* plus a past tense verb is used when you have two things going on in the past and you want to indicate which action occurred earlier. Here, you could change *doesn't* to *didn't*, or use *saw* instead of *had seen*.

5. You need to indicate an action that began in the past and will end in the future. Think of it this way: At some future time, what will have happened? She will have saved enough money.

6. *Closed, occurred,* and *wasn't able to get back in* are all in the simple past tense. But you need to indicate first, that she closed the door before something occurred to her, and second, that she wouldn't be able to do something in the future. So you need to say *had already closed,* and *wouldn't be able to get back in.*

6. Similar elements in a sentence must be parallel to each other.

Similar elements in a sentence must be in similar form. These elements include items in a list and verbs in a series. Also, two-part constructions (such as *from . . . to . . .* and *(n)either . . .(n)or . . .*) have to introduce similar terms. Finally, items linked by *and* should be structurally similar. Although this principle has several components, the basic concept behind parallelism is pretty simple: Ideas with the same importance and function—nouns, verbs, phrases, or whatever—should be expressed in the same grammatical form.

You should look out for:

- Lists of items or a series of events
- Such expressions as *both* X *and* Y, *either* X *or* Y, *prefer* X *to* Y

Parallelism Drill

Directions: In the following sentences, put parallel items into the same form. Use the lines below the sentences for your rewrites.

1. The city's decay stems from governmental mismanagement, increasing unemployment, and many businesses are relocating.

_____

_____

_____

Review

Watch out for items in pairs or series, and also pair expressions; make sure these items are expressed in parallel form.

2. Tourists' images of France range from cosmopolitan to the pastoral.

3. Excited about visiting New York, Jasmine minded neither riding the subways nor to cope with the crowded sidewalks.

4. To visualize success is not the same as achieving it.

5. I remember my aunt making her own dandelion wine and that she played the fiddle.

6. In my favorite Armenian restaurant, the menu is fascinating and the entrées exquisite.

Answers and Explanations

1. The last four words, *many businesses are relocating*, should be replaced by *business relocation*, to parallel *governmental mismanagement* and *increasing unemployment*.

2. If you say *the pastoral* you have to say *the cosmopolitan*. Or you could just say *cosmopolitan to pastoral*.

3. In order to parallel *riding*, you need *coping* instead of *to cope*.

4. You need *visualizing* instead of *to visualize*.

5. It has to be either: *I remember my aunt making . . . and playing . . .* , or *I remember that my aunt made . . . and played . . .* .

6. You say *is fascinating*, so you must say, *are exquisite*.

Review

Compare people to people, groups to groups, and attributes to attributes.

Review

Check to see whether the comparison is logical (according to the standards of GMAT English), and grammatical.

7. Compare like things only.

You should compare only things that can be logically compared. Faulty comparisons account for a significant number of errors in GMAT Sentence Correction questions. Most relate to the very simple idea that *you can't compare apples and oranges.* You don't want to compare merely things that are grammatically similar; you also want to compare things that are logically similar. For instance, you can't logically compare a person to a quality or an item to a group. You have to compare one individual to another, one quality to another, one group to another.

You should look out for key comparison words, such as *like, as, compared to, less than, more than, other, that of,* and *those of.*

Comparisons Drill

Directions: Fix the comparisons in the sentences below, using the lines below the sentence for your rewrites.

1. Like a black bear I once saw in the Buenos Aires Zoo, the Central Park Zoo polar bear's personality strikes me as being sadly neurotic.

   _____

   _____

   _____

2. The article questioned the popularity of jazz compared to classical music.

   _____

   _____

3. The challenger weighed 20 pounds less than that of the defender.

   _____

   _____

4. The Boston office contributes less to total national sales than any other U.S. branch.

   _____

   _____

5. The host paid more attention to his celebrity guest than the others.

_____

_____

Answers and Explanations

1. *Like* creates a comparison, and you can compare only similar things. Here, you have to compare bears to bears or personalities to personalities. The simplest way to fix this sentence is to replace *polar bear's personality* with *polar bear*.

2. It has to be *the popularity of jazz* that's compared to *the popularity of classical music*, or *that of classical music*.

3. It has to be either: *The challenger weighed 20 pounds less than the defender did* or *The challenger's weight was 20 pounds less than that of the defender*.

4. You want to compare what the *Boston office contributes* to what any other U.S. branch contributes. In GMAT English, the most elegant way to fix this is to insert *does* after *U.S. branch. Does* will stand for *contributes*.

5. A similar problem—you need to repeat the verb after *than* (*than he or she paid to the others*). Or you can refer to the verb by placing *to* after *than* (*than to the others*).

Kaplan Rules

Listen for what sounds natural and right. If you have a faulty ear for idioms, study and even memorize them.

8. Use your "ear" for correct idioms.

This eighth (and frequently tested) principle concerns forms of expression that have established themselves in standard English as the "right" way to say things. There's no grammar rule that applies here; it's just that these particular expressions are generally agreed upon as correct by all English speakers.

If you're a native English speaker, you probably know most idioms already. Your "ear" will tell you what's correct. If you are not a native speaker, it's worth taking time to learn these expressions. In fact, keep a notebook and jot them down as you come across them in your practice.

You should look out for Sentence Corrections that contain idiomatic expressions.

Idioms Drill

Directions: In each of the following sentences, circle the word or words that "sounds" right in the sentence.

1. Mathew Brady is regarded (as/to be) one of the greatest nineteenth-century American photographers.

2. The destruction of tropical rain forests is generally considered (as/to be/_ _) a major threat to the environment.

3. It took me four times as long to write the report collaboratively (than/as) it would have taken me to write it by myself.

4. The Geneva Convention covers such questions (like/as) the proper treatment of prisoners of war.

5. Hiram plays guitar (like/as) his father does.

6. The gas was being produced (in/at) a rate of twelve million cubic feet a day.

7. I prefer Korean food (to/over) Japanese.

8. My mother tried to discourage me (from attending/to attend) law school.

9. Many consumers buy inferior products when forced to choose (among/between) price and value.

10. Off-off-Broadway theaters seat significantly (fewer/less) patrons than do Broadway theaters.

Answers and Explanations

1. The idiom is *regarded as*.

2. It's *considered* a threat. Although *considered to be* is also *considered to be* correct by most grammarians, it is *considered* wordy by the GMAT writers, who always prefer to drop the "to be." Moreover, *considered as* is considered wrong by all authorities.

3. The idiom is *as long . . . as*. This test lasted four times *as long as* that one did. *As far . . . as* works in the same way.

4. You have to say "the Geneva Convention covers such questions *as* proper treatment."

5. He plays *like* his father does.

6. It's "*at a* rate of," instead of "in a rate of."

7. The correct idiom is "prefer . . . to."

8. You don't discourage someone *to attend*; you discourage that person *from attending*.

9. Use *between* to distinguish two things, such as *price* and *value* here. Use *among* for more than two things. They divided the pie *between themselves* or *among the four of them.*

10. *Fewer* is correct. *Fewer* answers the question: "How many?" (for example, fewer people, cats, mushrooms, or lawnmowers) and *less* answers the question: "How much?" (for example, less sand or flour).

Now that you have the basics of GMAT Sentence Correction under your belt, try the Practice Quiz.

Sentence Correction Practice Quiz

Directions: The following questions consist of sentences that are either partly or entirely underlined. Below each sentence are five versions of the underlined portion of the sentence. Choice (A) duplicates the original version. The four other versions revise the underlined portion of the sentence. Read the sentence and the five choices carefully, and select the best version. If the original seems better than any of the revisions, select choice (A). If not, choose one of the revisions. Darken the oval corresponding to your choice. (Answers and explanations follow the quiz.)

These questions test your recognition of correct grammatical usage and your sense of clear and economical writing style. Choose answers according to the norms of standard written English for grammar, word choice, and sentence construction. Your selected answer should express the intended meaning of the original sentence as clearly and precisely as possible, while avoiding ambiguous, awkward, or unnecessarily wordy constructions.

Question 1

The concert this weekend promises to attract <u>an even greater amount of people</u> than attended the last one.

- (A) an even greater amount of people
- (B) an even larger amount of people
- (C) an amount of people even greater
- (D) a number of people even larger
- (E) an even greater number of people

Question 2

<u>Compared with the time period of John Steinbeck's *The Grapes of Wrath*</u>, the poor of today would be considered wealthy.

- (A) Compared with the time period of John Steinbeck's *The Grapes of Wrath*
- (B) Compared with the time period during which John Steinbeck's *The Grapes of Wrath* took place
- (C) Compared with the characters in John Steinbeck's *The Grapes of Wrath*
- (D) In comparison to the time of John Steinbeck's *The Grapes of Wrath*
- (E) In comparison to John Steinbeck's *The Grapes of Wrath*

Question 3

Although the square root of a negative number has no real value, it is not necessarily true that <u>equations involving imaginary numbers like these are practically inapplicable</u>.

- (A) equations involving imaginary numbers like these are practically inapplicable
- (B) equations involving such imaginary numbers have no practical applications
- (C) equations involving these inapplicable imaginary numbers are practical
- (D) equations involving imaginary numbers such as these are inapplicable practically
- (E) there is no practical applications for equations involving such imaginary numbers as these

Question 4

Anarchists believe that the ideal society is one in which the motivation to maintain law and order <u>lies in the innate reasonableness of human nature rather than in the threat of force</u>.

- (A) lies in the innate reasonableness of human nature rather than in the threat of force
- (B) lie in the innate reasonableness of human nature rather than in the threat of force
- (C) lays in the innate reasonableness of human nature rather than the threat of force
- (D) lay in the innate reasonableness of human nature instead of the threat of force
- (E) lies in the innate reasonableness of human nature instead of the threat of force

Question 5

The public's widespread belief in the existence of <u>UFOs and their general curiosity about extraterrestrial life has</u> generated considerable interest in science fiction.

- (A) UFOs and their general curiosity about extraterrestrial life has
- (B) UFOs and they are generally curious about extraterrestrial life which has
- (C) UFOs, as well as their general curiosity about extraterrestrial life, have
- (D) UFOs, as well as its general curiosity about extraterrestrial life, has
- (E) UFOs, as well as general curiosity about extraterrestrial life, have

Question 6

In some countries, the political system works by a simple logic: the more an organization contributes to politicians' campaign funds, <u>its interests are better served by the policies and actions of the government</u>.

- (A) its interests are better served by the policies and actions of the government
- (B) its interests are the better served through the policies and actions of the government
- (C) the better its interests are served by the policies and actions of the government
- (D) by the policies and actions of the government, its interests being better served
- (E) by the policies and actions of the government, service is the better for its interests

Question 7

Many of the thousands of students currently enrolled in night courses hope <u>for the exchanging of their drab jobs for new careers that are challenging</u>.

- (A) for the exchanging of their drab jobs for new careers that are challenging
- (B) for exchanging drab jobs for new careers that will challenge them
- (C) to exchange their drab jobs with new careers that will be new and challenging
- (D) to exchange their drab jobs for new and challenging careers
- (E) to exchanging their drab jobs and find careers that will be new and challenging

Question 8

Records of the first 736 British convicts deported to Australia reveal <u>convictions for crimes against property in all cases and they ranged</u> from highway robbery to forgery.

- Ⓐ convictions for crimes against property in all cases and they ranged
- Ⓑ convictions in all cases were crimes against property and ranging
- Ⓒ the ranging of convictions for crimes against property in all cases
- Ⓓ that all were convicted of crimes against property ranging
- Ⓔ that all of them had convictions for crimes that were against property; the range was

Question 9

The symptoms of the participants in a recent decongestant effectiveness study, including a required "stuffy nose," <u>parallel that of the multitudes of Americans afflicted with</u> the common cold each winter.

- Ⓐ parallel that of the multitudes of Americans afflicted with
- Ⓑ parallel the multitudes of Americans afflicted with
- Ⓒ parallel those of the multitudes of Americans afflicted with
- Ⓓ parallels those of the multitudes of Americans afflicted from
- Ⓔ parallels that of the multitudes of Americans afflicted from

Question 10

A group of students who have begun to clean up Frederick Law Olmsted's Morningside Park in New York City <u>believes that the park needs not to be redesigned but to</u> be returned to its former condition.

- Ⓐ believes that the park needs not to be redesigned but to
- Ⓑ believe that the park needs to not be redesigned but to
- Ⓒ believes that the park needs not to be redesigned but could
- Ⓓ believe that the park needs to be not redesigned but to
- Ⓔ believe that the park needs not to be redesigned but that it

Question 11

<u>Having recently published a series of science fiction books influenced by Sufism, Doris Lessing will likely</u> be remembered best for her early novels about Africa.

- Ⓐ Having recently published a series of science fiction books influenced by Sufism, Doris Lessing will likely
- Ⓑ Although she has recently published a series of science fiction books influenced by Sufism, Doris Lessing is likely to
- Ⓒ She has recently published a series of science fiction books influenced by Sufism, and Doris Lessing will likely
- Ⓓ In spite of recently publishing a series of science fiction books influenced by Sufism, Doris Lessing should likely
- Ⓔ Recently publishing a series of science fiction books influenced by Sufism, Doris Lessing may likely

Question 12

In February, 1983, brush fires <u>had swept the drought-parched southeastern coast of Australia, at least 69 people being killed, and thousands of homes and acres of farmland were left smoldering</u>.

A. had swept the drought-parched southeastern coast of Australia, at least 69 people being killed, and thousands of homes and acres of farmland were left smoldering

B. swept the drought-parched southeastern coast of Australia, having killed at least 69 people, and thousands of home and acres of farmland were left smoldering

C. swept the drought-parched southeastern coast of Australia, killing at least 69 people, and had left thousands of homes and acres of farmland smoldering

D. swept the drought-parched southeastern coast of Australia, killing at least 69 people, and leaving thousands of homes and acres of farmland smoldering

E. swept the drought-parched southeastern coast of Australia, killing at least 69 people, and left smoldering thousands of homes and acres of farmland

Question 13

Scoliosis, <u>a condition when the spine curves abnormally and throws the body out of line</u>, can cause heart and lung problems as well as physical deformity.

A. a condition when the spine curves abnormally and throws the body out of line

B. an abnormal curvature of the spine that throws the body out of line

C. a condition of the spine curving abnormally and in which the body is thrown out of line

D. where the body is thrown out of line by an abnormal curvature of the spine

E. a condition of an abnormal curvature of the spine throwing the body out of line

Question 14

<u>Although some ornithologists contend that the precursors of birds are arboreal creatures that glide from tree to tree</u>, others believe that they were runners whose front limbs evolved into wings.

A. Although some ornithologists contend that the precursors of birds are arboreal creatures that glide from tree to tree

B. However it may be that some ornithologists contend that the precursors of birds were arboreal creatures that glide from tree to tree

C. Despite that the precursors of birds were, according to some ornithologists, arboreal creatures that glide from tree to tree

D. Although some ornithologists contend that the precursors of birds were arboreal creatures that glided from tree to tree

E. According to some ornithologists gliding from tree to tree, the precursors of birds are arboreal creatures, that

Question 15

The recently reelected president of Cyprus has asked <u>that the United States would encourage Turkey, which invaded the island in 1974 and now controls their</u> northern regions, to withdraw from his country.

A. that the United States would encourage Turkey, which invaded the island in 1974 and now controls their

B. of the United States that it would encourage Turkey, which invaded the island in 1974 and now controls their

C. that the United States would encourages Turkey, which invaded the island in 1974 and now controls its

D. that the United States encourage Turkey, which invaded the island in 1974 and now controls their

E. the United States to encourage Turkey, which invaded the island in 1974 and now controls its

Question 16

In the conflict between the Israelis and the Palestinians, <u>the refusal of each side to acknowledge the other as a legitimate national movement is closer to the heart of the problem than</u> is any other issue.

Ⓐ the refusal of each side to acknowledge the other as a legitimate national movement is closer to the heart of the problem than

Ⓑ that the refusal of each side to acknowledge the other as a legitimate national movement is closer to the heart of the problem as

Ⓒ the refusal of each side to acknowledge another as a legitimate national movement is closer to the heart of the problem than

Ⓓ that the refusal of each side to acknowledge another as a legitimate national movement is closer to the heart of the problem than

Ⓔ the refusal of each side to acknowledge the other as a legitimate national movement is closer to the heart of the problem as

Question 17

In this year's negotiations unionized workers will be fighting to improve job security in many industries, but will be seeking large wage increases in some, <u>as in the prospering telecommunications industry</u>.

Ⓐ as in the prospering telecommunications industry

Ⓑ such industries like telecommunications, which is prospering

Ⓒ as in that of the prospering telecommunications industry

Ⓓ as is the prospering telecommunications industry

Ⓔ as in an industry like telecommunications, which is prospering

Question 18

To tackle the issue of Congressional campaign spending is <u>becoming embroiled in a war which is raging between those who support public financing with</u> those who would lift the limits on the amount political parties and individuals may donate.

Ⓐ becoming embroiled in a war which is raging between those who support public financing with

Ⓑ becoming embroiled in a war raging among those who support public financing with

Ⓒ to become embroiled in a war raging between those who support public financing and

Ⓓ to become embroiled in a war which is raging among those who support public financing and

Ⓔ becoming embroiled in a war raging between those who support public financing and

Question 19

A scientist has determined that a recently discovered ancient Chinese weapon, buried since approximately 1300 B.C., is encrusted with silk, a fabric previously thought to have been invented 1,000 years later.

- (A) A scientist has determined that a recently discovered ancient Chinese weapon, buried since approximately 1300 B.C., is encrusted with silk, a fabric previously thought to have been invented 1,000 years later.
- (B) Buried since approximately 1300 B.C., an ancient Chinese weapon had been recently determined by a scientist to be encrusted with silk, a fabric previously thought to be invented 1,000 years later.
- (C) A scientist had determined that a recently discovered ancient Chinese weapon is encrusted with silk, a fabric previously thought to be invented 1,000 years later, after having been buried since approximately 1300 B.C.
- (D) After being buried since approximately 1300 B.C., a scientist has determined that a recently discovered ancient Chinese weapon is encrusted with silk, a fabric previously thought to have been invented 1,000 years later.
- (E) A recently discovered ancient Chinese weapon, buried since approximately 1300 B.C., has been determined to be covered with silk by a scientist, a fabric previously thought to have been invented 1,000 years later.

Question 20

When he had run for mayor of Cleveland in 1968, Carl Stokes won the election, proving that an African American candidate can be elected in a city in which African Americans constitute a minority of the population.

- (A) When he had run for mayor of Cleveland in 1968,
- (B) He ran for mayor of Cleveland in 1968, and
- (C) Running, in 1968, for Mayor of Cleveland,
- (D) When he ran for mayor of Cleveland in 1968,
- (E) In 1968 he had run for mayor of Cleveland, and

Question 21

Brief psychotherapy requires far fewer hours and costs far less money than traditional psychoanalysis, and so will hopefully prove to be an effective treatment for many of the large amount of people currently seeking therapy.

- (A) will hopefully prove to be an effective treatment for many of the large amount
- (B) will prove hopefully to be an effective treatment for many of the large amount
- (C) hopefully will prove to be an effective treatment for many of the large number
- (D) will, it is hoped, prove to be an effective treatment for many of the large number
- (E) will, it is hoped, prove to be an effective treatment for many of the large amount

Question 22

Having often been thought of as still a city of working-class neighborhoods, Chicago is increasingly populated by poor people.

(A) Having often been thought of as still a city of working-class neighborhoods, Chicago is increasingly populated by poor people.

(B) It is still often thought of as a city of working-class neighborhoods, and Chicago is increasingly populated by poor people.

(C) In spite of still often being thought of as a city of working-class neighborhoods, the people who populate Chicago are increasingly poor.

(D) It is still often thought of as a city of working-class neighborhoods, but the people who populate Chicago are increasingly poor.

(E) Although still often thought of as a city of working-class neighborhoods, Chicago is increasingly populated by poor people.

Question 23

To control public unease over the regime's impending economic collapse, the government ordered local officials should censor records of what were their communities' unemployment figures.

(A) should censor records of what were their communities' unemployment figures

(B) would do the censorship of records of their communities' unemployment figures

(C) censoring records of unemployment figures in their communities

(D) the censoring of a record of unemployment figures in their communities

(E) to censor records of unemployment figures in their communities

Question 24

As a result of having nostrils, called nares, connected to olfactory bulbs that go back to the brain, sharks are capable of smelling even a few molecules of blood in the water.

(A) As a result of having

(B) As a result of it having

(C) Because they have

(D) Because of having

(E) Because of their having

Question 25

In the past few months, there has been extensive dispute over if fare hikes should be a first or last recourse in improving the transit system.

(A) over if fare hikes should be a first or last recourse

(B) about if fare hikes is a first or last recourse

(C) about hiking fares being first or last recourses

(D) over whether fare hikes should be a first or last recourse

(E) concerning hikes in fares and their being first or last recourses

Question 26

Psycholinguists know that a child produces speech sounds <u>by imitating adults, but they do not know how he learns to distinguish significantly different phonemes or</u> how he comes to ignore meaningless variations between speech sounds.

- (A) by imitating adults, but they do not know how he learns to distinguish significantly different phonemes or
- (B) by imitating adults, but they do not know either how he learns to distinguish significantly different phonemes nor
- (C) through the imitation of adults, but they neither know how he learns to distinguish significantly different phonemes or
- (D) through the imitation of adults, but they do not know either how he learns to distinguish significantly different phonemes nor
- (E) by imitating adults, but they do not know how he learns to distinguish significantly different phonemes nor

Question 27

In response to higher oil prices, window manufacturers have improved the insulating capability of their products; their windows <u>have been built to conserve energy, and they are</u>.

- (A) have been built to conserve energy, and they are
- (B) are built to conserve energy, and they have
- (C) are built to conserve energy, and they do
- (D) are being built to conserve energy, and have
- (E) had been built to conserve energy, and they are

Question 28

Though initially opposed to the measure, the governor approved the new needle-exchange program <u>at the urging of his own doctor, his chief advisers, and a coalition of some</u> twenty social action groups.

- (A) at the urging of his own doctor, his chief advisers, and a coalition of some
- (B) as a consequence of having been urged by his own doctor, his chief advisers, and a coalition of some
- (C) on account of being urged by his own doctor, chief advisers, and a coalition of
- (D) as he was urged to do by his own doctor, his chief advisers, and a coalition of some
- (E) as his own doctor was urging him to do, along with his chief advisers, and a coalition of

Answer Key

1. E	8. D	15. E	22. E
2. C	9. C	16. A	23. E
3. B	10. A	17. A	24. C
4. A	11. B	18. C	25. D
5. D	12. D	19. A	26. A
6. C	13. B	20. D	27. C
7. D	14. D	21. D	28. A

Explanations

Question 1

Scanning the answer choices, notice that three choices contain the word *amount* and two choices contain *number*. People, because they can be counted, come in numbers, rather than amounts. This eliminates choices (A), (B), and (C). (E) is best because the phrase *an even greater number of people* clearly refers to more people, while a *number of people even larger* could be referring to bigger people.

Question 2

In standard written English, you can compare only similar things. So people, in this case "the poor," can be compared only with other people, including fictional characters (C). People cannot be compared with a "time period," as in (A) and (B); or with a "time," as in (D); or with "a . . . book," as in (E).

Question 3

Choices (A), (C), (D), and (E) use the plural pronoun *these* to refer to the singular noun *square root*. That's not a problem in (B); the phrase *such imaginary numbers* means "numbers like the one mentioned."

Question 4

You can start by choosing between *lies, lie, lays,* and *lay*. We need a singular, present tense, intransitive verb, so *lies* (A) is correct here. (If you're not sure about the difference between *lie* and *lay*, look them up in the dictionary; the distinction is important in Sentence Correction.) Choices (C), (D), and (E) fail to observe parallelism: We have to say that the motivation *lies in* one thing instead of (or rather than) *in* something else.

Question 5

The original has two mistakes. First, there's a problem with subject/verb agreement. The subject consists of two nouns, *belief* and *curiosity*. There's a plural subject, then, but the verb *has* is singular. It is also unclear what the word *their* refers to—*public* or *UFO*s. Logically, it would seem the reference is to the public, but *public* is singular; so we would have to use *its*, not *their*. Eliminate (A) right away, on the basis of this one mistake. Choice (B) is awkward. This structure has no main verb. Also, it's not clear whom the word *they* refers to. (C), (D), and (E) change the sentence's structure so that the word *belief* becomes the only subject—now we need a singular verb. Only (D) contains the singular verb *has*.

Question 6

The relevant part begins after the colon. Note that the second part of the sentence (immediately after the colon) begins with *the more*. Idiomatically, the best way to start the second part of the clause is *the better*. The only choice that fits is (C). All other choices muddy the construction, making the sentence awkward and unclear.

Question 7

One idiom being tested here is *hope for* versus *hope to*. One can hope for something to happen or for a thing; for example we can *hope for* a peaceful resolution to the problem. One can also hope to do something; for example, I can *hope to* travel the world one day.

In this sentence, the students want to do something (change careers); the proper idiom is *hope to*. Eliminate (A) and (B). Another idiom tested here is the proper use of *exchange for*. The correct idiom is *exchange for* (when one thing is replaced with another). So *exchange with* in (C) is wrong. In choice (E) something's missing; this version of the sentence doesn't specify what the "drab jobs" are being exchanged for.

Question 8

This sentence attempts to describe the crimes committed by the deported British convicts. The original (A) is awkwardly wordy and the pronoun *they* has more than one possible antecedent. In choice (B) the two verbs linked by *and* aren't parallel; "were convicted" doesn't match "ranging." In choice (C) "the ranging of convictions" is awkward and unidiomatic. Choice (E) is wordy. Also, the second part of the sentence doesn't relate clearly to the first part; this raises the question, "The range of what?" (D) is the best choice. Note that it's also the shortest. The most concise answer choice is often (but not always) the correct answer on the GMAT.

Question 9

This question tests comparison. We have to compare "symptoms" with symptoms, not with "multitudes," so (B) is wrong. *Symptoms* is plural, so the comparison has to be with the plural *those* in (C) or (D), not with the singular *that*, as in (A) and (E). Finally, the correct idiom is *afflicted with*, as in (A), (B), and (C), not *afflicted from*, as in (D) and (E).

Question 10

The subject of the sentence is *group*, which is singular, so the main verb has to be *believes*, not *believe*. Also, the things linked by *not* and *but* have to be in parallel form: the infinitive *to be redesigned* has to be paired with the infinitive *to be returned*.

Question 11

Choice (B), with its use of the word *although*, makes clear the contrast between Lessing's recent work and her better-known early work. Choices (A), (C), and (E) don't make that contrast clear. Also, *is likely to be* is more idiomatic than *will likely be* in (A) and (C), *should likely be* in (D), and *may likely be* in (E).

Question 12

Choice (A) uses the past perfect *had swept* for no reason given that there's no sequence of events; they all took place at essentially the same time. Choice (B) illogically implies that the fires killed people before sweeping through the area. Choices (A), (B), (C), and (E) all fail to describe the effects of the fires— the deaths of people and the destruction of property—in parallel form.

Question 13

Choices (A) and (D) are wrong because *when* should be used only to refer to a time, and *where* should be used only to refer to a place. Choices (C) and (E) are wordy and awkward.

Question 14

Since the sentence is about "precursors" or forerunners, and since the part of the sentence that's not underlined uses the past tense verb *were*, the correct answer has to use *were* as in (D), not *are* as in (A) and (E). Also, *however it may be that* in (B) and *despite that* in (C) are unidiomatic. Choice (E) makes it sound as though the ornithologists are the ones gliding from tree to tree.

Question 15

Asked that the United States would encourage, in (A), *asked of the United States that it encourage,* in (B), and *asked that the United States encourages,* in (C), are all awkward and unidiomatic. Choice (D) uses a correct form, *asked that the United States encourage,* but it also uses the plural pronoun *their* when the antecedent is the singular noun island. (Choices (A) and (B) also incorrectly use the plural *their*.) Choice (E) uses the correct pronoun, and another correct form: *asked the United States to encourage.*

Question 16

The subject of the sentence is *the refusal*, not *that the refusal*, as in (B) and (D). The idiomatic form of the comparison is *closer than*, not *closer as* in (B) and (E). And each of two sides needs to acknowledge "the other," not "another," as in (C) and (D), in order to make clear just what the relationship is between the two sides.

Question 17

Such . . . like in (B) is unidiomatic. *That of* in (C) is illogical: *that* can stand only for *industry*, and it doesn't make sense to talk about the industry of an industry. *Is* in (C) doesn't have an object. In (E), the use of both *as* and *like* is redundant. Also, (B) and (E) both use the phrase *which is prospering*, when the single word *prospering* will do. The most concise choice, (A), is correct; this will often, but not always, be the case on the GMAT.

Question 18

The rule of parallelism demands that the infinitive *to tackle* be paired with the infinitive *to become*, as in (C) and (D), not with the participle *becoming* in the other choices. A war rages between one side *and* another, not between one side *with* another, as in (A) and (B), nor *among those*, as in (D). *Among*, which appears in (B) and (D), should be used only in discussions of three or more things; here there are only two sides, so *between* is correct. Finally, the phrase *which is* in (A) and (D) can be omitted without the sentence losing anything.

Question 19

Choices (B) and (C) contain errors of verb tense. The invention of silk is something that happened in the past, so *be* is wrong. Also, the past perfect *had been* in (B) makes it sound as if the analysis of the weapon took place before its burial, which makes no sense. What's more, (C), (D), and (E) all contain misplaced modifiers. In (C), *after having been buried since approximately 1300 B.C.* seems to modify the word *silk;* besides, *silk* could hardly have been invented after being buried. In (D), the phrase a*fter being buried since approximately 1300 B.C.* seems to modify *a scientist.* (E) has a nearly identical modification problem.

Question 20

Choice (D) is the only choice that makes the sequence of events perfectly clear; Stokes ran for mayor at essentially the same time as he won the election. Other choices are more awkwardly worded or use confusing verb tenses. Choices (A) and (E) use the past perfect *had run*, which makes it sound as if Stokes ran for mayor long before actually winning. (C)'s phrasing is awkward and (C) use of *running* tends to obscure the sense of the victory as the conclusion of the campaign. (B)'s phrasing is awkward and it's unclear who the antecedent of the pronoun *he* is.

Question 21

People can be individually counted, so they come in numbers, as in (C) and (D), not in amounts, as in (A), (B), and (E). And strictly speaking, the adverb *hopefully* cannot be used to mean "it is hoped." That knocks out (C). *Hopefully* can't modify an entire sentence; it can modify only a single verb or adjective, in this case, the verb *prove*. Although most of us use the word *hopefully* to mean "it is hoped" in everyday speech, standard written English has different, more rigorous requirements.

Question 22

Choice (A) uses the complicated passive construction *having often been thought of* for no good reason; there's no sequence of past events. The point of the sentence is that people now still think something that's no longer entirely correct. In choice (B), it's not clear what the pronoun *it* refers to, and (B) also fails to convey the contrast between the truth and what people think. Choice (C) has a misplaced modifier: it seems to be saying that *the people* are thought of as a city of working-class neighborhoods. In choice (D), *it* appears to refer to *the people*, and that makes no sense. Choice (E) uses correct sequence of tenses—(simple) past and present—and it also uses the phrase *although still often thought of* to set up the contrast.

Question 23

Read the sentence carefully, but don't get preoccupied with correcting it. Get right to the choices. Your ear for correct English will tell you that "ordered [local officials] to censor" (E) is correct. Listen to how (A), (B), (C), and (D) sound: "Ordered [local officials] should censor"; "ordered [local officials] would do the censorship"; "ordered [local officials] censoring"; and "ordered [local officials] the censoring" all sound weird.

Question 24

-*Ing* verbs often make a GMAT sentence correction sentence or phrase unnecessarily wordy. That's the case here. The correct answer is a concise choice that eliminates the unnecessary phrase *As a result of having.* (If you ever need to guess, stay away from *ing*s in the answer choices and avoid long answer choices.) (C) takes out the -*ing* and is shortest; it's right. It also clears up ambiguity in the sentence by including the pronoun *they*, which refers to *sharks* in the second half of the sentence.

KAPLAN

Question 25

The difference between if and whether is a favorite GMAT issue. A dispute concerns whether, not if, one alternative or the other is better. As a rule of thumb, *whether* will always beat out *if* on the GMAT. If you can't rely on your ear to rule out funny-sounding constructions like dispute over if or dispute about *if,* try to eliminate choices for other reasons. First, keep steering away from really long answer choices, like choice (E) here. Second, stay away from wordy constructions using being like the verbose constructions in (C) and (E). Finally, dispose of choice (B), which has a subject/verb agreement problem. In (B), the singular is disagrees with the plural fare hikes.

Question 26

This choice illustrates the importance of knowing your idioms, and of working strategically. Scan the answer choices quickly to zero in on the significant differences, which all occur around *or.* This lets you eliminate all choices but (A) for their incorrect usage. You can't say *either . . . nor* in (B) and (D), or *neither . . . or,* in (C). Choice (E)'s out as well. Think of it this way: You would say, "They do not know *X* or *Y,*" not "They do not know *X* nor *Y.*"

Question 27

GMAT English is very precise. Think about what the sentence correction is really saying, rather than what it means to say. The windows in question "have been built to conserve energy, and they are." Are what? Conserving energy, of course. The verb that follows *are* is left out, but its meaning is implied. Problem is, the verb is *to conserve energy,* not *conserving. Are* makes no sense with it. You can't say "they are (conserve energy)." You have to say, "they do (conserve energy)," in choice (C).

Question 28

An important rule on the GMAT is "Avoid wordiness." Ask yourself whether a longer choice adds meaning or just hot air. Here, all the choices except (A) add unnecessary words. For instance in (B), *as a consequence of having been urged* doesn't add anything. In (D), *as he was urged to do* is not so obvious, but still longer than it needs to be. *At the urging* is the most compact and elegant version.

Reading Comprehension

....

- Learn the Four Basic Principles of Reading Comp
- Study the Kaplan Method for answering Reading Comp questions
- Focus on the different types of Reading Comp questions and the targeted strategies for answering each type
- Complete the Reading Comp Practice Quiz

....

The directions for Reading Comprehension on the GMAT look like this:

> <u>Directions:</u> **Answer the questions after reading through the passage. Base your answers on information that is either stated or implied in the passage.**

On the GMAT, expect to see three or four Reading Comprehension passages—in areas of business, social science, and natural science—and a total of about 14 questions (approximately three to four questions for each passage). You'll see only one question at a time on the monitor, however.

Reading Comp Tally

Expect to see three to four passages (related to business, social science, or natural science) followed by a total of approximately 14 questions.

Reading the first paragraph of the passage is a zooming-in process. First, you get a sense of the general topic. Then you pin down the more specific scope of the passage. Finally, you glean the author's purpose in writing the passage.

The Four Basic Principles of Reading Comprehension

1. Be sensitive to issues of topic, scope, and author's purpose and structure, and to the author's voice.

Reading for the GMAT means reading with different goals and employing different techniques than you do in the course of everyday life. Most of us usually read for one or both of two simple reasons: to learn something or to pass the time pleasantly. Needless to say, neither of these purposes has anything to do with the GMAT. We also tend to read for content. "What's this author saying?" we ask ourselves, or "What's this book about?" But anyone who tries to read for content during the GMAT is going about it all wrong. There's just no time under strict test conditions to understand everything that's being said, and, as we'll see, there's no payoff in it, either.

So what does GMAT reading involve? Broadly stated, it involves reading to identify three general elements: topic and scope, the author's purpose and passage structure, and the author's voice. And all of these elements will normally be clear from a strategic reading of the first paragraph alone.

Topic and Scope

As you work through the first few sentences, you need to determine the passage's topic. If it's a science passage, for example, ask yourself what branch of science it's about. If it's about astronomy, ask yourself what part of astronomy. If it's about stars, then zero in on the passage's topic: stars.

When it comes to determining the scope of a passage, you need to understand what we mean by *scope.* Think of scope as a narrowing of the topic. If the topic is industrial safety regulations, what narrower definition can we present that still describes all of the passage? Is there a comparison to another type of safety regulation? Is there a comparison between safety regulations in different historical eras? Is there an analysis of the regulations' histories? Or is the passage concerned only with a small aspect of the regulations—the ones pertaining to pregnant workers, for example?

Notice the questions in the previous paragraph. They may not read well, but we left them that way for a reason. Those questions nicely illustrate the kind of thinking that you'll need to do as you work through a passage on test day. Once you have the topic and narrowed down its scope, you've finished the first step in Reading Comprehension. But what then? You still don't have a firm grasp of the passage.

Author's Purpose and Structure

Almost every single GMAT Reading Comp question (and Critical Reasoning question, for that matter) hinges on your ability to step back from the text and analyze why the author is writing in the first place and how she puts her text together. The GMAT demands that you figure out the author's purpose and the passage structure, because that's the best way for the test makers to test how you think about the prose you read. And thinking is always being tested, one way or another, on every GMAT question.

Now, it would be nice, not to mention helpful, if the authors of the reading passages came right out and announced *why* they are writing, *what* they have to say, and *how* they intend to accomplish their goal. No such luck. The prose that you will see on the GMAT, like most sophisticated writing, doesn't reveal its secrets quite so explicitly. Authors always have a purpose, of course, and always have a structural plan for carrying out that purpose. What they don't do is announce them, and that puts an extra burden on the reader—to analyze what's stated, read between the lines, and make inferences.

Baldly laying out the why and how of a passage up front isn't a hallmark of GMAT Reading Comp passages. And even more importantly (as far as the test makers are concerned), if ideas were blatantly laid out, the test makers couldn't ask probing questions about them. So, in order to set up the questions—to test how we think about the prose we read—the GMAT uses passages in which authors hide or disguise their statement of purpose and challenge us to extract it. If you came across the following first sentence of a typical passage, could you identify the topic and scope?

> The great migration of European intellectuals to the United States in the second quarter of the twentieth century prompted a transmutation in the character of Western social thought.

First, what's the topic? The migration of European intellectuals to the United States in the second quarter of the twentieth century. That's clear. Second, what's the scope? (How can we narrow the topic?) Well, the passage looks as if it will discuss the effects of this migration on social thought.

So, using what we know about topic and scope, we can easily deduce why the author is writing. His purpose, we might say, is "to explore how the arrival of European eggheads during the period 1926–1950 changed Western social thought" (your phrasing might be a bit different, but the gist is probably the same). And notice the implied structure of what will follow. Don't you expect the author to first describe the migration westward and then explain what the "transmutation" was? (And it probably will be in that order; GMAT authors are nothing if not logical.) There is a definite purpose and structure here; we just have to work a little harder at figuring them out than we're used to doing. So, the author will never say, "Here's why I write." But unless you figure out why the author is

Teacher Tip

Ordinary reading is too slow to find things and too fast to analyze text. Good test takers scan quickly to find what they need and then analyze intensely. Structural keywords and references from the stem are crucial. Looking for a conclusion? Scan for keywords and for words with heavy emotional content. If the stem asks for an assumption made by a researcher, scan for the word 'research' or 'researcher.' Then read up and down from that spot.
—Eirik Johnson
  Chicago, IL

writing, you won't be able to analyze why each piece—each paragraph and each detail—is there and how it's being used.

Author's Voice

An important part of GMAT critical reading is distinguishing between factual assertions—things that you could go and look up—and opinions or interpretations. It's the latter that GMAT Reading Comp passages are built on, and you should pay the most attention to them every step of the way. Let's say that while reading a passage, you come upon a paragraph that reads:

> The coral polyps secrete calceous exoskeletons, which cement themselves into an underlayer of rock, while the algae deposit still more calcium carbonate, which reacts with sea salt to create an even tougher limestone layer.

You have to stop and say to yourself, "So what? These are statements of fact. What's the point? Why are you telling me this?" And instead of getting all wrapped up in the facts, push yourself forward until the author explains *why* he's writing on the topic of coral reef formation. What should grab your attention is the following sentence:

> All of this accounts for the amazing renewability of coral reefs despite the endless erosion caused by wave activity.

Consider how different this sentence is from the first one. The phrase *this accounts for* should set off an alarm in your brain: That's the author talking, saying, "I believe this to be proven cause-and-effect." The same goes for the word *amazing.* It indicates the author's personal interpretation. Your response to this sentence should be: "Great! Now, how so? Where's your evidence?" In other words, as an active reader, you are now demanding support for the author's opinions. You're forcing the author to defend his view—to tell you just what accounts for the "amazing renewability of coral reefs."

Attacking a passage is what critical reading is all about: stepping back from the sheer factual content, figuring out the author's views on a topic and how she arrived at them, and looking for the evidence that must be provided. Always be on the lookout for sentences in which the author's voice is coming through, and try to skip past the sentences that are purely factual or simply there for support.

As you identify the author's viewpoints, be sure not to "argue with" the author. If your own personal understanding or view of the issue happens to be a bit different, keep it to yourself. The questions are going to test your command of the *author's* views, and you can only get in trouble by imposing your own opinions.

Kaplan Rules

Being able to distinguish opinions or interpretations from factual assertions is an important skill in Reading Comp. Questions usually revolve around the author's point of view and the support for that viewpoint.

Kaplan Rules

Attack the passage for the author's views; don't worry about jargon, facts, and details.

2. Get the gist of each paragraph.

The paragraph is the main structural unit of any passage. After you've read the first paragraph of the passage carefully, you need only find the "gist," or general purpose, of each succeeding paragraph and then relate each paragraph to the passage as a whole. To find the gist of each paragraph, ask yourself:

- Why did the author include this paragraph?
- What shift did the author have in mind when moving on to this paragraph?
- What bearing does this paragraph have on the author's main idea?

This process allows you to create a "mental road map" of the passage. When questions arise that require you to look back into the passage, having a roadmap will help you locate the place in the text that contains the answer. For example, it's helpful to know that the author's critique of a recommendation is in paragraph three. This will allow you to zero in on the relevant information quickly.

3. Look for the main idea.

At this point I can hear some of you asking: "Hey, you haven't mentioned the main idea yet. I thought that was crucial." Well, it is and it isn't. If you get in the habit of reading the way we're describing, for purpose and structure, you can't help but notice the author's main idea.

The term *main idea* refers to a single thesis that the author may be trying to prove in the course of the passage. It's always a personal interpretation, a strong authorial point of view that demands evidence. And in the end, it's the main thought that the author wants you to come away with as you finish the passage.

Lincoln was the sixteenth president will never be a main idea on a GMAT Reading Comp passage. Count on it. But *As president, Lincoln set uncomfortable precedents for the curtailing of civil liberties*—now there's a promising main idea! There's a statement that demands evidence (What *precedents*? Why were they *uncomfortable*?), and an entire 350-word passage might be used to try to prove it true.

Not every GMAT reading passage features what you'd call a strong main idea. Sometimes the author has no major axe to grind, and so he or she just sets out to tell you about a topic in a style that we at Kaplan call "storytime." When there is a strong main idea, the test makers usually highlight it by asking a pointed question, such as:

Which of the following is the main idea of the passage?

Teacher Tip

Many times when I ask my students for the main idea, they will give me the topic of the passage, for example, "it's about the Rocky Mountains." I remind them that the main idea is more than just a topic, it is the author's point of view on the topic.
–Jennifer Killmer
 Coral Gables, FL

Kaplan Rules

You should always keep the main idea in mind, even when answering questions that don't explicitly ask for it. Correct answers on even the detail questions tend to echo the main idea in one way or another.

And then you pick the answer choice that best sums up the author's topic, scope, and point of view: exactly what we've been talking about up to now. So don't sweat it; "main idea" isn't an especially problematic concept, insofar as GMAT Reading Comprehension is concerned.

4. Don't obsess over details.

On the GMAT, you'll need to read only for short-term, as opposed to long-term, retention. When you finish the questions on a certain passage, that passage is over, gone, done with. You're free to promptly forget everything about it.

What's more, there's certainly no need to memorize details. You always have the option of relocating details if a particular question requires you to do so. If you have a good sense of a passage's structure and paragraph topics and your mental roadmap is clear, then you should have no problem navigating back through the text when the need arises.

Typical Reading Comp Question Types

Although it might be convenient to break the Reading Comprehension section down into the types of *passages* that typically appear on it—business, natural science, and social science—we at Kaplan feel that's not the best way to master the section. While passages differ, we read them in essentially the same way, employing the same critical reading techniques for each. We find it more efficient to break the section down into the four main *question types* that accompany passages: Global, Inference, Logic, and Explicit Detail. Let's look at each of these more closely.

Global Questions

A Global question asks us to recognize the author's overall intentions, ideas, or passage structure. It's really a question whose scope is the entire passage. In general, any answer choice that grabs onto a small detail, or zeroes in on the content of only one paragraph, will be wrong for a Global question. Often, scanning the verbs in a Global question's answer choices is a good way to take a first cut at the question. The verbs must agree with the author's tone and chosen structure, so scanning the verbs can narrow down the options quickly. The correct answer must be consistent with the overall tone and structure of the passage, while the wrong choices will be too broad or narrow in scope or inconsistent with the author's tone. You'll often find Global questions at the beginning of question sets, and often one of the wrong choices will play on some side issue discussed at the tail end of the passage.

Kaplan Rules

Don't feel that you have to memorize or understand every little thing as you read the passage. Remember, you can always refer to the passage to clarify the meaning of any specific detail.

Global Questions at a Glance

- They sum up the author's overall intention or the passage structure.
- Nouns and verbs must be consistent with the author's tone and the passage's scope.

Main Idea and Primary Purpose Questions

The two main types of Global questions are Main Idea and Primary Purpose questions. Main idea and purpose are inextricably linked, because the author's purpose is to convey his or her main idea. The format for these question types are pretty self-evident:

- Which one of following best expresses the main idea of the passage?

- The author's primary purpose is to . . .

Structure Questions

Another type of Global question asks you to recognize a passage's overall structure. Here's what this type of question might look like:

- Which of the following best describes the organization of the passage?

Answer choices to this kind of Global question are usually worded very generally; they force you to recognize the broad layout of the passage, as opposed to the specific content. For example, here are three possible ways that a passage could be organized:

1. A hypothesis is stated and then analyzed.

2. A proposal is evaluated and alternatives are explored.

3. A viewpoint is set forth and then subsequently defended.

When choosing from among these choices, ask yourself: "Was there a hypothesis here? Was there an evaluation of a proposal or a defense of a viewpoint?" These terms might all seem similar, but, in fact, they're very different. Learn to recognize the difference between a proposal, a viewpoint, and so on. Try to keep an eye on what the author is *doing*, as well as what the author is *saying*, and you'll have an easier time with this type of question. By the way, you'll get to try your hand at an actual Global question later in this chapter (question 3 of the sample passage to come).

Inference Questions

Inference questions, as you can easily guess, concern inferences arising from the passage. An inference is something that is almost certainly true, based on the passage, but that is contained "between the lines." The answer is something that the author strongly implies or hints at but does not state explicitly. Inference questions ask about large points or small.

Extracting valid inferences from Reading Comp passages requires the ability to recognize that information in the passage can be expressed in different ways. The ability to bridge the gap between the way information is presented in the passage and the way it's presented in the correct answer choice is vital. In fact, Inference questions often boil down to an exercise in "translation."

Inference Questions at a Glance

Inference Questions:

- Involve the ability to read between the lines
- Often boil down to translating the author's points
- Usually provide a clue as to where in the passage the answer will be found
- Will ask for either something that can be inferred from a specific part of the passage or else for something the author would agree with

Regular Inference Questions

The most common type of Inference question simply asks what can be inferred from the passage but it can do so in a variety of different ways:

- It can be inferred from the passage that . . .
- The passage/author suggests that . . .
- The passage/author implies that . . .
- The passage supports which one of the following statements regarding . . .

Agreement Questions

Another common form of Inference question is one that asks you to find a statement that the author (or some character or group mentioned in the passage) would agree with. The question stem will usually provide a hint about where in the passage the answer can be found:

> With which one of the following statements . . . would the author most likely agree?

You need to have a good handle on the author's point of view or position in order to infer what the author would think about a particular situation or a new premise. Just remember to choose an answer that stays within the scope and tone of the passage. Also, remember that anything that seems to contradict any of the author's ideas will almost certainly be wrong.

Logic Questions

Logic questions ask about *why* the author does something—cites a source, brings up a detail, puts one paragraph before another, and so forth. Answer choices that discuss the actual content or a detail will be wrong for these questions. (Question 2 in the upcoming sample passage is a Logic question, so you'll see exactly what one looks like.)

Logic questions will look like this:

- The author refers to/mentions . . . primarily/most probably in order to . . .
- Which of the following best describes the relationship of the [first, second, etcetera] paragraph to the rest of the passage?

Just be careful with line references in Logic questions—they'll bring you to the right area, but usually the actual answer will be found in the lines immediately before or after the referenced line.

Explicit Detail Questions

The fourth major type of Reading Comprehension questions is the Explicit Detail question. As the name implies, an Explicit Detail question is one whose answer can be pinpointed in the text. It's fairly simple to identify an Explicit Detail question from its stem:

- According to the passage/author . . .
- The author states that . . .
- The author mentions which one of the following as . . .

Often, these questions provide very direct clues about where an answer may be found, such as line references or some text that links up with the passage structure.

You may recall that we advised you to skim over details in Reading Comp passages and to focus on the topic, scope, and purpose. But now here's a question type that's specifically concerned with details, so what's the deal? The fact is, most of the details that appear in a typical passage aren't tested in the questions. Of the few that are, you'll either:

- Remember them from your reading;
- Be given a line reference to bring you right to them; or
- Simply have to find them on your own in order to track down the answer.

If that's the case—if your mental roadmap and understanding of the purpose of each paragraph are both clear in your mind—it shouldn't take long to locate the relevant detail and then choose an answer. Despite this question type, the winning strategy is still to note the purpose of details in each paragraph's argument but not to attempt to memorize the details themselves.

Most students find Explicit Detail questions to be the easiest type of Reading Comp question because they're the most concrete. Unlike inferences, which hide somewhere between the lines, explicit details reside in the lines themselves.

The Kaplan Four-Step Method for Reading Comp

There's absolutely nothing to stop you from simply reading a passage from beginning to end and answering the questions. That's as simple as can be, and test takers have been attempting Reading Comp that way for decades. But not the best test takers.

Explicit Detail Questions at a Glance

- The answer can be found in the text.
- They sometimes includes line references to help you locate the relevant material.
- They are concrete and, therefore, the easiest RC question type for most people.

Teacher Tip

Read for the moment, not for memory. Unlike in a school class, you're not going to be tested on the details two weeks from now. Don't try to remember them, pronounce them, even totally understand them. If there's a question about a particular detail, then you'll go back and figure it out. If there's no question, forget it!
—Marilyn Engle
Encino, CA

The best test takers use a strategic plan for attacking passages and questions in an aggressive, energetic, and critical way. Working this way pays off because it's the kind of pragmatic and efficient approach that the GMAT rewards—the same type of approach that business schools like their students to take when faced with intellectual challenges.

The Kaplan Four-Step Method for Reading Comp

1. Attack the opening paragraph.
2. Create a mental road map.
3. Stop to sum up before answering questions.
4. Attack the questions.

1. Attack the opening paragraph.

Be an active reader. This means thinking about what you're reading; paraphrasing the complicated parts; determining the topic, scope, the author's purpose and passage structure, and author's voice; and asking yourself questions about the passage.

2. Create a mental road map.

Try labeling each paragraph so you know what's covered and how it fits into the overall structure of the passage. This will help you get a fix on the passage as a whole, and it will help you locate specific details later on.

3. Stop to sum up.

Before answering the questions, take a few seconds to summarize your mental road map.

4. Attack the questions.

Answer the questions based on your mental road map of the passage.

Using the Kaplan Four-Step Method

Now let's try the Four-Step Method on an actual GMAT-length Reading Comp passage.

> Since 1980, the notion that mass extinctions at the end of the Cretaceous period 65 million years ago resulted from a sudden event has slowly gathered support, although even today there is no scientific consensus. In the Alvarez
> (5) scenario, an asteroid struck the earth, creating a gigantic crater. Beyond the immediate effects of fire, flood, and storm, dust darkened the atmosphere, cutting off plant life. Many animal species disappeared as the food chain was snapped at its base.
> (10) Alvarez's main evidence is an abundance of iridium in the KT boundary, a thin stratum dividing Cretaceous rocks from rocks of the Tertiary period. Iridium normally accompanies the slow fall of interplanetary debris, but in KT boundary strata iridium is 10–100 times more

(15) abundant, suggesting a rapid, massive deposition. Coincident with the boundary, whole species of small organisms vanish from the fossil record. Boundary samples also yield osmium isotopes, basaltic sphericles, and deformed quartz grains, all of which could have resulted from high-
(20) velocity impact.

Paleontologists initially dismissed the theory, arguing that existing dinosaur records showed a decline lasting millions of years. But recent studies in North America, aimed at a comprehensive collection of fossil remnants rather than rare
(25) or well-preserved specimens, indicate large dinosaur populations existing immediately prior to the KT boundary. Since these discoveries, doubts about theories of mass extinction have lessened significantly.

Given the lack of a known impact crater of the necessary
(30) age and size to fit the Alvarez scenario, some scientists have proposed alternatives. Courtillot, citing huge volcanic flows in India coincident with the KT boundary, speculates that eruptions lasting many thousands of years produced enough atmospheric debris to cause global devastation. His analyses
(35) also conclude that iridium in the KT boundary was deposited over a period of 10,000–100,000 years. Alvarez and Asaro reply that the shock of an asteroidal impact could conceivably have triggered extensive volcanic activity. Meanwhile, exploration at a large geologic formation in
(40) Yucatan, found in 1978 but unstudied until 1990, has shown a composition consistent with extraterrestrial impact. But evidence that the formation is indeed the hypothesized impact site remains inconclusive.

1. It can be inferred from the passage that supporters of the Alvarez and Courtillot theories would hold which of the following views in common?

   Ⓐ   The KT boundary was formed over many thousands of years.

   Ⓑ   Large animals such as the dinosaurs died out gradually over millions of years.

   Ⓒ   Mass extinction occurred as an indirect result of debris saturating the atmosphere.

   Ⓓ   It is unlikely that the specific cause of the Cretaceous extinctions will ever be determined.

   Ⓔ   Volcanic activity may have been triggered by shock waves from the impact of an asteroid.

2. The author mentions "recent studies in North America" (line 23) primarily in order to
   (A) point out the benefits of using field research to validate scientific theories
   (B) suggest that the asteroid impact theory is not consistent with fossil evidence
   (C) describe alternative methods of collecting and interpreting fossils
   (D) summarize the evidence that led to wider acceptance of catastrophic scenarios of mass extinction
   (E) show that dinosaurs survived until the end of the Cretaceous period

3. In the passage, the author is primarily concerned with doing which one of the following?
   (A) describing recent fossil discoveries in North America
   (B) offering a solution to a scientific problem
   (C) summarizing the history of a geologic period
   (D) revising the research methods of paleontologists
   (E) delineating hypotheses about a mass extinction

4. According to the passage, the discoveries described in paragraph three
   (A) support the notion that dinosaurs died out gradually over a long period of time
   (B) undermine Courtillot's volcanic theory of mass extinction
   (C) convinced scientists to investigate the Yucatan formation
   (D) caused scientists to reassess their views about extinctions
   (E) suggested that dinosaurs may have survived into the Tertiary period

Here's how the Kaplan method works with this passage.

1. Attack the opening paragraph.

Take 30 to 45 seconds to read the opening paragraph. Aim at the topic, scope, and author's purpose or point of view. Get a decent sense of where the whole thing is going. Here's roughly what you should have gotten out of the paragraph on your first pass:

The topic is clearly announced in the opening sentence: *mass extinctions at the end of the Cretaceous period.* . . . Noting the general topic is the first step in wading into any passage. At the same time, you want to start seeing the scope, which also happens in the first sentence.

Specifically, that same sentence does two things: (1) It introduces the theory that the mass extinctions may have resulted from *a sudden*

KAPLAN

event; (2) The words *although even today* are a signal that the passage will explain that there are still differences about what exactly happened. Savvy test takers notice such signal words and phrases. They're clues as to where the passage is going.

Beyond the first sentence, the paragraph delivers fundamentals about the Alvarez theory of mass extinction. The idea is that an asteroid hit the earth and exploded, filled the atmosphere with dust, which killed off plant life, wrecked the food chain, and caused mass extinctions. Simple enough.

2. Create a road map.

Not surprisingly, paragraph two delves deeper into the Alvarez theory, summarizing evidence that supports it. This is a common construction of science passages: They'll start by citing a theory and then turn to the evidence (detailed and often convoluted) supporting it. You absolutely shouldn't get bogged down at this point. Be sure to note the gist—the thrust of the detail—but don't linger. For example, you might have made a mental note about the part about iridium and its unusual abundance at the KT boundary. Or you might simply have noted "EVIDENCE" (mentally or on your scratch paper) and then pushed on. All you need for a road map is a general (and hopefully accurate) sense of what each paragraph is up to. Save the complexity for later, if a question asks for further details.

The word *initially* unlocks paragraph three, and the idea is simple. At first paleontologists doubted the theory, but they've since become less resistant because of fossil evidence found in North America. Note that this paragraph falls in line with the larger structure, echoing the paragraph one suggestion that there's ongoing uncertainty about what really happened.

Paragraph four continues the discussion and ties everything up. The lack of a known impact crater to support the Alvarez hypothesis has encouraged alternative scenarios, one being Courtillot's volcanic theory, which is also based on the notion of a catastrophe, but a purely earthly one this time. The final sentences swing back to Alvarez and then end on the familiar note that the evidence, while growing, remains inconclusive.

Now, instead of throwing yourself into the waiting jaws of the questions, our suggestion is to take a few seconds to prepare.

3. Stop to sum up.

So your next move is to sum up the road map—meaning a quick review of paragraph gists. After that, it's time to dance. As long as we know where the various details are to be found, we'll be able to find them.

Kaplan Rules

When a passage becomes top-heavy with detail (especially a science passage), creating a rough mental picture of the situation may be invaluable in making sense of it all.

Kaplan Rules

Before moving on to the questions, spend a few moments to sum up each of the paragraphs and decide how they fit together as a whole.

Paragraph one gives the basics: the idea of mass extinctions stemming from a sudden catastrophe. And it cites the Alvarez hypothesis, which is then detailed in paragraph two. Paragraph three explains why doubts about mass extinction have decreased, and paragraph four compares the Alvarez and Courtillot theories, which agree about catastrophe but diverge over cause.

Armed with that recap, we should be able to move confidently into the questions. Maybe we can't answer every question on sight. But there'll be some that we can answer on sight, and with the rest we'll know where to go, which means quick, right answers.

4. Attack the questions.

Work through the questions as they appear. Most of the questions here are ones that should yield some quick points after checking details, an easy matter with your road map.

Answers and Explanations

1. C

Paragraph one describes mass extinctions in the Alvarez scenario as resulting from the devastating effects of atmospheric dust on the food chain. Paragraph four describes Courtillot's volcanic theory as an alternative explanation for a similar ecological effect. (A) is inconsistent with Alvarez. (B) and (D) contradict both theorists—they agree that the extinctions were pretty sudden and they have clear ideas about causes. (E) contradicts Courtillot, who doesn't buy the asteroid causal notion.

2. D

Note how the answer to this detail question dovetails with your road map—the gist of paragraph three: The North American studies are cited as the main reason why *initially* skeptical paleontologists opened up to the idea of catastrophic mass extinctions. (D) paraphrases the last sentence: "Since these discoveries, doubts about theories of mass extinction have lessened significantly." Beware of choices like (A), (C), and (E). They're baited to sound plausible (i.e., you can infer that the author wouldn't disagree with any of them), but they miss the point that the studies changed people's minds. (B) is inconsistent with the passage—the fossil evidence is consistent with catastrophe scenarios, asteroidal or otherwise.

3. E

(E) is the only choice that fits the topic (mass extinction), scope (the evidence for catastrophic scenarios like Alvarez's) and purpose (to suggest the plausibility of such scenarios despite lack of proof). (A) focuses on detail in paragraph three. (B) slips away from the scope. The author isn't giving a solution of his own, but rather outlines what others believe. (C) and (D)

KAPLAN

are also outside the scope—a mere historical summary of an era (C) never happens, and "revising research methods of paleontologists" (D) is a distortion of paragraph three.

4. D

Choice (D) here repeats the gist of paragraph three: After the discoveries, doubts about mass extinction theory dropped. (A) is an *au contraire* choice. The discoveries point to a mass extinction. Likewise with (B), the discoveries support Courtillot, an alternative catastrophic view. (C) doesn't work because no direct link is drawn between the Yucatan and these other studies. (E) is *au contraire:* The studies suggest that dinosaurs disappeared suddenly.

For even more practice, take a stab at the Reading Comprehension Practice Quiz.

So there you are—a demonstration of how to use the ideas and tactics outlined in this chapter to work through the complete Reading Comprehension process. Try to use these tips with the Reading Comp questions in the Practice Test. And check out our explanations for further suggestions.

Reading Comprehension Practice Quiz

Directions: Answer the questions after reading through the passage. Base your answers on information that is either stated or implied in the passage. Answers and Explanations can be found at the end of the Quiz.

Passage for Questions 1–7:

(5)

The rich analyses of Fernand Braudel and his fellow *Annales* historians have made significant contributions to historical theory and research. In a departure from traditional historical approaches, the *Annales* historians assume (as do Marxists) that history cannot be limited to a simple recounting of conscious human actions, but must be understood in the context of forces and material conditions that underlie human behavior. Braudel was the first *Annales* historian to gain widespread support for the idea that history should synthesize data from various social sciences, especially economics, in order to provide a broader view of human societies over time (although Febvre and Bloch, founders of the *Annales* school, had originated this approach).

(10)

(15)

Braudel conceived of history as the dynamic interaction of three temporalities. The first of these, the *événementielle*, involved short-lived dramatic "events," such as battles, revolutions, and the actions of great men, which had preoccupied traditional historians like Carlyle. *Conjonctures* was Braudel's term for larger, cyclical processes that might last up to half a century. The *longue durée*, a historical wave of great length, was for Braudel the most fascinating of the three temporalities. Here he focused on those aspects of everyday life that might remain relatively unchanged for centuries. What people ate, what they wore, their means and routes of travel—for Braudel these things create "structures" that define the limits of potential social change for hundreds of years at a time.

(20)

(25)

(30)

(35)

Braudel's concept of the *longue durée* extended the perspective of historical space as well as time. Until the *Annales* school, historians had taken the juridical political unit—the nation-state, duchy, or whatever—as their starting point. Yet, when such enormous time spans are considered, geographical features may well have more significance for human populations than national borders. In his doctoral thesis, a seminal work on the Mediterranean during the reign of Philip II, Braudel treated the geohistory of the entire region as a "structure" that had exerted myriad influences on human lifeways since the first settlements on the shores of the Mediterranean Sea.

(40)

(45)

(50)

And so the reader is given such arcane information as the list of products that came to Spanish shores from North Africa, the seasonal routes followed by Mediterranean sheep and their shepherds, and the cities where the best ship timber could be bought.

(55)

Braudel has been faulted for the imprecision of his approach. With his Rabelaisian delight in concrete detail, Braudel vastly extended the realm of relevant phenomena; but this very achievement made it difficult to delimit the boundaries of observation, a task necessary to beginning any social investigation. Further, Braudel and other *Annales* historians minimize the differences among the social sciences. Nevertheless, the many similarly designed studies aimed at both professional and popular audiences indicate that Braudel asked significant questions which traditional historians had overlooked.

(60)

(65)

(70)

Question 1

The primary purpose of the passage is to

(A) show how Braudel's work changed the conception of Mediterranean life held by previous historians

(B) evaluate Braudel's criticisms of traditional and Marxist historiography

(C) contrast the perspective of the longue durée with the actions of major historical figures

(D) illustrate the relevance of Braudel's concepts to other social sciences

(E) outline some of Braudel's influential conceptions and distinguish them from conventional approaches

Question 2

The author refers to the work of Febvre and Bloch in order to

(A) illustrate the limitations of the *Annales* tradition of historical investigation

(B) suggest the relevance of economics to historical investigation

(C) debate the need for combining various sociological approaches

(D) show that previous *Annales* historians anticipated Braudel's focus on economics

(E) demonstrate that historical studies provide broad structures necessary for economic analysis

Question 3

According to the passage, all of the following are aspects of Braudel's approach to history EXCEPT that he

(A) attempted to unify various social sciences

(B) studied social and economic activities that occurred across national boundaries

(C) pointed out the link between increased economic activity and the rise of nationalism

(D) examined seemingly unexciting aspects of everyday life

(E) visualized history as involving several different time frames

Question 4

The passage suggests that, compared to traditional historians, *Annales* historians are

(A) more interested in other social sciences than in history

(B) more critical of the achievements of famous historical figures

(C) more skeptical of the validity of most economic research

(D) more interested in the underlying context of human behavior provided by social structure

(E) more inclined to be dogmatic in their approach to history

Question 5

The author is critical of Braudel's perspective for which of the following reasons?

(A) It seeks structures that underlie all forms of social activity.

(B) It assumes a greater similarity among the social sciences than actually exists.

(C) It fails to consider the relationship between short-term events and long-term social activity.

(D) It clearly defines boundaries for social analysis.

(E) It attributes too much significance to conscious human actions.

Question 6

The passage implies that Braudel would consider which of the following as exemplifying the *longue durée*?

I. The prominence of certain crops in the diet of a region
II. The annexation of a province by the victor in a war
III. A reduction in the population of an area following a disease epidemic

(A) I only
(B) III only
(C) I and II only
(D) II and III only
(E) I, II, and III

Question 7

Which of the following statements is most in keeping with the principles of Braudel's work as described in the passage?

(A) All written history is the history of social elites.
(B) The most important task of historians is to define the limits of potential social change.
(C) Those who ignore history are doomed to repeat it.
(D) People's historical actions are influenced by many factors that they may be unaware of.
(E) History is too important to be left to historians.

Questions 8–13 are based on the following passage.

In many underdeveloped countries, the state plays an important and increasingly varied role in economic development today. There are four general arguments, all of them
(5) related, for state participation in economic development. First, the entrance requirements in terms of financial capital and capital equipment are very large in certain industries, and the size of these obstacles will serve as barriers
(10) to entry on the part of private investors. One can imagine that these obstacles are imposing in industries such as steel production, automobiles, electronics, and parts of the textile industry. In addition, there are what Myint calls
(15) "technical indivisibilities in social overhead capital." Public utilities, transport, and communications facilities must be in place before industrial development can occur, and they do not lend themselves to small-scale improve-
(20) ments.

A related argument centers on the demand side of the economy. This economy is seen as fragmented, disconnected, and incapable of using inputs from other parts of the economy.
(25) Consequently, economic activity in one part of the economy does not generate the dynamism in other sectors that is expected in more cohesive economies. Industrialization necessarily involves many different sectors; economic
(30) enterprises will thrive best in an environment in which they draw on inputs from related economic sectors and, in turn, release their own goods for industrial utilization within their own economies.
(35) A third argument concerns the low-level equilibrium trap in which less developed countries find themselves. At subsistence levels, societies consume exactly what they produce. There is no remaining surplus for reinvestment. As per-capita income rises, how-
(40) ever, the additional income will not be used for savings and investment. Instead, it will have the effect of increasing the population that will eat up the surplus and force the society to its

KAPLAN

(45) former subsistence position. Fortunately, after a certain point, the rate of population growth will decrease; economic growth will intersect with and eventually outstrip population growth. The private sector, however, will not be able to provide the one-shot large dose of
(50) capital to push economic growth beyond those levels where population increases eat up the incremental advances.

The final argument concerns the relationship between delayed development and the
(55) state. Countries wishing to industrialize today have more competitors, and these competitors occupy a more differentiated industrial terrain than previously. This means that the available niches in the international system are more
(60) limited. For today's industrializers, therefore, the process of industrialization cannot be a haphazard affair, nor can the pace, content, and direction be left solely to market forces. Part of the reason for a strong state presence,
(65) then, relates specifically to the competitive international environment in which modern countries and firms must operate.

Question 8

According to the passage, all of the following are arguments for state economic intervention EXCEPT

(A) the start-up costs of initial investments are beyond the capacities of many private investors

(B) the state must mediate relations between the demand and supply sides of the economy

(C) the pace and processes of industrialization are too important to be left solely to market trends

(D) the livelihoods and security of workers should not be subject to the variability of industrial trends

(E) public amenities are required to facilitate a favorable business environment

Question 9

Which of the following best states the central point of the passage?

(A) Without state intervention, many less developed countries will not be able to carry out the interrelated tasks necessary to achieve industrialization.

(B) Underdeveloped countries face a crisis of overpopulation and lack of effective demand that cannot be overcome without outside assistance.

(C) State participation plays a secondary role as compared to private capital investment in the industrialization of underdeveloped countries.

(D) Less developed countries are trapped in an inescapable cycle of low production and demand.

(E) State economic planning can ensure the rapid development of nonindustrialized countries' natural resources.

Question 10

The author suggests all of the following as appropriate roles for the state in economic development EXCEPT

(A) safeguarding against the domination of local markets by a single source of capital

(B) financing industries with large capital requirements

(C) helping to coordinate demand among different economic sectors

(D) providing capital inputs sufficient for growth to surpass increases in per capita consumption

(E) developing communication and transportation facilities to service industry

Question 11

The author suggests which of the following about the "technical indivisibilities in social overhead capital" (lines 15–16) and the "low-level equilibrium trap" (lines 34–35)?

Ⓐ The first leads to rapid technological progress; the second creates demand for technologically sophisticated products.
Ⓑ Both enhance the developmental effects of private sector investment.
Ⓒ Neither is relevant to formulating a strategy for economic growth.
Ⓓ The first is a barrier to private investment; the second can attract it.
Ⓔ The first can prevent development from occurring; the second can negate its effects.

Question 12

Which of the following, if true, would cast doubt on the author's argument that state participation is important in launching large-scale industries?

   I. Coordination of demand among different economic sectors requires a state planning agency.
  II. Associations of private-sector investors can raise large amounts of capital by pooling their resources.
 III. Transportation and communications facilities can be built up through a series of small-scale improvements.

Ⓐ I only
Ⓑ II only
Ⓒ I and II only
Ⓓ II and III only
Ⓔ I, II, and III

Question 13

According to the passage, the "low-level equilibrium trap" in underdeveloped countries results from

Ⓐ the tendency for societies to produce more than they can use
Ⓑ intervention of the state in economic development
Ⓒ the inability of market forces to overcome the effects of population growth
Ⓓ the fragmented and disconnected nature of the demand side of the economy
Ⓔ one-shot, large doses of capital intended to spur economic growth

Answer Key

1. E	6. A	11. E
2. D	7. D	12. D
3. C	8. D	13. C
4. D	9. A	
5. B	10. A	

Explanations

Passage One: Questions 1–7

This is a social science passage about historian Fernand Braudel; notice that all the French expressions are explained in plain English. The first paragraph says that Braudel and his precursors, the *Annales* historians, look at history in broad social and economic context. The second paragraph describes Braudel's three major time frames: the *événementielle,* specific one-time historical events; *conjonctures,* historical trends that take place over several decades; and the *longue durée,* aspects of life that can stay the same for centuries. The third paragraph elaborates on the idea of the *longue durée:* Over long periods of time, geographical features may be more important national borders. The last paragraph says that Braudel has been criticized, but is nevertheless very important.

Question 1

Primary purpose is another term for main idea, so this is a Main Idea question. The purpose, or main idea, of this passage is to explain Braudel's ideas and discuss how they differ from those of traditional historians. Choices (A) and (D) focus on details, and (B) and (C) focus on inaccurately stated details.

Question 2

Febvre and Bloch are mentioned only in the first paragraph. There, it's said that they "anticipated [Braudel's] approach."

Question 3

Here, you have to find which detail is not mentioned in the passage. Choice (A) is mentioned in the first paragraph, (D) and (E) in the second, and (B) in the third.

Question 4

In this Inference question, the correct answer choice (D) refers to a point made in the opening paragraph. ("[H]istory . . . must be understood in the context of forces and material conditions that underlie human behavior.") Choice (A) is wrong because there's no

indication that the *Annales* historians were more interested in other social sciences than in history (they were historians, after all). Choice (E) is wrong because, although it's clear that the *Annales* historians had a dogma of their own, there's no indication that they were any more dogmatic than anyone else.

Question 5

Criticism of Braudel's perspective can be found in the last paragraph, which says that *Annales* historians "minimize the differences between social sciences." Choices (C), (D), and (E) are contradicted by the passage. Choice (A) is correct, but it's not really a criticism. Choice (B) is the best answer.

Question 6

The *longue durée* is defined in the second paragraph. Item I gives us the example of a *longue durée* that's actually given in the passage at line 31. Item II, as a dramatic, one-time event, is an example of what Braudel calls the *événementielle.* Item III describes a change, not necessarily permanent, in response to a specific event, so this is probably an example of *conjoncture.*

Question 7

Choices (A) and (B) are defensible claims, and choices (C) and (E) are familiar sayings, but none of them are supported by the passage. The correct answer (D) accurately states the assumptions underlying Braudel's work (see in particular lines 4–10).

Passage Two: Questions 8–13

This business-related passage presents four reasons (one in each paragraph) for government participation in economic development in underdeveloped countries. First, the capital necessary to begin development is more than private investors can muster. Second, several sectors of the economy must be coordinated. Third, a large boost is necessary to put the economy beyond the stage at which increased populations eat up increased capital. Finally, the state can best oversee development in such a way as to make the country competitive in an international market.

Question 8

You need to find a reason that's not given in the passage. Choices (A) and (E) are mentioned in the first paragraph, (B) in the second, and (C) in the fourth.

Question 9

The passage as a whole presents reasons state intervention is necessary for the industrialization of many less developed countries. Choice (B) introduces the idea of outside assistance, (C) contradicts the passage by saying that start participation is not as important as private investment, (D) says that less developed countries can't be industrialized at all, and (E) overstates the case by saying that state economic planning "can ensure" a "rapid" development.

Question 10

Here, as in question 8, you're looking for something that's not in the passage. Choices (B) and (E) are mentioned in the first paragraph, (C) in the second, and (D) in the third.

Question 11

Both of the phrases quoted in the question refer to problems in underdeveloped countries that can make state participation necessary. The wrong answer choices all say that at least one of these things are good, or at least neutral.

Question 12

Here we're looking for statements that essentially weaken the author's argument (something that's often tested in Critical Reasoning, too). Statement I is not part of the correct answer, because it restates the author's opinion. Because they all include Statement I, choices (A), (C), and (E) are out. Statement II contradicts the author's statement, in the first and third paragraphs, that only the government can come up with the amount of capital necessary to launch large-scale industries. Statement III also contradicts the author's statement, in the first paragraph, that transportation and communications facilities "do not lend themselves to small-scale improvements." Correct choice (D) specifies accurate Statements II and III.

Question 13

The quoted phrase comes from the third paragraph; it explains how economic growth in subsistence-level economies tends to produce population growth, which negates the effects of the economic growth.

CHAPTER SIX

Quantitative Section Overview

HIGHLIGHTS

- Learn how to manage the Quantitative section
- Get to know the two Quantitative section question types
- Find out how to get your best score

A little less than half of the multiple-choice questions on the GMAT appear in the Quantitative section. You'll have 75 minutes to answer 37 math questions in two formats: Problem Solving and Data Sufficiency. These two formats are mingled throughout the Quantitative section, so you never know what's coming next. Here's what you can expect to see.

Quantitative Question Type	Approximate Number of Questions
Problem Solving	22
Data Sufficiency	15
Total: 37 questions in 75 minutes	

The range of math topics tested on the GMAT is actually fairly limited. The same concepts are tested again and again in remarkably similar ways. Arithmetic is the most commonly tested topic; about half of all GMAT math questions test arithmetic. The second most commonly tested subject is algebra; about one quarter of GMAT math questions are algebra questions. Less than one-sixth of all GMAT math questions are geometry questions. The other questions relate to a variety of less frequently tested topics, such as graphs and logic.

The good news is that if you're comfortable with arithmetic and algebra, you've already taken a big step towards doing well on the GMAT. Don't

Top GMAT Math Topics

The three most commonly tested topics in the math sections are:
- Arithmetic (about half of the questions)
- Algebra (a little more than one-fourth of the questions)
- Geometry (less than one-sixth of the questions)

worry if you haven't done math in school for a long time. You're using it all the time in daily life; every time you leave a 15 percent tip you're practicing one of your most important GMAT math skills—percents. And to help you brush up on math concepts, we've included Kaplan's GMAT Math Reference in the back of the book.

In the next few chapters, we'll show you strategies for specific Quantitative question types. But first, let's look at some techniques for managing the whole section.

Set Your Own Goals

To get your best possible score on the Math section of the GMAT, you'll need to work strategically. The key is to spend your time answering the questions you can and piling up points. Don't overextend yourself and miss questions that you could answer. Remember, you're not trying to be perfect; you're trying to get the absolute best score you can get. You can make mistakes (after the first 5–7 questions) and still do very well—as long as you get the questions early on right.

Adapting to the Computer-Adaptive Test (CAT)

The Quantitative section of the GMAT is quite different from the Quantitative sections of most paper-and-pencil tests. The major difference between the test formats is that the CAT "adapts" to your performance. Each test taker is given a different mix of questions depending on how well he or she is doing on the test. This means the questions get harder or easier depending on whether you answer them correctly or not. Your score is not directly determined by how many questions you get right, but by how hard the questions you get right are.

How a Computer-Adaptive Test Finds Your Score

When you start a section, the computer:

- Assumes you have an average score (500)
- Gives you a medium-difficulty question. About half the people who take the test will get this question right, and half will get it wrong

What happens next depends on whether you answered the question correctly.

If you answer the question correctly:

- Your score goes up
- You are given a slightly harder question

If you answer a question incorrectly:

- Your score goes down
- You are given a slightly easier question

This pattern continues for the rest of the section. Every time you get the question right, the computer raises your score, then gives you a slightly harder question. Every time you get a question wrong, the computer lowers your score, then gives you a slightly easier question. In this way the computer tries to "home in" on your score.

Theoretically, as you get to the end of a section, you will reach a point where every time the computer raises the difficulty level of a question, you get it wrong, but every time it lowers the difficulty level of a question, you get it right. Your score at this point will supposedly be an accurate measure of your ability.

How to Manage the Quantitative Section

The best way to attack the computer-adaptive GMAT is to exploit the way it determines your score. Since early questions are worth more, spend more time on those questions. Since you can't skip any questions, you'll have to guess intelligently if you get stuck. Having a systematic approach to each section will ensure that you spend your time as wisely as possible.

You should spend more time on the first 10-15 questions, double-checking your answers before you move on. These questions are crucial in determining your ability estimate, so invest the necessary time and try to answer these questions correctly.

Make sure, however, to pace yourself so that you have time to mark an answer for every question in the section, because you will be penalized for questions you don't reach. If you don't have time to give some thought to the answer to every question, guess if necessary during the final minutes allotted to you in order to get to the end of the section.

Make Educated Guesses

Whether it is because you are running short of time or have hit a question that totally flummoxes you, you will have to guess occasionally. However, if you are test savvy you will not just guess at random. You should try to narrow down the answer choices before you guess. This will greatly improve your chances of guessing the right answer. When you guess, you should follow this plan:

1. Eliminate answer choices you know are wrong. Even if you don't know the right answer, you can often tell that some of the answer

> **Teacher Tip**
>
> Because you can't skip questions and come back to them, it is essential that you make good judgements about how much time to invest in any one question.
> —Tiffany Sanders
>   Downers Grove, IL

choices are wrong. For instance, on Data Sufficiency questions, you can eliminate at least two answer choices by determining the sufficiency of one statement.

2. Avoid answer choices that make you suspicious. These are the answer choices that just "look wrong" or conform to a common wrong-answer type. For example, if only one of the answer choices in a Problem Solving question is negative, chances are that it will be incorrect.

3. Choose one of the remaining answer choices.

Avoid the Penalty

There is a penalty for not completing a section. Every question that you leave unanswered at the end of a section is twice as damaging to your score as an incorrect answer. For this reason it is very important that you answer all the questions. If you have only a minute or two to go, and you have questions remaining, guess at random to get to the end of the section.

Experimental Questions

About a quarter of the questions on the test are experimental—questions that the test makers are checking out for possible use on future tests. These questions do not contribute to your score, and there is no way of identifying them. Treat every question as if it were scored.

The Art of Using Scratch Paper

One of the skills you will have to master to ace the GMAT is the systematic use of scratch paper. Since you can't write on the screen, you will need to transfer some information to your scratch paper to be able to solve many problems. Although this sounds simple, it takes practice; otherwise you may find yourself transferring reams of data, or not enough at all. To practice using scratch paper efficiently, use scratch paper as you work through the questions in this book. Treat all testlike questions in this book as if they were on a computer screen. Make your notes and calculations on a separate piece of paper. Don't mark up questions in the book.

Kaplan Rules

Practice using scratch paper by treating all test-like questions in this book as though they were on a computer screen. Make your calculations on a separate piece of paper.

KAPLAN

CHAPTER SEVEN

Problem Solving

HIGHLIGHTS

- Learn the Four Basic Principles of Problem Solving
- Study the Kaplan Method for Problem Solving
- Find out about shortcuts and alternative methods for solving problems
- Complete the Problem Solving Practice Quiz

The instructions for the Problem Solving questions on the GMAT look like this:

> <u>Directions:</u> **Solve the problems and choose the best answer.**
>
> **Note: Unless otherwise indicated, the figures accompanying questions have been drawn as accurately as possible and may be used as sources of information for answering the questions.**
>
> **All figures lie in a plane except where noted.**
>
> **All numbers used are real numbers.**

There are about 22 Problem Solving questions on each GMAT Quantitative section. The directions indicate that some diagrams on the GMAT are drawn to scale, which means that you can use them to estimate measurements and size relationships. Other diagrams are labeled "Not drawn to scale," so you can't "eyeball" them. In fact, when a diagram says "Not drawn to scale," the unpredictability of the picture is often the key to the problem.

The directions also let you know that you won't have to deal with imaginary numbers, such as $\sqrt{-1}$, and that you'll be dealing with flat figures, such as squares and circles, unless they tell you otherwise.

Problem Solving Tally

Expect to see 22 questions in this format on the GMAT.

The Four Basic Principles of Problem Solving

By adopting a systematic approach to Problem Solving, you will have a clear, concise method for thinking your way to a response. You won't waste time by attacking a problem in a tentative or haphazard manner. A systematic approach will ensure that you find the most efficient solution to the problem and that you make as few careless and unnecessary errors as possible.

1. Develop the ability to decipher question stems quickly.

With practice, you'll quickly recognize exactly what you're being asked. For example, you might get this question early on during the GMAT.

> At a certain diner, Joe ordered 3 doughnuts and a cup of coffee and was charged $2.25. Stella ordered 2 doughnuts and a cup of coffee and was charged $1.70. What is the price of two doughnuts?
>
> (A) $0.55
> (B) $1.00
> (C) $1.10
> (D) $1.30
> (E) $1.80

Did you read carefully and avoid the potential trap? You're asked for the price of 2 doughnuts, not 1 doughnut. Many GMAT Problem Solving questions invite you to misread them. If you're careless when you read the question—for instance, solving for the price of one doughnut in this example—you can be sure that the test maker will include that answer among the four wrong answer choices.

2. Decide how much effort to put into each question.

Depending on where you are on the test, you might be better off guessing and saving time for other questions. Only you know what type of questions give you particular trouble. If you're lousy at ratios and hit a ratio question in the second half of the test, you should move through it quickly to allow time to answer other questions more completely.

3. Consider alternative methods.

If the question seems as if it will take too long to solve, look for shortcuts. There are many different ways to solve a given math question. Remember, you're not looking for an ideal method for everybody but the fastest method for you. Time is a key element on standardized exams, so you should maximize the value of your time with shortcuts or alternative methods. The Kaplan Method is all about time management. The right method is whatever method is quickest for you.

In the doughnut example above, you could power your way through using algebra and substitutions:

$$3d + 1c = 2.25, \text{ therefore } c = 2.25 - 3d$$
$$2d + 1c = 1.70$$

Now, substituting for c:

$$2d + (2.25 - 3d) = 1.70$$
$$2d - 3d = 1.70 - 2.25$$
$$-d = -.55$$
$$d = .55; \text{ therefore } 2d = 1.10.$$

Note

There are many ways to solve math questions, and alternative methods, such as picking numbers and backsolving, can save time.

A better way might be to notice that Joe orders the same thing Stella does, *except that he orders one more doughnut*. So the difference in the price of their orders, 2.25 − 1.70, or .55, is just the price of one doughnut. Algebraically, this looks like:

$$(3d + 1c = 2.25)$$
$$-\underline{(2d + 1c = 1.70)}$$
$$(d \quad = .55)$$

The lesson: It saves time to *think* about what you're doing before setting up your equations.

Picking Numbers
Picking numbers is a powerful alternative to solving problems by brute force. Rather than trying to work with unknown variables, you pick concrete values for the variables. Any answer choice that does not work for the concrete values cannot be the correct answer.

How does picking numbers work?

- Pick simple numbers to stand in for the variables. The usefulness of the strategy depends in large part on your ability to pick convenient numbers.

- Try all the answer choices, ditching those that don't agree with the question information. Remember to keep the values you've picked for the variables constant throughout the problem.

- Try different values when more than one answer choice works. Sometimes more than one choice will give the right answer. If that happens, pick some new numbers. The correct choice must work for all possible numbers.

Note

Shortcuts and alternative approaches to Problem Solving are the key to success on the GMAT CAT.

When you encounter a problem that contains variables, think of Kaplan alternative approaches to Problem Solving. Very often, picking numbers and substituting is quicker than any mathematical calculation.

Now let's try using the picking numbers technique on a few problems. You might run into this kind of question:

Carol spends $\frac{1}{4}$ of her savings on a stereo and $\frac{1}{3}$ less than she spent on the stereo for a television. What fraction of her savings did she spend on the stereo and television?

- (A) $\frac{1}{4}$
- (B) $\frac{2}{7}$
- (C) $\frac{5}{12}$
- (D) $\frac{1}{2}$
- (E) $\frac{7}{12}$

In this case, the common denominator is 12; so let the number 12 (12 dollars) represent Carol's total savings. That means she spends $\frac{1}{4} \times 12$ dollars, or 3 dollars, on her stereo, and $\frac{2}{3} \times 3$ dollars, or 2 dollars, on her television. That comes out to be 3 + 2 = 5 dollars; that's how much she spent on the stereo and television combined. You're asked what *fraction* of her savings she spent. Because her total savings are 12 dollars, she spent $\frac{5}{12}$ of her savings; (C) is correct. Notice how picking a common denominator for the variable (Carol's savings) made it easy to convert each of the fractions ($\frac{1}{4}$ and $\frac{2}{3} \times \frac{1}{4}$ of her savings) to a simple number.

Kaplan Rules

When picking a number for fraction problems, pick a common denominator.

A tricky part of this question is understanding how to figure the price of the television. Remember your first Basic Principle of Problem Solving: Understand exactly what's being asked. The television does not cost $\frac{1}{3}$ of her savings, it costs $\frac{1}{3}$ *less* than the stereo; that is, it costs $\frac{2}{3}$ as much as the stereo.

A quick overview could have helped you eliminate (A), (D), and (E). (A) is too small; the stereo alone costs $\frac{1}{4}$ of her savings. (D) and (E) are too large, because the television costs LESS than the stereo, so the two together must cost less than $2 \times \frac{1}{4}$, or half, of Carol's savings.

This next problem is of medium difficulty:

If $a > 1$, what is the value of $\dfrac{2a+6}{a^2+2a-3}$?

- (A) a

- (B) $a + 3$

- (C) $\dfrac{2}{a-1}$

- (D) $\dfrac{2a}{a-3}$

- (E) $\dfrac{a-1}{2}$

If a question has variables in the answer choices, that's your signal it can be attacked by picking numbers.

Note the condition you're given: $a > 1$. You might start by picking 2 for a. Then the expression we're given is 2(2) + 6 divided by $(2)^2$ + 2(2) − 3. This equals 10 over 5, or 2. Check the answer choices: which of the expressions equals 2 when $a = 2$? Unfortunately, both (A) and (C) equal 2. This narrows the possibilities down to (A) and (C). When you have more than one answer choice that gives the right answer, you have to pick another number.

Try $a = 3$. Then the expression in the question stem is $2(3) + 6$ divided by $(3)^2 + 2(3) - 3$. This equals 12 over 12, or 1. Now when $a = 3$, (A) has value 3 and (C) has value 1, so (C) is the correct answer.

Remember to try out *all* the answer choices with the picking numbers strategy. If you neglected to do this, you might have picked (A) before seeing that (C) also works with $a = 2$.

You might run into the following difficult problem.

> A car rental company charges for mileage as follows: x dollars per mile for the first n miles and $x + 1$ dollars per mile for each mile over n miles. How much will the mileage charge be, in dollars, for a journey of d miles, where $d > n$?
>
> (A) $d(x + 1) - n$
> (B) $xn + d$
> (C) $xn + d(x + 1)$
> (D) $x(n + d) + d$
> (E) $(x + 1)(d - n)$

Picking numbers can often simplify complex word problems.

This is a late problem, so you know to expect traps. Reading it might make your head spin, but it becomes much simpler when you substitute numbers for the variables. For instance, suppose you pick $x = 4$, $n = 2$, $d = 5$. The problem now reads: 4 dollars per mile for the first 2 miles, and 5 dollars a mile for each mile over 2 miles. How much will the mileage charge be for a journey of 5 miles? That's easily calculated: the first 2 miles cost 2×4 dollars and the remaining 3 cost 3×5 dollars for a total cost of $8 + 15$, or 23 dollars. Of the answer choices, only (A) has value 23 when $x = 4$, $n = 2$, and $d = 5$. Without the picking-numbers strategy at their disposal, many test takers might be stumped by a question like this one on test day. With the picking numbers strategy in mind, however, *you* can answer it fairly quickly.

Picking numbers is almost always the best way to attack odd/even questions. The following problem is of medium difficulty.

If *a* and *b* are odd integers, which of the following is an even integer?

(A) $a(b - 2)$
(B) $ab + 4$
(C) $(a + 2)(b - 4)$
(D) $3a + 5b$
(E) $a(a + 6)$

You can run through the answer choices quite quickly using the picking numbers strategy. Try $a = 3$, $b = 5$. Only (D), $9 + 25 = 34$, is even. There's no trick here; this question simply rewards the careful test taker.

Backsolving
Backsolving is a strategy that allows you to use the answer choices to work backwards through the question stem. The answer choice that agrees with the information in the question stem is correct. You've probably used this strategy unconsciously when you ran into a multiple-choice question that you found difficult. Backsolving can save a great deal of time if you use it wisely. It is an exceptional method for solving questions when you have no idea where to begin on a problem.

We want you to learn to use backsolving systematically. On the GMAT, answers are arranged in ascending or descending order. Start backsolving with the middle choice. If that isn't the answer, you'll usually be able to tell whether the correct answer is larger or smaller than the middle choice, which means you'll have narrowed the choices down to two.

Solve the following problem by backsolving; this problem is of medium difficulty.

A crate of apples contains one bruised apple for every 30 apples in the crate. If 3 out of every 4 bruised apples are considered unsalable, and there are 12 unsalable apples in the crate, how many apples are there in the crate?

(A) 270
(B) 480
(C) 600
(D) 740
(E) 840

Start backsolving with answer choice (C); assume there are 600 apples in the crate. Then 600/30, or 20 apples are bruised. Three-fourths of these apples are unsaleable, so 15 apples are unsellable. That's too many. Since we want a smaller number of unsellable apples, we need a smaller number of *total* apples. So we can eliminate (D) and (E) as well, since they are larg-

Definition

Backsolving is a strategy in which you plug answer choices into the question to see which one works.

Kaplan Rules

Always start with the middle answer choice when backsolving. The choices are arranged in ascending or descending order. If the third choice isn't the answer, you'll usually be able to tell whether the correct answer is larger or smaller than choice (3)—narrowing the choices down to two.

er. The correct answer must be either (A) or (B). Try either one the same way: if (A) works, it's the answer. If (A) doesn't work, you don't even need to try (B), because (B) must be the answer. (And it is: 480/30 = 16; $\frac{3}{4} \times 16 = 12$).

This is also a medium-difficulty problem.

What is the value of x if $\dfrac{x+1}{x-3} - \dfrac{x+2}{x-4} = 0$?

- (A) −2
- (B) −1
- (C) 0
- (D) 1
- (E) 2

Note

Backsolving is often the quickest and easiest way to solve complicated equations on the GMAT.

Backsolving is often simpler and faster than solving equations (especially when the equations look like this). Again, start with (C): $\dfrac{1+1}{0-3} - \dfrac{0+2}{0-4} = \dfrac{1}{-3} - \dfrac{2}{-4}$ which is not equal to 0. It's not immediately clear if the right answer should be larger or smaller, so go to an answer choice that looks easy to work with. Try (D):

$$\dfrac{1+1}{1-3} - \dfrac{1+2}{1-4} = \dfrac{2}{-2} - \dfrac{3}{-3} = -1 - (-1) = 0. \text{ Bingo!}$$

4. Guess if you're stumped.

If you simply cannot solve an equation using regular math or an alternative method, sometimes that's the time to make an educated guess. The key to good guessing is the elimination of wrong answer choices. Many questions will have answer choices that are obviously wrong or don't make sense. If you can eliminate some wrong choices using common sense, make a good guess and move on.

For example, try to eliminate some answer choices on the following medium-difficulty question.

A container holding 12 ounces of a solution that is 1 part alcohol to 2 parts water is added to a container holding 8 ounces of a solution that is 1 part alcohol to 3 parts water. What is the ratio of alcohol to water in the resulting solution?

- Ⓐ 2:5
- Ⓑ 3:7
- Ⓒ 3:5
- Ⓓ 4:7
- Ⓔ 7:3

Note

Guessing is often the best approach on difficult Roman numeral questions.

Right away you can eliminate (E). It's the only choice that has more alcohol than water; not only does it stand out from the others, but it doesn't make sense because both solutions had less alcohol than water. You can use common sense to eliminate some other choices. One of the solutions is 1:2 alcohol to water, the other is 1:3. A combination of the two should have a ratio somewhere between 1:2 and 1:3. But (C) and (D) both have a higher proportion of alcohol than the 1:2 solution, so you can eliminate them. Guess (A) or (B); you have a 50 percent chance of being right.

(Point of information: The answer is (B). The 12-ounce solution has 4 oz alcohol and 8 oz water. The 8 oz solution has 2 oz alcohol and 6 oz water. Add them for a solution with 6 oz alcohol and 14 oz water for a ratio of 3:7 alcohol to water.)

Kaplan Rules

Before you guess, eliminate some answer choices through common sense, picking numbers, or back-solving.

Guessing can also be useful on Roman numeral questions. If you can figure out one statement, you can eliminate a few answer choices. Try the following medium-level Roman numeral question.

If $x - y = 8$, which of the following must be true?

I. Both x and y are positive.
II. If x is positive, y must be positive.
III. If x is negative, y must be negative.

- Ⓐ I only
- Ⓑ II only
- Ⓒ III only
- Ⓓ I and II
- Ⓔ II and III

You want to figure out one statement and thus eliminate as many answer choices as you can while doing as little work as possible. Statement II occurs in three answer choices, so we'll try it. You can use the picking-numbers technique to evaluate the truth of this statement. Can II be false? Can you pick numbers to fit the equation such that x is positive and y is negative? Suppose $x = 2$. Then $y = -6$. So II need not be true. That eliminates (B), (D), and (E), and leaves you with a 50-50 shot at guessing.

As a matter of fact, you've done better than that. Did you notice? If II can be false, if it's possible for x to be positive and y to be negative, then Statement I need not be true either, and the answer is (C).

An important point to take with you about guessing is that it works in alliance with the techniques we've discussed. Don't guess blindly: Use anything you can—common sense, picking numbers, backsolving—to eliminate some choices and improve your odds.

You've already seen how Problem Solving techniques can help your guessing. But what happens when you're totally at a loss? Suppose you were confronted with the following medium-difficulty question. How might you go about it using guesswork?

> If a and b are prime numbers, such that $a > b$, which of the following cannot be true?
> (A) $a + b$ is prime.
> (B) ab is odd.
> (C) $a(a - b)$ is odd.
> (D) $a - b$ is prime.
> (E) a^b is even.

Definition

A prime number is a positive integer that has only two positive factors—itself and 1. The first eight prime numbers are 2, 3, 5, 7, 11, 13, and 17.

Guessing anything when you have no clue at all is usually smart—with one exception. Let's say you were totally clueless on this problem beyond knowing the definition of a prime number. Think like the test maker. If you were the test maker and your goal was to make some students spend too much time on a problem, where would you hide the answer? In a problem in which there's no alternative but to work with the answer choices to solve, the answer will more often than not be (D) or (E). So if you decide to guess, which should you guess? (Or if you decide to solve it, where should you begin trying out answer choices?) How about (E)? For the record, the answer *is* (E): Because a can't be even ($a > b$), no integer power of a can be even.

By now you've seen that there's more than one way to solve a math problem. All the ways are equally legitimate, as long as they get you to the right answer. Your concern is to pick the one that will solve the problem fastest for you. You can always, at a minimum, get started on a problem, eliminate a few answer choices, and guess.

The Kaplan Four-Step Method for Problem Solving

Now that you've got a grip on the basic principles of Problem Solving, let's look at how to attack the questions you'll see on the test.

1. Read through the whole question.

Determine exactly what the question is asking. Is the question or situation complicated?

2. Decide how much effort to put into the question.

Is this the sort of question you normally do well on? Will you be able to solve it quickly? Be aware of where you are in the test and how much time you have left.

3. Choose the fastest approach to the answer.

Choose the approach that you feel most comfortable with. Questions are often deliberately confusing and contain traps for the unwary.

4. Select an answer.

Answer every question. Eliminate answer choices whenever you can. The more unlikely answer choices you can eliminate, the better your chances of guessng correctly. And if you're running out of time and several questions remain, make sure to answer each question by guessing something.

Using the Kaplan Method

Try the Four-Step Method on the following example:

> If $w > x > y > z$ on the number line and y is halfway between x and z, and x is halfway between w and z,
>
> then $\dfrac{y - x}{y - w}$ =

- (A) $\dfrac{1}{4}$
- (B) $\dfrac{1}{3}$
- (C) $\dfrac{1}{2}$
- (D) $\dfrac{3}{4}$
- (E) 1

The Kaplan Four-Step Method for Problem Solving

1. Read through the whole question.
2. Decide how much effort to put into the question.
3. Choose the fastest approach to the answer.
4. Select an answer.

1. Read through the whole question.

You should immediately notice that the question has four variables and that you need to figure out the relative values for x, y, and w.

2. Decide how much effort to put into the problem.

It's up to you, but let's go for it.

3. Choose the fastest approach to the answer.

This could have been a long day at the office if you didn't see that picking numbers is the fastest way here. The question essentially gives you instructions on how to pick numbers. Say $z = 2$ and $y = 4$; then $x = 6$. That would make $w = 10$, so: $\dfrac{y-x}{y-w} = \dfrac{4-6}{4-10} = \dfrac{-2}{-6} = \dfrac{1}{3}$. If you missed this strategy you might have elected to skip this one and come back later.

4. Select an answer.

Eliminate unlikely choices, and guess. If you're running out of time, guess something.

Now that you have a handle on Problem Solving, try the Practice Quiz.

Problem Solving
Practice Quiz

Directions: Solve the problems and choose the best answer. (Answers and explanations follow the quiz.)

Question 1

7.38 + 10.075 =

- (A) 10.813
- (B) 17.113
- (C) 17.355
- (D) 17.383
- (E) 17.455

Question 2

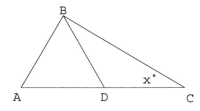

In the diagram above, if $AB = AD = BD = DC$, then $x =$

- (A) 30
- (B) 35
- (C) 40
- (D) 45
- (E) 60

Question 3

If $2x - 4y = -2$ and $3x - 2y = 3$, then $2y + x =$

- (A) $\dfrac{3}{2}$
- (B) 2
- (C) $3\dfrac{1}{2}$
- (D) 5
- (E) $5\dfrac{1}{2}$

Question 4

Joan spends 20 percent of her income on taxes and 20 percent of the remainder on rent. What percent of her income does she spend on rent?

- (A) 8%
- (B) 10%
- (C) 16%
- (D) 20%
- (E) 24%

Question 5

An overnight courier service charges $5.00 for the first 2 ounces of a package and $0.75 for each additional ounce. If there is a 6 percent sales tax added to these charges, how much does it cost to send a 6-ounce package?

- (A) $4.24
- (B) $8.00
- (C) $8.48
- (D) $9.28
- (E) $10.60

Question 6

If $\dfrac{3M}{2N} = 0.125$, what is the value of N in terms of M?

(A) $\dfrac{M}{8}$

(B) $\dfrac{M}{4}$

(C) $4M$

(D) $8M$

(E) $12M$

Question 7

Company C sells a line of 25 products with an average retail price of $1,200. If none of these products sells for less than $420, and exactly 10 of the products sell for less than $1,000, what is the greatest possible selling price of the most expensive product?

(A) $2,600
(B) $3,900
(C) $7,800
(D) $11,800
(E) $18,200

Question 8

If $\dfrac{n}{2}$ is an even integer, what is the remainder when n is divided by 4?

(A) 0
(B) 1
(C) 2
(D) 3
(E) 4

Question 9

A certain industrial loom weaves 0.128 meters of cloth every second. Approximately how many seconds will it take for the loom to weave 25 meters of cloth?

(A) 178
(B) 195
(C) 204
(D) 488
(E) 512

Question 10

If $a - b = \dfrac{a^2 - b^2}{b^2 - a^2}$ and $b^2 - a^2 \neq 0$, then $b - a =$

(A) −1
(B) 0
(C) 1
(D) 2
(E) It cannot be determined from the information given.

Question 11

If a sequence of consecutive integers of increasing value has a sum of 63 and a first term of 6, how many integers are in the sequence?

(A) 11
(B) 10
(C) 9
(D) 8
(E) 7

Question 12

A cube of white chalk is painted red, and then cut parallel to the sides to form two rectangular solids of equal volume. What percent of the surface area of each of the new solids is not painted red?

(A)   15%

(B) $16\frac{2}{3}$ %

(C)   20%

(D)   25%

(E) $33\frac{1}{3}$ %

Question 13

Ann and Bob drive separately to a meeting. Ann's average driving speed is $\frac{1}{3}$ greater than Bob's, and Ann drives twice as many miles as Bob. What is the ratio of the number of hours Ann spends driving to the meeting to the number of hours Bob spends driving to the meeting?

(A) 8:3
(B) 3:2
(C) 4:3
(D) 2:3
(E) 3:8

Question 14

If $0 < p < 1$, which of the following has the least value?

(A) $\dfrac{1}{p^2}$

(B) $\dfrac{1}{\sqrt{p}}$

(C) $\dfrac{1}{p^2+1}$

(D) $\dfrac{1}{\sqrt{p+1}}$

(E) $\dfrac{1}{(p+1)^2}$

Question 15

In a certain game, each player scores either 2 points or 5 points. If n players score 2 points and m players score 5 points, and the total number of points scored is 50, what is the least possible positive difference between n and m ?

(A) 1
(B) 3
(C) 5
(D) 7
(E) 9

Question 16

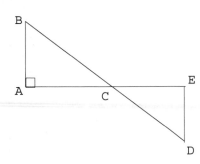

$AB \parallel ED$

<u>Note</u>: Figure not drawn to scale.

In the figure above, $ED = 1$, $CD = 2$, and $AE = 6\sqrt{3}$. What is the perimeter of $\triangle ABC$?

  (A) $3\sqrt{3}$

  (B) $5\sqrt{3}$

  (C) $10\sqrt{3}$

  (D) $15 + 5\sqrt{3}$

  (E) $25\sqrt{3}$

Question 17

James's library contains reference, biography, and fiction books only, in the ratio of 1:2:7, respectively. If James's library contains 30 books, how many biographies does he own?

  (A)   2
  (B)   3
  (C)   4
  (D)   6
  (E)   10

Question 18

Which of the following fractions is smaller than $\dfrac{2}{5}$?

  (A) $\dfrac{7}{16}$

  (B) $\dfrac{4}{11}$

  (C) $\dfrac{3}{7}$

  (D) $\dfrac{4}{9}$

  (E) $\dfrac{9}{20}$

Question 19

A sink contains exactly 12 liters of water. If water is drained from the sink until it holds exactly 6 liters of water less than the quantity drained away, how many liters of water were drained away?

  (A)   2
  (B)   3
  (C)   4.5
  (D)   6
  (E)   9

Question 20

In a certain state, a person may inherit up to $8,000 tax free, but any amount in excess of $8,000 is taxed at a rate of 6 percent. If Tony inherits a total of $11,500, how much tax will he have to pay?

  (A) $210
  (B) $270
  (C) $300
  (D) $420
  (E) $510

Question 21

The amount of gas in a gas storage tank is halved by draining 15 gallons of gas from it. If p gallons of gas are then added to the tank, how many gallons of gas are there in the storage tank?

(A) $15 + p$
(B) $30 - p$
(C) $30 + p$
(D) $2p - 30$
(E) $p - 15$

Question 22

A rectangular parking space is marked out by painting three of its sides white. If the length of the unpainted side is 9 feet, and the sum of the lengths of the painted sides is 37 feet, what is the area of the parking space in square feet?

(A) 46
(B) 81
(C) 126
(D) 252
(E) 333

Question 23

on time	x %
up to 15 minutes delayed	43 %
15–30 minutes delayed	17 %
30–60 minutes delayed	12 %
more than 60 minutes delayed	3 %

The chart above shows how long departures from a certain airport were delayed on a certain day. If 1,200 flights were delayed, how many flights departed on time?

(A) 250
(B) 300
(C) 350
(D) 400
(E) 900

Question 24

Cheese, bologna, and peanut butter sandwiches were made for a picnic in a ratio of 5 to 7 to 8. If a total of 120 sandwiches were made, how many bologna sandwiches were made?

(A) 15
(B) 30
(C) 38
(D) 42
(E) 48

Question 25

If a rectangle with width 49.872 inches and length 30.64 inches has an area that is 15 times the area of a certain square, which of the following is the closest approximation to the length, in inches, of a side of that square?

(A) 5
(B) 10
(C) 15
(D) 20
(E) 25

Answer Key

1. E	8. A	15. B	22. C
2. A	9. B	16. D	23. D
3. D	10. C	17. D	24. D
4. C	11. E	18. B	25. B
5. C	12. D	19. E	
6. E	13. B	20. A	
7. D	14. E	21. A	

Explanations

Question 1

It doesn't get any more basic than this, which is why you need to be on the lookout for silly errors. If you wanted to double-check your decimal arithmetic, you could reason that 7.38 plus an even 10 is going to be 17.38. Therefore, since we're adding more than 10, (A), (B), and (C) are all out. Adding .075 to .38 is actually .455, so (E) gets the nod.

Question 2

This question quickly tests your knowledge of a few triangle "rules." Triangle *ABD* is an equilateral triangle, which means that in addition to having sides of the same length, it has angles of the same measure (namely, 60°). Triangle *BDC* is an isosceles triangle, meaning that it has two sides of the same length, and that the angles opposite these sides are of the same measure. This allows us to conclude that angle *DBC* is $x°$ also. The last triangle "rule" is that angle *BDC* is 120°. This is because it is supplementary to angle *BDA*, so its measure and angle *BDA*'s measure sum to 180°. (Angle *BDA*, remember, is 60°.) So, if angle *BDC* is 120°, then the other two angles in triangle *BDC* must sum to 60°. Since they are equal angles, each is half of 60°, or 30°.

Question 3

Two equations, two variables. We can express one variable in terms of the other using one equation, and then plug this expression for the variable we solved for into the other equation, but there's a faster method. If we subtract the first equation from the second, we get—on the left side—exactly the expression that we are asked the value of:

$$3x - 2y = 3$$
$$- \quad (2x - 4y = -2)$$
$$\overline{x + 2y = 5}$$

Although the order of *x* and *y* is reversed from the expression in the question, the left side of the last equation contains the same expression. Choice (D) it is.

Question 4

If Joan spends 20 percent of her income on taxes, then the remainder is 80 percent of her income. If she spends 20 percent of this remaining 80 percent on rent, she spends:

$$.2(.8) = .16$$

Sixteen percent of her income goes to rent.

Question 5

Take it one step at a time. We want to send a 6-ounce package. The first 2 ounces cost $5.00. Each of the remaining 4 ounces costs $0.75. So the total for all 6 ounces, exclusive of tax is:

$$\$5.00 + 4(\$0.75) = \$8.00$$

To this is added a 6 percent tax, resulting in a total cost of:

$$\$8.00 + .06(\$8.00) =$$
$$\$8.00 + \$0.48 = \$8.48.$$

Question 6

We want to isolate *N*. First we'll multiply both sides by $2N$ in order to separate *N* and *M*. Then we'll divide both sides by 0.125:

$$\frac{3M}{2N} = 0.125$$
$$3M = 2N(0.125)$$
$$\frac{3M}{0.125} = 2N$$
$$24M = 2N$$

Now we can solve for *N* by just dividing both sides by 2:

$$12M = N.$$

Question 7

Since the 25 products sell at an average of $1,200, to buy one of each we'd have to spend 25 × $1,200 = $30,000. We want to find the greatest possible selling price of the most expensive product. The way to maximize this price is to minimize the prices of the other 24 products. Ten of these products sell for less than \$1,000, but all sell for at least \$420. This means that (in trying to minimize the price of 24 items) we can have 10 sell at \$420. That leaves 14 more that sell for \$1,000 or more. So, in order to keep minimizing, we'll price these at \$1,000. That means that, out of the \$30,000 we know it will take to purchase one of each item, only 10(\$420) + 14(\$1,000) = \$18,200 is needed in order to purchase the 24 cheap items. The final, most expensive item can thus cost as much as \$30,000 − \$18,200 = \$11,800.

Question 8

You either see this one right away, through your knowledge of number properties, or you just pick numbers. Any even integer multiplied by 2 will be evenly divisible by 4 because either the even integer itself is already divisible by 4 or it leaves a remainder of 2 when divided by 4. If it leaves a reminder of 2, then when this number is multiplied by 2, we'll have 2 remainders of 2, which when divided by 4 leaves no remainder. If you didn't see that, you could have picked numbers for n that resulted in an even integer when divided by 2 and seen what happens:

$$\frac{4}{2} = 2; \qquad \frac{4}{4} = 1$$

$$\frac{8}{2} = 4; \qquad \frac{8}{4} = 2$$

$$\frac{12}{2} = 6; \qquad \frac{12}{4} = 3$$

$$\frac{16}{2} = 8; \qquad \frac{16}{4} = 4$$

. . .

Already we can see the pattern: When divided by 2, only multiples of 4 will result in an even integer. Multiples of 4, of course, will have a remainder of 0 when divided by 4.

Question 9

Work = rate × time. The work here is 25 meters; the rate is 0.128 meters/second; we want to solve for the number of seconds:

25 meters = 0.128 meters/second × x seconds

$$\frac{25 \text{ meters}}{0.128 \text{ meter/seconds}} = x \text{ seconds}$$

$$\frac{25 \text{ meters}}{0.128 \text{ meter/seconds}} \approx 195 \text{ seconds}$$

Question 10

We have to factor the numerator and denominator. Since both are the difference of two squares, this should be automatic:

$$a - b = \frac{(a+b)(a-b)}{(b-a)(b+a)}$$

Since $a + b$ is the same as $b + a$, these terms are the same and can be canceled:

$$a - b = \frac{a-b}{b-a}$$

This equation can just be manipulated to give a value for $b - a$:

$$(b-a)(a-b) = a - b$$

$$b - a = \frac{a-b}{a-b}$$

Although we never find a value for either a or b, we can see that the value of the right hand side is just 1.

Question 11

It may look ugly, but it's easiest to just add up the integers, stopping when the sum hits 63:

$$6 + 7 = 13$$
$$13 + 8 = 21$$
$$21 + 9 = 30$$
$$30 + 10 = 40$$
$$40 + 11 = 51$$
$$51 + 12 = 63$$

The sequence runs from 6 to 12, which is 7 integers total.

Question 12

If you aren't good at visualizing, you might want to scratch out a figure:

In the figure above, meant to represent one of the two half cubes, the three unseen sides (the back, bottom, and left side) are also red (shaded). It's the top—the surface that used to be "inside" the cube—that's still white. Let's count up the surfaces, calling a full cube face (a face on the original cube) 1 unit.

Okay, we have the bottom and top here, which makes 2 units. Each of the other four faces is a half unit, so that's another 2 units. The total surface area, then, is 4 cube faces. One whole cube face (the top) is still white, so $\frac{1}{4}$ or 25 percent of the surface area is not red.

Question 13

Picking numbers is the strategy that works here. Since Ann drives $\frac{1}{3}$ faster than Bob, let's pick a number for Bob that's a multiple of 3. Why not 3? Let's say that Bob drives 3 miles per hour. Then Ann drives $\frac{1}{3}$ faster, or 4 miles per hour.

Now, the other information we have to consider is how far each travels. Ann drives twice as far as Bob. Let's pick 12 as the number of miles she drives (it's a multiple of both 3 and 4, the numbers we've already chosen—that's usually a good idea). If Ann drives 12 miles, then Bob drives 6 miles.

So now how much time will each spend driving? Ann will drive 12 miles at 4 miles per hour:

4 miles per hour $\times$ x hours = 12 miles

$$x \text{ hours} = \frac{12 \text{ miles}}{4 \text{ miles per hour}}$$
$$x = 3$$

Bob will drive for 6 miles at 3 miles per hour:

3 miles per hour $\times$ x hours = 6 miles

$$x \text{ hours} = \frac{6 \text{ miles}}{3 \text{ miles per hour}}$$
$$x = 2$$

So the ratio of the amount of time that Ann will drive to amount of time that Bob will drive is 3:2.

Question 14

Since p is a positive fraction less than 1, let's pick a value for it. Since we'll be taking a root (in choice (B)), let's choose $\frac{1}{9}$. Notice that since all of the choices are fractions whose numerators are 1, we need compare only the denominators. To find the smallest value, we'll want the fraction with the largest denominator. So the question is essentially asking which denominator is largest. (A)'s is $\left(\frac{1}{9}\right)^2 = \frac{1}{81}$. (B)'s is $\sqrt{\frac{1}{9}} = \frac{1}{3}$. (B)'s is larger. (C)'s denominator is (A)'s but with 1 added. That'll be a number larger than 1 (namely $1\frac{1}{81}$), so (C)'s is clearly larger than (B)'s. The denominator of (E) is $\left(\frac{1}{9}+1\right)^2 = \left(\frac{10}{9}\right)^2 = \frac{100}{81} = 1\frac{19}{81}$, which is greater than the denominator of (C). Since $p + 1$ is greater than 1, the denominator of (E)—which is the square of $p + 1$—must be greater than the denominator of (D), which is the square *root* of $p + 1$. Since (E) has the largest denominator, it's the smallest fraction.

Question 15

The quickest solution is to pick numbers for n and m. Since $n = 1$ and $m = 1$ would amount to 7 points, and since we want to minimize the difference between n and $m,$ and since $50 \div 7$ is just a bit more than 7, we'll start with values near 7.

The key is to discover what values for n, when multiplied by 2 points, will leave a multiple of 5 as the remaining points. The solution turns out to be 5 for n (10 points), which allows 8 for m (40 points). That's a total of 50 points, and the positive difference between the two values is only 3. If you investigate further, you find that it's impossible for there to be a difference of only 1 (choice (A)).

Question 16

The key is to recognize similar triangles. If AB is parallel to ED, then these alternate interior angles are equal: Angle ABC is equal to angle CDE and right angle BAC is equal to angle CED. Angle BCA is opposite angle ECD so the two of them are equal. Once we see that the triangles are similar, we know that the ratio between their corresponding sides is the same for all 3 pairs of sides. That in turn tells us that the same ratio will hold for their perimeters (which are, after all, just the sums of the sides).

Further inspection shows us that triangle CED is a special right triangle. With a leg of length 1 and a hypotenuse of length 2, the other leg (side CE) must be $\sqrt{3}$. Now if CE plus AC is $6\sqrt{3}$, and CE alone is just $\sqrt{3}$, then AC must be $5\sqrt{3}$. AC is the side corresponding to CE. Therefore, whatever ratio exists between the lengths of these sides also exists between the perimeters. Since AC is 5 times the length of CE, the perimeter of triangle BAC is 5 times that of triangle CED. Triangle CED has a perimeter of $1 + 2 + \sqrt{3}$, or $3 + \sqrt{3}$. Five times this is $15 + 5\sqrt{3}$.

Question 17

Since a ratio gives relative size rather than absolute size, we need to figure out what number, multiplied by the ratio, will give us the actual number of each type of book. Of course, we're only concerned with one type of book—biographies. If we call the unknown number x, we can create an algebraic equation. $1x + 2x + 7x$ is equal to the total number of books, which we've been told is 30. Therefore, $x + 2x + 7x = 30$; $10x = 30$; $x = 3$. So James owns $2(3) = 6$ biographies.

As a savvy Kaplan test taker, you might have solved this even more quickly, by *noticing that the parts of the ratio (1, 2, and 7) add up to 10*. So for every 10 books there must be 1 reference, 2 biographies, and 7 fiction books. Since there are 30 books, which is 3 × 10, we can find the actual number of any type of book by multiplying that part of the ratio by 3.

Question 18

When you see a question like this on the day of the test (and you will), compare fractions as quickly as possible. For choice (A), the least common denominator of $\frac{2}{5}$ and $\frac{7}{16}$ is 5×16, or 80, so convert $\frac{2}{5}$ to $\frac{32}{80}$ and convert $\frac{7}{16}$ to $\frac{35}{80}$; $\frac{35}{80}$ is obviously larger than $\frac{32}{80}$. For (B), the least common denominator of $\frac{2}{5}$ and $\frac{4}{11}$ is 5×11, or 55. Convert $\frac{2}{5}$ to $\frac{22}{55}$ and

convert $\frac{4}{11}$ to $\frac{20}{55}$. $\frac{20}{55}$ is less than $\frac{22}{55}$. That is, $\frac{4}{11}$ is less than $\frac{2}{5}$, so (B) is correct and we don't have to check the other choices.

Question 19

The key to this somewhat confusing word problem is to concentrate on what the question asks for: the quantity of water drained away, which we'll call x. We're told that x liters of water are drained away, and $x - 6$ liters are left. So x (liters taken away) plus $x - 6$ (liters left) equals 12 (total liters originally in sink). Therefore $2x - 6 = 12$, and $x = 9$.

The algebra here was easy, but if you had trouble setting up the equation you could have gotten the answer by *backsolving*. Can 2 liters have been taken away? No, because then –4 liters would be left. That reasoning eliminates choices (A), (B), and (C). As for (D), if 6 liters are drained away, that means 0 gallons are left, and there couldn't have been 12 liters in the tank originally.

Question 20

The only trick here is understanding what quantity is being taxed: the amount of inheritance in excess of $8,000. Tony will have to pay the 6 percent inheritance tax on $11,500 – $8,000, or $3,500. The problem then becomes a matter of straightforward calculation: 6 percent of $3,500 is just .06 × $3,500, which is 6 × 35, or $210. *In percent word problems, always make sure you're taking the proper percent of the proper quantity.*

Question 21

The key is interpreting the first sentence, which tells you how many gallons of gas are left in the tank after 15 gallons are drained. Since draining 15 gallons cuts the amount of gas in half, there must originally have been 2×15, or 30 gallons in the tank. After the 15 gallons are drained away, there are 15 gallons left. (This should be intuitively obvious. If it's not, you can set up an algebraic equation, letting x stand for the amount in the tank at the beginning: $x - 15 = \frac{1}{2}x$; $\frac{1}{2}x = 15$; $x = 30$.) Since p gallons are added to the 15 gallons left in the tank, the number of gallons at the end is $15 + p$.

If for some reason you were confused by the wording of this problem you should at least have been able to narrow it down to (A) and (C). Since p gallons of gas are added to some other quantity, the correct answer should be in the form some quantity *plus p*.

Question 22

The key to solving this one is knowing that the opposite sides of a rectangle are equal in length. If the unpainted side is 9 feet long, then the opposite, *painted* side is also 9 feet long. The total length of the three painted sides is 37 feet; this means that the other two painted sides are $37 - 9$ (the length of the painted side opposite the unpainted side) = 28 feet in length combined. Since these two sides are also opposite and equal, each one is $\frac{28}{2}$ = 14 feet long. The area of the rectangle is then 14 (the length of one of the two painted sides) $\times$ 9 (the length of one of the other sides—only one of which is painted) = 126 square feet.

Question 23

The chart tells us what percent of the flights were late, and the text tells us what number of flights were late (the number of flights that the percentage represents). We have to figure out the number of flights that were *not* late (that were on time). 43% + 17% + 12% + 3% = 75% of the flights were late. That's a nice, neat percentage, representing $\frac{3}{4}$. So $\frac{3}{4}$ of the flights were late, which means $\frac{1}{4}$ of the flights were on time. That makes the calculation very easy: 1,200 flights were late, which is equal to $\frac{3}{4}$ of all the flights. Therefore, $\frac{3}{4}$ of the flights is just $\frac{1200}{3}$ = 400 flights. So 400 flights were on time. When possible, it's often a good idea to avoid messy calculations by reducing percents to simple fractions like $\frac{1}{2}$, $\frac{1}{4}$, and $\frac{1}{5}$.

Question 24

There's a shortcut to solving this one. We're told that cheese, bologna, and peanut butter sandwiches are made in the ratio of 5 to 7 to 8. Every time they make 5 cheese sandwiches, they also have to make 7 bologna and 8 peanut butter sandwiches. So there must be $5x$ cheese sandwiches (and we don't know what x is at this point), $7x$ bologna sandwiches, and $8x$ peanut butter sandwiches. How many bologna sandwiches were made? Well, the number of bologna sandwiches must be some multiple of 7. But only choice (D), 42, is a multiple of 7.

If you didn't notice that, you'd have solved the problem algebraically, which is also pretty simple. If you add $5x$, the number of cheese sandwiches, $7x$, the number of bologna sandwiches, and $8x$, the number of peanut butter sandwiches, you get 120 total sandwiches. In other words: $5x + 7x + 8x = 120$, $20x = 120$, $x = 6$. So there were $7(6) = 42$ bologna sandwiches.

Question 25

Follow the question carefully. We're ultimately interested in the length of a side of "a certain square." We've been given a clue: the square's area is $\frac{1}{15}$ the area of a rectangle measuring 49.872 by 30.64. Fortunately, we've been told we need only the "approximate" length of a side, so we can work with approximates throughout. The area of the rectangle, then, is approximately 50×30, or 1,500. The area of the square will be approximately $\frac{1}{15}$ of that, or 100. The length of the side of a square is always the square root of the area (side $\times$ side = area), so this square has sides of approximately 10 inches.

KAPLAN

CHAPTER EIGHT

Data Sufficiency

HIGHLIGHTS

- Learn the Five Basic Principles of Data Sufficiency
- Study the Kaplan Method for Data Sufficiency questions
- Focus on step-by-step solutions to sample questions
- Complete the Data Sufficiency Practice Quiz

The instructions for the Data Sufficiency section look like this:

> <u>Directions:</u> In each of the problems, a question is followed by two statements containing certain data. You are to determine whether the data provided by the statements are sufficient to answer the question. Choose the correct answer based upon the statements' data, your knowledge of mathematics, and your familiarity with everyday facts (such as the number of minutes in an hour or cents in a dollar). Choose choice
>
> (A) if statement (1) by itself is sufficient to answer the question, but statement (2) by itself is not;
>
> (B) if statement (2) by itself is sufficient to answer the question, but statement (1) by itself is not;
>
> (C) if statements (1) and (2) taken together are sufficient to answer the question, even though neither statement by itself is sufficient;
>
> (D) if either statement by itself is sufficient to answer the question;
>
> (E) if statements (1) and (2) taken together are not sufficient to answer the question, requiring more data pertaining to the problem.

Data Sufficiency Tally

Expect to see about 15 questions in Data Sufficiency format on the GMAT.

Note: Diagrams accompanying problems agree with information given in the questions, but may not agree with additional information given in statements (1) and (2).

All numbers used are real numbers.

Confused? No wonder. The directions for these questions are pretty complicated. Let's look at a simple example.

What is the length of segment *AC* ?
(1) *B* is the midpoint of *AC*
(2) *AB* = 5

Statement (1) tells you that *B* is the midpoint of *AC*, so *AB* = *BC* and *AC* = 2*AB* = 2*BC*. Since statement (1) does not give a value for *AB* or *BC*, you cannot answer the question using statement (1) alone. Statement (2) says that *AB* = 5. Since statement (2) does not give you a value for *BC*, the question cannot be answered by statement (2) alone. Using both statements together you can find a value for both *AB* and *BC*; therefore you can find *AC*, so the answer to the problem is choice (C).

Kaplan Rules

Your goal on Data Sufficiency questions is to determine when you have enough information to make a decision or solve a problem.

Data Sufficiency is just a fancy name for a skill that you use all of the time, and it's one that's actually very important in business. The basic idea in Data Sufficiency questions is to determine when you have enough information to make a decision or solve a problem. The big difference between Data Sufficiency on the GMAT and most of the "data sufficiency" problems you come across in real life is that the GMAT problems are concerned solely with math facts and relationships.

For example, let's say you want to know whether a particular manager is doing a good job in her department. If you were informed that her department spent $50,000 more than it took in this year, would you be justified in saying that she was doing a bad job? Of course not—there could be all kinds of factors causing the loss that were beyond her control. For instance, the department might have spent $250,000 more than it took in last year when she wasn't in charge, and so she could be making great improvements, even though the department is still losing money.

The Five Basic Principles
of Data Sufficiency

1. Know the Data Sufficiency answer choices cold.

The directions and answer choices for Data Sufficiency questions never change. As we pointed out earlier, you can't afford to fumble with the answer choices on test day. You've got to become familiar with them now, so you can save time and minimize errors when you actually take the test. Let's take another look at the five answer choices:

- (A) Statement (1) by itself is sufficient to answer the question, but statement (2) by itself is not.
- (B) Statement (2) by itself is sufficient to answer the question, but statement (1) by itself is not.
- (C) Statements (1) and (2) taken together are sufficient to answer the question, even though neither statement by itself is sufficient.
- (D) Either statement by itself is sufficient to answer the question.
- (E) Statements (1) and (2) taken together are not sufficient to answer the question, requiring more data pertaining to the problem.

A statement provides sufficient information only if it leads to one and only one answer to the question. For example, if a question asked. "What is the value of x?" and a statement told you that x was equal to either 1 or 2, that statement would *not* be sufficient to answer the question.

2. Learn to work with the stem and two statements.

There are two basic questions that you must ask yourself on every Data Sufficiency question: Can you answer the question using the information from statement (1) only? Can you answer the question using the information from statement (2) only? If the answer to both of these questions is "no," then you ask yourself a third question: Can you answer the question if you combine the information from both statements?

Let's look at an example:

stem   If Augie's restaurant needs daily revenues of at least $3,000 to cover operating costs, is the restaurant making a profit from its operations?

statement (1) At Augie's restaurant, the average amount that each customer spends is $10.00.

statement (2) An average of 400 customers per day dine at Augie's restaurant.

1. Can you answer the question in the stem using only the information from statement (1)? *No.* You don't know how many customers come to the restaurant per day.

2. Can you answer the question using only the information from statement (2)? *No.* You don't know how much the customers will spend. *(You must ignore what statement (1) tells you when you consider statement (2).)*

   Now, because the answer to both of these questions is "no," you must ask yourself a third question:

3. Can you answer it if you combine the information from both statements? *Yes.* You can determine that the restaurant makes a profit because you know that revenues are higher than $3,000. (400 customers per day × $10.00 per customer = an average of $4,000 per day).

3. Know the two types of Data Sufficiency questions.

You should start to conceptualize Data Sufficiency questions into two types—those for which you have to consider the statements in combination, and those for which you don't. Recall the first two questions we asked about Augie's restaurant. Had the answer to either of these questions been "yes," we wouldn't have had to ask the third question—the one that involved combining the statements. If at least one of the statements is sufficient, your answer can be only (A), (B), or (D), depending on whether statement (1) is sufficient or statement (2) is sufficient or both are sufficient. Only in a case (such as Augie's) in which neither statement is sufficient do you have to consider the statements in combination. These then are the two general "types" of Data Sufficiency question:

- At least one of the statements is sufficient, and the answer is either (A), (B), or (D).

- Neither statement by itself is sufficient, forcing you to the additional step of combining the statements in order to choose between (C) and (E).

4. Know the topics.

As with the other GMAT question types, knowing what to expect from Data Sufficiency is half the battle. In addition to knowing the question type and how to deal with it efficiently (which we'll discuss shortly), it also helps to know the topics that you're likely to be tested on. The more you know about the inner workings of the GMAT, the better you can budget your time and maximize your score. The following table shows what topics are tested on Data Sufficiency and with what frequency:

TOPIC	PERCENTAGE
Ratios, Rates, Percentages	30%
Algebra	25%
Number Properties	25%
Geometry	15%
Other	5%

5. Think sufficiently.

Get into the habit of thinking about the sufficiency of information from the moment you read the question. The goal of the following exercise is getting you to think about what sort of information you need to answer a question, not about what the answer is. Read each statement below and ask yourself whether that statement alone is enough to answer the question. Don't bother about coming up with an actual value.

> A particular company made a profit of 4.5 million dollars in 1991. What was the value of its profit in 1993?

Can you answer this question if you know that:

1. The company earned 10 percent less profit in 1991 than in 1993?
2. In 1993, the company earned the same amount of profit as in 1992?
3. The company's profit was larger in 1993 than in 1991?
4. In 1991, the company's profit was $4.5 million less than in 1993?

Statement 1 is sufficient. You could solve this by letting the 1993 profit equal x and solving the equation for x : 4.5 million = $.9x$.

Statement 2 is insufficient. How much did the company earn in 1992? There's no way to tell.

Statement 3 is insufficient. Larger, but by how much?

Statement 4 is sufficient. You could add another $4.5 million to 1991's $4.5 million profit.

Kaplan Rules

The goal of Data Sufficiency questions is to find out what sort of information you need to answer a question, not what the answer is.

The Kaplan Three-Step Method for Data Sufficiency

This is the essential systematic approach to mastering Data Sufficiency. Use this approach for every Data Sufficiency question. It will allow you to answer questions quickly and will guarantee that you avoid the common GMAT mistake of subconsciously combining the statements instead of using them separately.

Here's how the method works:

> Team X won 40 basketball games. What percent of its basketball games did Team X win?
>
> (1) Team X played the same number of basketball games as Team Y.
>
> (2) Team Y won 45 games, representing 62.5 percent of the basketball games it played.

1. Focus on the question stem.

First think about what information would be sufficient to answer the question. You must be able to decipher the question stem quickly and focus on what information is needed to answer it. Do you need a formula? Do you need to set up an equation? Do you need to know the value of a variable?

You should be able to recognize this sample question as a percent question. (Helpful hint: Percent × Whole = Part.) You're given the part (the number of games team X won) and asked for the percent (that is, the percentage of its games that team X won). What do you need? The whole—the total number of games team X played.

2. Look at each statement separately.

Be sure you ignore the other statement! Remember, while determining the sufficiency of a particular statement, you must not carry over the other statement's information. When you look at Statement (1), cover up Statement (2), and vice versa. That's a practical and easy way to avoid falling into this very, very common GMAT error. As you evaluate each statement, eliminate the appropriate answer choices.

In our example, with (1) we know that Team X played the same number of games as Team Y, but we don't know what that number is. With (2), we get plenty of information about Team Y, but nothing at all that relates to Team X. So neither statement by itself is sufficient.

The Kaplan Three-Step Method for Data Sufficiency

1. Focus on the question stem.
2. Look at each statement separately.
3. Look at both statements in combination.

3. Look at both statements in combination.

You need to proceed to Step 3 only when both statements (1) and (2) are insufficient. This happens less than half the time. Note that if you reach this point on a problem, you know the answer is either (C) or (E). When considering the two statements together, simply treat them and the stimulus as one long problem and ask yourself: Can it be solved? STOP as soon as you know whether it can be solved! Don't carry out any unnecessary calculations.

In general, these questions are a lot easier when taken in parts; don't try to cram all the information into your head at once. In the example, when we combine the two statements, we know that the number of games Team X played is the same as the number Team Y played, *and* we can find out how many games Team Y played by using the percent formula (Percent × Whole = Part; 62.5% × Games Played = 45). Therefore, we can figure out how many games Team X played, which is all we need to know in order to figure out what percent of its games Team X won. So we have the answer for this example, (C), without doing any calculation at all.

Using the Kaplan Three-Step Method

The key to doing well in Data Sufficiency is becoming adept at determining the sufficiency or insufficiency of the statements without doing unnecessary calculations. It just takes practice. In the following problems, just decide whether the statements are sufficient to answer the question.

If $2b - 2a^2 = 18$, what is the value of b ?

(1) $a^2 = 1,156$

(2) $a > 0$

- (A) Statement (1) by itself is sufficient to answer the question, but statement (2) by itself is not.
- (B) Statement (2) by itself is sufficient to answer the question, but statement (1) by itself is not.
- (C) Statements (1) and (2) taken together are sufficient to answer the question, even though neither statement by itself is sufficient.
- (D) Either statement by itself is sufficient to answer the question.
- (E) Statements (1) and (2) taken together are not sufficient to answer the question, requiring more data pertaining to the problem.

Here's how the three-step method works with the first example.

Step 1: Focus on the question stem.
What would we need to get the value of b? We need the value of the equation's only other variable, a.

Step 2: Look at each statement separately.
(1) alone does give us what we need. We could just substitute the value (1) gives for a^2 into the equation and solve. Right off that eliminates choices (B), (C), and (E). (2) alone, however, gives us nothing, because a could be 1 or 1,000,000. So eliminate (D) and the answer is (A).

Step 3: Look at both statements in combination.
There is no Step 3 for this problem. Remember, Step 3 is necessary only when neither statement by itself is sufficient, which is true less than half the time (about 40 percent of the time, actually).

Now let's look at another problem, which is easier than it looks. When a question appears to be complicated, take it apart and deal with it piece by piece. Keep focused on exactly what information you need in order to solve the problem.

> A certain company produces exactly three products, X, Y, and Z. In 1990, what was the total income for the company from the sale of its products?
>
> (1) In 1990, the company sold 8,000 units of product X, 10,000 units of product Y, and 16,000 units of product Z.
>
> (2) In 1990, the company charged $28 per unit for product X, and twice as much for product Z.
>
> (A) Statement (1) by itself is sufficient to answer the question, but statement (2) by itself is not.
> (B) Statement (2) by itself is sufficient to answer the question, but statement (1) by itself is not.
> (C) Statements (1) and (2) taken together are sufficient to answer the question, even though neither statement by itself is sufficient.
> (D) Either statement by itself is sufficient to answer the question.
> (E) Statements (1) and (2) taken together are not sufficient to answer the question, requiring more data pertaining to the problem.

Step 1: Focus on the question stem.

What do you need to solve this problem? You need to know the total income of the company from the three products, and so far you've been told nothing.

Step 2: Look at each statement separately.

(1) by itself is insufficient; it gives you just the number of **units** of each product, but it says nothing about income. Eliminate choices (A) and (D). (2) by itself is also insufficient; it gives you the price per unit of X and Z, but it doesn't even mention Y. Eliminate choice (B) as well.

Step 3: Look at both statements together.

Both together still leave us lacking the unit price of Y, and so we have no way of figuring the income derived from the sale of Y. The statements together are insufficient and the answer is (E).

Note that focusing on exactly what you needed to answer the question— the total income from all three products—allowed you to avoid wasting time calculating the profits for X and Z. You knew that without Y, such calculations were fruitless. You can avoid calculations (on a math test no less) by determining exactly what information you need to solve the problem. Then you can recognize straight off when you have that necessary information. When you use the three-step method and take an overview of the problem at the beginning (our Step 1), you save yourself unnecessary labor.

> A number of bacteria were placed in a petri dish at 5:00 A.M. If the number of bacteria in the petri dish grew for 5 days, by doubling every 12 hours, how many bacteria were in the petri dish at 5:00 P.M. on the third day?
>
> (1) From 5:00 A.M. to 5:00 P.M. on the second day the number of bacteria increased by 100 percent.
>
> (2) 20 bacteria were placed in the petri dish at 5:00 A.M. the first day.

   (A) Statement (1) by itself is sufficient to answer the question, but statement (2) by itself is not.

   (B) Statement (2) by itself is sufficient to answer the question, but statement (1) by itself is not.

   (C) Statements (1) and (2) taken together are sufficient to answer the question, even though neither statement by itself is sufficient.

   (D) Either statement by itself is sufficient to answer the question.

   (E) Statements (1) and (2) taken together are not sufficient to answer the question, requiring more data pertaining to the problem.

Step 1: Focus on the question stem.

You're given the rate of growth of the number of bacteria, and the time at which the growth started. You're asked for the number of bacteria at the end of the growth. You need to know a number: How many bacteria did they start with? (Actually, if they gave you the number of bacteria in the dish at *any* time prior to 5:00 P.M. on the third day, you would be able to figure out how many bacteria wound up in the petri dish by using the rate of growth.)

Step 2: Look at each statement separately.

Forget what (1) gives us; you have to realize what it doesn't: anything about numbers, so it is insufficient. (As a matter of fact, it just repeats the information in the stimulus that the number of bacteria doubles every 12 hours.) Eliminate choices (A) and (D). (2) gives us exactly what we're looking for—the number of bacteria in the dish at the beginning. You *could* do calculations from here to get the actual numbers, but because you *know* that you could, you don't have to bother. So choice (B) is the answer, and we can skip step 3.

As you'll see in the next example, geometry also shows up on Data Sufficiency. Be very careful with any diagrams you are given! Things may not be what they seem. Try the problem below. (Helpful hint: The key to multiple figures is to pass information from one figure to the next.)

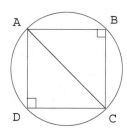

If points *A*, *B*, *C*, and *D* are points on the circumference of the circle in the figure above, what is the area of *ABCD* ?

(1) The radius of the circle is $\dfrac{\sqrt{2}}{2}$.

(2) *ABCD* is a square.

KAPLAN

- (A) Statement (1) by itself is sufficient to answer the question, but statement (2) by itself is not.
- (B) Statement (2) by itself is sufficient to answer the question, but statement (1) by itself is not.
- (C) Statements (1) and (2) taken together are sufficient to answer the question, even though neither statement by itself is sufficient.
- (D) Either statement by itself is sufficient to answer the question.
- (E) Statements (1) and (2) taken together are not sufficient to answer the question, requiring more data pertaining to the problem.

Step 1: Focus on the question stem.

Be careful! The trap is that many, if not most, students will assume that *ABCD* is a square. You can't trust diagrams in Data Sufficiency. Straight lines are straight, that's true, and angles marked as right angles are right angles, but they want to test your ability to look at a shape and re-imagine it based on the facts, and this is how they do it. Here you could slide the points around the circumference without changing the angle measures, so *ABCD* may not be a square. So we need confirmation that *ABCD* is a square, and we need either a radius, a diameter (*AC*), or a side. (Note: We know *AC* is a diameter because angle *ADC*—and angle *ABC*, for that matter—is a right angle. Whenever a right angle is inscribed in a circle, the two chords that form this right angle are the legs of a right triangle with a hypotenuse that is a diameter of the circle.)

Step 2: Look at both statements separately.

(1) gives you the radius, but you still don't know whether *ABCD* is a square, so you can't calculate its area from the length of diameter *AC*. Insufficient: Eliminate (A) and (D). (2) tells you *ABCD* is indeed a square but not how big a square. Because (2) provides no numbers, it is insufficient, and we can eliminate (B).

Step 3: Look at both statements together.

With the two statements together, however, we have what we were looking for. We know *ABCD* is a square, we have the length of its diagonal *AC* (which is also the diameter of the circle; remember to pass information between figures), so we're set. The answer is (C).

If you drew a complete blank on the geometry in this problem, don't worry. Geometry is a fairly small part of GMAT and should never become your top priority. Moreover, you could have eliminated some answer choices even if you know almost nothing about squares and circles. You might have been baffled by (1), but look at (2). No numbers! There are no numbers in the stimulus either, so (2) can't possibly be sufficient to provide a number for the area. So you could eliminate (B) and (D), which leaves you with a one-in-three chance of guessing correctly.

Value Problems
Many GMAT Data Sufficiency questions ask for the value of a particular variable. When they ask for a value on GMAT Data Sufficiency, it means the one and only value. Statement (1) and statement (2) will never give contradictory values for the same variable.

The next example is a fairly basic value problem.

What is the value of x ?

(1) $x^2 - 9 = 16$

(2) $3x(x - 5) = 0$

(A) Statement (1) by itself is sufficient to answer the question, but statement (2) by itself is not.

(B) Statement (2) by itself is sufficient to answer the question, but statement (1) by itself is not.

(C) Statements (1) and (2) taken together are sufficient to answer the question, even though neither statement by itself is sufficient.

(D) Either statement by itself is sufficient to answer the question.

(E) Statements (1) and (2) taken together are not sufficient to answer the question, requiring more data pertaining to the problem.

Step 1: Focus on the question stem.
No question about what you need; you're looking for x. Don't expect to be given the value directly, though (that almost never happens), but instead a way of finding it, perhaps through an equation.

Step 2: Look at each statement separately.
(1) is an example of a dangerous GMAT trap. The minute you see x^2 in Data Sufficiency, expect a trap. Here, $x^2 = 25$, but x can equal +5 or –5. So (1) is not sufficient; eliminate choices (A) and (D).

As for (2), again you have two possible values for x, 0 and 5. So, (2)'s insufficient, and we eliminate (B).

Step 3: Look at both statements together.
Many students may jump to the conclusion that the answer must be (E) when they see what looks like three possible values for x (–5, 0, +5). But look carefully at what's going on. (1) says x is either +5 or –5; (2) says x

is either 0 or +5. *Both* these statements must be true, and that means the only possible value for x is +5. We know that x can't be 0, because that contradicts statement (1), and x can't be −5, because that contradicts statement (2). If in one statement the variable has two values, and in the other statement the variable has two values, but the statements share just one value, then these statements are sufficient for answering the question.

Here's another value problem:

If z is an integer, what is the units' digit of z^3 ?

(1) z is a multiple of 5.

(2) $\sqrt{z}$ is an integer.

- (A) Statement (1) by itself is sufficient to answer the question, but statement (2) by itself is not.
- (B) Statement (2) by itself is sufficient to answer the question, but statement (1) by itself is not.
- (C) Statements (1) and (2) taken together are sufficient to answer the question, even though neither statement by itself is sufficient.
- (D) Either statement by itself is sufficient to answer the question.
- (E) Statements (1) and (2) taken together are not sufficient to answer the question, requiring more data pertaining to the problem.

Kaplan Rules

For a Data Sufficiency question that asks for the value of a particular variable, the question is looking for one and only one value.

Step 1: Focus on the question stem.

The question isn't actually asking for z, though of course figuring out z would do it. We're looking for the value of a digit of z^3; on the GMAT that's a pretty strong signal that we're going to be dealing with the concept of multiples.

Step 2: Look at each statement separately.

How does the concept "multiple of 5" in (1) relate to the units' digit (what we're looking for)? All multiples of 5 (and of course that includes the cubes of all multiples of 5) have units' digits of 0 or 5. Therefore, (1) tells us only that the units' digit of z^3 is 0 or 5. It's insufficient, so eliminate (A) and (D). In statement (2), z^3 can have any units' digit. If you can't see this immediately, it becomes obvious when you pick a couple of numbers: say $z = 1$, then the units' digit of z^3 is 1. Say $z = 100$, then the units' digit of z^3 is 0. So (2) is insufficient, and we can eliminate (B).

Step 3: Look at both statements together.

Even when you combine the statements you can still have 0 and 5 as possible values for the units' digit of z^3 (again, pick numbers, say $z = 25$, and

$z = 100$). As you can see, some Data Sufficiency problems cannot be intuited. In such cases, picking numbers is really the only way to go. If more than one value works for a statement, then that statement is insufficient.

"Yes or No" Questions
Usually about a third of the Data Sufficiency questions you'll see on the GMAT are "Yes or No" questions. Although these questions are sometimes hard to get a handle on immediately, don't get into the habit of giving up on them too easily. The important thing is to remember that they're looking for a definite, unambiguous "yes" or a definite, unambiguous "no." Generally, if a statement provides sufficient information, the answer to the question is almost always "yes." But don't forget that a solid "no" is adequate too.

Here's a fairly basic "yes or no" question.

Is $4 + \dfrac{n}{6}$ an integer?

(1) n is a multiple of 3.

(2) n divided by 6 has a remainder of 0.

(A) Statement (1) by itself is sufficient to answer the question, but statement (2) by itself is not.
(B) Statement (2) by itself is sufficient to answer the question, but statement (1) by itself is not.
(C) Statements (1) and (2) taken together are sufficient to answer the question, even though neither statement by itself is sufficient.
(D) Either statement by itself is sufficient to answer the question.
(E) Statements (1) and (2) taken together are not sufficient to answer the question, requiring more data pertaining to the problem.

Step 1: Focus on the question stem.
Simple. We need to know whether n is a multiple of 6, because the 4 drops out (if $\dfrac{n}{6}$ is an integer, $\dfrac{n}{6} + 4$ is an integer).

Step 2: Look at each statement separately.
(1) is insufficient; n could be 3, 9, 15, etcetera, in which case $n/6$ is not an integer; or it could be 6, 12, 18, etcetera, in which case $n/6$ is an integer. Eliminate choices (A) and (D).

(2) tells us that n is a multiple of 6 by definition, so it's sufficient (the answer to the question is "yes"); (B) is the answer and we can skip step 3.

Note that picking numbers came in handy again, but remember: If you pick numbers, you must be thorough. You must pick different types of numbers: Here in statement (1) it was important that you picked both odd and even multiples of 3.

The following is a middle-level "yes or no" question, one that involves the common GMAT concepts of primes and odds-and-evens. When the GMAT brings the primes together with a question about oddness and evenness, it's a pretty sure bet that the answer is going to test whether you know that 2 is the only even prime.

If x and y are prime numbers, is $y(x - 3)$ odd?

(1) $x > 10$
(2) $y < 3$

- (A) Statement (1) by itself is sufficient to answer the question, but statement (2) by itself is not.
- (B) Statement (2) by itself is sufficient to answer the question, but statement (1) by itself is not.
- (C) Statements (1) and (2) taken together are sufficient to answer the question, even though neither statement by itself is sufficient.
- (D) Either statement by itself is sufficient to answer the question.
- (E) Statements (1) and (2) taken together are not sufficient to answer the question, requiring more data pertaining to the problem.

Step 1: Focus on the question stem.
We're asked whether the product $y(x - 3)$ is odd. We can answer that if we know either that *both $x - 3$* and y are odd, which would mean that the product is odd, or by showing that *either $x - 3$* or y is even, which would mean that the product is even (because an even integer times any integer is even).

Step 2: Look at each statement separately.
(1): If x is a prime greater than 10, then x is an odd prime. Therefore $x - 3$ is even, and $y(x - 3)$ must also be even, so (1) is sufficient. Eliminate answer choices (B), (C), and (E). (2) tells us that y is 2, the only prime less than 3, so y is even. Once again this is sufficient to prove that $y(x - 3)$ is even. Eliminate (A). (D) is the answer.

Note that these statements were sufficient to answer the question in the negative, which is rare but does happen. A "no" is as good as a "yes" in answering "yes or no" questions.

Kaplan Rules

A "no" is as good as a "yes" in "yes or no" questions.

Kaplan Rules

Try this next "yes or no" question, which is basic. It's a natural for the picking numbers strategy.

Is the product of x, y, and z equal to 1?

(1) $x + y + z = 3$

(2) x, y, and z are each greater than 0.

A Statement (1) by itself is sufficient to answer the question, but statement (2) by itself is not.

B Statement (2) by itself is sufficient to answer the question, but statement (1) by itself is not.

C Statements (1) and (2) taken together are sufficient to answer the question, even though neither statement by itself is sufficient.

D Either statement by itself is sufficient to answer the question.

E Statements (1) and (2) taken together are not sufficient to answer the question, requiring more data pertaining to the problem.

Step 1: Focus on the question stem.

You want the product xyz; that may mean knowing the values of x, y, and z or it may mean having some other way of determining their product (if you were told $xy = 1$, for instance, you wouldn't need to know the values of x and y separately).

Step 2: Look at each statement separately.

When you run into a straightforward question like this, it sometimes pays to give some thought to the math oddity that's being tested. Here the test makers know that some people will pick only positive integers. You, on the other hand, should always be aware of the importance of picking negative numbers and fractions and zero.

(1): Pick a couple of possibilities for x, y, and z; remember to try fractions, negative numbers, and zero, as well as positive integers. If $x = 1$, $y = 1$, and $z = 1$, then xyz does equal 1. But if $x = 3$, $y = 0$, $z = 0$, then xyz does not equal 1. (1) is insufficient. Eliminate (A) and (D).

(2) is obviously insufficient; you could have $x = y = z = 1$ again, where xyz does equal 1, or you could have $x = y = z = 100$, and xyz equals 1,000,000. Eliminate (B).

Step 3: Look at both statements together.

Combining the steps is still insufficient. You could again pick $x = y = z = 1$, which makes xyz equal 1. You could also pick $x = 2$, $y = \dfrac{1}{2}$, $z = \dfrac{1}{2}$, where $xyz = \dfrac{1}{2}$. So the two statements together don't tell us if $xyz = 1$, and the answer is (E).

Guessing in Data Sufficiency
When you run into a real horror-show question, like the following, don't forget to use sound Data Sufficiency guessing strategy. That means skipping a statement that looks too daunting and trying to eliminate some answer choices by looking at the easier statement. Try your hand at the tough question below. Don't try to solve it; instead see if you can narrow the possibilities down quickly.

What was the maximum temperature in City A on Saturday, May 14?

(1) The average (arithmetic mean) of the maximum daily temperatures in City A from Sunday May 8 to Saturday, May 14 was 72°, which was two degrees less than the average (arithmetic mean) of the maximum daily temperatures in City A from Monday, May 9 to Friday, May 13.

(2) The maximum temperature on Saturday, May 14 was 5° greater than the maximum temperature in City A on Sunday, May 8.

(A) Statement (1) by itself is sufficient to answer the question, but statement (2) by itself is not.

(B) Statement (2) by itself is sufficient to answer the question, but statement (1) by itself is not.

(C) Statements (1) and (2) taken together are sufficient to answer the question, even though neither statement by itself is sufficient.

(D) Either statement by itself is sufficient to answer the question.

(E) Statements (1) and (2) taken together are not sufficient to answer the question, requiring more data pertaining to the problem.

Even on a difficult question, you can still use the Three-Step Method.

1. Focus on the question stem.

Clear enough: We need a number—the maximum temperature on a certain date. It's hard to say what sort of information we might need to answer this, before we look at the statements.

2. Look at each statement separately.

(1): This is a mess. You're in a hurry. Skip it and look at Statement (2), which only compares the maximum on May 14 with the maximum on May 8, without telling us what that earlier temperature was. There's no way you can get a number from (2), so it's insufficient. That eliminates (B) and (D), so guess from the remaining choices. On harder questions, answer choices tend to be more sufficient than they might seem, so don't choose (E). Pick between (A) and (C), depending on how much you think you can extract from the first statement, and lean towards (A). In this case, the answer is (C), though historically (A) has been slightly more common in this GMAT situation.

Don't let this one leave you with a bad taste in your mouth; you're unlikely to run into anything as horrible as Statement (1) on test day. The point of this exercise is to show you that even if you do hit something this bad, you're still in control. You don't just sit there and feel mistreated. You work the odds, you look for the strategic approach, and you increase your likelihood of picking up a point. This is your test. Never relinquish control to the test makers.

Here's the solution. If the average maximum temperature from May 8 to May 14 was 72 degrees, then the sum of the maximum temperatures of those days is $7 \times 72 = 504$ degrees. If the average maximum temperature from May 9 to May 13 was $72 + 2$, or 74 degrees, then the sum of the maximum temperatures of those days was $5 \times 74 = 370$ degrees.

The difference between those numbers is just the sum of the maximum temperature on May 8, which we'll call x, and the maximum temperature on May 14, which we'll call y (since these two days were left out of the second time period). So $x + y = 504 - 370 = 134$. But Statement (2) tells us that $y - x = 5$. Adding these two equations we get $2y = 139$; $y = 69.5$ (and $x = 64.5$).

This example demonstrates how guessing can be more practical for some questions. One thing that you can do to improve your chances of guessing correctly is to learn to use the rules to your advantage by eliminating choices. By looking at only one statement you can narrow the possibilities down to 2 or 3 choices. This can be a great help, particularly on difficult problems for which you think you might have to guess. Note that

KAPLAN

for this, and other Data Sufficiency strategies, you must be sure you know the rules absolutely cold by test day.

- If statement (1) is sufficient, eliminate (B), (C), and (E): the answer must be (A) or (D).

- If statement (2) is sufficient, eliminate (A), (C), and (E): the answer must be (B) or (D).

- If statement (1) is insufficient, eliminate (A) and (D): the answer must be (B), (C), or (E).

- If statement (2) is insufficient, eliminate (B) and (D): the answer must be (A), (C), or (E).

Helpful Hint: If Statement (1) looks too confusing, don't skip the problem. Look at Statement (2); sometimes it's a lot easier. If you can figure out if even one statement is sufficient or insufficient, you've enormously improved the odds of guessing correctly. This is one of the many ways in which you can take control of the test.

The best way to master Data Sufficiency questions is to practice. Try your hand at the Data Sufficiency Practice Quiz.

Kaplan Rules

If statement (2) looks easier than statement (1), look at that statement first.

Data Sufficiency Practice Quiz

Directions: In each of the problems, a question is followed by two statements containing certain data. You are to determine whether the data provided by the statements are sufficient to answer the question. Choose the correct answer based upon the statements' data, your knowledge of mathematics, and your familiarity with everyday facts (such as the number of minutes in an hour or cents in a dollar). Choose choice

  (A) if statement (1) by itself is sufficient to answer the question, but statement (2) by itself is not;

  (B) if statement (2) by itself is sufficient to answer the question, but statement (1) by itself is not;

  (C) if statements (1) and (2) taken together are sufficient to answer the question, even though neither statement by itself is sufficient;

  (D) if either statement by itself is sufficient to answer the question;

  (E) if statements (1) and (2) taken together are not sufficient to answer the question, requiring more data pertaining to the problem.

Note: Diagrams accompanying problems agree with information given in the questions, but may not agree with additional information given in statements (1) and (2).

All numbers used are real numbers.

Example:

$$A \quad\quad B \quad\quad\quad C$$

What is the length of segment AC?
  (1) B is the midpoint of AC.
  (2) $AB = 5$

Choose answer choice

  (A) if statement (1) BY ITSELF is sufficient to answer the question, but statement (2) by itself is not;

  (B) if statement (2) BY ITSELF is sufficient to answer the question, but statement (1) by itself is not;

  (C) if statements (1) and (2) TAKEN TOGETHER are sufficient to answer the question, even though NEITHER statement BY ITSELF is sufficient;

  (D) if EITHER statement BY ITSELF is sufficient to answer the question;

  (E) if statements (1) and (2) TAKEN TOGETHER are NOT sufficient to answer the question, requiring more data pertaining to the problem.

Explanation: Statement (1) tells you that B is the midpoint of AC, so $AB = BC$ and $AC = 2AB = 2BC$. Since statement (1) does not give a value for AB or BC, you cannot answer the question using statement (1) alone. Statement (2) says that $AB = 5$. Since statement (2) does not give you a value for BC, the question cannot be answered by statement (2) alone. Using both statements together you can find a value for both AB and BC; therefore you can find AC, so the answer to the problem is choice (C).

Question 1

What is the ratio of the discounted price of an item to the list price?

(1) The discounted price is $4 less than the list price.
(2) The discounted price is 20 percent less than the list price.

  (A)
  (B)
  (C)
  (D)
  (E)

Choose answer choice

① if statement (1) BY ITSELF is sufficient to answer the question, but statement (2) by itself is not;
② if statement (2) BY ITSELF is sufficient to answer the question, but statement (1) by itself is not;
③ if statements (1) and (2) TAKEN TOGETHER are sufficient to answer the question, even though NEITHER statement BY ITSELF is sufficient;
④ if EITHER statement BY ITSELF is sufficient to answer the question;
⑤ if statements (1) and (2) TAKEN TOGETHER are NOT sufficient to answer the question, requiring more data pertaining to the problem.

Question 2

Does $x = y$?

(1) $x^2 - y^2 = 0$
(2) $(x - y)^2 = 0$

Ⓐ
Ⓑ
Ⓒ
Ⓓ
Ⓔ

Question 3

Does rectangle A have a greater perimeter than rectangle B ?

(1) The length of a side of rectangle A is twice the length of a side of rectangle B.
(2) The area of rectangle A is twice the area of rectangle B.

Ⓐ
Ⓑ
Ⓒ
Ⓓ
Ⓔ

Question 4

How many students scored less than the class average on a test?

(1) The class average was 83.
(2) Fourteen students scored above the class average.

Ⓐ
Ⓑ
Ⓒ
Ⓓ
Ⓔ

Question 5

If $ab < ac$, which is greater, b or c ?

(1) $a < 0$
(2) $c < 0$

Ⓐ
Ⓑ
Ⓒ
Ⓓ
Ⓔ

Choose answer choice

(A) if statement (1) BY ITSELF is sufficient to answer the question, but statement (2) by itself is not;

(B) if statement (2) BY ITSELF is sufficient to answer the question, but statement (1) by itself is not;

(C) if statements (1) and (2) TAKEN TOGETHER are sufficient to answer the question, even though NEITHER statement BY ITSELF is sufficient;

(D) if EITHER statement BY ITSELF is sufficient to answer the question;

(E) if statements (1) and (2) TAKEN TOGETHER are NOT sufficient to answer the question, requiring more data pertaining to the problem.

Question 6

If p, q, and r are even numbers, and $2 < p < q < r$, what is the value of q ?

(1) $r < 10$
(2) $p < 6$

(A)
(B)
(C)
(D)
(E)

Question 7

If there are an average of 250 words on each page, how many pages can Michael read in an hour?

(1) There is an average of 25 ten-word lines on each page.
(2) Michael can read 30 ten-word lines per minute.

(A)
(B)
(C)
(D)
(E)

Question 8

Is $m > n$?

(1) $\dfrac{3}{7} < m < \dfrac{5}{7}$

(2) $\dfrac{2}{7} < n < \dfrac{4}{7}$

(A)
(B)
(C)
(D)
(E)

Question 9

What is the value of $a^4 - b^4$?

(1) $a = 3$
(2) $b = a$

(A)
(B)
(C)
(D)
(E)

Choose answer choice

Ⓐ if statement (1) BY ITSELF is sufficient to answer the question, but statement (2) by itself is not;

Ⓑ if statement (2) BY ITSELF is sufficient to answer the question, but statement (1) by itself is not;

Ⓒ if statements (1) and (2) TAKEN TOGETHER are sufficient to answer the question, even though NEITHER statement BY ITSELF is sufficient;

Ⓓ if EITHER statement BY ITSELF is sufficient to answer the question;

Ⓔ if statements (1) and (2) TAKEN TOGETHER are NOT sufficient to answer the question, requiring more data pertaining to the problem.

Question 10

If R is an integer, is R evenly divisible by 3?

(1) $2R$ is evenly divisible by 3.
(2) $3R$ is evenly divisible by 3.

Ⓐ
Ⓑ
Ⓒ
Ⓓ
Ⓔ

Question 11

Susan flipped a fair coin N times. What fraction of the flips came up heads?

(1) $N = 24$

(2) The number of flips that came up tails was $\frac{3}{8}N$.

Ⓐ
Ⓑ
Ⓒ
Ⓓ
Ⓔ

Question 12

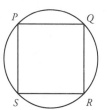

If the vertices of quadrilateral $PQRS$ above lie on the circumference of a circle, is $PQRS$ a square?

(1) Side PS is equal in length to a radius of the circle.
(2) The degree measure of minor arc QR is 45°.

Ⓐ
Ⓑ
Ⓒ
Ⓓ
Ⓔ

Question 13

If he did not stop along the way, what speed did Bill average on his 3-hour trip?

(1) He traveled a total of 120 miles.
(2) He traveled half the distance at 30 miles per hour, and half the distance at 60 miles per hour.

Ⓐ
Ⓑ
Ⓒ
Ⓓ
Ⓔ

Choose answer choice

    Ⓐ if statement (1) BY ITSELF is sufficient to answer the question, but statement (2) by itself is not;

    Ⓑ if statement (2) BY ITSELF is sufficient to answer the question, but statement (1) by itself is not;

    Ⓒ if statements (1) and (2) TAKEN TOGETHER are sufficient to answer the question, even though NEITHER statement BY ITSELF is sufficient;

    Ⓓ if EITHER statement BY ITSELF is sufficient to answer the question;

    Ⓔ if statements (1) and (2) TAKEN TOGETHER are NOT sufficient to answer the question, requiring more data pertaining to the problem.

Question 14

What is the value of $\dfrac{x+z}{x-y}$?

(1) $x + z = 3$
(2) $y + z = 2$

    Ⓐ
    Ⓑ
    Ⓒ
    Ⓓ
    Ⓔ

Question 15

If x is a positive integer less than 10, and $x + 2$ is a prime number, what is the value of x ?

(1) $x + 3$ is the square of an integer.
(2) $x + 7$ is the cube of an integer.

    Ⓐ
    Ⓑ
    Ⓒ
    Ⓓ
    Ⓔ

Question 16

On a certain construction crew there are 3 carpenters for every 2 painters. What percent of the entire crew are carpenters or painters?

(1) Eighteen percent of the crew are carpenters.
(2) Twelve percent of the crew are painters.

    Ⓐ
    Ⓑ
    Ⓒ
    Ⓓ
    Ⓔ

Question 17

A rectangular aquarium provides 36 square centimeters of water-surface area per fish. How many fish are there in the aquarium?

(1) The edges of the aquarium have lengths of 60, 42, and 30 centimeters.
(2) The aquarium is filled to a depth of 40 centimeters.

    Ⓐ
    Ⓑ
    Ⓒ
    Ⓓ
    Ⓔ

Choose answer choice

(A) if statement (1) BY ITSELF is sufficient to answer the question, but statement (2) by itself is not;

(B) if statement (2) BY ITSELF is sufficient to answer the question, but statement (1) by itself is not;

(C) if statements (1) and (2) TAKEN TOGETHER are sufficient to answer the question, even though NEITHER statement BY ITSELF is sufficient;

(D) if EITHER statement BY ITSELF is sufficient to answer the question;

(E) if statements (1) and (2) TAKEN TOGETHER are NOT sufficient to answer the question, requiring more data pertaining to the problem.

Question 18

At Consolidated Foundries, for a resolution to become policy, a quorum of at least half the 20 directors must pass the resolution by at least a two-thirds majority. At a meeting of the board of directors, did resolution *X* pass or fail?

(1) Ten directors voted for the resolution.
(2) Seven directors voted against the resolution.

(A)
(B)
(C)
(D)
(E)

Question 19

Is $x + y$ positive?

(1) $x - y$ is positive.
(2) $y - x$ is negative.

(A)
(B)
(C)
(D)
(E)

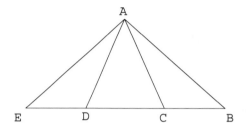

Question 20

In the figure above, segments *AD* and *AC* divide $\angle EAB$ into three nonoverlapping angles that are equal in measure. Are *AE* and *AB* equal in length?

(1) $AD = AC$
(2) $AC = CB$

(A)
(B)
(C)
(D)
(E)

Choose answer choice

    (A) if statement (1) BY ITSELF is sufficient to answer the question, but statement (2) by itself is not;

    (B) if statement (2) BY ITSELF is sufficient to answer the question, but statement (1) by itself is not;

    (C) if statements (1) and (2) TAKEN TOGETHER are sufficient to answer the question, even though NEITHER statement BY ITSELF is sufficient;

    (D) if EITHER statement BY ITSELF is sufficient to answer the question;

    (E) if statements (1) and (2) TAKEN TOGETHER are NOT sufficient to answer the question, requiring more data pertaining to the problem.

Question 21

If x and y are positive, x is what percent of y ?

(1) $x = \dfrac{1}{16}$

(2) $\dfrac{x}{y} = 4$

    (A)
    (B)
    (C)
    (D)
    (E)

Question 22

A shopper bought a tie and a belt during a sale. Which item did he buy at the greater dollar discount?

(1)   He bought the tie at a 20 percent discount.

(2)   He bought the belt at a 25 percent discount.

    (A)
    (B)
    (C)
    (D)
    (E)

Question 23

Joyce has a recipe for a batch of brownies and a recipe for a coffee cake. How much flour does her recipe for a batch of brownies require?

(1)   When Joyce bakes a batch of brownies and a coffee cake following her recipes, she uses a total of $4\dfrac{1}{2}$ cups of flour.

(2)   When Joyce bakes 2 batches of brownies and 3 coffee cakes following her recipes, she uses a total of 11 cups of flour.

    (A)
    (B)
    (C)
    (D)
    (E)

Question 24

Calvin has a total of 64 compact discs and cassettes. How many compact discs does he have?

(1)   If he buys 10 more cassettes, he will have 58 cassettes.

(2)   He has three times as many cassettes as compact discs.

    (A)
    (B)
    (C)
    (D)
    (E)

Answer Key

1. B	8. E	15. D	22. E
2. B	9. B	16. D	23. C
3. C	10. A	17. E	24. D
4. E	11. B	18. B	
5. A	12. D	19. E	
6. A	13. D	20. A	
7. B	14. C	21. B	

Explanations

Question 1

We need to determine a ratio.

(1) *Insufficient.* Merely knowing that there is a four dollar difference won't suffice. The list price could be $40, making the ratio 36:40, which is 9:10. Or the list price could be $10, making the ratio 6:10.

(2) *Sufficient.* Knowing the percentage difference, as opposed to the actual dollar difference, allows us to determine the ratio. The ratio between a quantity and another quantity 20 percent less than the first is 10:8, or 5:4.

Question 2

We want to know whether x equals y. If and only if a statement allows us to answer "yes" or to answer "no," definitively, is it sufficient.

(1) *Insufficient.* There's a common trap here, one you need to learn for test day. It may look like the two variables are equal, but not necessarily. All the statement tells us is that x^2 is equal to y^2. That doesn't mean that x equals y, because one could be negative and the other positive. Suppose x equals 2; y could also equal 2, or it can equal -2.

(2) *Sufficient.* This tells us that $(x - y)(x - y) = 0$. So, $(x - y) = 0$. The only way the difference between the two variables can be 0 is if they are the same.

Question 3

Perimeter, remember, is the sum of the lengths of the sides. We'll need to consider different rectangles to test whether the statements are sufficient.

(1) *Insufficient.* The two rectangles could be exactly the same. Let's say they are both 5 by 10. In this case the question is answered "no." On the other hand, B could be 5 by 10 while A is 10 by 10. In this case, the answer is "yes."

(2) *Insufficient.* This one is tricky. The key though, is to envision a very long, thin rectangle for B. If it is 50 by 1, its perimeter is greater than a rectangle A that is 10 by 10, even though B's area is only half that of A. The answer then would be "no." It's easy to see how the answer could be "yes," as it's not hard to envision A as having a greater perimeter in addition to its greater area.

Since neither is sufficient, we have to combine them. If we combine the two, however, we can answer the question. If A has one side twice the length of one of B's, and A's area is twice that of B, then the other side of A is equal to the other side of B and A must have a greater perimeter.

Question 4

The question is clear: How many students scored less than the average?

(1) *Insufficient.* Merely knowing the average tells us nothing about how anyone scored. There could be a lot of students under the average, or only a few.

(2) *Insufficient.* There could be any number of number of students under the average.

Combining the statements still leaves the question unanswered. Fourteen students above 83 could be balanced by a lot of students under 83 or very few who happen to have scored way under 83. We don't even know what those 14 scores were.

Question 5

A key here will be determining whether *a* is positive or negative. If we know that, we'll be able to divide both sides of the inequality and settle the issue. (Remember, if you divide an inequality by a negative number, you must reverse the inequality. Since we don't know whether *a* is positive or negative, we cannot do the division yet.)

(1) *Sufficient.* If *a* is negative, we can cancel it from both sides of the inequality as long as we reverse the inequality. We're left with $b > c$, and the question is answered.

(2) *Insufficient.* The fact that *c* is negative tells us nothing. Let's say *a* is 1. Then it's just a straight comparison between *b* and *c*, and *c* is greater. On the other hand, suppose *a* is −1. In this case, we get $-b < -c$. Divide by −1 and we find that *b* is greater.

Question 6

We know that all three variables are even numbers greater than 2, and that *q* is greater than *p* but less than *r*. Notice also that we cannot assume *p*, *q*, and *r*, are consecutive even numbers.

(1) *Sufficient.* If *r* is less than 10, it can be only 8. So *p* and *q*, respectively, must be 4 and 6.

(2) *Insufficient.* If *p* is less than 6, it can be only 4. However, *q* can be any even number greater than 4, and *r* can be any even number greater than 6.

Question 7

To find the pages per hour that Michael reads, we need a rate. Most helpful would be words per hour, but in fact, any rate will do—words per day, year, etcetera.

(1) *Insufficient.* This tells us merely how the words are arranged on the page. It provides no information about Michael's reading speed.

(2) *Sufficient.* This is a rate, exactly what we wanted. Since we know that he reads 300 words per minute, and the question told us there are 250 words per page, we can compute how many pages he reads per hour. On Test Day you wouldn't bother doing this computation. For the record, it's

$$\frac{300 \text{ (words/min.)} \times 60 \text{(min./hour)}}{250 \text{ (words/page)}} = 72 \text{ (pages/hour)}.$$

Question 8

Not much to pull out of the question; on to the statements.

(1) *Insufficient.* Spend no time thinking about this. Since *n* is never mentioned, the statement cannot be sufficient.

(2) *Insufficient.* Same principle here. We get a range of values for *n*, but are told nothing about *m*.

In combining the two statements, we want to see whether we can make each variable greater than the other. If we can, the answer is (E); if we can't, it's (C).

Certainly *m* can be greater. It could be just less than $\frac{5}{7}$ and thus greater than the entire range of values for *n*. The question then becomes: Can *n* be larger than *m*? Yes, *n* could be just a hair less than $\frac{4}{7}$, while *m* is just a hair more than $\frac{3}{7}$. ($\frac{10}{21}$ for *m* and $\frac{11}{21}$ for *n* illustrate this.) The answer is (E).

Question 9

We need to know, or be able to derive, the values of both a^4 and b^4, or the difference between them.

(1) *Insufficient*. This allows us to derive a value for a^4, but tells us nothing about b^4. Therefore, we can't determine the difference between the two.

(2) *Sufficient*. If the variables are equal, then their values when raised to the fourth power are equal, and so $a^4 - b^4 = 0$.

Question 10

There isn't anything special to pull out of this question. We just want to know whether R is a multiple of—evenly divisible by—3.

(1) *Sufficient*. Since the quantity $2R$ is divisible by 3, one of those two factors (2 or R) must be divisible by 3. (If you don't see this, plug in some numbers and try it out.) Since 2 isn't evenly divisible by 3, R must be.

(2) *Insufficient*. Similar reasoning is at work here. We know that the quantity $3R$ is evenly divisible by 3, which means that at least one of the factors (3 or R) must be divisible by 3. The problem, though, is that 3 is evenly divisible by 3, making it impossible for us to tell whether R is also evenly divisible by 3.

Question 11

The fraction described is just the number of times the coin came up heads over the number of flips, N. Of course, this fraction can be expressed in many different ways.

(1) *Insufficient*. This tells us how many coin tosses there were, but leaves us clueless as to how many came up heads. (Note that you cannot infer that 12 of the tosses were heads just because the coin is described as "fair." Although a fair coin tends to come up heads half the time, in any given series of flips the number of times it comes up heads can vary significantly.)

(2) *Sufficient*. By telling us what fraction came up tails, this statement tells us what fraction came up heads. Since only heads or tails is possible, and since $\frac{3}{8}$ were tails, the remaining $\frac{5}{8}$ were heads.

Question 12

PQRS is described only as a quadrilateral, which means that none of its sides needs to be the same length as any other. We want to know whether or not it's also a square, meaning that all four sides are the same length. (Because the quadrilateral is inscribed in a circle, we don't need to worry about whether the angles are all 90°; if the four sides are all the same length, the angles must each be 90°.) Notice how Data Sufficiency diagrams can be misleading. *PQRS* could look quite different from what's depicted. It could look like this:

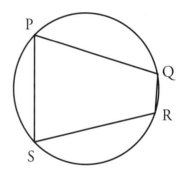

(1) *Sufficient*. Interestingly, the answer to the question turns out to be "no." That's unusual, but it does happen. In order for *PQRS* to be a square, all four sides must have the same length. This is impossible if *PS* is equal to the circle's radius. Draw in the triangle formed by *PSR*. If it's half of a square, it has to be an isosceles right triangle. Is it? The hypotenuse *PR* is equal to the diameter. If *PS* and *SR* are each equal to the radius—half of the diameter—the triangle collapses. The sum of any two sides of a triangle must be greater than the third; here they would equal only the third.

(2) *Sufficient*. In order for *PQRS* to be a square, the degree measure of all four minor arcs (*PQ*, *QR*, *RS*, and *SP*) must be one quarter of the circle. Since every circle is 360°, the degree measure of the arcs would have to be 90°. Since minor arc *QR* is 45°, *PQRS* isn't a square.

Question 13

We want Bill's average rate. The rate formula is: *Distance = Rate × Time.* We know the time (3 hours), so merely finding out the distance he traveled would be sufficient.

(1) *Sufficient.* Exactly as hoped for. With the distance known, we could plug it into the rate formula and compute Bill's rate. We won't, however, because all we need to know is that we could solve for the rate; doing so would waste valuable time.

(2) *Sufficient.* If he covered the same distance at 30 mph as he did at 60 mph, he must have been traveling at 30 mph for twice as long as he was at 60 mph. Given that he traveled for 3 hours, he traveled at 30 mph for 2 hours and 60 mph for 1 hour. That comes to 120 miles total distance, and again we can solve for the rate.

Question 14

We need values for these variables, or at least values for the sum and difference used in the fraction.

(1) *Insufficient.* This supplies the numerator, but as we have no idea what the value of the denominator is, we cannot evaluate the fraction.

(2) *Insufficient.* We cannot determine the value of either part of the fraction.

Since we know the value of the numerator from statement (1), combining the two is just a matter of trying to determine the value of the denominator, $x - y$. As it turns out, we can do this. Statement (2) can be rewritten as $z = 2 - y$. Substituting that value for z into statement (1) yields: $x + 2 - y = 3$. Subtracting 2 from both sides yields $x - y = 1$. We now have a value for the denominator as well as the numerator, so we can evaluate the fraction.

Question 15

This question is worth working out ahead of time. For x to be less than 10 and for $x + 2$ to be prime, x must be 1, 3, 5, or 9. Those are the only numbers that fit the description. Answering the question,

then, will really be a matter of seeing whether the statements narrow x down to only one of these.

(1) *Sufficient.* Just plug in the values above: $1 + 3 = 4$; $3 + 3 = 6$; $5 + 3 = 8$; $9 + 3 = 12$. Only 4 is the square of an integer, so we know the value of x.

(2) *Sufficient.* Just plug in the values again: $1 + 7 = 8$; $3 + 7 = 10$; $5 + 7 = 12$; $9 + 7 = 16$. Only 8 is the cube of an integer, so again we know the value of x.

Question 16

We want to know what percent of the crew is made up of carpenters and painters. Because we're given the ratio of carpenters to painters, if we're told how many there are of either, we can compute the total of both. We'd still need to know, though, how many people are in the crew. Another way to solve this would be to get a ratio for the total crew to either the carpenters or the painters. This additional ratio would allow us to compute the percent of the crew that is comprised of carpenters and painters.

(1) *Sufficient.* This is essentially a ratio between carpenters and the whole crew. For every 100 members of the crew, there are 18 carpenters. From the question itself, we can solve for the number of painters (12) and determine the percentage of the whole crew that carpenters and painters comprise (18 + 12 = 30% of 100).

(2) *Sufficient.* Same idea, just the other way around. If 12 percent are painters, then 18 percent are carpenters (this comes from the 3:2 ratio) and so 30 percent are either carpenters or painters.

Question 17

It's simple division, once you've figured out what needs to be divided. The number of fish will be determined by dividing 36 (each fish's allotment) into the number of square centimeters of "water-surface area." All we need, essentially, is that—the amount of surface area the water in the tank has. As the tank is a rectangle, we'll need to know the length, width, and depth of the water.

(Note: The volume of the water won't be sufficient. The same volume can have different surface areas.)

(1) *Insufficient.* Here's a tricky one. These dimensions provide the surface area of the tank, but not of the water. Since we don't know how full the tank is, we can't solve for surface area.

(2) *Insufficient.* This gives us the depth of the water, but without its length or width, we can't determine its surface area.

You might have thought that combining the two would do the trick, since we know the tank's dimensions and how deep the water is. The problem, though, is that we don't know which dimension is which. That is, we don't know whether the 40 cm deep water is 60 cm by 30 cm, or 42 by 30. (It can't be 60 by 42, because that would leave 30 for the depth, yet we know the depth of the water is 40.) Until we learn the length and width of the tank, we don't have sufficient information.

Question 18

The rules say that a resolution must be passed by at least two-thirds of half of the 20 directors. Half of 20 is 10, and two-thirds of that is $6\frac{2}{3}$. Since we can't have fractional directors, we're left with 7—the absolute minimum number of directors required to pass a resolution. Of course, if more directors are voting, more votes are needed to pass the resolution. Twenty directors voting, for example, would require 14 votes in favor.

(1) *Insufficient.* Ten votes might or might not pass a resolution, depending on how many directors vote. If only 10 vote, it passes; if 20 vote, it doesn't.

(2) *Sufficient.* Seven votes against means that even if all 20 directors vote a 2/3 majority is impossible. The resolution doesn't pass.

Question 19

The best strategy is to "pick numbers."

(1) *Insufficient.* Pick 10 for x and 5 for y. This satisfies the statement and would allow us to answer "yes" to the question. We can't stop here, though; we have to try different values to see if we can answer the question "no." Try 5 for x and –10 for y. These values satisfy statement (1) but allow us to answer the question "no."

(2) *Insufficient.* Try the same values: 5 for x and –10 for y. Those values allow us to answer "no" to the question. But we need to consider other values. If we set y equal to –5 and x equal to 10, we can answer "yes" to the question.

You could guess between (C) and (E) or you could plug in some more numbers. As it turns out the two statements are equivalent. So they are just as insufficient together as they are separate.

Question 20

All three triangles have an equal angle. Since we want to know if two of them have an equal side, we should think in terms of identical triangles.

(1) *Sufficient.* This tells us that the middle triangle (*ACD*) is isosceles. The angles facing the two equal sides are, therefore, equal (these are angles *ADC* and *ACD*). Since these angles are equal, their supplementary angles (*ADE* and *ACB*) are also equal. Since those two supplementary angles are equal, the third and final angles (*AED* and *ABC*) in the two outside triangles must also be equal. Looking at the whole figure then, we see that triangle *ABE* is isosceles. Therefore, *AE* is equal to *AB*.

(2) *Insufficient.* This allows us to conclude that angles *CAB* and *CBA* are equal, but that's of no help. We learn nothing about the other triangle in question (*ADE*), so we cannot answer the question.

Question 21

From the stem: x and y are positive, so we're considering values like .5, 1, π, etcetera. We want to know what percent of y, x is. That's most easily thought of as a fraction: $\frac{x}{y}$. If you thought of it that way, you probably jumped to statement 2 first.

(2) *Sufficient.* If we're given a value for $\frac{x}{y}$, then we can determine the percent we're asked about. This is, in fact, how you would do so—you'd divide x by y. In fact, and know this for GMAT day, we could also have solved for the percent if we'd been given the value for the reciprocal, for $\frac{x}{y}$. Eliminate (A), (C), and (E).

(1) *Insufficient.* The value of x has been given, but the value of y has not, and thus the desired percentage could be anything. Choose (B).

Question 22

From the stem: We can see that we want to compare the number of dollars discounted from the price of the tie with the number of dollars discounted from the sale of the belt. Notice that we need dollars; mere percentages won't suffice. Also notice that since we aren't given information on either item, a statement can be sufficient only if it talks about both items or compares the two items.

(1) *Insufficient.* only information about the tie is given. We know nothing about the belt. Eliminate (A) and (D).

(2) *Insufficient.* only information about the belt is given. We know nothing about the tie. Eliminate (B).

In combination: All we can determine is that a greater percentage discount was obtained on the belt. Whether this translates into a greater *dollar* discount cannot be determined. Twenty percent of the tie's original price may amount to more or fewer dollars than 25 percent of the belt's original price. Choose (E).

Question 23

Your Data Sufficiency sense probably alerted you to the fact that this looks very much like a setup for an algebra problem. We should be ready to work with equations, employing b for brownies and c for coffee cakes.

(1) *Insufficient.* One batch of brownies (b) and (+) one coffee cake (c) together require 4.5 cups of flour. We get one equation, $b + c = 4.5$, with two variables. We can't solve for either variable. Eliminate (A) and (D).

(2) *Insufficient.* Same story. Two batches of brownies and three coffee cakes together require 11 cups of flour. Therefore, $2b + 3c = 11$. We can't solve the problem for either variable. Eliminate (B).

In combination: Since the equations are different, and since there are only two variables, we can solve for the values of the variables. Remember, you can solve for a variable if you have as many different equations as you have variables in the equations. Choose (C).

Question 24

From the stem: Since Calvin has 64 total discs and cassettes, the number of his discs (d) plus the number of his cassettes (c) equals 64: $d + c = 64$. Thus, to find the number of discs, we need only *one* more equation with d or c or both in it. (It must be a different equation, of course.)

(1) *Sufficient.* Here's a different equation: $c + 10 = 58$. We could solve for c and plug that value into our original equation to solve for d. There's no need, though, to even think it that far through. Merely seeing that we have two different equations with two variables is enough. Eliminate (B), (C), and (E).

(2) *Sufficient.* Same story: $c = 3d$. This is another, different equation and so we can solve for d. Choose (D).

CHAPTER NINE

Word Problems

HIGHLIGHTS

- Learn the Three Basic Principles of Word Problems
- Study the Kaplan Method for Word Problems in Problem Solving questions
- Review Kaplan's strategies for Word Problems in Data Sufficiency questions

Word problems appear throughout the Quantitative section. Because word problems can be particularly tricky, we're going to discuss them separately in this section. We'll begin by looking at word problems in Problem Solving format.

The primary skill used in word problems is to take a tedious, little story and conceptualize it mathematically. If you have trouble with word problems, it's probably because you're having trouble with this technique. Don't get frustrated. Just keep practicing until you can see a word problem and visualize the math as you are reading. That is, if you get a problem that tells you, "George has ten dollars less than twice as much as Bill," you should be thinking, "Oh, I'll use *G* for how much George has, and *B* for how much Bill has. *Twice as much as Bill* means *2B,* and *ten dollars less* means -10, so $G = 2B - 10$." *Once you have mastered this skill, you will have mastered the most difficult part of GMAT word problems.*

Word problems are ultimately an exercise in translation. The actual math in GMAT word problems tends to be fairly easy—it's the translation that's often the hard part. All of us, at some time or other, come across a word problem that makes us scratch our head and ask, "What are these people talking about?!" The word problems translation table on the next page should help.

Teacher Tip

Everybody wants to know the easiest way to a higher score. I say: Practice. Practice. Practice problems.
—Suzanne Riskin
  Miami, FL

Word Problems Translation Table

English	Math
Equals, is, was, will be, has, costs, adds up to, the same as, as much as	$=$
Times, of, multiplies by, product of, twice, double, by	$\times$
Divided by, per, out of, each, ratio	$\div$
Plus, added to, and, sum, combined	$+$
Minus, subtracted from, smaller than, less than, fewer, decreased by, difference between	$-$
A number, how much, how many, what	x, n, etcetera

The Three Basic Principles of Word Problems

1. Before plunging into word problems, read through the entire question and the answer choices to gain a general understanding of the situation.

Some people follow this principle instinctively. If you are such a person, great! If you aren't, you need to practice until it becomes a reflex. This step shouldn't take more than 10 to 15 seconds.

2. Always keep track of exactly what you're after.

Locate the specific question itself: Exactly what is it asking? To solve word problems efficiently, it helps to make sure you know exactly what the question is asking.

3. Learn to recognize the types of problems that you find easy and those that you find difficult.

You should ask yourself whether the question is one that you normally do well on. If this is the type of question you typically ace and if you think you will be able to solve it quickly, go ahead and tackle it. If you think the question looks complicated or you have less confidence solving this particular type of question and if it isn't one of the first few questions, eliminate answer choices and guess.

Kaplan's Four-Step Method for Word Problems in Problem Solving Format

1. Look for the best approach to the question—and apply it.

In most cases the best approach to use in solving word problems is to translate the prose into a mathematical equation. But sometimes you can solve the problem by using an alternative method, such as picking numbers and backsolving.

2. Reread the question, figuring out what you're given and what you need to know.

Before trying to solve the problem, be sure that you know exactly what information the problem gives you and what you need to figure out yourself.

3. Translate the problem from English to an equation.

Your ability to translate word problems from prose to math is the single most important skill that you need to develop to master this problem type. For geometry word problems, you'll need to translate from English to a diagram.

4. If you're stuck translating, or if you just don't understand the problem, consider using an alternative method.

Sometimes translating is too complicated, or the problem doesn't click for you. You can use such alternative methods as picking numbers or backsolving.

Go through this fairly typical word problem about age, referring to the Word Problem Translation Table if you need to. Then compare how you translated the word problem with how Kaplan translated it.

> Jacob is now 12 years younger than Michael. If in 9 years Michael will be twice as old as Jacob, how old will Jacob be in 4 years?
>
> (A) 3
> (B) 7
> (C) 15
> (D) 21
> (E) 25

The Kaplan Four-Step Method for Word Problems

1. Look for the best approach to the question and apply it.
2. Reread the question to figure out what you're given and what you need to know.
3. Translate the problem from English to an equation.
4. If you're stuck, consider using an alternative method.

Here's Kaplan's solution:

Jacob's age   is now   Michael's age   (but) 12 years younger
J $=$ M $- 12$

In this case, we switched the order of the sentence as we translated it from English to math. "12 years younger than Michael" became "Michael's age (but) 12 years younger."

Sometimes the order of the terms in English will differ slightly from the order in math. If you get confused, pick some sample values: If Michael is 15 years old, then Jacob is 12 years younger, or 3. Therefore, $J = M - 12$.

To continue, here's the rest of the solution.

Michael   in 9 years   will be   twice as old as Jacob
M $+ 9$ $=$ $2(J + 9)$

So we know that: $J = M - 12$ and $M + 9 = 2(J + 9)$. The question asks for $J + 4$. Solve for J by substituting.

$$J = M - 12$$
$$J + 12 = M$$

$$M + 9 = 2(J + 9)$$
$$(J + 12) + 9 = 2J + 18$$
$$J + 21 = 2J + 18$$
$$J + 3 = 2J$$
$$3 = J$$
$$7 = J + 4$$

Remember that we're looking for $J + 4$, not J, so (B) is correct.

Another way to solve this problem is with simultaneous equations. When you have two equations, you can add or subtract them from one another just as though they were regular numbers. You just have to set it up right, with like variables directly above one another.

$$M + 9 = 2J + 18$$
$$- \underline{(M - 12 = J)}$$
$$21 = J + 18$$
$$3 = J$$
$$7 = J + 4$$

So that's how to translate word problems into math. We said before that we'd look at how Kaplan's math strategies can be applied to word problems. The two most useful are picking numbers and backsolving. Let's look at them now and later turn to detailed attacks on two of the most annoying types of GMAT word problems.

Picking Numbers

There are two times to pick numbers. First, when the problem is made easier by trying out possibilities rather than by hassling with the algebra involved. Second, when you simply don't understand the algebra and cannot solve the problem. What you do in either case is pick a few simple numbers—keeping them small, if possible, so the arithmetic will be simple—and do to them what has been described in the word problem.

Here are a few guidelines for when to plug in numbers and what numbers you should try:

- In problems involving **percents**, a good number to start with is often 100, because it is so easy to find a percent of 100.

- In problems with two or more **fractions**, try using the least common denominator of the fractions involved.

- Picking numbers is almost always the fastest way to do problems about **remainders.**

- In algebra, in which the problem and its answer choices are all expressed in terms of such **variables** as *x* or *y*, you can avoid algebra by simply making up values for *x* and *y*. When you plug in numbers for the variables and do the arithmetic involved, you will get another number as a result. Take the numbers you used for *x* and *y* and plug them into the variables in the answer choices—assuming only one choice results in the same number as in the problem, that choice is the answer. (Avoid using 0 or 1, because they have special properties. Often, when you use 0 or 1, more than one answer choice will work, and then you have to try plugging in another number to decide between the remaining choices.)

Kaplan Rules

Tips for Picking Numbers

- For percents problems, use 100.
- For fractions problems, use the least common denominator.

Let's take a look at picking numbers in action.

The value of a certain antique car increased by 30 percent from 1986 to 1990 and then decreased by 20 percent from 1990 to 1994. The car's value in 1994 was what percent of its value in 1986?

- (A) 90%
- (B) 100%
- (C) 104%
- (D) 110%
- (E) 124%

Let's say the car was originally worth $100: $100 in 1986. It increases by 30% of $100, or $30, which means it was worth $130 in 1990. Then it decreases 20%: $\frac{1}{5} \times 130 = 26$. So it decreased by $26. Therefore it was worth $104 in 1994. The car was worth $104, which is 104% of $100. The answer, therefore, is (C).

Try each of the next two word problems on your own, using the strategy of picking numbers. Feel free to refer back to the bullet point guidelines for picking numbers on the previous page. After you've worked through each question, consult the Kaplan solution.

At an international dinner $\frac{1}{5}$ of the people attending were from South America. If the number of North Americans at the dinner was $\frac{2}{3}$ greater than the number of South Americans, what fraction of people at the dinner were from neither South America nor North America?

(A) $\frac{1}{5}$

(B) $\frac{2}{5}$

(C) $\frac{7}{15}$

(D) $\frac{8}{15}$

(E) $\frac{2}{3}$

You should notice immediately that the problem contains two fractions: $\frac{1}{5}$ and $\frac{2}{3}$. The least common denominator is 15, so let's say the total number of people at the dinner was 15. That means we have 3 South Americans in the room. We also have North Americans numbering two-thirds more than that, or 5. So there were 8 people from South America or North America, which means 7 people were not from either place. So $\frac{7}{15}$ of the people in the room were from neither South America nor North America. The correct answer, therefore, is (C).

Here's another picking numbers example.

> If the price of item X increased by 20%, and then by a further 20%, what percent of the original price is the increase in price?
>
> (A)   24%
>
> (B)   40%
>
> (C)   44%
>
> (D) $66\frac{2}{3}$%
>
> (E)   140%

Let's say the price was originally $100. It increases by 20% of $100 ($20), so the price is $120. The price then increases by 20% of $120 ($\frac{1}{5} \times \$120 = \$24$) which means an increase of $24. So the price is now $144, or 44% more than its original price of $100. The correct answer, therefore, is (C).

Backsolving
You will remember that in backsolving, you plug in the answer choices and see which one works. This approach might seem time-consuming, but you already know that you can make it more efficient (the choices are almost always in ascending or descending order) by trying choice (C) first. If it's too small, you know right away that the answer must be (D) or (E) (assuming the choices are in ascending order), and trying just one of those will tell you the answer. For instance, if (D) is also too small, the answer must be (E). Conversely, if (C) is too big, you know the answer must be either (A) or (B), and you can try one of those. If the one you pick doesn't work, the answer must be the other (assuming you haven't made an arithmetic error—if you're worried about it and have the time, go ahead and check the third choice).

It takes a while to get used to backsolving, but with practice it can be nearly as fast as solving the problem the traditional way. Follow along as we backsolve through this word problem:

An insurance company provides coverage for a certain dental procedure according to the following rules: the policy pays 80% of the first $1,200 of cost, and 50% of the cost above $1,200. If a patient had to pay $490 of the cost for this procedure himself, how much did the procedure cost?

- (A) $1,200
- (B) $1,300
- (C) $1,500
- (D) $1,600
- (E) $1,700

Definition

The distance formula: Distance (*D*) equals Rate (*R*) times Time (*T*):

$$D = RT$$

Because the policy pays 80% of the first $1,200 of cost, the patient must pay 20% of $1,200. One-fifth of $1,200 is $240.

Let's try (C), because it's the middle value. If the procedure cost $1,500, then the patient pays: $240 + 50% of $300; $240 + $150 = $390, which is too small, by $100. So the 50% of $300 didn't add enough to the original $240 payment.

We need a larger number, so we're down to (D) or (E). Let's try (E). If the procedure cost $1,700, then the patient pays: $240 plus 50% of $500, which is $250, totaling $490, which is correct. The answer is (E).

Rate Problems

Some word problems deal with rates. Don't let them psych you out because they aren't really that difficult. They typically spell out some kind of rate early in the problem, like the following example. Follow along as we show you two ways to solve this typical rate problem.

If José does GMAT word problems at a constant rate of 2 problems every 5 minutes, how many seconds will it take him to do *N* problems?

- (A) $\dfrac{2}{5}N$

- (B) $2N$

- (C) $\dfrac{5}{2}N$

- (D) $24N$

- (E) $150N$

There are two common ways of doing rate problems—algebraically and by plugging in numbers. Let's try both for the problem above.

Algebraic Solution
Let's call the number of seconds that we've been asked to find T.

$$\frac{2}{5(60)} = \frac{N}{T}$$

Now we cross multiply and solve for T.

$$2T = 300N$$
$$T = 150N$$

The answer is (E).

Picking Numbers Solution
Let's say that $N = 2$. That means José does exactly 2 problems every 5 minutes, or 300 seconds (5 × 60 seconds = 300 seconds). Now look for the answer choices that yield 300 when $N = 2$. The only one that does is (E), so that must be the answer.

By the way, here's a tip while we're on the topic of rates: It'll help if you know the Distance formula, $D = R \times T$, as it usually shows up once or twice on the test. It just means that the distance you traveled equals the rate you were going at multiplied by the time it took you to get there. For instance, if you travel for 2 hours at 30 miles per hour, then you travel 2 × 30, or 60 miles.

Work Problems
Word problems involving work occasionally show up on the GMAT. They will be easy if you use this formula:

> The inverse of the time it takes everyone working together = the sum of the inverses of the times it would take each working individually.

Now let's look at a problem and use the formula.

> Working together, John, David, and Roger require $2\frac{1}{4}$ hours to complete a certain task, if each of them works at his respective constant rate. If John alone can complete the task in $4\frac{1}{2}$ hours, and David alone can complete the

Definition

Work Equation: The inverse of the time it takes everyone working together = the sum of the inverses of the times it would take each working individually.

task in 9 hours, how many hours would it take Roger to complete the task, working alone?

- (A) $2\frac{1}{3}$
- (B) $4\frac{1}{2}$
- (C) $6\frac{3}{4}$
- (D) 9
- (E) 12

Here's the solution, employing the work equation.

$$\frac{1}{T} = \frac{1}{J} + \frac{1}{D} + \frac{1}{R}$$

$$\frac{1}{2.25} = \frac{1}{4.5} + \frac{1}{9} + \frac{1}{R}$$

$$\frac{4}{9} = \frac{2}{9} + \frac{1}{9} + \frac{1}{R}$$

$$\frac{1}{9} = \frac{1}{R}$$

$$R = 9$$

An alternative approach to this kind of problem that some find intuitive and quick is to break down the work on an hour-by-hour basis.

Take David first. By himself, he could do the entire task in 9 hours. Therefore, during every *single* hour that the guys work together, David will be doing $\frac{1}{9}$ of the task (it's just the reciprocal of 9 hours). In the second hour he'll do another $\frac{1}{9}$. And in that extra $\frac{1}{4}$ hour, he'll do $\frac{1}{4} \times \frac{1}{9}$ or $\frac{1}{36}$ of the task. Add them up: David will be doing $\frac{1}{9} + \frac{1}{9} + \frac{1}{36} = \frac{1}{4}$ of the entire task during the period in question.

Review

The GMAT Math Reference section in the next chapter contains math facts and formulas you might need to review.

How about John? He's much faster than David—working alone, he could do the entire task in $4\frac{1}{2}$ (or $\frac{9}{2}$) hours. So during each hour he works, he'll do the reciprocal of $\frac{9}{2}$, or $\frac{2}{9}$ of the task. Multiply that $\frac{2}{9}$ of a task per hour by the $2\frac{1}{4}$ hours the guys work, and you see that John himself will account for $\frac{2}{9} \times \frac{9}{4}$, or $\frac{1}{2}$ the task.

With David and John accounting for $\frac{1}{4}$ and $\frac{1}{2}$ of the task respectively, that leaves exactly $\frac{1}{4}$ of the task to be performed by Roger. You can either see that this means that Roger and David are identical workers—so it'll take Roger 9 hours, too—or just divide $2\frac{1}{4}$ hours by $\frac{1}{4}$ task to get 9 hours per task, choice (D).

Note that even where backsolving helps, it does not absolve you of thoroughly understanding the question. You must understand what's being asked before you can apply backsolving.

Data Sufficiency Word Problems

Data Sufficiency word problems often require very little calculation, and if you attack them without thinking first, you will nearly always waste time and end up crunching numbers. If a Data Sufficiency word problem is based on some kind of formula, such as the distance formula ($D = RT$) or the area of a circle, you should ask yourself what kind of information would give you the area of a circle. Then, if statement (1) tells you the circle's circumference, don't calculate! It is sufficient to know that you could have calculated. Your motto should be, "Think—don't crunch!"

The Kaplan Three-Step Method for Data Sufficiency Word Problems

1. Quickly skim the question stem.
Determine what you're looking for and what kind of information would be sufficient to find it. Often that information will be the missing variable in a common formula, such as the distance formula or the average formula.

2. If stuck, try translating the question stem and the statements into math.
If a statement clearly isn't sufficient, though, don't waste time trying to translate it. Instead move on.

3. If and when each statement is insufficient by itself and you need to consider them together, think of the problem as one long word problem and translate it as one unit.
You should keep in mind what kind of information is needed to answer the question. Do only as much work as you need in order to determine sufficiency and remember to ignore the other statement!

Practice Data Sufficiency Word Problems

Let's put these strategies into practice. Now let's try the two problems below. Try to conceptualize what you need, without actually solving for it. Keep the relevant formulas in mind and ask yourself, "What do I need?" and "What kind of statement would give it to me?"

> If there are 32 guests at a party, what is the average (arithmetic mean) age of the guests?
>
> (1) The sum of the ages of the guests is 1,536 years.
> (2) The youngest guest, Tracy, is 24 years old and the oldest guest, Pat, is 68 years old.
>
> (A) Statement (1) by itself is sufficient to answer the question, but statement (2) by itself is not.
> (B) Statement (2) by itself is sufficient to answer the question, but statement (1) by itself is not.
> (C) Statements (1) and (2) taken together are sufficient to answer the question, even though neither statement by itself is sufficient.
> (D) Either statement by itself is sufficient to answer the question.
> (E) Statements (1) and (2) taken together are not sufficient to answer the question, requiring more data pertaining to the problem.

Remember the average formula:

$$Average = \frac{Sum\ of\ the\ terms}{Number\ of\ the\ terms} = \frac{Sum}{32}$$

So we just need the sum to calculate the average. Does either of the statements give us the sum? Yes, Statement (1) does. Statement (2) does not give us the sum; there's no way to figure it out from (2) because the guests in between can be of all sorts of ages. So the answer is (A).

Here's a second example.

A rectangle has length y feet and width z feet. What is its area in square feet?

(1) z is the reciprocal of y.
(2) The fence around the perimeter of the rectangle is 720 feet.

(A) Statement (1) by itself is sufficient to answer the question, but statement (2) by itself is not.
(B) Statement (2) by itself is sufficient to answer the question, but statement (1) by itself is not.
(C) Statements (1) and (2) taken together are sufficient to answer the question, even though neither statement by itself is sufficient.
(D) Either statement by itself is sufficient to answer the question.
(E) Statements (1) and (2) taken together are not sufficient to answer the question, requiring more data pertaining to the problem.

First recall the formula for the area of a rectangle:

$$Area = length \times width$$

Here you might want to draw a picture of a rectangle with the length and width labeled y and z respectively.

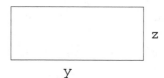

This would be a hard problem, but if you focus on what you need to know, you're less likely to be fooled. We need the area of this rectangle, which is length $\times$ width or, in this case, $y \times z$. We need a number. Would statement (1) give us a number? It's not clear on a first glance, so let's test it: $z = \dfrac{1}{y}$, so $y \times z = y \times \dfrac{1}{y} = 1$. The area must be 1, and Statement (1) is sufficient.

How about Statement (2)? It gives us the perimeter. But this doesn't give us $y \times z$. It tells us that $2(y + z) = 720$, or $y + z = 360$. But this doesn't tell us the individual values of y and z, or the product of y and z, so this statement is insufficient. (A) is correct.

Remember this mathematical principle: **Whatever number of different variables you need to solve for, you will need that same number of different equations relating at least one of those variables.**

There are usually a few tough Data Sufficiency problems that can be made easy by applying this principle and the Kaplan Method for Data Sufficiency Word Problems. If you get such a problem, ask yourself, "How many variables do I need to solve for? How many equations do I have?"

The following is a typical question involving simultaneous equations.

> Jessica has a limited investment portfolio of stocks and bonds. If she sells half her stocks, how many stocks and bonds will she be left with?
>
> (1) If she were to buy six more stocks, she would have twice as many stocks as bonds.
> (2) If she were to triple the number of her bonds, she would have three less than twice the number of her stocks.

- (A) Statement (1) by itself is sufficient to answer the question, but statement (2) by itself is not.
- (B) Statement (2) by itself is sufficient to answer the question, but statement (1) by itself is not.
- (C) Statements (1) and (2) taken together are sufficient to answer the question, even though neither statement by itself is sufficient.
- (D) Either statement by itself is sufficient to answer the question.
- (E) Statements (1) and (2) taken together are not sufficient to answer the question, requiring more data pertaining to the problem.

We get one equation in Statement (1) and another equation in Statement (2). You need both equations to answer the question, so you need both statements. The answer is (C). Thus, you solve a difficult problem in 10 seconds, and the time you save can help you get another question right.

Try to apply these techniques as best you can on the Practice Test. Use the Math Reference in the next chapter to brush up on any basic concepts that are troubling you.

CHAPTER TEN

GMAT Math Reference

HIGHLIGHTS

- Review the 100 most important math concepts you need to know for the GMAT
- Find your math level
- Brush up on math skills and formulas

The math on the GMAT covers a lot of ground—from basic algebra to symbol problems to geometry. Don't let yourself be intimidated. The GMAT Quantitative section tests your understanding of a relatively limited number of mathematical concepts. It is possible to learn all the math you need to know for the GMAT in a short time. We've highlighted the 100 most important concepts that you need to know and divided them into three levels.

Level 1 is the most basic. Most people preparing to take the GMAT are already pretty good at Level 1 math. Look over the Level 1 list just to make sure you're comfortable with the basics.

Level 2 is the place for most people to start their review of math. These skills and formulas come into play quite frequently on the GMAT. If you're like a lot of students, your Level 2 math is probably rusty.

Level 3 is the hardest math you'll find on the GMAT. These are skills and formulas that you might find difficult. Don't spend a lot of time on Level 3 if you still have gaps in Level 2. But once you've about mastered Level 2, then tackling Level 3 can put you over the top.

Level 1 (Math You Probably Already Know)

1.   How to add, subtract, multiply, and divide WHOLE NUMBERS

2.   How to add, subtract, multiply, and divide FRACTIONS

3.   How to add, subtract, multiply, and divide DECIMALS

4.   How to convert FRACTIONS TO DECIMALS and DECIMALS TO FRACTIONS

5.   How to add, subtract, multiply, and divide POSITIVE AND NEGATIVE NUMBERS

6.   How to plot points on the NUMBER LINE

7.   How to plug a number into an ALGEBRAIC EXPRESSION

8.   How to SOLVE a simple EQUATION

9.   How to add and subtract LINE SEGMENTS

10. How to find the THIRD ANGLE of a TRIANGLE, given the other two angles

Level 2 (Math You Might Need to Review)

11. How to use PEMDAS

When you're given an ugly arithmetic equation, it's important to know the order of operations. Just remember PEMDAS (as in "Please excuse my dear Aunt Sally"). What PEMDAS means is this: Clean up **Parentheses** first; then deal with **Exponents**; then do the **Multiplication** and **Division** together, going from left to right; and finally do the **Addition** and **Subtraction** together, again going from left to right.

Example:

$9 - 2 \times (5 - 3)^2 + 6 \div 3 =$

Begin with parentheses: $9 - 2 \times (2)^2 + 6 \div 3.$
Then do the exponent: $9 - 2 \times 4 + 6 \div 3$
Now do the multiplication and division from left to right: $9 - 8 + 2$
Finally, do addition and subtraction fron left to right: $9 - 8 + 2 = 1 + 2 = 3.$

12. How to use the PERCENT FORMULA

Identify the part, the percent, and the whole.

$$Part = percent \times whole$$

HINT: You'll usually find the part near the word *is* and the whole near the word *of*.

Example: (Find the part)

What is 12 percent of 25?

Setup:

Part $= \dfrac{12}{100} \times 25 = 3$

Example: (Find the percent)

45 is what percent of 9?

Setup:

$45 = \text{Percent} \times 9 = 5 \times 9$

$\text{Percent} = 5 \times 100\% = 500\%$

Example: (Find the whole)

15 is $\dfrac{3}{5}$ percent of what number?

Setup:

$\dfrac{3}{5}$ percent $= \dfrac{3}{500}$

$15 = \dfrac{3}{500} \times \text{whole}$

$\text{Whole} = 2,500$

13. How to use the PERCENT INCREASE/DECREASE FORMULAS

Identify the original whole and the amount of increase/decrease.

$$Percent\ increase = \frac{amount\ of\ increase}{original\ whole} \times 100\%$$

$$Percent\ decrease = \frac{amount\ of\ decrease}{original\ whole} \times 100\%$$

Example:

The price goes up from $80 to $100. What is the percent increase?

Setup:

Percent increase = $\frac{20}{80} \times 100\% = 25\%$

HINT: Be sure to use the original whole—not the new whole—for the base.

---

14. How to predict whether a sum, difference, or product will be ODD or EVEN

Don't bother memorizing the rules. Just take simple numbers like 1 and 2 and see what happens.

Example:

If m is even and n is odd, is the product mn odd or even?

Setup:

Say $m = 2$ and $n = 1$.

2×1 is even, so mn is even.

15. How to recognize MULTIPLES OF 2, 3, 4, 5, 6, 9, 10, and 12.

2: Last digit is even.
3: Sum of digits is a multiple of 3.
4: Last two digits are a multiple of 4.
5: Last digit is 5 or 0.
6: Sum of digits is a multiple of 3 and last digit is even.
9: Sum of digits is a multiple of 9.
10: Last digit is 0.
12: Sum of digits is a multiple of 3 and last two digits are a multiple of four.

16. How to find a COMMON FACTOR

Break down both numbers to their prime factors to see what they have in common. Then multiply the shared prime factors to find all common factors.

Example:

What factors greater than 1 do 135 and 225 have in common?

Setup:

First find the prime factors of 135 and 225. $135 = 3 \times 3 \times 3 \times 5$, and $225 = 3 \times 3 \times 5 \times 5$. The number share $3 \times 3 \times 5$ in common. Thus, aside from 3 and 5, the remaining common factors can be found by multiplying 3, 3, and 5 in every possible combination: $3 \times 3 = 9$, $3 \times 5 = 15$, and $3 \times 3 \times 5 = 45$.

17. How to find a COMMON MULTIPLE

The product is the easiest common multiple to find. If the two numbers have any factors in common, you can divide them out of the product to get a lower common multiple.

Example:

What is the least common multiple of 28 and 42?

Setup:

The product $28 \times 42 = 1,176$ is a common multiple, but not the least. $28 = 2 \times 2 \times 7$, and $42 = 2 \times 3 \times 7$. They share a 2 and a 7, so divide the product by 2 and then by 7. $1,176 \div 2 = 588$. $588 \div 7 = 84$. The least common multiple is 84.

18. How to find the AVERAGE

$$Average = \frac{sum\ of\ terms}{number\ of\ terms}$$

Example:

What is the average of 3, 4, and 8 ?

Setup:

$$Average = \frac{3 + 4 + 8}{3} = \frac{15}{3} = 5$$

19. How to use the AVERAGE to find the SUM

$$Sum = (average) \times (number\ of\ terms)$$

Example:

17.5 is the average (arithmetic mean) of 24 numbers. What is the sum?

Setup:

$Sum = 17.5 \times 24 = 420$

20. How to find the AVERAGE of CONSECUTIVE NUMBERS

The average of evenly spaced numbers is simply the average of the smallest number and the largest number. The average of all the integers from 13 to 77, for example, is the same as the average of 13 and 77:

$$\frac{13 + 77}{2} = \frac{90}{2} = 45$$

21. How to COUNT CONSECUTIVE NUMBERS

The number of integers from A to B inclusive is $B - A + 1$.

Example:

How many integers are there from 73 through 419, inclusive?

Setup:

$419 - 73 + 1 = 347$

HINT: Don't forget to add 1.

---

22. How to find the SUM OF CONSECUTIVE NUMBERS

$$Sum = (average) \times (number\ of\ terms)$$

Example:

What is the sum of the integers from 10 through 50, inclusive?

Setup:

Average = $(10 + 50) \div 2 = 30$;

number of terms = $50 - 10 + 1 = 41$

Sum = $30 \times 41 = 1,230$

23. How to find the MEDIAN

Put the numbers in numerical order and take the middle number. (If there's an even number of numbers, the average of the two numbers in the middle is the median.)

Example:

What is the median of 88, 86, 57, 94, and 73?

Setup:

Put the numbers in numerical order and take the middle number:

$$57, 73, 86, 88, 94$$

The median is 86. (If there's an even number of numbers, take the average of the two in the middle.)

24. How to find the MODE

Take the number that appears most often. For example, if your test scores were 88, 57, 68, 85, 98, 93, 93, 84, and 81, the mode of the scores is 93 because it appears more often than any other score. (If there's a tie for most often, then there's more than one mode.)

25. How to find the RANGE

Simply take the difference between the highest and the lowest values. Using the previous example, if your test scores were 88, 57, 68, 85, 98, 93, 84, and 81, the range of the scores is 41, the difference between the highest and lowest values (98 − 57 = 41).

26. How to use actual numbers to determine RATIO

To find a ratio, put the number associated with *of* on the top and the word associated with *to* on the bottom.

$$Ratio = \frac{of}{to}$$

The ratio of 20 oranges to 12 apples is $\frac{20}{12}$, or $\frac{5}{3}$.

27. How to use ratio to determine an ACTUAL NUMBER

Set up a proportion.

Example:

The ratio of boys to girls is 3 to 4. If there are 135 boys, how many girls are there?

Setup:

$$\frac{3}{4} = \frac{135}{x}$$
$$3 \times x = 4 \times 135$$
$$x = 180$$

28. How to use actual numbers to determine a RATE

Identify the quantities and the units to be compared. Keep the units straight.

Example:

Anders typed 9,450 words in $3\frac{1}{2}$ hours. What was his rate in words per minute?

Setup:

First convert $3\frac{1}{2}$ hours to 210 minutes. Then set up the rate with words on top and minutes on bottom:

$$\frac{9,450 \text{ words}}{210 \text{ minutes}} = 45 \text{ words per minute}$$

HINT: The unit before *per* goes on top, and the unit after *per* goes on the bottom.

---

29. How to deal with TABLES, GRAPHS, AND CHARTS

Read the question and all labels extra carefully. Ignore extraneous information and zero in on what the question asks for. Take advantage of the spread in the answer choices by approximating the answer whenever possible.

30. How to count the NUMBER OF POSSIBILITIES

In most cases, you won't need to apply the combination and permutation formulas on the GMAT. The number of possibilities is generally so small that the best approach is just to write them out systematically and count them.

Example:

How many three-digit numbers can be formed with the digits 1, 3, and 5?

Setup:

Write them out. Be systematic so you don't miss any: 135, 153, 315, 351, 513, 531. Count them: six possibilities.

31. How to calculate a simple PROBABILITY

$$Probability = \frac{number\ of\ favorable\ outcomes}{total\ number\ of\ possible\ outcomes}$$

Example:

What is the probability of throwing a 5 on a fair six-sided die?

Setup:

There is one favorable outcome—throwing a 5.

There are six possible outcomes—one for each side of the die.

Probability $= \frac{1}{6}$

32. How to work with new SYMBOLS

If you see a symbol you've never seen before, don't freak out: It's a made-up symbol. Everything you need to know is in the question stem. Just follow the instructions.

33. How to SIMPLIFY POLYNOMIALS

First multiply to eliminate all parentheses. Each term inside one parentheses is multiplied by each term inside the other parentheses. All like terms are then combined.

Example:

$(3x^2 + 5x)(x - 1) =$

$3x^2(x - 1) + 5x(x - 1)$

$3x^3 - 3x^2 + 5x^2 - 5x =$

$3x^3 + 2x^2 - 5x$

34. How to FACTOR certain POLYNOMIALS

Learn to spot these classic factorables:

$$ab + ac = a(b + c)$$
$$a^2 + 2ab + b^2 = (a + b)^2$$
$$a^2 - 2ab + b^2 = (a - b)^2$$
$$a^2 - b^2 = (a - b)(a + b)$$

35. How to solve for one variable IN TERMS OF ANOTHER

To find x "in terms of" y : isolate x on one side, leaving y as the only variable on the other.

36. How to solve an INEQUALITY

Treat it much like an equation—adding, subtracting, multiplying, and dividing both sides by the same thing. Just remember to reverse the inequality sign if you multiply or divide by a negative.

Example:

Rewrite $7 - 3x > 2$ in its simplest form:

Setup:

$7 - 3x > 2$ Subtract 7 from both sides.
$7 - 3x - 7 > 2 - 7$
So $-3x > -5$. Now divide both sides by -3, and remember to reverse the inequality sign:

$x < \dfrac{5}{3}$

37. How to handle ABSOLUTE VALUES

The *absolute value* of a number n, denoted by $|n|$, is defined as n if $n \geq 0$ and $-n$ if $n < 0$. It's also referred to as the distance from zero to the number on the number line:

$|-5| = 5$

If $|x| = 3$, the x could be 3 or -3.

Example:

If $|x - 3| < 2$, what is the range of possible values for x ?

Setup:

$|x - 3| < 2$ so $(x - 3) < 2$ and $-(x - 3) < 2$.
So $x - 3 < 2$ and $x - 3 > -2$
So $x < 2 + 3$ and $x > -2 + 3$.
So $x < 5$ and $x > 1$.
So $1 < x < 5$.

38. How to TRANSLATE ENGLISH INTO ALGEBRA

Look for the key words and systematically turn phrases into algebraic expressions and sentences into equations. Here's a table of key words that you may have to translate into mathematical terms.

Operation	Key Words
Addition	sum, plus, and, added to, more than, increased by, combined with, and, exceeds, total, greater than
Subtraction	difference between, minus, subtracted from, decreased by, diminished by, less than, reduced by
Multiplication	of, product, times, multiplied by, twice, double, triple, half
Division	quotient, divided by, per, out of, ratio of__ to__
Equals	equals, is, was, will be, the result is, adds up to, costs, is the same as

---

HINT: Be extra careful of the order in which you place numbers when subtraction is called for.

---

39. How to find an ANGLE formed by INTERSECTING LINES

Vertical angles are equal. Adjacent angles add up to 180°.

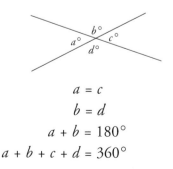

$$a = c$$
$$b = d$$
$$a + b = 180°$$
$$a + b + c + d = 360°$$

40. How to find an angle formed by a TRANSVERSAL across PARALLEL LINES

All the acute angles are equal. All the obtuse angles are equal. An acute plus an obtuse equals 180°.

Example:

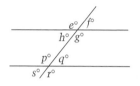

$$e = g = p = r$$
$$f = h = q = s$$
$$e + q = g + s = 180°$$

41. How to find the AREA of a TRIANGLE

$$Area = \frac{1}{2}(base)(height)$$

Example:

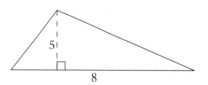

Setup:

Area = $\frac{1}{2}(5)(8) = 20$

HINT: You might have to construct an altitude, as we did in the triangle above.

---

42. How to work with ISOSCELES TRIANGLES

Isosceles triangles have two equal sides and two equal angles. If a GMAT question tells you that a triangle is isosceles, you can bet that you'll need to use that information to find the length of a side or a measure of an angle.

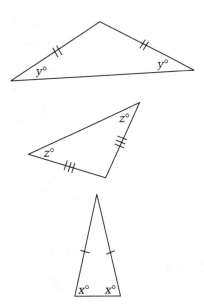

43. How to work with EQUILATERAL TRIANGLES

Equilateral triangles have three equal sides and three 60° angles. If a GMAT question tells you that a triangle is equilateral, you can bet that you'll need to use that information to find the length of a side or a measure of an angle.

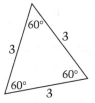

44. How to work with SIMILAR TRIANGLES

In similar triangles, corresponding angles are equal and corresponding sides are proportional. If a GMAT question tells you that triangles are similar, you'll probably need that information to find the length of a side or the measure of an angle.

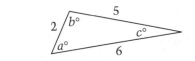

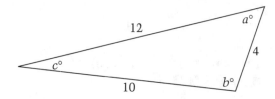

45. How to find the HYPOTENUSE or a LEG of a RIGHT TRIANGLE

Pythagorean theorem: $a^2 + b^2 = c^2$

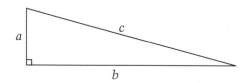

HINT: Most right triangles on the GMAT are "special" right triangles (see number 46), so you can often bypass the Pythagorean theorem.

---

46. How to spot SPECIAL RIGHT TRIANGLES

3-4-5
5-12-13
30-60-90
45-45-90

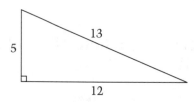

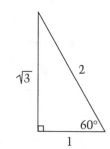

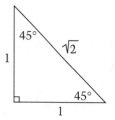

HINT: Learn to spot special right triangles—the less often you have to calculate using the Pythagorean theorem, the more time you save.

---

47. How to find the PERIMETER of a RECTANGLE

Perimeter = 2(length + width)

Example:

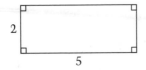

Setup:

Perimeter = 2(2 + 5) = 14

48. How to find the AREA of a RECTANGLE

Area = (length)(width)

Example:

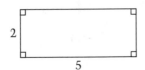

Setup:

Area = 2 × 5 = 10

49. How to find the AREA of a SQUARE

Area = (side)^2

Example:

Setup:

Area = 3^2 = 9

50. How to find the AREA of a PARALLELOGRAM

Area = (base)(height)

Example:

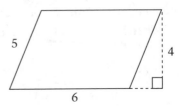

Setup:

Area = 6 × 4 = 24

51. How to find the AREA of a TRAPEZOID

A trapezoid is a quadrilateral having only two parallel sides. You can always drop a line or two to break the figure into a rectangle and a triangle or two triangles. Use the area formulas for those familiar shapes. You could also apply the general formula for the area of a trapezoid: *Area = (average of parallel sides) × (height)*.

Example:

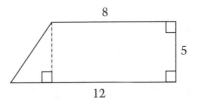

Setup:

Area of rectangle = 8 × 5 = 40

Area of triangle = $\frac{1}{2}$ (4 × 5) = 10

Area of trapezoid = 40 + 10 = 50

HINT: Any time you're asked to find the area of an unfamiliar shape, try dropping lines to break it into familiar shapes that you can work with.

KAPLAN

52. How to find the CIRCUMFERENCE of a CIRCLE

$$Circumference = 2\pi r$$

Example:

Setup:

$$Circumference = 2\pi(5) = 10\pi$$

53. How to find the AREA of a CIRCLE

$$Area = \pi r^2$$

Example:

Setup:

$$Area = \pi \times 5^2 = 25\pi$$

54. How to find the DISTANCE BETWEEN POINTS on the coordinate plane

If two points have the same x's or the same y's—that is, they make a line segment that is parallel to an axis—all you have to do is subtract the numbers that are different.

Example:

What is the distance from (2, 3) to (–7, 3)?

Setup:

The y's are the same, so just subtract the x's.

$$2 - (-7) = 9$$

If the points have different x's and different y's, make a right triangle and use the Pythagorean theorem.

Example:

What is the distance from (2, 3) to (–1, –1)?

Setup:

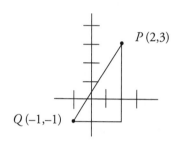

It's a 3-4-5 triangle!

$$PQ = 5$$

HINT: Look for "special" right triangles.

---

55. How to find the SLOPE of a LINE

$$Slope = \frac{rise}{run} = \frac{change\ in\ y}{change\ in\ x}$$

Example:

What is the slope of the line that contains the points (1, 2) and (4, –5)?

Setup:

$$Slope = \frac{2 - (-5)}{1 - 4} = -\frac{7}{3}$$

Level 3 (Math You Might Find Difficult)

56. How to determine COMBINED PERCENT INCREASE/DECREASE

Start with 100 and see what happens.

Example:

A price rises by 10 percent one year and by 20 percent the next. What's the combined percent increase?

Setup:

Say the original price is $100.

Year 1: $100 + (10% of 100) = 100 + 10 = 110.

Year 2: 110 + (20% of 110) = 110 + 22 = 132.

From 100 to 132—that's a 32 percent increase.

57. How to find the ORIGINAL WHOLE before percent increase/decrease

Think of a 15% increase over x as $1.15x$, and set up an equation.

Example:

After decreasing by 5 percent, the population is now 57,000. What was the original population?

Setup:

.95 × (Original Population) = 57,000

Original Population = 57,000 ÷ .95 = 60,000

58. How to solve a SIMPLE INTEREST problem

With simple interest, the interest is computed on the principal only and is given by:

interest = (principal) × (interest rate*) × (time**)

* expressed as a decimal
** expressed in years

Example:

If $12,000 is invested at 6 percent simple annual interest, how much interest is earned after nine months?

Setup:

$$(12{,}000) \times (.06) \times \left(\frac{9}{12} \right) = \$540$$

59. How to solve a COMPOUND INTEREST problem

If interest is compounded, the interest is computed on the principal as well as on any interest earned. To compute compound interest:

$$(\text{final balance}) = (\text{principal}) \times \left(1 + \frac{\text{interest rate}}{C} \right)^{(\text{time})(C)}$$

where C = the number of times compounded anually

Example:

If $10,000 is invested at 8 percent annual interest, compounded semiannually, what is the balance after 1 year?

Setup:

Final balance

$$= (10{,}000) \times \left(1 + \frac{.08}{2}\right)^{(1)(2)}$$

$$= (10{,}000) \times (1.04)^2$$

$$= \$10{,}816$$

HINT: Often on the GMAT, you don't have to do the work of calculating compound interest. Try calculating the simple interest and looking for the answer that's just a little bit larger.

---

60. How to solve a REMAINDERS problem

Pick a number that fits the given conditions and see what happens.

Example:

When n is divided by 7, the remainder is 5. What is the remainder when $2n$ is divided by 7?

Setup:

Find a number that leaves a remainder of 5 when divided by 7. A good choice would be 12. If $n = 12$, then $2n = 24$, which, when divided by 7, leaves a remainder of 3.

61. How to solve a DIGITS problem

Use a little logic—and some trial and error.

Example:

If A, B, C, and D represent distinct digits in the addition problem below, what is the value of D?

$$\begin{array}{r} AB \\ + \, BA \\ \hline CDC \end{array}$$

Setup:

Two 2-digit numbers will add up to at most something in the 100s, so $C = 1$. B plus A in the units' column gives a 1, and since it can't simply be that $B + A = 1$, it must be that $B + A = 11$, and a 1 gets carried. In fact, A and B can be just about any pair of digits that add up to 11 (3 and 8, 4 and 7, etcetera), but it doesn't matter what they are, they always give you the same thing for D:

$$\begin{array}{r} 47 \\ +74 \\ \hline 121 \end{array} \qquad \begin{array}{r} 83 \\ +38 \\ \hline 121 \end{array}$$

62. How to find a WEIGHTED AVERAGE

Give each term the appropriate "weight."

Example:

The girls' average score is 30. The boys' average score is 24. If there are twice as many boys as girls, what is the overall average?

Setup:

$$\text{Weighted Avg.} = \frac{1 \times 30 + 2 \times 24}{3} = \frac{78}{3} = 26$$

HINT: Don't just average the averages.

---

63. How to find the NEW AVERAGE when a number is added or deleted

Use the sum of the terms of the old average to help you find the new average.

Example:

Michael's average score after four tests is 80. If he scores 100 on the fifth test, what's his new average?

Setup:

Find the original sum from the original average:

Original sum = 4 × 80 = 320

Add the fifth score to make the new sum:

New sum = 320 + 100 = 420

Find the new average from the new sum:

New average = $\frac{420}{5}$ = 84

64. How to use the ORIGINAL AVERAGE and NEW AVERAGE to figure out WHAT WAS ADDED OR DELETED

Use the sums.

Number added = (new sum) – (original sum)

Number deleted = (original sum) – (new sum)

Example:

The average of five numbers is 2. After one number is deleted, the new average is –3. What number was deleted?

Setup:

Find the original sum from the original average:

Original sum = 5 × 2 = 10

Find the new sum from the new average:

New sum = 4 × (–3) = –12

The difference between the original sum and the new sum is the answer.

Number deleted = 10 – (–12) = 22

65. How to find an AVERAGE RATE

Convert to totals.

Average A per B = $\frac{Total\ A}{Total\ B}$

Example:

If the first 500 pages have an average of 150 words per page, and the remaining 100 pages have an average of 450 words per page, what is the average number of words per page for the entire 600 pages?

Setup:

Total pages = 500 + 100 = 600

Total words = 500 × 150 + 100 × 450 = 120,000

Average words per page = $\frac{120,000}{600}$ = 200

To find an average speed, you also convert to totals.

Average speed = $\frac{total\ distance}{total\ time}$

Example:

Rosa drove 120 miles one way at an average speed of 40 miles per hour and returned by the same 120-mile route at an average speed of 60 miles per hour. What was Rosa's average speed for the entire 240-mile round trip?

Setup:

To drive 120 miles at 40 mph takes 3 hours. To return at 60 mph takes 2 hours. The total time, then, is 5 hours.

Average speed = $\frac{240\ miles}{5\ hours}$ = 48 mph

HINT: Don't just average the rates.

66. How to solve a WORK problem

In a work problem, you are given the rate at which people or machines perform work individually, and asked to compute the rate at which they work together (or vice versa). The work formula states: The inverse of the time it would take everyone working together equals the sum of the inverses of the times it would take each working individually. In other words:

$$\frac{1}{r} + \frac{1}{s} = \frac{1}{t}$$

Where r and s are, for example, the number of hours it would take Rebecca and Sam, respectively, to complete a job working by themselves, and t is the number of hours it would take the two of them working together.

Example:

If it takes Joe 4 hours to paint a room and Pete twice as long to paint the same room, how long would it take the two of them, working together, to paint the same room, if each of them works at his respective individual rate?

Setup:

Joe takes 4 hours, so Pete takes 8 hours; thus:

$$\frac{1}{4} + \frac{1}{8} = \frac{1}{t}$$

$$\frac{1}{4} + \frac{1}{8} = \frac{3}{8} = \frac{\frac{1}{8}}{3}$$

So it would take them $\frac{8}{3}$ hours, or 2 hours 40 minutes, to paint the room together.

67. How to determine a COMBINED RATIO

Multiply one or both ratios by whatever you need to in order to get the terms they have in common to match.

Example:

The ratio of a to b is 7:3. The ratio of b to c is 2:5. What is the ratio of a to c?

Setup:

Multiply each member of a:b by 2 and multiply each member of b:c by 3 and you get a:b = 14:6 and b:c = 6:15. Now that the b's match, you can just take a and c and say a:c = 14:15.

68. How to solve a DILUTION or MIXTURE problem

In dilution or mixture problems, you have to determine the characteristics of the resulting mixture when substances with different characteristics are combined. Or, alternatively, you have to determine how to combine substances with different characteristics to produce a desired mixture. There are two approaches to such problems—the straightforward setup and the balancing method.

Example:

If 5 pounds of raisins that cost $1.00 per pound are mixed with 2 pounds of almonds that cost $2.40 per pound, what is the cost per pound of the resulting mixture?

Setup:

The straightforward setup:

$$5(1.00) + 2(2.40) = 9.80$$

The cost per pound is $\frac{9.80}{7} = \$1.40$

Example:

How many liters of a solution that is 10 percent alcohol by volume must be added to 2 liters of a solution that is 50 percent alcohol by volume to create a solution that is 15 percent alcohol by volume?

Setup:

The balancing method:

Make the weaker and stronger (or cheaper and more expensive, etcetera) substances balance. That is: (percent/price difference between the weaker solution and the desired solution) × (amount of weaker solution) = (percent/price difference between the stronger solution and the desired solution) × (amount of stronger solution).

In this case:

$$n(15 - 10) = 2(50 - 15)$$

$$n \times 5 = 2(35)$$

$$n = \frac{70}{5} = 14$$

So 14 liters of the 10 percent solution must be added.

HINT: The balancing method is also effective on weighted average questions.

---

69. How to solve a GROUP problem involving BOTH/NEITHER

Some GMAT word problems involve two groups with overlapping members, and possibly elements that belong to neither group. It's easy to identify this type of question because the words "both" and/or "neither" appear in the question. These problems are quite easy if you just memorize the following formula:

$$\text{Group}_1 + \text{Group}_2 + \text{Neither} - \text{Both} = \text{Total}$$

Example:

Of the 120 students at a certain language school, 65 are studying French, 51 are studying Spanish, and 53 are studying neither language. How many are studying both French and Spanish?

Setup:

$$65 + 51 + 53 - \text{Both} = 120$$
$$169 - \text{Both} = 120$$
$$\text{Both} = 49$$

70. How to solve a GROUP problem involving EITHER/OR categories

Other GMAT word problems involve groups with distinct "either/or" categories (male/female, blue-collar/white collar, etcetera). The key to solving this type of problem is to organize the information in a grid.

Example:

At a certain professional conference with 130 attendees, 94 of the attendees are doctors and the rest are dentists. If 48 of the attendees are women, and $\frac{1}{4}$ of the dentists in attendance are women, how many of the attendees are male doctors?

Setup:

To complete the grid, each row and column adds up to the corresponding total:

	Doctors	Dentists	Total
Male	55	27	82
Female		9	48
Total	94	36	130

After you've filled in the information from the question, simply fill in the remaining boxes until you get the number you are looking for—in this case, that 55 of the attendees are male doctors.

71. How to work with FACTORIALS

You may see a problem involving factorial notation. If n is an integer greater 1, then n factorial, denoted by $n!$, is defined as the product of all the integers from 1 to n. In other words:

$$2! = 2 \times 1 = 2$$
$$3! = 3 \times 2 \times 1 = 6$$
$$4! = 4 \times 3 \times 2 \times 1 = 24, \text{ etcetera}$$

By definition, $0! = 1! = 1$.

Also note: $6! = 6 \times 5! = 6 \times 5 \times 4!$, etcetera. Most GMAT factorial problems test your ability to factor and/or cancel.

Example:

$$\frac{8!}{6! \times 5!} = \frac{\cancel{8} \times 7 \times \cancel{6!}}{\cancel{6!} \times 5 \times \cancel{4} \times 3 \times \cancel{2} \times 1} = \frac{7}{15}$$

72. How to solve a PERMUTATION problem

Factorials are useful for solving questions about permutations, i.e., the number of ways to arrange elements sequentially. For instance, to figure out how many ways there are to arrange 7 items along a shelf, you would multiply the number of possibilities for the first position times the number of possibilities remaining for the second position, and so on—in other words: $7 \times 6 \times 5 \times 4 \times 3 \times 2 \times 1$, or $7!$.

If you're asked to find the number of ways to arrange a smaller group that's being drawn from a larger group, you can either apply logic or you can use the permutation formula:

$$P = \frac{n!}{(n-k)!}$$

Where n = (# in the larger group) and k = (# you're arranging)

Example:

Five runners run in a race. The runners who come in first, second, and third place will win gold, silver, and bronze medals, respectively. How many possible outcomes for gold, silver, and bronze medal winners are there?

Setup:

Any of the 5 runners could come in first place, leaving 4 runners who could come in second place, leaving 3 runners who could come in third place, for a total of 5 $\times$ 4 $\times$ 3 = 60 possible outcomes for gold, silver, and bronze medal winners. Or, using the formula:

$$P = \frac{5!}{(5-3)!} = \frac{5!}{2!} = 5 \times 4 \times 3 = 60$$

73. How to solve a COMBINATION problem

If the order or arrangement of the smaller group that's being drawn from the larger group does NOT matter, you are looking for the numbers of combinations, and a different formula is called for:

$$C = \frac{n!}{k!(n-k)!}$$

Where n = (# in the larger group) and k = (# you're choosing)

Example:

How many different ways there are to choose 3 delegates from 8 possible candidates?

Setup:
$$C = \frac{8!}{3! \times 5!} = \frac{8 \times 7 \times 6 \times 5!}{3 \times 2 \times 1 \times 5!} = 56$$

So there are 56 different possible combinations.

74. How to solve a MULTIPLE-EVENT PROBABILITY problem

Many hard probability questions involve finding the probability of a certain outcome after multiple events (a coin being tossed several times, et cetera). These questions come in two forms: those in which each individual event must occur a certain way, and those in which individual events can have different outcomes.

To determine multiple-event probability where each individual event must occur a certain way:

• Figure out the probability for each individual event.
• Multiply the individual probabilities together.

Example:

If 2 students are chosen at random from a class with 5 girls and 5 boys, what's the probability that both students chosen will be girls?

Setup:

The probability that the first student chosen will be a girl is $\frac{5}{10} = \frac{1}{2}$, and since there would be 4 girls left out of 9 students, the probability that the second student chosen will be a girl is $\frac{4}{9}$. Thus the probability the both students chosen will be girls is

$$\frac{1}{2} \times \frac{4}{9} = \frac{2}{9}.$$

To determine multiple-event probability where individual events can have different outcomes:

• Find the *total number of possible outcomes* by determining the number of possible outcomes for each individual event and multiplying these numbers together.

• Find the *number of desired outcomes* by listing out the possibilities.

Example:

If a fair coin is tossed 4 times, what's the probability that at least 3 of the 4 tosses will come up heads?

Setup:

There are 2 possible outcomes for each toss, so after 4 tosses there are a total of $2 \times 2 \times 2 \times 2 = 16$ possible outcomes.

List out all the possibilities where "at least 3 of the 4 tosses" come up heads:

H, H, H, T
H, H, T, H
H, T, H, H
T, H, H, H
H, H, H, H

So there's a total of 5 possible desired outcomes. Thus, the probability that at least 3 of the 4 tosses will come up heads is

$$\frac{\text{number of desired outcomes}}{\text{number of possible outcomes}} = \frac{5}{16}$$

75. How to deal with STANDARD DEVIATION

Like mean, mode, median, and range, standard deviation is a term used to describe sets of numbers. Standard deviation is a measure of how spread out a set of numbers is (how much the numbers deviate from the mean). The greater the spread, the higher the standard deviation. You'll never actually have to calculate the standard deviation on test day, but here's how it's calculated:

- Find the average (arithmetic mean) of the set.
- Find the differences between the mean and each value in the set.
- Square each of the differences.
- Find the average of the squared differences.
- Take the positive square root of the average.

Although you won't have to calculate standard deviation on the GMAT, you may be asked to compare standard deviations between sets of data, or otherwise demonstrate that you understand what standard deviation means.

Example:

High temperatures, in degrees Fahrenheit, in 2 cities over 5 days:

September	1	2	3	4	5
City A	54	61	70	49	56
City B	62	56	60	67	65

For the 5-day period listed, which city had the greater standard deviation in high temperatures?

Setup:

Even without trying to calculate them out, you can see that City A has the greater spread in temperatures, and therefore the greater standard deviation in high temperatures. If you were to go ahead and calculate the standard deviations following the steps described above, you would find that the standard deviation in high temperatures for City $A = \sqrt{\dfrac{254}{5}}$ ≈ 7.1, while the same for City $B = \sqrt{\dfrac{74}{5}} \approx 3.8$.

76. How to MULTIPLY/DIVIDE POWERS

Add/subtract the exponents.

$$x^a \times x^b = x^{(a+b)}$$
$$2^3 \times 2^4 = 2^7$$
$$\frac{x^c}{x^d} = x^{(c-d)}$$
$$\frac{5^6}{5^2} = 5^4$$

77. How to RAISE A POWER TO A POWER

Multiply the exponents.

$$(x^a)^b = x^{ab}$$

Example:

$$(3^4)^5 = 3^{20}$$

78. How to handle ZERO POWERS

Zero raised to any power equals zero.

Example:

$0^4 = 0^{12} = 0^1 = 0$

Any number raised to the 0 power equals 1.

Example:

$3^0 = 15^0 = (0.34)^0 = -345^0 = \pi^0 = 1$

The lone exception is 0 raised to the 0 power, which is *undefined*.

79. How to handle NEGATIVE POWERS

A number raised to the exponent $-x$ is the reciprocal of that number raised to the exponent x.

Example:

$5^{-3} = \dfrac{1}{5^3} = \dfrac{1}{5 \times 5 \times 5} = \dfrac{1}{125}$

$n^{-1} = \dfrac{1}{n}$, $n^{-2} = \dfrac{1}{n^2}$, and so on

80. How to handle FRACTIONAL POWERS

Fractional exponents relate to roots. For instance, $x^{\frac{1}{2}} = \sqrt{x}$. Likewise, $x^{\frac{1}{3}} = \sqrt[3]{x}$, $x^{\frac{2}{3}} = \sqrt[3]{x^2}$, and so on.

Example:

$4^{\frac{1}{2}} = \sqrt{4} = 2$

$\left(x^{-2}\right)^{\frac{1}{2}} = x^{(-2)\left(\frac{1}{2}\right)} = x^{-1} = \dfrac{1}{x}$

HINT: The rules for multiplying powers, dividing powers, and raising powers to powers also apply nicely to negative, zero and fractional exponents.

---

81. How to handle CUBE ROOTS

The cube root of x is just the number that multiplied by itself 3 times (i.e., cubed) gives you x. Both positive and negative numbers have one and only one cube root, denoted by the symbol $\sqrt[3]{}$, and the cube root of a number is always the same sign as the number itself.

Example:

$(-5) \times (-5) \times (-5) = -125$, so $-\sqrt[3]{125} = -5$

$\dfrac{1}{2} \times \dfrac{1}{2} \times \dfrac{1}{2} = \dfrac{1}{8}$, so $\sqrt[3]{\dfrac{1}{8}} = \dfrac{1}{2}$

82. How to ADD, SUBTRACT, MULTIPLY, and DIVIDE ROOTS

You can add/subtract roots only when the parts inside the $\sqrt{}$ are identical.

Example:

$$\sqrt{2} + 3\sqrt{2} = 4\sqrt{2}$$
$$\sqrt{2} - 3\sqrt{2} = -2\sqrt{2}$$

$\sqrt{2} + \sqrt{3}$—cannot be combined.

To multiply/divide, deal with what's inside the $\sqrt{}$ and outside the $\sqrt{}$ separately.

Example:

$(2\sqrt{3})(7\sqrt{5}) = (2 \times 7)(\sqrt{3 \times 5}) = 14\sqrt{15}$

$\dfrac{10\sqrt{21}}{5\sqrt{3}} = \dfrac{10}{5}\sqrt{\dfrac{21}{3}} = 2\sqrt{7}$

KAPLAN

83. How to SIMPLIFY A SQUARE ROOT

Look for perfect squares (4, 9, 16, 25, 36. . .) inside the $\sqrt{}$. Factor them out and "unsquare" them.

Example:

$$\sqrt{48} = \sqrt{16} \times \sqrt{3} = 4\sqrt{3}$$
$$\sqrt{180} = \sqrt{36} \times \sqrt{5} = 6\sqrt{5}$$

84. How to solve certain QUADRATIC EQUATIONS

Forget the quadratic formula. Manipulate the equation (if necessary) into the "_____ = 0" form, factor the left side, and break the quadratic into two simple equations.

Example:

$$x^2 + 6 = 5x$$
$$x^2 - 5x + 6 = 0$$
$$(x - 2)(x - 3) = 0$$
$$x - 2 = 0 \text{ or } x - 3 = 0$$
$$x = 2 \text{ or } 3$$

Example:

$$x^2 = 9$$
$$x = 3 \text{ or } -3$$

HINT: Watch out for x^2.
There can be two solutions.

---

85. How to solve MULTIPLE EQUATIONS

When you see two equations with two variables on the GMAT, they're probably easy to combine in such a way that you get something closer to what you're looking for.

Example:

If $5x - 2y = -9$ and $3y - 4x = 6$, what is the value of $x + y$?

Setup:

The question doesn't ask for x and y separately, so don't solve for them separately if you don't have to. Look what happens if you just rearrange a little and "add" the equations:

$$5x - 2y = -9$$
$$-4x + 3y = 6$$
$$\overline{}$$
$$x + y = -3$$

HINT: Don't do more work than you have to. Look for the shortcut.

---

86. How to solve a SEQUENCE problem

The notation used in sequence problems scares many test takers, but these problems aren't as bad as they look. In a sequence problem, the nth term in the sequence is generated by performing an operation, which will be defined for you, on either n or on the previous term in the sequence. Familiarize yourself with sequence notation and you should have no problem.

Example:

What is the difference between the fifth and fourth terms in the sequence 0, 4, 18, . . . whose nth term is $n^2(n - 1)$?

Setup:

Use the operation given to come up with the values for your terms:

$$n_5 = 5^2(5 - 1) = 25(4) = 100$$
$$n_4 = 4^2(4 - 1) = 16(3) = 48$$

So the difference between the fifth and fourth terms is $100 - 48 = 52$.

HINT: Many GMAT sequence problems invite you to backsolve.

---

87. How to solve a FUNCTION problem

You may see classic function notation on the GMAT. An algebraic expression of only one variable may be defined as a function, f or g, of that variable.

Example:

What is the minimum value of the function $f(x) = x^2 - 1$?

Setup:

In the function $f(x) = x^2 - 1$, if x is 1, then $f(1) = 1^2 - 1 = 0$. In other words, by inputting 1 into the function, the output $f(x) = 0$. Every number inputted has one and only one output (although the reverse is not necessarily true). You're asked here to find the minimum value, that is, the smallest possible value of the function. Minimums are usually found using calculus, but there is no need to use anything that complicated on the GMAT. Any minimum (or maximum) value problem on the test can be solved in one of two simple ways. Either plug the answer choices into the function and find which gives you the lowest value, or use some common sense. In the case of $f(x)\ x^2 - 1$, the function will be at a minimum when

x^2 is as small as possible. Since x^2 gets larger the farther x is from 0, x^2 is as small as possible when $x = 0$. Consequently the smallest value of $x^2 - 1$ occurs when $x = 0$. So $f(0) = 0^2 - 1 = -1$, which is the minimum value of the function.

88. How to handle GRAPHS of FUNCTIONS

You may see a problem that involves a function graphed onto the xy-coordinate plane, often called a "rectangular coordinate system" on the GMAT. When graphing a function, the output, $f(x)$, becomes the y-coordinate. For example, in the previous example, $f(x) = x^2 - 1$, you've already determined 2 points, $(1, 0)$ and $(0, -1)$. If you were to keep plugging in numbers to determine more points and then plotted those points on the xy-coordinate plane, you would come up with something like this:

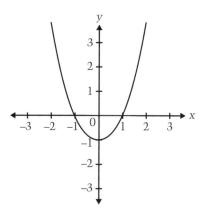

This curved line is called a *parabola*. In the event that you should see a parabola on the GMAT (it could be upside down or squatter or more elongated the one shown), you will most likely be asked to choose which equation the parabola is describing. These questions can be surprisingly easy to answer. Pick out obvious points on the graph, such as $(1, 0)$ and $(0, -1)$ above, plug these values into the answer choices, and eliminate choices that don't jibe with those values until only one answer is left.

KAPLAN

89. How to handle LINEAR EQUATIONS

You may also encounter linear equations on the GMAT. A linear equation is often expressed in the form

$$y = mx + b, \text{ where:}$$

- m = the slope of the line = $\dfrac{\text{rise}}{\text{run}}$.

  For instance, a slope of 3 means that the line rises 3 steps for every 1 step it makes to the right.
  A positive slope slopes up from left to right.
  A negative slope slopes down from left to right.
  A slope of zero (e.g., $y = 5$) is a flat line.

- b = the y-intercept (where the line passes the y-axis).

Example:

The graph of the linear equation $y = \dfrac{-3}{4x} + 3$ is:

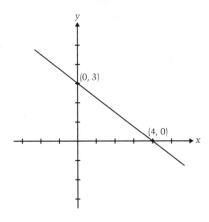

To get a better handle on an equation written in this form, you can solve for y to write it in its more familiar form. Or, if you're asked to choose which equation the line is describing, you can pick obvious points such as (0, 3) and (4, 0) above, and use these values to eliminate answer choices until only one answer is left.

90. How to find the x- and y-INTERCEPTS of a line

The x-intercept of a line is the value of x where the line crosses the x-axis. In other words, it's the value of x when $y = 0$. Likewise, the y-intercept is the value of y where the line crosses the y-axis, i.e., the value of y when $x = 0$, also the value b when the equation is in the form: $y = mx + b$. For instance, in the line shown above, the x-intercept is 4 and the y-intercept is 3.

91. How to find the MAXIMUM and MINIMUM lengths for a SIDE of a TRIANGLE

If you know two sides of a triangle, then you know that the third side is somewhere between the difference and the sum.

Example:

The length of one side of a triangle is 7. The length of another side is 3. What is the range of possible lengths for the third side?

Setup:

The third side is greater than the difference $(7 - 3 = 4)$ and less than the sum $(7 + 3 = 10)$.

92. How to find one angle or the sum of all the ANGLES of a REGULAR POLYGON

Sum of the interior angles in a polygon with n *sides =* $(n - 2) \times 180$

Degree measure of one angle in a Regular Polygon with n *sides =*

$$\frac{(n-2) \times 180}{n}$$

Example:

What is the measure of one angle of a regular pentagon?

Setup:

Plug $n = 5$ into the formula:

Degree measure of one angle =

$$\frac{(5-2) \times 180}{5} = \frac{540}{5} = 108$$

93. How to find the LENGTH of an ARC

Think of an arc as a fraction of the circumference of a circle.

$$Length\ of\ arc = \frac{n}{360} \times 2\pi r$$

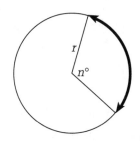

94. How to find the AREA of a SECTOR

Think of a sector as a fraction of the circle's area.

$$Area\ of\ sector = \frac{n}{360} \times \pi r^2$$

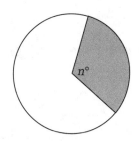

95. How to find the dimensions or area of an INSCRIBED or CIRCUMSCRIBED FIGURE

Look for the connection. Is the diameter the same as a side or a diagonal?

Example:

If the area of the square is 36, what is the circumference of the circle?

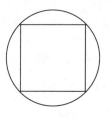

Setup:

To get the circumference, you need the diameter or radius. The circle's diameter is also the square's diagonal, which (it's a 45-45-90 triangle!) is $6\sqrt{2}$.

Circumference = π(diameter) = $6\pi\sqrt{2}$.

96. How to find the VOLUME of a RECTANGULAR SOLID

$$Volume = length \times width \times height$$

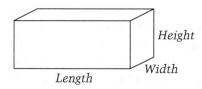

97. How to find the SURFACE AREA of a RECTANGULAR SOLID

To find the surface area of a rectangular solid, you have to find the area of each face and add them together. Here's the formula.

Surface area = 2(length × width + length × height + width × height)

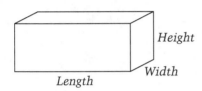

98. How to find the DIAGONAL of a RECTANGULAR SOLID

Use the Pythagorean theorem twice, unless you spot special triangles. This will often be the case on the GMAT.

Example: What is the length of *AG* ?

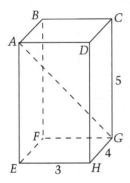

Setup: Draw diagonal *AC*.

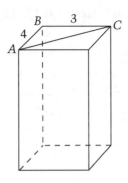

ABC is a 3-4-5 triangle, so *AC* = 5. Now look at triangle *ACG*:

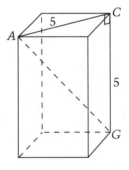

ACG is another special triangle, so you don't need to use the Pythagorean theorem. *ACG* is a 45-45-90, so *AG* = $5\sqrt{2}$.

99. How to find the VOLUME of a CYLINDER

Volume $= \pi r^2 h$

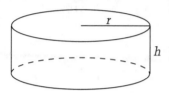

100. How to find the VOLUME of a SPHERE

Volume $= \dfrac{4}{3}\pi r^3$

KAPLAN

Analytical Writing Assessment

....

- Learn the Four Basic Principles and the Kaplan Method for Analytic Writing

- Focus on the two types of essay: Analysis of an Issue and Analysis of an Argument

- Find out what the e-rater computer grader wants

- Complete the two Practice Essays

- Review the GMAT style checklist

....

The GMAT begins with Analytical Writing Assessment, which consists of two timed essay sections. For each section, you not only have to analyze the given topic and plan your attack, but you must also type your essays into a simple word processing program.

One of the two writing assignments is what ETS calls an "Issue" essay: You'll be shown an essay topic—a single sentence or paragraph that expresses an opinion on an issue of general interest. You then have 30 minutes to plan and write an essay that communicates your own view on the issue. Whether you agree or disagree with the opinion on the screen is irrelevant: What matters is that you support your view with relevant examples and statements.

The other of the two writing assignments is the "Argument" essay. Here, you will be shown a paragraph that argues a certain point. You will then be given 30 minutes to assess that argument's logic. As with the "Issue" essay, it won't matter whether you agree with what you see on the screen.

The "Issue" and the "Argument" essays may appear in either order on your exam. Since the two essays require different specific tasks, make sure

Analytical Writing Tally

- Two 30-minute sections
- One essay topic per section
- One Analysis of an Issue topic
- One Analysis of an Argument topic

E-Rater

GMAT essays had been graded by two real human beings since these questions were added to the GMAT several years ago. But since early 1999, each GMAT essay has been graded by a human grader as well as a computerized essay grader—called the "e-rater."

Teacher Tip

The computer grader focuses on structure, so it is especially important to plan your essays in advance. Rambling or jumping back and forth will confuse the e-rater, and you might not get credit for your arguments. Make sure that you structure your argument clearly, and use clear structural signals.
—Tiffany Sanders
   Downers Grove, IL

you look at your first essay assignment to see whether it is labeled "Analysis of an Issue" or "Analysis of an Argument."

How the Analytical Writing Assessment Is Administered

At the start of the Analytical Writing Assessment, you will be given a brief tutorial on how to use the word processor. If you aren't comfortable with complex word processing programs, don't worry. The program you'll use on the GMAT is quite simple, as the only commands you'll use are *cut, paste,* and *undo.* You'll be well acquainted with the program's commands by the time you start writing. If you're worried about having to type your essay for the GMAT, you should spend some time practicing typing and getting comfortable with a keyboard between now and Test Day.

Your essays will be graded on a scale from a low of 0 to a high of 6. You'll get one score, which will be an average of the scores that you receive for each of the two essays. Your essay will be graded by a human grader as well as a computerized essay grader (the "e-rater"). If the human and the e-rater agree on a score, that's the grade your essay will receive. If they disagree by more than one point, a second human will grade the essay to resolve any differences.

What is the e-rater looking for?

The e-rater was designed to make the same judgments that a good human grader would make. In fact, part of GMAC's argument for the validity of the e-rater is the fact that in the vast majority of cases the e-rater gives the same grade a human would give. Even so, there are steps you can take to improve your chances of getting a great score from the e-rater. The computer is not a great judge of creativity or humor, but it does know what it likes. We'll have more to say on this topic later in this chapter, but here are some tips to get started with:

- Before you begin to write, outline your essay. Good organization always counted, and now it's more important than ever.
- Since your essay will be compared against other essays, think about the points that the best essays will make.
- The length of your essay is not a factor; the computer does not count the number of words in your response.
- Use transitional phrases like *first, therefore, since,* and *for example* so that the computer can recognize structured arguments.
- Avoid spelling and grammar errors. Although the e-rater doesn't grade spelling per se, if it can't understand you or thinks you used the wrong words, it could give you a lower score.

The Four Basic Principles of Analytical Writing

GMAT writing is a two-stage process: First you decide what you want to say about a topic, and then you figure out how to say it. If your writing style isn't clear, your ideas won't come across, no matter how brilliant they are. Good GMAT English is not only grammatical but also clear and concise. Keeping these principles in mind will help you to express your ideas clearly and effectively in both of your essays.

1. Your control of language is important.

Writing that is grammatical, concise, direct, and persuasive displays the "superior control of language" (as the test makers term it) that earns top GMAT Analytical Writing scores. To achieve effective GMAT style in your essays, you should pay attention to the following points.

Grammar

Your writing must follow the same general rules of standard written English that are tested by Sentence Correction questions. If you're not confident of your mastery of grammar, review the Sentence Correction section.

Diction

Diction means word choice. For example, do you use the words *affect* and *effect* correctly? Be careful with such commonly confused words as *its/it's*, *there/their*, *precede/proceed*, *principal/principle*, and *whose/who's*.

Syntax

Syntax refers to sentence structure. Do you construct your sentences so that your ideas are clear and understandable? Do you vary your sentence structure, sometimes using simple sentences and other times using sentences with clauses and phrases?

2. It's better to keep things simple.

Perhaps the single most important thing to bear in mind when writing GMAT essays is to keep everything simple. This rule applies to word choice, sentence structure, and organization. If you obsess about how to spell an unusual word, you can lose your flow of thought. The more complicated your sentences are, the more likely it is that they will be plagued by errors. The more complex your organization gets, the more likely it is that your argument will get bogged down in convoluted sentences that obscure your point. But keep in mind that simple does not mean simplistic. A clear, straightforward approach can still be sophisticated and convey perceptive insights.

3. Minor grammatical flaws won't torpedo your score.

Many test takers mistakenly believe that they'll lose a few points because of a few mechanical errors such as misplaced commas, misspellings, or other minor glitches. Occasional mistakes of this type will not dramatically affect your GMAT essay score. In fact, the test makers' description

The Basic Principles of GMAT Writing

1. Use language effectively.
2. Keep it simple.
3. Don't worry excessively about making minor errors.
4. Keep sight of your goal.

Note

For both essay types, you must:

- Analyze a topic
- Take a position
- Explain your position

Teacher Tip

Use your scratch paper to write a first draft of your opening sentence (starting strong is great!), and then outline the points you want to make in order. Good logical planning will impress every reader.
—Bob Verini
   Los Angeles, CA

of a top-scoring essay (the highest score) acknowledges that there may be minor grammatical flaws. The essay graders understand that you are writing first-draft essays. They will not be looking to take points off for minor errors, provided you don't make them consistently. If your essays are littered with misspellings and grammar mistakes, then the graders may conclude that you have a serious communication problem. To write an effective essay, you must be concise, forceful, and correct. An effective essay wastes no words, makes its point in a clear, direct way, and conforms to the generally accepted rules of grammar and form.

4. Keep sight of your goal.

Remember, your goal isn't to become a prize-winning stylist. It's to write two solid essays that will convince B-school admissions officers you can write well enough to clearly communicate your ideas to a reader—or business associate. GMAT essay graders don't expect rhetorical flourishes, but they do expect effective expression.

This chapter will give you the chance to sharpen your GMAT writing skills.

The Kaplan Five-Step Method for the Writing Assessment

Here's the deal: You have a limited amount of time to show the business school admissions people that you can think logically and express yourself in clearly written English. They don't care how many syllables you can cram into a sentence or how fancy your phrases are. They care that you're making sense. Whatever you do, don't try to hide beneath a lot of hefty words and abstractions. Just make sure that everything you say is clearly written and relevant to the topic. Get in there, state your main points, back them up, and get out.

1. **Digest the Issue/Argument.**
   - Read it through to get a sense of the scope of the matter.
   - Note any terms that are ambiguous and need defining.
   - Frame the issue/argument.

2. **Select the points you will make.**
   - In the "Analysis of Issue" essay, think of the arguments for both sides and make a decision as to which side you will support or the exact extent to which you agree with the stated position.
   - In the "Analysis of Argument" essay, identify all the important gaps between the evidence and the conclusion. Think of remedies for the problems you discover.

Kaplan Rules

Essay topics require thinking and writing skills, *not* knowledge of technical information or specialized learning.

3. Organize.

- Outline your essay.

- Lead with your best arguments.

- Think about how the essay as a whole will flow.

4. Write/Type.

- Be direct.

- Use paragraph breaks to make your essay easier to read.

- Make transitions, link related ideas; it will help your writing flow.

- Finish strongly.

5. Proofread.

- Save enough time to read through the entire essay.

- Have a sense of the errors you are liable to make.

As explained before, the two essay types you'll meet on the GMAT, the Issue and the Argument, require generally similar tasks. You must analyze a subject, take an informed position, and explain that position in writing. The two essay types, however, require different specific tasks.

Analysis of an Issue

The stimulus and question stem of an Analysis of an Issue topic will look something like the example below.

> Many assert that individuals allowed to work flexible schedules at home will be both more productive and happier than colleagues working under more traditional arrangements. But others assert that the close supervision of an office workplace is necessary to ensure productivity and quality control and to maintain morale.
>
> Which argument do you find more compelling, the case for flexible work conditions or the opposing viewpoint? Explain your position using relevant reasons or examples drawn from your own experience, observations, or reading.

The Stimulus

In this example, the stimulus consists of a few sentences that discuss two points of view on a broad, general issue. Sometimes the stimulus is a single sentence. You don't need prior knowledge of any specific subject matter to discuss the issue.

The first sentence or two introduces the general issue and expresses one point of view. Sometimes, a key word—here, it's the word *but*—will sig-

Analysis of an Issue Essay

Analysis of an Issue questions ask you to choose which of two viewpoints you find more convincing and argue your position.

nal the introduction of the contrasting point of view. In other cases, the transition might not be so obvious. The last part of this stimulus presents the contrary view of the issue.

The Question Stem
The stem asks you which of the two viewpoints you find more convincing and instructs you to explain your position using reasons or examples. Although the specific wording may vary by question, the basic task will be essentially the same.

Not all issue topics will look exactly like our example. Some may present only a sentence in which the two conflicting viewpoints are not specified. For instance:

> Allowing individuals to work flexible schedules is an idea that makes sense.

Notice how this is just a reworking of our original topic. Here, the two viewpoints are implicit, so your task includes a little digging: What are the two viewpoints? From here, your basic task is the same. Explain what the issue is and make a case for one opinion on that issue.

Applying the Kaplan Five-Step Method to an Issue Essay

Let's use the Kaplan Five-Step Method on the Analysis of an Issue topic we saw before:

> Many assert that individuals allowed to work flexible schedules at home will be both more productive and happier than colleagues working under more traditional arrangements. Others assert that the close supervision of an office workplace is necessary to ensure productivity and quality control and to maintain morale.
>
> Which argument do you find more compelling, the case for flexible work conditions or the opposing viewpoint? Explain your position using relevant reasons or examples drawn from your own experience, observations, or reading.

1. Digest the issue.
It's simple enough. Some people think flexible schedules make for happier and more productive workers. Other people think a traditional office workplace makes for happier and more productive workers. Your job, as stated in the second paragraph, is to pick one of the sides and defend it.

2. Select the points you will make.
So which side do you take? Remember, this isn't about showing the admissions people what your politics are—it's about showing you can formulate

---

Teacher Tip

When trial lawyers recognize a weakness in their case, they usually try to bring it up under favorable conditions during direct examination rather than allow their opponents to bring it up under cross examination. You can use this same concept, effectively, in your analysis of issue. In other words, forthrightly admit (but downplay the significance of) weaknesses in your case or strengths of the opposing side. In this way, you can not be accused of having ignored something. Instead, you have considered it but found it to be relatively less important.
—Vince LoCascio
　New Brunswick, NJ

an argument and write it down. Quickly think through the pros and cons of each side, and choose the side for which you have the most relevant things to say. For this topic, that process might go something like this:

Arguments for flexible schedules:	Arguments for office workplace:
• People feel more valued, work better	• People less likely to waste time if boss is there
• Decreases absence due to child care emergencies, etc.	• People need to feel part of team to be happy
• People happier if they don't have to commute	• More supervision and quality control possible

Note

You can take either side in an Analysis of an Issue essay. Take the position that you prefer and argue it well.

Again, it doesn't matter which side you take. Let's say that in this case you decide to argue in favor of traditional office workplaces. Remember, the question is asking you to argue *why* traditional schedules lead to greater happiness and productivity—happiness and productivity are the ends you're arguing towards, so don't list them as supporting arguments.

3. Organize your argument.

You've already begun to think out your arguments—that's why you picked the side you did in the first place. Now's the time to write them all out, including ones that weaken the opposing side.

Traditional office workplaces lead to greater happiness and productivity because:
- People work harder under supervision (more productive)
- People need co-workers, team spirit (happier)
- People who work at home feel isolated (weakens opposing argument)
- Healthier to separate work and home life (happier, weakens opposing argument)
- Support of other staff members for problem solving (more productive)
- Greater technical resources in office environment (more productive)

4. Compose your essay.

Remember, open up with a general statement and then assert your position. From there, get down your main points. Your essay for this assignment might look like the following.

Sample Essay 1
Many companies face the decision to either allow employees flexible work schedules or to maintain traditional work environments. A close examination of the issue reveals that workers are happier and more productive in a traditional office environment.

A main reason that people are happier in traditional offices is the team spirit and personal satisfaction that come from working in a group. People who spend their workday at home are more likely to feel isolated from the company and divorced from the final product. Additionally, people who work in an office environment are more likely to form close friendships with co-workers than those who are rarely in the office, an occurrence that fosters greater happiness and stability within the company.

The bottom line for businesses is, of course, productivity, and there are several reasons why the traditional workplace promotes greater productivity than work at home. One reason is the increased resources the workplace provides. An office space is more likely to have better technical resources than a home work space. Also, the company staff provides problem-solving resources to which a home worker would not have direct access.

Traditional work space is far better from a managerial standpoint, as well. An office environment makes for easier supervision and quality control. Managers can make sure employees aren't wasting time or doing shoddy work. Also, a manager can more quickly spot and fix problems if they are occurring in the office, increasing productivity significantly.

While there are arguments to be made for both sides, it is clear that there are greater advantages to the traditional work environment. The traditional office space allows for workers to be happier and more productive than those who work at home.

5. Proofread your work.
Take that last couple of minutes to catch any glaring errors.

Analysis of an Argument

The stimulus and question stem of an Analysis of an Argument topic should look something like this:

> The problem of poorly trained teachers that has plagued the state public school system is bound to become a good deal less serious in the future. The state has initiated comprehensive guidelines

that oblige state teachers to complete a number of required credits in education and educational psychology at the graduate level before being certified.

Explain how logically persuasive you find this argument. In discussing your viewpoint, analyze the argument's line of reasoning and its use of evidence. Also explain what, if anything, would make the argument more valid and convincing or help you to better evaluate its conclusion.

The Stimulus

Analysis of an Argument topics that present an argument will probably remind you of those in Critical Reasoning questions. The basic idea is similar. Just as in Critical Reasoning, the writer tries to persuade you of something—her conclusion—by citing some evidence. So look for these two basic components of an argument: a conclusion and supporting evidence. You should read the arguments in the Analysis of an Argument topics in much the same way you read Critical Reasoning questions; be on the lookout for assumptions—the ways the writer makes the leap from evidence to conclusion.

The Question Stem

The question stem above instructs you to decide how convincing you find the argument, explain why, and discuss what might *improve* the argument. In some topics, the question stem may ask you to decide why the argument is *not* persuasive, explain why, and outline how to further *weaken* the argument. (It's the flip side of the same assignment.) To perform either task, you'll need to do essentially the same things. First, analyze the argument itself and evaluate its use of evidence; second, explain how a different approach or more information would make the argument better (or worse).

Applying the Kaplan Five-Step Method to an Argument Essay

Let's use the Kaplan Five-Step Method on the Analysis of an Argument topic we saw before:

The problem of poorly trained teachers that has plagued the state public school system is bound to become a good deal less serious in the future. The state has initiated comprehensive guidelines that oblige state teachers to complete a number of required credits in education and educational psychology at the graduate level before being certified.

Analysis of an Argument Essay

Your tasks in the Analysis of an Argument essay are to decide how convincing you find an argument, explain why the argument is convincing (or unconvincing), and discuss what might improve the argument (or weaken it).

Explain how logically persuasive you find this argument. In discussing your viewpoint, analyze the argument's line of reasoning and its use of evidence. Also explain what, if anything, would make the argument more valid and convincing or help you to better evaluate its conclusion.

1. Digest the argument.

First, identify the conclusion—the point the argument's trying to make. Here, the conclusion is:

> The problem of poorly trained teachers that has plagued the state public school system is bound to become a good deal less serious in the future.

Next, identify the evidence—the basis for the conclusion. Here, the evidence is:

> The state has initiated comprehensive guidelines that oblige state teachers to complete a number of required credits in education and educational psychology at the graduate level before being certified.

Finally, sum up the argument in your own words:

> The problem of badly trained teachers will become less serious because they'll be getting better training.

Explain how logically persuasive you find this argument. In explaining your viewpoint, analyze the argument's line of reasoning and its use of evidence.

Also explain what, if anything, would make the argument more valid and convincing or would help you to better evaluate its conclusion.

- Credits in education will improve teachers' classroom performance.
- Present bad teachers haven't already met this standard of training.
- Current poor teachers will not still be teaching in the future, or will have to be trained, too.

2. Select the points you will make.

Analyze the use of evidence in the argument.

Determine whether there's anything relevant that's not discussed.

Kaplan Rules

To attack the argument:

- Identify the argument's conclusion
- Identify the evidence
- Sum up the argument in your own words

- Whether the training will actually address the cause of the problems
- How to either improve or remove the poor teachers now teaching

Also determine what types of evidence would make the argument stronger or more logically sound. In this case, we need some new evidence supporting the assumptions.

- Evidence verifying that this training will make better teachers
- Evidence making it clear that present bad teachers haven't already had this training
- Evidence suggesting why all or many bad teachers won't still be teaching in the future (or why they'll be better trained)

3. Organize.

For an essay on this topic, your opening sentence might look like this:

> The writer concludes that the present problem of poorly trained teachers will become less severe in the future because of required course work in education and psychology.

Then use your notes as a working outline. Remember to lead with your best arguments. You might also recommend new evidence you'd like to see and explain why.

The argument says that:

> The problem of poorly trained teachers will become less serious with better training.

It assumes that:

- Course work in education will improve teachers' classroom performance.
- Present bad teachers haven't already met this standard of classroom training.
- Current poor teachers will not be teaching in the future or will get training, too.

4. Compose your essay.

Begin typing or writing your essay now. Keep in mind the basic principles of writing that we discussed earlier. And remember the following issues:

What assumptions are made by the author?

- Are these assumptions valid? Why or why not?
- What additional information or evidence would make the argument stronger?

Kaplan Rules

In writing your essay, cover each point in your outline and employ the four basic principles of Analytical Writing.

Your essay might look something like this:

Sample Essay 2

The writer concludes that the present problem of poorly trained teachers will become less severe in the future because of required credits in education and psychology. However, the conclusion relies on assumptions for which there is no clear evidence.

First, the writer assumes that the required courses will make better teachers. In fact, the courses might be entirely irrelevant to the teachers' failings. If, for example, the prevalent problem is cultural and linguistic gaps between teacher and student, graduate level courses that do not address these specific issues probably won't do much good. The argument that the courses will improve teachers would be strengthened if the writer provided evidence that the training will be relevant to the problems.

In addition, the writer assumes that current poor teachers have not already had this training. In fact, the writer doesn't mention whether or not some or all of the poor teachers have had similar training. The argument would be strengthened considerably if the writer provided evidence that current poor teachers have not had training comparable to the new requirements.

Finally, the writer assumes that poor teachers currently working will either stop teaching in the future or will have received training. The writer provides no evidence, though, to indicate that this is the case. As the argument stands, it's highly possible that only brand-new teachers will receive the training, and the bright future to which the writer refers is decades away. Only if the writer provides evidence that all teachers in the system will receive training—and will then change their teaching methods accordingly—does the argument hold.

5. Proofread.

Save a few minutes to go back over your essay and catch any obvious errors. The best way to improve your writing style is to write, so tackle the two topics below.

Practice Essays

Directions: Write an essay on each of the topics below. While writing, pay particular attention to making your essay concise, forceful, and grammatically correct. After you've finished with each essay, proofread to catch your errors. Allow yourself 30 minutes to complete each essay.

Essay Topic 1

Some people believe that second-language fluency is crucial to individual development and international accord, and maintain that language training should begin very early. Others feel that second-language fluency is not necessary to most Americans, and that elementary school should be devoted to basic skills.

Which argument do you find more compelling, the case for early foreign language learning or the opposing viewpoint? Explain your position using relevant reasons or examples drawn from your own experience, observations, or reading.

Essay Topic 2

Many lives might be saved if inoculations against cow flu were routinely administered to all people in areas in which the disease is detected. However, since there is a small possibility that a person will die as a result of the inoculations, we cannot permit inoculations against cow flu to be routinely administered.

Explain how logically persuasive you find this argument. In discussing your viewpoint, analyze the argument's line of reasoning and its use of evidence. Also explain what, if anything, would make the argument more valid and convincing or help you to better evaluate its conclusion.

After writing these two essays, evaluate your work using the checklist on the following page.

Essays at a Glance

Remember that an effective GMAT essay should be:

- Concise
- Forceful
- Grammatically correct

GMAT Style Checklist

Cut the fat.

❑ Cut out words, phrases, and sentences that don't add any information or serve a purpose.

❑ Watch out for repetitive phrases such as *refer back* or *serious crisis.*

❑ Don't use conjunctions to join sentences that would be more effective as separate sentences.

Be forceful.

❑ Avoid jargon and pompous language; it won't impress anybody.

❑ Avoid clichés and overused terms or phrases. (For example, *beyond the shadow of a doubt.*)

❑ Don't be vague. Avoid generalizations and abstractions when more specific words would be clearer. (For example, write *a waste of time and money* instead of *pointless temporal and financial expenditure.*)

❑ Don't use weak sentence openings. Avoid beginning a sentence with *there is* or *there are.*

❑ Don't refer to yourself needlessly. Avoid pointless phrases like *in my personal opinion.*

❑ Don't be monotonous: Vary sentence length and style.

❑ Use transitions to connect sentences and make your essay easy to follow. Paragraphs should clarify the different parts of your essay.

Be correct.

❑ Stick to the rules of standard written English.

Part Two

Taking Control of the Test

CHAPTER TWELVE

Test Mentality

- How to prepare mentally for the GMAT
- How test awareness can help
- Developing stamina, confidence, and a winning attitude
- Managing test stress

In the earlier parts of this book, we looked at the content covered by the various sections of the GMAT, focusing on the strategies and methods you'll need to tackle individual questions, passages, and problems. Then we discussed the test expertise involved in moving from individual items to working through full-length sections. Now we're ready to turn our attention to the often overlooked topic of test mentality. In this chapter we'll show you how to get into peak mental condition for the GMAT.

How to Develop Good Mental Conditioning

We arm you with the weapons you need to do well on the GMAT. But you must wield those weapons with the right frame of mind and in the right spirit. This involves taking a certain stance towards the entire test. Here's what's involved in developing the best GMAT test mentality.

Test Awareness

To do your best on the GMAT, you must always keep in mind that the test is unlike other tests that you've taken, both in terms of content and in terms of the scoring system. If you took a test in high school or college and got a quarter of the questions wrong, you'd probably receive a pretty lousy grade. But on the GMAT, if you can get the first ten questions right, you can get lots of later questions wrong and still get a high percentile score! The test is designed to push test takers to their limits, so people rarely get every question right. In fact, you can get a handful of questions wrong and still score in the top one percent.

> ## Teacher Tip
>
> I always tell my students that the best gift that Kaplan can give them is that we can help them avoid being tested "by ambush." You will always know what is coming. I also tell them that they are in control of the test and that "you do the test, the test does not do you." They can dictate the questions, but not how you handle them.
> —Fran Longo
>   Boston, MA

Test Your Best

Work on your test mentality as you prep for the GMAT:

- Test awareness
- Stamina
- Confidence
- The right attitude

Test Tip

Remember that the GMAT isn't like most tests you've taken. You can get a number of questions wrong and still get a great score. So don't get rattled if you miss a few questions. Even those with "perfect" scores of 800 can get some questions wrong.

What does this mean for you? Well, just as you shouldn't let one bad problem or passage ruin an entire section, you shouldn't let what you consider to be a subpar performance on one section ruin your performance on the other. A lousy performance on a section will not, by itself, spoil your score (unless you literally miss almost every question). However, if you allow that subpar section to rattle you, it can have a cumulative negative effect that can ruin your performance on the other section. It's that kind of thing that could potentially do serious damage to your score. Missing a few points won't do you in, but losing your head will.

Remember, the test is designed to find your limits, so it should be challenging. If you feel you've done poorly on a section, don't sweat it. The point is, you must remain calm and collected. Simply do your best on each section, and once a section is over, forget about it and move on.

Never try to figure out which questions are unscored. This practice has gotten countless test takers into trouble. They somehow convince themselves that a certain section is the one that doesn't count, and then don't take it seriously. Are they upset when they find out they guessed wrong. You can't know which questions are experimental, so treat each one as if it counts. That way, you're covered no matter what. If a question you had trouble with turns out to be experimental, it's gravy.

Stamina

You have to work on your test-taking stamina. The GMAT is a fairly grueling experience, and some test takers simply run out of gas when they reach the final questions. To avoid this, you must prepare by taking several practice tests in the week or two before the test, so that on test day, two 75-minute sections plus two essays will seem like a breeze—at least not a hurricane.

One option is to download GMAC's *Powerprep* software, which contains two full-length tests and is now available free from the official GMAC Website at www.gmac.com. If for some reason you prefer not to download it from the Internet, you can have a free CD-ROM version mailed to you when you make an appointment to take the GMAT. The one drawback to the software is that it recycles questions from *The Official Guide to the GMAT Review*, GMAC's own test-prep book, and these questions come from previously administered "paper-and-pencil" GMATs. The computer-adaptive tests on the software have been normed and should give you good indication of what you're likely to score on the actual exam. But the flavor of the test—particularly the Quantitative section—has changed somewhat since it went CAT, so expect that your experience on Test Day will be a little different from your experience with *Powerprep*, especially if you're doing well on the math section.

Another option, if you have some time, would be to take the full Kaplan course. We'll give you access to every released test plus loads of additional material, so you can really build up your GMAT stamina. You'll also get the benefit of our expert live instruction in every aspect of the GMAT. If you decide to go this route, call (800) KAP-TEST for a Kaplan center location near you.

Confidence

Confidence feeds on itself, and unfortunately, so does self-doubt. Confidence in your ability leads to quick, sure answers, and a sense of confidence that translates into more points. If you lack confidence, you end up reading sentences and answer choices two, three, or four times, to the point where you confuse yourself and get off track. This ruins your timing, which only perpetuates a downward spiral, causing anxiety and a tendency to rush in order to finish sections.

If you subscribe to the GMAT mindset that we described at the beginning of the book, however, you'll gear all of your practice towards the major goal of taking control of the test. When you've achieved that goal—armed with the principles, techniques, strategies, and approaches explained in this book—you'll be ready to face the GMAT with supreme confidence. And that's the best way to score your best on Test Day.

The Right Attitude

Those who approach the GMAT as an obstacle, and who rail against the necessity of taking it, usually don't fare as well as those who see the GMAT as an opportunity to show off the thinking and writing skills that business schools are looking for. Those who look forward to doing battle with the GMAT—or, at least, who enjoy the opportunity to distinguish themselves from the rest of the applicant pack—tend to score better than do those who resent or dread it.

Take our word for it: Attitude adjustment is a proven test-taking technique. Here are a few steps you can take to make sure you develop the right GMAT attitude:

- Look at the GMAT as a challenge, but try not to obsess over it; you certainly don't want to psyche yourself out of the game.

- Remember that, yes, the GMAT is obviously important, but, contrary to popular belief, this one test will not single-handedly determine the outcome of your life.

- Try to have fun with the test. Learning how to match your wits against the test makers can be a very satisfying experience, and the reading and thinking skills you'll acquire will benefit you in business school, as well as in your future career.

> **Teacher Tip**
>
> Don't overcorrect yourself and don't think that just because the answer comes easily, it's got to be wrong. Stay confident!
> —Marilyn Engle
> Encino, CA

> **Test Tip**
>
> It sounds touchy-feely, we know. But your attitude towards the test really does affect your performance.

- Remember that you're more prepared than most people. You've trained with Kaplan. You have the tools you need, plus the ability to use those tools.

Managing Stress

The countdown has begun. Your date with the test is looming on the horizon. Anxiety is on the rise. The butterflies in your stomach have gone ballistic and your thinking is getting cloudy. Maybe you think you won't be ready. Maybe you already know your stuff, but you're going into panic mode anyway. Don't freak! It's possible to tame that anxiety and stress—before and during the test.

Remember, some stress is normal and good. Anxiety is a motivation to study. The adrenaline that gets pumped into your bloodstream when you're stressed helps you stay alert and think more clearly. But if you feel that the tension is so great that it's preventing you from using your study time effectively, here are some things you can do to get it under control.

Take Control
Lack of control is a prime cause of stress. Research shows that if you don't have a sense of control over what's happening in your life, you can easily end up feeling helpless and hopeless. Try to identify the sources of the stress you feel. Which ones of these can you do something about? Can you find ways to reduce the stress you're feeling about any of these sources?

Focus on Your Strengths
Make a list of areas of strength you have that will help you do well on the test. We all have strengths, and recognizing your own is like having reserves of solid gold at Fort Knox. You'll be able to draw on your reserves as you need them, helping you solve difficult questions, maintain confidence, and keep test stress and anxiety at a distance. And every time you recognize a new area of strength, solve a challenging problem, or score well on a practice test, you'll increase your reserves.

Imagine Yourself Succeeding
Close your eyes and imagine yourself in a relaxing situation. Breathe easily and naturally. Now, think of a real-life situation in which you scored well on a test or did well on an assignment. Focus on this success. Now turn your thoughts to the GMAT and keep your thoughts and feelings in line with that successful experience. Don't make comparisons between them; just imagine yourself taking the upcoming test with the same feelings of confidence and relaxed control.

Set Realistic Goals

Facing your problem areas gives you some distinct advantages. What do you want to accomplish in the time remaining? Make a list of realistic goals. You can't help feeling more confident when you know you're actively improving your chances of earning a higher test score.

Exercise Your Frustrations Away

Whether it's jogging, biking, pushups, or a pickup basketball game, physical exercise will stimulate your mind and body, and improve your ability to think and concentrate. A surprising number of students fall out of the habit of regular exercise, ironically because they're spending so much time prepping for exams. A little physical exertion will help you to keep your mind and body in sync and sleep better at night.

Avoid Drugs

Using drugs (prescription or recreational) specifically to prepare for and take a big test is definitely self-defeating. (And if they're illegal drugs, you may end up with a bigger problem than the GMAT on your hands.) Mild stimulants, such as coffee or cola can sometimes help as you study, since they keep you alert. On the down side, too much of these can also lead to agitation, restlessness, and insomnia. It all depends on your tolerance for caffeine.

Eat Well

Good nutrition will help you focus and think clearly. Eat plenty of fruits and vegetables, low-fat protein such as fish, skinless poultry, beans, and legumes, and whole grains such as brown rice, whole wheat bread, and pastas. Don't eat a lot of sugar and high-fat snacks, or salty foods.

Keep Breathing

Conscious attention to breathing is an excellent way to manage stress while you're taking the test. Most of the people who get into trouble during tests take shallow breaths: They breathe using only their upper chests and shoulder muscles, and may even hold their breath for long periods of time. Conversely, those test takers who breathe deeply in a slow, relaxed manner are likely to be in better control during the session.

Stretch

If you find yourself getting spaced out or burned out as you're studying or taking the test, stop for a brief moment and stretch. Even though you'll be pausing for a moment, it's a moment well spent. Stretching will help to refresh you and refocus your thoughts.

Now you're ready to take on the challenge of the GMAT. You're going to get a great score. Take a look at the suggestions in the next chapter for the last few days before the test, and then relax!

Stress Tip

Don't work in a messy or cramped area. Before you sit down to study, clear yourself a nice, open space. And make sure you have books, paper, pencils—whatever tools you will need—within easy reach before you sit down to study.

CHAPTER THIRTEEN

Tips for the Final Week

![HIGHLIGHTS]

- What to do just before the test
- How to do well on Test Day
- Canceling scores

Is it starting to feel like your whole life is a buildup to the GMAT? You've known about it for years, worried about it for months, and now spent at least a few weeks in solid preparation for it. As the test gets closer, you may find your anxiety is on the rise. You shouldn't worry. After the preparation you've received from this book, you're in good shape for the day of the test.

To calm any pretest jitters you may have, though, let's go over a few strategies for the couple of days before and after the test.

The Week Before Test Day

In the week or so leading up to Test Day, you should do the following:

- Visit the testing center if you can. Sometimes seeing the actual room where your test will be administered and taking notice of little things—such as the kind of desk you'll be working on, whether the room is likely to be hot or cold, etcetera—may help to calm your nerves. And if you've never been to the test center, visiting beforehand is a good way to ensure that you don't get lost on Test Day. Remember, you must be on time—the computers at the test centers are booked all day long.

- Practice working on test material, preferably a full-length test, at the same time of day that your test is scheduled for, as if it were the real Test Day.

Test Tip

The tendency among test takers is to study too hard during the last few days before the test, and then to forget the important practical matters until the last minute. Part of taking control means avoiding this last-minute crush.

- Time yourself accurately, with the same device and in the same manner in which you plan to keep track of time on Test Day. (The computer has a clock on the screen that you'll see during the test, but it's good to track your own time as well.)

- Evaluate thoroughly where you stand. Use the time remaining before the test to shore up your weak points, rereading the appropriate sections of this book. But make sure not to neglect your strong areas; after all, this is where you'll rack up most of your points.

The Day Before the Test

Try to avoid doing intensive studying the day before the test. There's little you can do to help yourself at this late date, and you may just wind up exhausting yourself and burning out. Our advice is to review a few key concepts, get together everything you'll need for Test Day (see the note on your GMAT survival kit), and then take the night off entirely. Go to see a movie, rent a video, or watch some TV. Try not to think too much about the test.

The Day of the Test

Leave early, giving yourself plenty of time. Read something to warm up your brain; you don't want the GMAT to be the first written material your brain tries to assimilate that day.

Dress in layers for maximum comfort. That way, you'll be able to adjust to the testing room's temperature. In traveling to the test center, leave yourself enough time for traffic or mass transit delays.

Be ready for a long day. Total testing time, remember, is three and a half hours. When you add the administrative paperwork before and after, and the two 5-minute breaks, you're looking at an experience of four hours or more.

It's also best to practice using a timing routine that you'll follow during the real test, so that keeping track of time on Test Day is second nature. Of course, the GMAT has a clock on the screen for you.

Here are some other last-minute reminders to help guide your work on Test Day:

- Read each question stem carefully, and reread it before making your final selection.

- Don't get bogged down in the middle of any section. You may find questions that appear later to be more to your liking. So don't freak. Eliminate answer choices, guess, and move on.

- Start strong. The first few questions are important, so spend as much time as necessary on the early ones.

- Don't bother trying to figure out which questions are unscored. It can't help you, and you might very well be wrong. Instead, just determine to do your best on every question.

- Confidence is key. Accentuate the positives, and don't dwell on the negatives! Your attitude and outlook are crucial to your performance on test day.

- During the exam, try not to think about how you're scoring. It's like a baseball player who's thinking about the crowd's cheers and the sportswriters and his contract as he steps up to the plate: There's no surer way to strike out. Instead, focus on the question-by-question task of picking an answer choice. The correct answer is there: You don't have to come up with it; it's sitting right there in front of you! Concentrate on each question, each passage, each problem and you'll be much more likely to hit a home run.

Cancellation and Multiple Scores Policy

Unlike many things in life, the GMAT allows you a second chance. If you walk out of the test feeling that you've really not done as well as you can, you always have the option to cancel your score—before you see it, of course. Canceling a test means that it won't be scored. It will just appear on your score report as a canceled test. No one will know how well or poorly you really did—not even you.

When deciding whether to cancel your score, a good rule of thumb is to make an honest assessment of whether you'll do better on the next test. Wishful thinking doesn't count; you need to have a valid reason to believe that the next time will be different. Remember, no test experience is going to be perfect, and the test is designed to find the limits of your ability.

Two *legitimate* reasons to cancel your test are illness and personal circumstances that cause you to perform unusually poorly on that particular day. Also, if you feel that you didn't prepare sufficiently, then it may be advisable to cancel your score and approach your test preparation a little more seriously the next time.

But keep in mind that test takers historically underestimate their performance, especially immediately following the test. They tend to forget about all of the things that went right and focus on everything that went

Test Tip

Don't rely on the computer to do the timekeeping. Be your own timer.

Canceling Scores

- You have to cancel before seeing your score. Don't simply cancel because the test felt hard; it's designed to challenge everyone.
- Cancel only under extreme circumstances.

Do You Really Want to Cancel?

The key question to ask yourself when deciding whether to cancel is this: Will I really do significantly better next time?

wrong. So unless your performance is terribly marred by unforeseen circumstances, don't cancel your test. Just remember, cancellations are permanent. Once you hit that button, you can't change your mind.

If you do cancel your test and then take it again for a score, your score report will indicate that you've canceled a previous score. If you take more than one test without canceling, then the three most recent scores will show up on each score report, so the business schools will see them all. Many business schools either count your highest GMAT score or average your scores. Check with individual schools for their policy on multiple scores.

A Final Note

After all the hard work you've done preparing for and taking the GMAT, you want to make sure you take time to celebrate afterwards. Plan to get together with friends the evening after the test. Relax, have fun, let loose. After all, you have lots to celebrate: You prepared for the test ahead of time. You did your best. You're going to get a good score.

So start thinking about all of the great times you'll be having at the business school of your choice!

KAPLAN

Part Three

The
Practice Test

THE PRACTICE TEST
FOR THE GMAT

How to Take This Test

Before taking this practice test, find a quiet place where you can work uninterrupted for four hours or so. Make sure you have a comfortable desk and several No. 2 pencils.

This practice test includes two scored multiple-choice sections and two Analytical Writing sections. Use the answer grid that follows to record your multiple-choice answers. Write the essays on the pages provided, or type them into a word processing program for a more testlike experience.

Once you start the practice test, don't stop until you've gone through all four sections. Remember, you can review any question within a section, but you may not go back or forward a section.

You'll find the answer key, scoring information, and explanations following the test.

Good luck!

GMAT PRACTICE TEST ANSWER SHEET

Start with number 1 for each new section. If a section has fewer questions than answer spaces, leave the extra spaces blank.

QUANTITATIVE SECTION

1. Ⓐ Ⓑ Ⓒ Ⓓ Ⓔ   14. Ⓐ Ⓑ Ⓒ Ⓓ Ⓔ   27. Ⓐ Ⓑ Ⓒ Ⓓ Ⓔ
2. Ⓐ Ⓑ Ⓒ Ⓓ Ⓔ   15. Ⓐ Ⓑ Ⓒ Ⓓ Ⓔ   28. Ⓐ Ⓑ Ⓒ Ⓓ Ⓔ
3. Ⓐ Ⓑ Ⓒ Ⓓ Ⓔ   16. Ⓐ Ⓑ Ⓒ Ⓓ Ⓔ   29. Ⓐ Ⓑ Ⓒ Ⓓ Ⓔ
4. Ⓐ Ⓑ Ⓒ Ⓓ Ⓔ   17. Ⓐ Ⓑ Ⓒ Ⓓ Ⓔ   30. Ⓐ Ⓑ Ⓒ Ⓓ Ⓔ
5. Ⓐ Ⓑ Ⓒ Ⓓ Ⓔ   18. Ⓐ Ⓑ Ⓒ Ⓓ Ⓔ   31. Ⓐ Ⓑ Ⓒ Ⓓ Ⓔ
6. Ⓐ Ⓑ Ⓒ Ⓓ Ⓔ   19. Ⓐ Ⓑ Ⓒ Ⓓ Ⓔ   32. Ⓐ Ⓑ Ⓒ Ⓓ Ⓔ
7. Ⓐ Ⓑ Ⓒ Ⓓ Ⓔ   20. Ⓐ Ⓑ Ⓒ Ⓓ Ⓔ   33. Ⓐ Ⓑ Ⓒ Ⓓ Ⓔ
8. Ⓐ Ⓑ Ⓒ Ⓓ Ⓔ   21. Ⓐ Ⓑ Ⓒ Ⓓ Ⓔ   34. Ⓐ Ⓑ Ⓒ Ⓓ Ⓔ
9. Ⓐ Ⓑ Ⓒ Ⓓ Ⓔ   22. Ⓐ Ⓑ Ⓒ Ⓓ Ⓔ   35. Ⓐ Ⓑ Ⓒ Ⓓ Ⓔ
10. Ⓐ Ⓑ Ⓒ Ⓓ Ⓔ   23. Ⓐ Ⓑ Ⓒ Ⓓ Ⓔ   36. Ⓐ Ⓑ Ⓒ Ⓓ Ⓔ
11. Ⓐ Ⓑ Ⓒ Ⓓ Ⓔ   24. Ⓐ Ⓑ Ⓒ Ⓓ Ⓔ   37. Ⓐ Ⓑ Ⓒ Ⓓ Ⓔ
12. Ⓐ Ⓑ Ⓒ Ⓓ Ⓔ   25. Ⓐ Ⓑ Ⓒ Ⓓ Ⓔ
13. Ⓐ Ⓑ Ⓒ Ⓓ Ⓔ   26. Ⓐ Ⓑ Ⓒ Ⓓ Ⓔ

VERBAL SECTION

1. Ⓐ Ⓑ Ⓒ Ⓓ Ⓔ   15. Ⓐ Ⓑ Ⓒ Ⓓ Ⓔ   29. Ⓐ Ⓑ Ⓒ Ⓓ Ⓔ
2. Ⓐ Ⓑ Ⓒ Ⓓ Ⓔ   16. Ⓐ Ⓑ Ⓒ Ⓓ Ⓔ   30. Ⓐ Ⓑ Ⓒ Ⓓ Ⓔ
3. Ⓐ Ⓑ Ⓒ Ⓓ Ⓔ   17. Ⓐ Ⓑ Ⓒ Ⓓ Ⓔ   31. Ⓐ Ⓑ Ⓒ Ⓓ Ⓔ
4. Ⓐ Ⓑ Ⓒ Ⓓ Ⓔ   18. Ⓐ Ⓑ Ⓒ Ⓓ Ⓔ   32. Ⓐ Ⓑ Ⓒ Ⓓ Ⓔ
5. Ⓐ Ⓑ Ⓒ Ⓓ Ⓔ   19. Ⓐ Ⓑ Ⓒ Ⓓ Ⓔ   33. Ⓐ Ⓑ Ⓒ Ⓓ Ⓔ
6. Ⓐ Ⓑ Ⓒ Ⓓ Ⓔ   20. Ⓐ Ⓑ Ⓒ Ⓓ Ⓔ   34. Ⓐ Ⓑ Ⓒ Ⓓ Ⓔ
7. Ⓐ Ⓑ Ⓒ Ⓓ Ⓔ   21. Ⓐ Ⓑ Ⓒ Ⓓ Ⓔ   35. Ⓐ Ⓑ Ⓒ Ⓓ Ⓔ
8. Ⓐ Ⓑ Ⓒ Ⓓ Ⓔ   22. Ⓐ Ⓑ Ⓒ Ⓓ Ⓔ   36. Ⓐ Ⓑ Ⓒ Ⓓ Ⓔ
9. Ⓐ Ⓑ Ⓒ Ⓓ Ⓔ   23. Ⓐ Ⓑ Ⓒ Ⓓ Ⓔ   37. Ⓐ Ⓑ Ⓒ Ⓓ Ⓔ
10. Ⓐ Ⓑ Ⓒ Ⓓ Ⓔ   24. Ⓐ Ⓑ Ⓒ Ⓓ Ⓔ   38. Ⓐ Ⓑ Ⓒ Ⓓ Ⓔ
11. Ⓐ Ⓑ Ⓒ Ⓓ Ⓔ   25. Ⓐ Ⓑ Ⓒ Ⓓ Ⓔ   39. Ⓐ Ⓑ Ⓒ Ⓓ Ⓔ
12. Ⓐ Ⓑ Ⓒ Ⓓ Ⓔ   26. Ⓐ Ⓑ Ⓒ Ⓓ Ⓔ   40. Ⓐ Ⓑ Ⓒ Ⓓ Ⓔ
13. Ⓐ Ⓑ Ⓒ Ⓓ Ⓔ   27. Ⓐ Ⓑ Ⓒ Ⓓ Ⓔ   41. Ⓐ Ⓑ Ⓒ Ⓓ Ⓔ
14. Ⓐ Ⓑ Ⓒ Ⓓ Ⓔ   28. Ⓐ Ⓑ Ⓒ Ⓓ Ⓔ

Use the answer key following the test to count up the number of questions you got right and the number you got wrong. (Remember not to count omitted questions as wrong.) The "Compute Your Score" section following the test will show you how to find your score.

ANALYSIS OF ISSUE ESSAY
Time—30 minutes

<u>Directions</u>: Analyze and present your point of view on the issue described below. There is no "right" point of view. In developing your point of view, you should consider the issue from a number of different viewpoints. Read the statement below and the directions that follow it. Write your final response on the page provided. Allow yourself 30 minutes to plan and write your response.

"Some people argue that those who do not send their children to public schools should not have to fund these schools through taxes, since neither parents nor children benefit from these schools. They ignore the fact that everyone benefits from the strong economy that a well-educated populace generates."

Which argument do you find more compelling, the case for forcing everyone to fund public schools or the opposing viewpoint? Explain your position using relevant reasons or examples taken from your own experience, observations, or reading.

S T O P
**IF YOU FINISH BEFORE TIME IS CALLED, YOU MAY CHECK YOUR WORK ON THIS SECTION ONLY.
DO NOT WORK ON ANY OTHER SECTION IN THE TEST.**

Use this space to write your essay. (Note: You will have to type your essay on the GMAT CAT.)

ANALYSIS OF ARGUMENT ESSAY
Time—30 minutes

<u>Directions</u>: Provide a critique of the argument below. Focus on one or all of the following, depending upon your considered opinion of the argument: questionable assumptions underlying the reasoning, alternative explanations or evidence that would weaken the reasoning, and/or additional information that would support or weaken the argument. Read the statement below and the directions that follow it. Write your final response on the pages provided. Allow yourself 30 minutes to plan and write your response.

The following appeared in the advertising literature of Travelshack.com, an online travel magazine and vacation resort catalogue.

"Your vacation resort can ill afford not to publicize its offerings on Travelshack.com. Our readership has more than doubled in the past year alone and is dominated by savvy consumers with large disposable incomes. Witness the experience of Snowbert Ski Lodge. Since it began advertising itself on our Website a year ago, it is regularly booked to capacity and its annual profits have increased more than threefold from the previous year."

Explain how logically persuasive you find this argument. In discussing your viewpoint, analyze the argument's line of reasoning and its use of evidence. Also explain what, if anything, would make the argument more valid and convincing or help you to better evaluate its conclusion.

S T O P
**IF YOU FINISH BEFORE TIME IS CALLED, YOU MAY CHECK YOUR WORK ON THIS SECTION ONLY.
DO NOT WORK ON ANY OTHER SECTION IN THE TEST.**

Use this space to write your essay. (Note: You will have to type your essay on the GMAT CAT.)

QUANTITATIVE SECTION
Time—75 minutes
37 questions

<u>Problem Solving Directions</u>: Solve the problems and choose the best answer.

<u>Data Sufficiency Directions</u>: In each of the problems, a question is followed by two statements containing certain data. You are to determine whether the data provided by the statements are sufficient to answer the question. Choose the correct answer based upon the statements' data, your knowledge of mathematics, and your familiarity with everyday facts (such as the number of minutes in an hour or cents in a dollar). Choose choice

  (A) if statement (1) by itself is sufficient to answer the question, but statement (2) by itself is not;
  (B) if statement (2) by itself is sufficient to answer the question, but statement (1) by itself is not;
  (C) if statements (1) and (2) taken together are sufficient to answer the question, even though neither statement by itself is sufficient;
  (D) if either statement by itself is sufficient to answer the question;
  (E) if statements (1) and (2) taken together are not sufficient to answer the question, requiring more data pertaining to the problem.

Note: Diagrams accompanying problems agree with information given in the questions, but may not agree with additional information given in statements (1) and (2).

Note: Unless otherwise indicated, the figures accompanying questions have been drawn as accurately as possible and may be used as sources of information for answering the questions. All figures lie in a plane except where noted. All numbers used are real numbers.

Example:

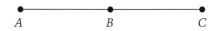

What is the length of segment AC ?

(1) B is the midpoint of AC.
(2) $AB = 5$

Explanation: Statement (1) tells you that B is the midpoint of AC, so $AB = BC$ and $AC = 2AB = 2BC$. Since statement (1) does not give a value for AB or BC, you cannot answer the question using statement (1) alone. Statement (2) says that $AB = 5$. Since statement (2) does not give you a value for BC, the question cannot be answered by statement (2) alone. Using both statements together you can find a value for both AB and BC; therefore you can find AC, so the answer to the problem is choice (C).

GO ON TO THE NEXT PAGE.

1. The price of copper rose by 25 percent and then fell by 20 percent. The price after these changes was

   (A) 20 percent greater than the original price
   (B) 5 percent greater than the original price
   (C) the same as the original price
   (D) 5 percent less than the original price
   (E) 15 percent less than the original price

2. If Sidney is taller than Roger, Roger is taller than Vernon, and Billy is taller than both Roger and Felix, then which of the following statements must be true?

   (A) Felix is shorter than Roger.
   (B) Sidney is taller than Billy.
   (C) Roger is shorter than Felix.
   (D) Sidney is taller than Felix.
   (E) Billy is taller than Vernon.

3. For each size of paper, a certain machine makes copies of an original document at a constant rate. How many copies of one original letter-size document does the machine make per minute?

   (1) The machine takes twice as long to make one 11" × 17" copy as it takes to make one letter-size copy.

   (2) The machine makes 100 copies of one original letter-size document in 6 minutes and 40 seconds.

   (A) Statement (1) by itself is sufficient to answer the question, but statement (2) by itself is not.
   (B) Statement (2) by itself is sufficient to answer the question, but statement (1) by itself is not.
   (C) Statements (1) and (2) taken together are sufficient to answer the question, even though neither statement by itself is sufficient.
   (D) Either statement by itself is sufficient to answer the question.
   (E) Statements (1) and (2) taken together are not sufficient to answer the question, requiring more data pertaining to the problem.

4. A television salesman makes a profit of 25 percent on all sales. How many televisions will he have to sell for $325 each to make a total profit of at least $200?

   (A) 3
   (B) 4
   (C) 6
   (D) 8
   (E) 15

GO ON TO THE NEXT PAGE.

KAPLAN

5. If $xy > 0$, which of the following CANNOT be true?

   (A) $x > 0$

   (B) $y < 0$

   (C) $x + y < 0$

   (D) $\dfrac{x}{y} < 0$

   (E) $\dfrac{x}{y} > 0$

6. What is the value of a if $27^{a-3} = 9^{2a+4}$?

   (A) -17
   (B) -7
   (C) -1
   (D) 1
   (E) 3

7.

Class	Average Age	No. of Students
A	15 years	6
B	16 years	12

Is the standard deviation of ages of students in class A greater than the standard deviation of the age of students in class B ?

(1) The difference between the ages of any two students in class A is always more than 1 year.

(2) No student in class B is more than 6 months older than any other student.

   (A) Statement (1) by itself is sufficient to answer the question, but statement (2) by itself is not.
   (B) Statement (2) by itself is sufficient to answer the question, but statement (1) by itself is not.
   (C) Statements (1) and (2) taken together are sufficient to answer the question, even though neither statement by itself is sufficient.
   (D) Either statement by itself is sufficient to answer the question.
   (E) Statements (1) and (2) taken together are not sufficient to answer the question, requiring more data pertaining to the problem.

GO ON TO THE NEXT PAGE.

8. A list contains 11 consecutive integers. What is the greatest integer on the list?

   (1) If x is the smallest integer on the list, then $(x + 72)^{\frac{1}{3}} = 4$.

   (2) If x is the smallest integer on the list, and y is the greatest integer on the list, then $16x^{-2} = y^{-2}$.

   (A) Statement (1) by itself is sufficient to answer the question, but statement (2) by itself is not.
   (B) Statement (2) by itself is sufficient to answer the question, but statement (1) by itself is not.
   (C) Statements (1) and (2) taken together are sufficient to answer the question, even though neither statement by itself is sufficient.
   (D) Either statement by itself is sufficient to answer the question.
   (E) Statements (1) and (2) taken together are not sufficient to answer the question, requiring more data pertaining to the problem.

9. The average (arithmetic mean) of $3a + 4$ and another number is $2a$. What is the average of the other number and a ?

   (A) $2a$
   (B) $a - 4$
   (C) $a - 2$
   (D) $a + 2$
   (E) $a + 4$

10. Tom reads at an average rate of 30 pages per hour, while Jan reads at an average rate of 40 pages per hour. If Tom starts reading a novel at 4:30, and Jan begins reading an identical copy of the same book at 5:20, at what time will they be reading the same page?

    (A) 9:30
    (B) 9:00
    (C) 8:40
    (D) 7:50
    (E) 7:00

11. Last month, what was the average (arithmetic mean) number of cups of coffee consumed per person by the 25 employees of a certain company?

    (1) A total of 75 one-pound cans of coffee grounds were consumed last month.

    (2) Each one-pound can of coffee grounds makes exactly 54 cups of coffee.

    (A) Statement (1) by itself is sufficient to answer the question, but statement (2) by itself is not.
    (B) Statement (2) by itself is sufficient to answer the question, but statement (1) by itself is not.
    (C) Statements (1) and (2) taken together are sufficient to answer the question, even though neither statement by itself is sufficient.
    (D) Either statement by itself is sufficient to answer the question.
    (E) Statements (1) and (2) taken together are not sufficient to answer the question, requiring more data pertaining to the problem.

GO ON TO THE NEXT PAGE.

12. What is the greatest possible common divisor of two different positive integers which are less than 144?

   Ⓐ 143
   Ⓑ 142
   Ⓒ 72
   Ⓓ 71
   Ⓔ 12

13. If x is a prime number, what is the value of x?

   (1) $x < 15$

   (2) $(x - 2)$ is a multiple of 5.

   Ⓐ Statement (1) by itself is sufficient to answer the question, but statement (2) by itself is not.
   Ⓑ Statement (2) by itself is sufficient to answer the question, but statement (1) by itself is not.
   Ⓒ Statements (1) and (2) taken together are sufficient to answer the question, even though neither statement by itself is sufficient.
   Ⓓ Either statement by itself is sufficient to answer the question.
   Ⓔ Statements (1) and (2) taken together are not sufficient to answer the question, requiring more data pertaining to the problem.

14. Steve gets on the elevator at the 11th floor of a building and rides up at a rate of 57 floors per minute. At the same time Joyce gets on an elevator on the 51st floor of the same building and rides down at a rate of 63 floors per minute. If they continue traveling at these rates, at which floor will their paths cross?

   Ⓐ 19
   Ⓑ 28
   Ⓒ 30
   Ⓓ 32
   Ⓔ 44

15. George takes 8 hours to copy a 50-page manuscript while Sonya can copy the same manuscript in 6 hours. How many hours would it take them to copy a 100-page manuscript, if they work together?

   Ⓐ $6\dfrac{6}{7}$

   Ⓑ 9

   Ⓒ $9\dfrac{5}{7}$

   Ⓓ $10\dfrac{2}{3}$

   Ⓔ 14

16. Which of the following expressions cannot be equal to zero when $x^2 - 2x = 3$?

   Ⓐ $x^2 - 6x + 9$
   Ⓑ $x^2 - 4x + 3$
   Ⓒ $x^2 - x - 2$
   Ⓓ $x^2 - 7x + 6$
   Ⓔ $x^2 - 9$

GO ON TO THE NEXT PAGE.

17. If both 5^2 and 3^3 are factors of $n \times 2^5 \times 6^2 \times 7^3$, what is the smallest possible positive value of n?

   (A) 25
   (B) 27
   (C) 45
   (D) 75
   (E) 125

18. If a rectangle has length a and width b, what is its area?

   (1) $2a = \dfrac{15}{b}$

   (2) $a = 2b - 2$

   (A) Statement (1) by itself is sufficient to answer the question, but statement (2) by itself is not.
   (B) Statement (2) by itself is sufficient to answer the question, but statement (1) by itself is not.
   (C) Statements (1) and (2) taken together are sufficient to answer the question, even though neither statement by itself is sufficient.
   (D) Either statement by itself is sufficient to answer the question.
   (E) Statements (1) and (2) taken together are not sufficient to answer the question, requiring more data pertaining to the problem.

19. If the only stocks that an investor owns are 75 shares of stock A and 100 shares of stock B, what is the total dollar value of his stocks?

   (1) The total value of 3 shares of stock A and 4 shares of stock B is $160.

   (2) The value of each share of stock A is twice the value of each share of stock B.

   (A) Statement (1) by itself is sufficient to answer the question, but statement (2) by itself is not.
   (B) Statement (2) by itself is sufficient to answer the question, but statement (1) by itself is not.
   (C) Statements (1) and (2) taken together are sufficient to answer the question, even though neither statement by itself is sufficient.
   (D) Either statement by itself is sufficient to answer the question.
   (E) Statements (1) and (2) taken together are not sufficient to answer the question, requiring more data pertaining to the problem.

20. How many different ways can 2 students be seated in a row of 4 desks, so that there is always at least one empty desk between the students?

   (A) 2
   (B) 3
   (C) 4
   (D) 6
   (E) 12

GO ON TO THE NEXT PAGE.

KAPLAN

21. What is the ratio of men to women enrolled in a certain class?

    (1) The number of women enrolled in the class is 3 less than half the number of men enrolled.

    (2) The number of women enrolled in the class is $\frac{2}{5}$ of the number of men enrolled.

    (A) Statement (1) by itself is sufficient to answer the question, but statement (2) by itself is not.
    (B) Statement (2) by itself is sufficient to answer the question, but statement (1) by itself is not.
    (C) Statements (1) and (2) taken together are sufficient to answer the question, even though neither statement by itself is sufficient.
    (D) Either statement by itself is sufficient to answer the question.
    (E) Statements (1) and (2) taken together are not sufficient to answer the question, requiring more data pertaining to the problem.

22. A clothing supplier stores 800 coats in a warehouse, of which 15 percent are full-length coats. If 500 of the shorter length coats are removed from the warehouse, what percent of the remaining coats are full length?

    (A)   5.62%
    (B)   9.37%
    (C) 35%
    (D) 40%
    (E) 48%

23. Are the integers q, r, and s consecutive?

    (1) The average (arithmetic mean) of q, r, and s is r.

    (2) $r - q = s - r$

    (A) Statement (1) by itself is sufficient to answer the question, but statement (2) by itself is not.
    (B) Statement (2) by itself is sufficient to answer the question, but statement (1) by itself is not.
    (C) Statements (1) and (2) taken together are sufficient to answer the question, even though neither statement by itself is sufficient.
    (D) Either statement by itself is sufficient to answer the question.
    (E) Statements (1) and (2) taken together are not sufficient to answer the question, requiring more data pertaining to the problem.

24. For a certain performance at a concert hall, a total of 2,350 tickets were sold in the orchestra, first mezzanine, and second mezzanine. How many orchestra tickets were sold?

(1) The number of first mezzanine tickets sold was one-half the number of second mezzanine tickets sold.

(2) The total number of first and second mezzanine tickets sold was 50 percent greater than the number of orchestra tickets sold.

(A) Statement (1) by itself is sufficient to answer the question, but statement (2) by itself is not.

(B) Statement (2) by itself is sufficient to answer the question, but statement (1) by itself is not.

(C) Statements (1) and (2) taken together are sufficient to answer the question, even though neither statement by itself is sufficient.

(D) Either statement by itself is sufficient to answer the question.

(E) Statements (1) and (2) taken together are not sufficient to answer the question, requiring more data pertaining to the problem.

25.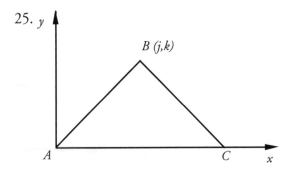

If the area of the triangle above is 8, what are the coordinates of point C?

(A) $(0, 2jk)$

(B) $(j^2 + k^2, 0)$

(C) $\left(\dfrac{8}{k}, 0\right)$

(D) $\left(0, \dfrac{16}{j}\right)$

(E) $\left(\dfrac{16}{k}, 0\right)$

GO ON TO THE NEXT PAGE.

26. If the probability of rain on any given day in City X is 50 percent, what is the probability that it rains on exactly 3 days in a 5-day period?

   (A) $\dfrac{8}{125}$

   (B) $\dfrac{2}{25}$

   (C) $\dfrac{5}{16}$

   (D) $\dfrac{8}{25}$

   (E) $\dfrac{3}{4}$

27. A recipe for soda requires w liters of water for every liter of syrup. If soda is made according to this recipe using m liters of syrup, and sold for j dollars a liter, what will be the gross profit if syrup costs k dollars a liter and water costs nothing?

   (A) $m(w + j - k)$

   (B) $jm(\frac{1}{w} + 1)$

   (C) $m(jw - k)$

   (D) $(j - k)m$

   (E) $jm(1 + w) - km$

28. A certain car dealership has two locations. Last month, an average (arithmetic mean) of 11 cars per salesperson was sold at location A and an average of 16 cars per salesperson was sold at location B. What was the average number of cars sold per salesperson at this dealership last month?

(1) Last month, the number of salespeople at location A was 3 times the number of salespeople at location B.

(2) Last month, the total number of cars sold at location A was 132, and the total number of cars sold at location B was 64.

   (A) Statement (1) by itself is sufficient to answer the question, but statement (2) by itself is not.

   (B) Statement (2) by itself is sufficient to answer the question, but statement (1) by itself is not.

   (C) Statements (1) and (2) taken together are sufficient to answer the question, even though neither statement by itself is sufficient.

   (D) Either statement by itself is sufficient to answer the question.

   (E) Statements (1) and (2) taken together are not sufficient to answer the question, requiring more data pertaining to the problem.

GO ON TO THE NEXT PAGE.

29. If an "anglet" is defined as 1 percent of 1 degree, then how many anglets are there in a circle?

  (A)   0.36
  (B)   3.6
  (C)   360
  (D)   3,600
  (E)   36,000

30. In a certain telephone poll, 600 people were asked whether they were in favor of, against, or undecided on a certain bill being debated in the legislature. How many of the people polled were in favor of the bill?

  (1) The number of people who were in favor of the bill was 200 greater than the number of people who were against it.

  (2) Two hundred people were undecided, which was twice as many as the number who were against the bill.

  (A) Statement (1) by itself is sufficient to answer the question, but statement (2) by itself is not.
  (B) Statement (2) by itself is sufficient to answer the question, but statement (1) by itself is not.
  (C) Statements (1) and (2) taken together are sufficient to answer the question, even though neither statement by itself is sufficient.
  (D) Either statement by itself is sufficient to answer the question.
  (E) Statements (1) and (2) taken together are not sufficient to answer the question, requiring more data pertaining to the problem.

31. A number of bricks were purchased to build a fireplace, at a cost of 40 cents each, but only $\frac{3}{4}$ of them were needed. If the unused 190 bricks were returned and their cost refunded, what was the cost of the bricks used to make the fireplace?

  (A) $76
  (B) $228
  (C) $304
  (D) $414
  (E) $570

32. If x is a number such that $-2 \leq x \leq 2$, which of the following has the largest possible absolute value?

  (A) $3x - 1$
  (B) $x^2 + 1$
  (C) $3 - x$
  (D) $x - 3$
  (E) $x^2 - x$

33. What is the smallest value of x for which $(\frac{12}{x} + 36)(4 - x^2) = 0$?

  (A) -3

  (B) -2

  (C) $-\frac{1}{2}$

  (D) $-\frac{1}{4}$

  (E) 2

GO ON TO THE NEXT PAGE.

KAPLAN

34. What is the value of b?

   (1) $2a - b = 3$

   (2) $a = b - (1 - a)$

    (A) Statement (1) by itself is sufficient to answer the question, but statement (2) by itself is not.

    (B) Statement (2) by itself is sufficient to answer the question, but statement (1) by itself is not.

    (C) Statements (1) and (2) taken together are sufficient to answer the question, even though neither statement by itself is sufficient.

    (D) Either statement by itself is sufficient to answer the question.

    (E) Statements (1) and (2) taken together are not sufficient to answer the question, requiring more data pertaining to the problem.

35. Which of the following is greater than 1,000.01?

    (A) 0.00001×10^8
    (B) 0.0101×10^4
    (C) 1.1×10^2
    (D) 1.00001×10^3
    (E) 0.00010001×10^7

36. If $a \neq b$, what is the value of $a + b$?

   (1) $\dfrac{a^2 - b^2}{a - b} = 6$

   (2) $(a + b)^2 = 36$

    (A) Statement (1) by itself is sufficient to answer the question, but statement (2) by itself is not.

    (B) Statement (2) by itself is sufficient to answer the question, but statement (1) by itself is not.

    (C) Statements (1) and (2) taken together are sufficient to answer the question, even though neither statement by itself is sufficient.

    (D) Either statement by itself is sufficient to answer the question.

    (E) Statements (1) and (2) taken together are not sufficient to answer the question, requiring more data pertaining to the problem.

GO ON TO THE NEXT PAGE.

37. If $2^{2m + 1} = 2^{n + 2}$, what is the value of $m + n$?

(1) $2^{3n - 1} = 256$

(2) $2^{m + 2n} = 256$

(A) Statement (1) by itself is sufficient to answer the question, but statement (2) by itself is not.

(B) Statement (2) by itself is sufficient to answer the question, but statement (1) by itself is not.

(C) Statements (1) and (2) taken together are sufficient to answer the question, even though neither statement by itself is sufficient.

(D) Either statement by itself is sufficient to answer the question.

(E) Statements (1) and (2) taken together are not sufficient to answer the question, requiring more data pertaining to the problem.

S T O P

IF YOU FINISH BEFORE TIME IS CALLED, YOU MAY CHECK YOUR WORK ON THIS SECTION ONLY. DO NOT WORK ON ANY OTHER SECTION IN THE TEST.

KAPLAN

VERBAL SECTION
Time—75 minutes
41 questions

<u>Reading Comprehension Directions</u>: Each passage will be followed by questions relating to that passage. After reading through the passage, choose the best response to each question and mark it on your answer sheet. Base your answers on information that is either stated or implied in the passage, and not on your own knowledge. You may refer to the passage while answering the questions.

<u>Sentence Correction Directions</u>: These questions consist of sentences that are either partly or entirely underlined. Below each sentence are five versions of the underlined portion of the sentence. The first of these, choice (A), duplicates the original version. The four other versions revise the underlined portion of the sentence. Read the sentence and the five choices carefully, and select the best version. If the original seems better than any of the revisions, select choice (A). If not, choose one of the revisions.

These questions test your recognition of correct grammatical usage and your sense of clear and economical writing. Choose answers according to the norms of standard written English for grammar, word choice, and sentence construction. Your selected answer should express the intended meaning of the original sentence as clearly and precisely as possible, while avoiding ambiguous, awkward, or unnecessarily wordy constructions.

<u>Critical Reasoning Directions</u>: Select the best answer for each question.

GO ON TO THE NEXT PAGE.

1. According to a recent study, advertisements in medical journals often contain misleading information about the effectiveness and safety of new prescription drugs. The medical researchers who wrote the study concluded that the advertisements could result in doctors prescribing inappropriate drugs to their patients.

The researchers' conclusion would be most strengthened if which of the following were true?

(A) Advertisements for new prescription drugs are an important source of revenue for medical journals.

(B) Editors of medical journals are often unable to evaluate the claims made in advertisements for new prescription drugs.

(C) Doctors rely on the advertisements as a source of information about new prescription drugs.

(D) Advertisements for new prescription drugs are typically less accurate than medical journal articles evaluating those same drugs.

(E) The Food and Drug Administration, the government agency responsible for drug regulation, reviews advertisements for new drugs before the ads have been printed.

2. Uninformed about students' experience in urban classrooms, critics often condemn schools' performance gauged by <u>an index, such as standardized test scores, that are called objective and can be quantified and overlook less measurable progress, such as that</u> in higher-level reasoning.

(A) an index, such as standardized test scores, that are called objective and can be quantified and overlook less measurable progress, such as that

(B) an index, such as standardized test scores, that are called objective and can be quantified and overlook less measurable progress, such as what is made

(C) an index, such as standardized test scores, that is called objective and can be quantified and overlook less measurable progress, such as what is made

(D) a so-called objective index, such as standardized test scores, that can be quantified and overlook less measurable progress, such as what is made

(E) a so-called objective index, such as standardized test scores, that can be quantified and overlook less measurable progress, such as that

GO ON TO THE NEXT PAGE.

3. A common social problem in the workplace occurs <u>when workers accept supervisory positions, and it causes them to lose</u> the trust of their former co-workers.

   (A) when workers accept supervisory positions, and it causes them to lose

   (B) by a worker accepting supervisory positions, which causes him to lose

   (C) when workers accept supervisory positions, and so lose

   (D) when a worker who accepts a supervisory position, thereby losing

   (E) if a worker accepts a supervisory position, he would lose

Questions 4–7 refer to the following passage.

An important feature of the labor market in recent years has been the increasing participation of women, particularly married
Line women. Many analysts suggest, however,
(5) that women comprise a secondary labor market where rates of pay and promotion prospects are inferior to those available to men. The principal reason is that women have, or are assumed to have, domestic
(10) responsibilities which compete with paid employment. Such domestic responsibilities are strongly influenced by social values which require women to give priority to home and family over paid employment.

(15) The difficulties which women face in the labor market and in their ability to reach senior positions in organizations are accentuated with the arrival of children. In order to become full-time employees, women with
(20) children must overcome the problems of finding good, affordable childcare and the psychological barriers of workplace marginality. Some women balance domestic and workplace commitments by working part-
(25) time. However, part-time work is a precarious form of employment. Women part-timers are often the first laid off in a difficult economy. These workers are often referred to as the "reserve army" of female labor.

(30) One researcher has found that approximately 80 percent of women in their twenties who have children remain at home. Such women who later return to work represent another sector of the workforce facing difficulties. When the typ-
(35) ical houseworker returns to the labor market she is unsure of herself in her new environment. This doubt is accentuated by her recent immersion in housework, a very private form of work. Without recent employment experience, these
(40) women confront a restricted range of opportunities and will almost certainly be offered low-status jobs with poor prospects.

Even women professionals who interrupt their careers to have children experience difficulties.
(45) Their technical skills may become rusty or obsolete, important networks of business contacts are broken, and their delayed return to work may mean that they are likely to come up for promotion well after the age that would be otherwise
(50) normal. Consequently, women, even those of high ability, may find themselves blocked in the lower echelons of an organization, overlooked, or even "invisible" to senior management.

GO ON TO THE NEXT PAGE.

4. The author of the passage is primarily concerned with

(A) advocating changes in employers' practices towards women with children

(B) examining some of the reasons women rarely reach the higher echelons of paid labor

(C) describing the psychological consequences for women of working outside the home

(D) taking issue with those who believe women should not work outside the home

(E) analyzing the contribution of women to industry and business

5. The passage provides information to support which of the following statements about women workers?

(A) It is the responsibility of employers to provide childcare accommodations for women workers with children.

(B) Women in high-status positions are easily able to integrate career and children.

(C) Conditions for working mothers are much better today than they were twenty years ago.

(D) The decision to work outside the home is often the source of considerable anxiety for women with children.

(E) With the expense of childcare, it is often not profitable for women with children to work.

6. The author's discussion of women professionals in the last paragraph serves to

(A) show that the difficulties of integrating careers and motherhood can be overcome

(B) indicate that even women of higher status are not exempt from the difficulties of integrating careers and children

(C) defend changes in the policies of employers towards working mothers

(D) modify a hypothesis regarding the increased labor force participation of women

(E) point out the lack of opportunities for women in business

7. According to the passage, men generally receive higher salaries and have a better chance of being promoted because women

(A) tend to work in industries that rely almost exclusively on part-time labor

(B) lack the technical and managerial experience of their male counterparts

(C) have responsibilities outside of the workplace that demand considerable attention

(D) are the first to be laid off when the economy grows at a very slow pace

(E) suffer discrimination in the male-dominated corporate environment

GO ON TO THE NEXT PAGE.

KAPLAN

8. A state legislator argues that her state's ban on casino gambling is inconsistent and impractical, since other forms of gambling such as bingo and the state lottery are legal. She claims that instead of vainly attempting to enforce the ban, the legislature should simply legalize all gambling, and that to do so would also have the positive effect of reducing the crime rate.

Which of the following, if true, most seriously weakens the legislator's argument above?

Ⓐ Since many people enjoy the thrill of participating in illegal practices, legalizing gambling would probably cause a decline rather than an increase in this activity.

Ⓑ Because prosecutors rarely seek prison terms for illegal gamblers, legalizing gambling would not result in a significant savings of money.

Ⓒ Long-term studies have shown that the number of people who participate in the lottery is higher now than it was when the lottery was prohibited.

Ⓓ Legalizing gambling would entice gamblers from states where it is still banned, and many of them are involved in other illegal activities such as drug smuggling.

Ⓔ Many people who participate in illegal gambling claim that they would risk their money on the stock market if they had more disposable income.

9. A researcher studying cats discovered that during the dream state of sleep, the cerebral cortex of a cat's brain fires messages to its body as rapidly as it does during wakefulness. In an effort to determine why the sleeping cat's body does not respond to the messages being fired by the brain, the researcher removed a cluster of neurons from a sleeping cat's brain stem, the part of the brain that connects the cerebral cortex to the spinal cord. After he had done so, the still sleeping cat got up, pounced as if it were chasing a mouse, and arched its back.

Which of the following, if true, taken together with the information above, best supports the conclusion that the sleeping cat was acting out its dreams?

Ⓐ The neurons that were removed from the brain stem normally serve to trigger the dream state of sleep and the rapid brain activity that accompanies it.

Ⓑ The cerebral cortex is able to receive and transmit sensory information even when the brain is in a sleeping state.

Ⓒ The neurons that were removed from the brain stem are normally responsible for transmitting messages from the cerebral cortex.

Ⓓ The neurons that were removed from the brain stem normally prevent messages fired by the cerebral cortex during sleep from being received by the spinal cord.

Ⓔ The types of brain waves produced by the cerebral cortex during sleep have distinctly different properties from those produced during a wakeful state.

GO ON TO THE NEXT PAGE.

10. Glaciologists believe that the frozen corpse recently found in a melting Alpine glacier, <u>apparently that of a shepherd who is thought to have lived</u> about 4,600 years ago, was preserved uncrushed by snow and ice because of the body's unique topographical position.

    (A) apparently that of a shepherd who is thought to have lived

    (B) that of a shepherd, apparently, who was thought to live

    (C) that of an apparent shepherd who was thought to live

    (D) that of a shepherd who is thought of as apparently living

    (E) that of a shepherd who was apparently thought to live

11. In contrast to Walt Whitman, <u>Ezra Pound considered that late 19th-century American poetry is not a distinct formal repertoire informed by its own ideology, and is</u> essentially an outgrowth of the British poetic tradition.

    (A) Ezra Pound considered that late 19th-century American poetry is not a distinct formal repertoire informed by its own ideology, and is

    (B) Ezra Pound considered late 19th-century American poetry not as a distinct formal repertoire informed by its own ideology, but

    (C) Ezra Pound considered late 19th-century American poetry not a distinct formal repertoire informed by its own ideology, but

    (D) it was considered by Ezra Pound that late 19th-century American poetry is not a distinct formal repertoire informed by its own ideology, but

    (E) late 19th-century American poetry was considered by Ezra Pound not to be a distinct formal repertoire informed by its own ideology, and is

GO ON TO THE NEXT PAGE.

KAPLAN

Questions 12–14 refer to the following passage.

A 1973 Supreme Court decision and related Senate hearings focused Congressional criticism on the 1966 Freedom of Information Act. Its
Line unconditional exemption of any material
(5) stamped "classified"—i.e., containing information considered relevant to national security—forced the Court to uphold non-disclosure in EPA v. Mink. Justice Potter Stewart explained that the Act provided "no means to question a
(10) decision to stamp a document 'secret.'" Senate witnesses testified that the wording of certain articles in the Act permitted bureaucrats to discourage requests for newsworthy documents.

In response, a House committee drafted HR
(15) 12471, proposing several amendments to the Act. A provision was reworded to ensure release of documents to any applicant providing a "reasonable description"—exact titles and numbers were no longer to be mandatory. The courts
(20) were empowered to review classified documents and rule on their status. The Senate companion bill, S 2543, included these provisions as well as others: standardization of search and copy fees, sanctions against non-compliant Federal
(25) employees, and a provision for non-exempt portions of a classified document to be released.

The Justice and Defense departments objected to the changes as "costly, burdensome, and inflexible." They argued that the time limits
(30) imposed on response "might actually hamper access to information." The Pentagon asserted that judicial review of exemptions could pose a threat to national security. President Ford, upon taking office in August 1974, concurred.

(35) HR 12471 passed in March 1974; S 2543 was approved in May after the adoption of further amendments to reduce the number of unconditional exemptions granted in 1966. The Hart Amendment, for instance, mandated disclosure
(40) of law enforcement records, unless their release would interfere with a trial or investigation,

invade personal privacy, or disclose an informer's identity. This amendment provoked another Presidential objection: Millions of pages of FBI
(45) records would be subject to public scrutiny, unless each individual section were proven exempt.

Before submitting the legislation to Ford, a joint conference of both houses amalgamated the two versions of the bill, while making further changes to
(50) incorporate Ford's criticisms. The administration of disciplinary sanctions was transferred from the courts to the executive branch; provisions were included to accord due weight to departmental expertise in the evaluation of "classified" exemptions. The identity of
(55) confidential sources was in all cases to be protected. Ford nevertheless vetoed the bill, but was overridden by a two-thirds vote in both houses.

12. According to the passage, the Justice and Defense Departments opposed the proposed revision of the Freedom of Information Act on the grounds that it

(A) was an attempt to block public access to information
(B) would violate national security agreements
(C) would pose administrative problems
(D) was an attempt to curtail their own departmental power
(E) would weaken the President's authority

GO ON TO THE NEXT PAGE.

13. Which of the following statements, if true, supports the assertion that "judicial review of exemptions could pose a threat to national security" (lines 32–33)?

    (A) Judges lack the expertise to evaluate the significance of military intelligence records.

    (B) Many of the documents which are presently stamped "classified" contain information which is inaccurate or outdated.

    (C) It would be time-consuming and expensive for judges to review millions of pages of classified records.

    (D) Some judges are likely to rule on exemptions in accordance with vested interests of political action groups.

    (E) The practice of judicial review of exemptions will succeed only if it meets with Presidential approval.

14. Which of the following statements is in accordance with President Ford's position on disclosure of FBI records?

    (A) FBI records should be exempt from the provisions of the Freedom of Information Act.

    (B) FBI records should only be withheld from release if such release constitutes a threat to national security.

    (C) It would be too expensive and time-consuming to identify exempt sections of FBI records.

    (D) Protection of the identity of confidential sources is more important than the protection of personal privacy or investigative secrecy.

    (E) FBI records should not be reviewed section by section before being released to the public.

15. Local reporters investigating the labor dispute reported that only half of the workers in the plant were covered by the union health plan; <u>at least as much as a hundred and more others had not any</u> health insurance whatsoever.

    (A) at least as much as a hundred and more others had not any

    (B) at least as much as more than a hundred others had no

    (C) more than a hundred others had not any

    (D) more than a hundred others had no

    (E) there was at least a hundred or more others without any

GO ON TO THE NEXT PAGE.

KAPLAN

16. According to a commonly held archaeological theory, the Neanderthals of Europe, an archaic version of *Homo sapiens*, competed with and were eventually replaced by modern humans, with little or no interbreeding between the two populations. A rival theory, developed more recently, suggests that Neanderthals were more similar to modern humans than previously supposed—that, in fact, modern humans evolved from them and from other archaic versions of *Homo sapiens*.

Evidence that would strongly support the more recent theory concerning the relationship between Neanderthals and modern humans would be

    (A) DNA analyses indicating that modern humans appeared in Africa 200,000 years ago, before migrating to Europe and other continents

    (B) archaeological evidence that Neanderthals and modern humans developed similar cultures, shared stone tools, and performed similar burial rituals

    (C) skulls of early modern humans in central Europe that exhibit a bone near the mandibular nerve that is a typical Neanderthal characteristic

    (D) evidence that the stone tools of Neanderthals remained unchanged for thousands of years, while the tools of modern humans in Europe were more specialized

    (E) biological evidence that Neanderthals had unique physical traits that enabled them to survive ice-age temperatures in Europe

17. Archaeologists have shown that ingesting lead in drinking water was a significant health hazard for the ancient Romans, <u>like that of modern Americans</u>.

    (A) like that of modern Americans

    (B) as that for modern Americans

    (C) just as modern Americans do

    (D) as do modern Americans

    (E) as it is for modern Americans

18. Born Nathan Weinstein in New York City on October 17, 1903, <u>Nathanael West's first novel, *The Dream Life of Balso Snell* was written during a stay in Paris and published when the author</u> was twenty-eight.

    (A) Nathanael West's first novel, *The Dream Life of Balso Snell* was written during a stay in Paris and published when the author

    (B) Nathanael West's first novel, *The Dream Life of Balso Snell*, written while he was staying in Paris, was published when the author

    (C) Nathanael West's *The Dream Life of Balso Snell*, his first novel, was written while the author was staying in Paris and published when he

    (D) Nathanael West wrote his first novel, *The Dream Life of Balso Snell*, during a stay in Paris and published it when he

    (E) when Nathanael West was staying in Paris, he wrote his first novel, *The Dream Life of Balso Snell*, publishing it when he

GO ON TO THE NEXT PAGE.

19. Aggressive fertility treatments are not responsible for the rise in the incidence of twin births. Rather, this increase can be attributed to the fact that women are waiting longer to become mothers. Statistically, women over 35 are more likely to conceive twins, and these women comprise a greater percentage of women giving birth than ever before.

The argument above is flawed in that it ignores the possibility that

(A) many women over 35 who give birth to twins are not first-time mothers

(B) women over 35 are not the only women who give birth to twins

(C) the correlation between fertility treatments and the increased incidence of multiple births may be a coincidence

(D) on average, women over 35 are no more likely to conceive identical twins than other women are

(E) women over 35 are more likely to resort to the sorts of fertility treatments that tend to yield twin births

Questions 20–23 refer to the following passage.

Modern methods of predicting earthquakes recognize that quakes, far from being geologic anomalies, are part of the periodic accumulation
Line and discharge of seismic energy. As continents
(5) receive the horizontal thrust of seafloor plates, crustal strains develop. Accumulation of strain can take anywhere from 100 years in certain coastal locations to over a millennium in some inland regions before a critical point is reached
(10) and a rupture occurs. In both areas, the buildup of strain is accompanied by long- and short-range precursory phenomena that are crucial to earthquake prediction.

Quakes along active faults—like those along the
(15) Pacific coasts—are usually frequent; scientists designate such areas as quake-prone. However, when the time interval between quakes is great, as in inland regions, locating active faults is only a beginning. Geological scars of past subsidence,
(20) cracks, and offsets are useful in determining potential quake locations, as are seismicity gaps, areas where no small quakes have been recorded. Seismologists may also consult the historical record. Primary sources range from eyewitness
(25) accounts of ancient quakes to recent official documentation of quake-related damage.

Once the perimeters of a quake-prone zone are established, a network of base stations can monitor precursory phenomena. Stations must
(30) extend over a wide area, yet be placed at measured intervals to obtain precise readings. Changes in geochemical readings (electric currents, radon concentrations) and in groundwater levels, as well as the occurrence of
(35) microearthquakes, are valuable precursors. Crustal movements—tilting, rising, and expansion or contraction of the ground surface—can be read through triangulation and leveling surveys taken over the course of decades.
(40) Theoretically, if an area's critical strain is

GO ON TO THE NEXT PAGE.

KAPLAN

known—the magnitude of strain necessary to produce a rupture—subtracting the measured accumulated crustal strain from the critical strain will indicate a time frame for an impend-
(45) ing quake.

Violent tilting and foreshocks are among phenomena classified as short-term precursors. Many are still being identified as new quakes occur. Such precursors are valuable since their
(50) appearance can permit prediction of a quake to within hours of the primary rupture. Here, too, historical documents are useful. Seismologists recognized the liquefaction of sand as a precursor after a 1964 quake in Japan.

20. According to the passage, a major difference between coastal regions and inland regions is that in coastal regions

    (A) crustal strain does not occur
    (B) earthquakes are less numerous
    (C) critical points are reached more quickly
    (D) precursory phenomena are seldom observed
    (E) seafloor plate action is less powerful

21. The primary purpose of the passage is to

    (A) clarify the way in which earthquakes develop in inland locations
    (B) show that earthquakes are a result of the normal accumulation and discharge of seismic energy
    (C) discuss the accumulation of crustal strain in coastal regions
    (D) argue that precursory phenomena should be disregarded in attempts at quake prediction
    (E) describe methods of earthquake prediction and explain the importance of precursory phenomena

22. The primary function of the third paragraph is to

    (A) explain the relationship between accumulated and critical strain
    (B) describe the use of precise intervals in establishing networks of base stations
    (C) summarize the differences between earthquakes in coastal and inland regions
    (D) outline some of the methods used by seismologists to predict earthquakes
    (E) suggest that critical strain is not spread evenly along most major fault lines

23. According to the passage, knowledge of an area's critical strain can help seismologists

    (A) estimate the date of a future earthquake
    (B) calculate the severity of an initial rupture
    (C) measure the seismic force along a fault
    (D) revise the distances between base stations
    (E) predict the rate of future crustal movement

GO ON TO THE NEXT PAGE.

24. Until the Federal government began providing low-cost flood insurance to coastal property owners, construction along beaches was limited by owners' fears that their property would be washed away. Since the insurance was made available, however, beachfront construction has boomed and land erosion has increased at a dangerous rate.

Which of the following, if feasible, offers the best prospects for the Federal government to put a stop to the problem of land erosion along beaches?

(A) prohibiting beachfront property owners from embellishing or adding to existing buildings

(B) utilizing computer science techniques to obtain detailed information on the extent and rapidity of land erosion along beaches

(C) enacting building codes requiring new beachfront structures in flood-threatened areas to be elevated above the high water level of a storm

(D) compensating beachfront property owners for moving to a new location off the coast while canceling flood insurance benefits for any new or remaining beachfront construction

(E) requiring beachfront property owners receiving flood insurance coverage to adopt construction standards that will protect their buildings from inundation

25. In commercial garment construction, one advantage of serging over single-needle sewing is that the seam allowance is overcast as the seam is sewn <u>instead of</u> a separate process requiring deeper seam allowances.

(A) instead of
(B) rather than in
(C) in contrast with
(D) as opposed to
(E) as against being done in

26. People with Williams syndrome, a rare mental disorder, are often highly articulate and sensitive. Not uncommonly, they are gifted in music and possess rich vocabularies. Yet these same people, because of their lack of ability in basic arithmetic and difficulty distinguishing left from right, are misleadingly labeled mentally retarded. As evaluated by conventional means such as IQ tests, their intelligence is no higher than that of people with Down's syndrome, despite the fact that people with Down's syndrome have uniformly limited cognitive abilities and show no specialized aptitudes.

The author is arguing that

(A) conventional methods of measuring intelligence, such as IQ tests, are inadequate for evaluating the capabilities of people with certain mental disorders such as Williams syndrome

(B) people with Down's syndrome usually have less verbal and musical ability but more mathematical and spatial ability than do people with Williams syndrome

(C) conventional methods of measuring intelligence tend to consider basic mathematical and spatial ability to be more important than verbal and musical skills

(D) people with Williams syndrome are only rarely given the opportunity to develop their unique musical and verbal abilities

(E) people with Williams syndrome need greater encouragement if they are to develop their mathematical spatial skills

GO ON TO THE NEXT PAGE.

27. When the nineteenth-century German bacteriologist Robert Koch identified a particular bacterium as responsible for cholera, Max von Pettenkoffer, a physician, expressed his skepticism by voluntarily drinking an entire bottle of the allegedly responsible bacteria. Although von Pettenkoffer took his failure to come down with the disease as a refutation of Koch's hypothesis that cholera was caused by bacteria, Koch argued that von Pettenkoffer had been protected by his own stomach acid. The acid secreted by the stomach, Koch explained, kills most ingested bacteria.

Which of the following, if true, provides the most evidence to support Koch's counterargument?

(A) Peptic ulcers, often associated with excessive secretions of stomach acid, are common in certain areas characterized by high rates of cholera.

(B) As von Pettenkoffer later admitted that he had previously had cholera, it is probable that he had developed antibodies that protected him from a second attack.

(C) Cholera is endemic in areas in which poor sanitation results in high concentrations of cholera bacteria in drinking water.

(D) Although stomach acid kills most ingested bacteria, large numbers of E. coli bacteria nonetheless manage to make their way to the lower intestine of the digestive tract.

(E) Cholera bacteria ingested with bicarbonate of soda, a neutralizer of stomach acid, is more likely to result in cholera than if the bacteria is ingested alone.

28. The Limón Dance Company believes that, since the death of José Limón in 1972, they have and will continue to perpetuate the shared artistic vision of Limón and his mentor and collaborator Doris Humphrey, who both choreographed works in the company's active repertory.

(A) they have and will continue to perpetuate the shared artistic vision of Limón and his mentor and collaborator Doris Humphrey,

(B) they have and will continue to perpetuate Limón and his mentor and collaborator Doris Humphrey's shared artistic vision,

(C) it has and will continue to perpetuate the shared artistic vision of Limón and his mentor and collaborator Doris Humphrey,

(D) it has perpetuated and will continue perpetuating the artistic vision that Limón and his mentor and collaborator Doris Humphrey shared,

(E) it has continued to perpetuate the shared artistic vision of Limón and his mentor and collaborator Doris Humphrey,

GO ON TO THE NEXT PAGE.

29. Agencies studying discrimination in housing have experimentally proved that minority clients are often discouraged as prospective buyers of residential real estate and <u>the antidiscrimination legislation of recent decades were only mitigating, rather than abolishing, inequity in housing practices</u>.

   (A) the antidiscrimination legislation of recent decades were only mitigating, rather than abolishing, inequity in housing practices

   (B) in recent decades, the antidiscrimination legislation only mitigated, rather than abolishing, inequity in housing practices

   (C) that antidiscrimination legislation of recent decades has only mitigated, rather than abolished, inequity in housing practices

   (D) that, in recent decades, antidiscrimination legislation has only mitigated, rather than abolishing, housing practices' inequity

   (E) that recent decades' antidiscrimination legislation only were mitigating, rather than abolishing, housing practices' inequity

30. Citing the legal precedent set by asbestos exposure cases, a state judge agreed to combine a series of workplace disability cases involving repetitive stress injuries to the hands and wrists. The judge's decision to consolidate hundreds of suits by data entry workers, word processors, newspaper employees, and other workers who use computers into one case is likely to prove detrimental for the computer manufacturing companies being sued, notwithstanding the defense's argument that the cases should not be combined because of the different individuals and workplaces involved.

Which of the following, if true, casts the most serious doubt on the validity of the judge's decision to consolidate the cases?

   (A) Unlike asbestos exposure cases, in which the allegedly liable product is the same in each situation, the type and quality of the allegedly liable office equipment is different in each case.

   (B) The fact that consolidation will accelerate the legal process may prove advantageous for the defense, as it limits the number of witnesses who can testify for the plaintiffs.

   (C) One of the most common causes of repetitive stress injuries is companies' failure to allow its employees adequate rest time from using computer keyboards.

   (D) Whereas exposure to asbestos often leads to fatal forms of cancer, repetitive stress injury typically results in personal discomfort and only rarely in unemployability.

   (E) The issue of responsibility for repetitive stress injury cannot be resolved without first addressing the question of its existence as an actual medical condition.

GO ON TO THE NEXT PAGE.

31. <u>Each of William Kennedy's novels in the "Albany Trilogy"—*Ironweed, Legs,* and *Billy Phelan's Greatest Game*—are set in the area around Albany, New York,</u> a region whose history also suggested some details of the novels' plots.

   (A) Each of William Kennedy's novels in the "Albany Trilogy"—*Ironweed, Legs,* and *Billy Phelan's Greatest Game*—are set in the area around Albany, New York,

   (B) *Ironweed, Legs,* and *Billy Phelan's Greatest Game*—each of them novels in William Kennedy's "Albany Trilogy"—are set in the area around Albany, New York,

   (C) William Kennedy's "Albany Trilogy" novels—*Ironweed, Legs,* and *Billy Phelan's Greatest Game*—are all set in the area around Albany, New York,

   (D) Novels by William Kennedy—*Ironweed, Legs,* and *Billy Phelan's Greatest Game*—each one of the "Albany Trilogy" novels, is set in the area around Albany, New York,

   (E) Novels by William Kennedy—*Ironweed, Legs,* and *Billy Phelan's Greatest Game*—every one of the "Albany Trilogy" novels are set in the area around Albany, New York,

32. Between 1977 and 1989, the percentage of income paid to federal taxes by the richest one percent of Americans decreased, from 40 percent to 25 percent. By the end of that same period, however, the richest one percent of Americans were paying a larger proportion of all federal tax revenues, from 12.7 percent in 1977 to 16.2 percent in 1989.

Which of the following, if true, contributes most to an explanation of the discrepancy described above?

   (A) Between 1977 and 1989, the Internal Revenue Service increased the percentage of its staff members responsible for audits and tax collection.

   (B) Between 1977 and 1989, the before-tax income of the richest one percent of Americans increased by over 75 percent when adjusted for inflation.

   (C) Between 1977 and 1989, many of the richest one percent of Americans shifted their investments from taxable to untaxable assets.

   (D) Between 1977 and 1989, the tax rate paid by middle-income Americans was reduced, but several tax loopholes were eliminated.

   (E) Between 1977 and 1989, the amount of federal taxes paid by the richest one percent of Americans increased by $45 billion, while the amount paid by all Americans rose by $50 billion.

GO ON TO THE NEXT PAGE.

Questions 33–35 refer to the following passage.

Contamination is the unintended presence of harmful substances or organisms in food. While it is true that recent scientific advances have
Line resulted in safer foods, better methods of preser-
(5) vation, and improved storage practices, it is still necessary to guard against the practices that can increase the likelihood of food contamination. Because foodborne illness poses a potentially serious threat to public health, preventing cont-
(10) amination of safe food needs to be a prime objective of every foodservice manager. Furthermore, a foodservice manager must possess accurate information on the different hazards associated with the contamination of food
(15) in the event that a foodborne illness crisis does arise. A full understanding of the biological, chemical, and physical hazards allows the food-service manager to implement the control measures necessary to minimize the health risks
(20) associated with food, and thus to decrease the possibility of contamination.

The most serious risk associated with food is the biological hazard. Biological hazards are dangers to food from pathogenic (disease-causing)
(25) microorganisms, such as bacteria, viruses, parasites, and fungi, and from toxins that occur in certain plants and fish. When biological hazards result in foodborne illnesses, these illnesses are generally classified as either infections or intoxi-
(30) cations. A foodborne infection is a disease that results from eating food containing living harmful microorganisms. One of the most frequently reported diseases of this type is Salmonellosis, which results from the consumption of food
(35) contaminated with live pathogenic Salmonella.

The other major form of biologically induced foodborne illness is the foodborne intoxication, which results when toxins, or poisons, from bacterial or mold growth are present in ingested
(40) food and cause illness in the host (the human body). These toxins are generally odorless and tasteless, and are capable of causing disease even after the microorganisms have been killed. Staphylococcus food intoxication is one of the
(45) most common types of foodborne illness reported in the United States.

33. Which of the following best expresses the main idea of the passage?

   Ⓐ Despite recent scientific advances, food-borne illness continues to present a serious risk to public health.
   Ⓑ Although chemical and physical hazards can cause a foodborne illness, biological hazards pose the most serious risk of food contamination.
   Ⓒ Knowledge of contamination sources is essential for a foodservice manager to safely operate a food establishment.
   Ⓓ Biological, chemical, and physical hazards represent the main sources of food contamination.
   Ⓔ The illnesses caused by the contamination of food by biological hazards take the form of either a foodborne infection or a food-borne intoxication.

34. The author of the passage would most likely agree that a foodservice manager's comprehension of the nature of potential food hazards is

   Ⓐ crucial to the safety of a foodservice operation
   Ⓑ necessarily limited due to the complexity of contamination sources
   Ⓒ the primary factor in an employer's decision to hire that manager
   Ⓓ utilized exclusively for the prevention of foodborne illness
   Ⓔ vitally important but nearly impossible to attain

GO ON TO THE NEXT PAGE.

35. According to the passage, pathogenic micro-organisms

    A are the most common form of biological hazard

    B can only trigger a foodborne illness when alive

    C are toxins that occur in certain plants and fish

    D include life forms such as bacteria and parasites

    E are difficult to detect because they are odorless and tasteless

36. Still employing the system of binomial nomenclature devised in the 18th century by Linnaeus, new technology enables modern day biological taxonomists to not only classify species, but to sort their evolutionary relationships by an approach that analyzes the sequences of DNA.

    A new technology enables modern day biological taxonomists to not only classify species, but to sort

    B modern day biological taxonomists using new technology can not only classify species, but also sort

    C using new technology enables modern day biological taxonomists to not only classify species, but they also sort

    D using new technology not only in classifying species, modern-day biological taxonomists are enabled to also sort them for

    E when modern day biological taxonomists are enabled by new technology, not only do they classify species, they also can sort

37. American executives, unlike their Japanese counterparts, have pressure to show high profits in each quarterly report, with little thought given to long-term goals.

    A have pressure to show

    B are under pressure to show

    C are under pressure of showing

    D are pressured toward showing

    E have pressure that they should show

GO ON TO THE NEXT PAGE.

38. The impact of the 1930s crisis on the different regions of Country *X* varied depending on the relationship of each region's economy to the international marketplace, with Region *A* most drastically affected. Interestingly, demand in foreign markets for Region *A*'s tropical crops was only slightly affected by the drop in income levels after 1929; the same was true of foreign demand for the temperate-zone basic foodstuffs produced by Region *B*. However, Region *B* was better able to survive the crisis because it could adjust the supply of its crops. Since Region *A* could not, its economy was devastated by the slight decrease in foreign demand.

Which one of the following provides the most reasonable explanation for the fact that Region *A*'s economy was more drastically affected by the slight decrease in demand than was Region *B*'s?

(A) Tropical crops like those produced by Region *A* usually command higher prices on the world market than do basic foodstuffs like those produced by Region *B*.

(B) Region *B*'s economy was dependent on annual crops, the supply of which is easily adjusted because the plants are renewed each year, in contrast to the perennial crops grown in Region *A*.

(C) Because tropical goods are generally bought by more affluent consumers, demand for these products rarely declines even when overall income levels drop.

(D) The temperate-zone basic foodstuffs produced in Region *B* directly competed with similar crops produced by the countries that imported Region *B*'s goods.

(E) Because Region *B*'s economy was dependent on the export of basic foodstuffs, there was only a slight decline in demand for its goods even after income levels dropped.

39. In the late 19th century, <u>when Vassar was a small, recently founded women's college, founding professor and astronomer Maria Mitchell taught as many Astronomy majors in a given year as there are today, when</u> Vassar is a much larger, coeducational college.

(A) when Vassar was a small, recently founded women's college, founding professor and astronomer Maria Mitchell taught as many Astronomy majors in a given year as there are today, when

(B) when Vassar was a small, recently founded women's college, in a given year, founding professor and astronomer Maria Mitchell taught just as many Astronomy majors as there are in a given year today, when

(C) while Vassar was a small, recently founded women's college, founding professor and astronomer Maria Mitchell taught a number of Astronomy majors in a given year such as there are today, when

(D) while Vassar was a small, recently founded women's college, founding professor and astronomer Maria Mitchell taught such a number of Astronomy majors in a given year as are there today, whereas

(E) when Vassar was a small, recently founded women's college, founding professor and astronomer Maria Mitchell taught a number of Astronomy majors just as large in a given year as the number that is there today, while

GO ON TO THE NEXT PAGE.

40. The work of short fiction writer Charles Chesnutt reflects characteristic interests of his contemporary "local colorists" <u>as much as the intellectual ferment and historical reassessments of Black American culture during the late 19th century</u>.

    Ⓐ as much as the intellectual ferment and historical reassessments of Black American culture during the late 19th century

    Ⓑ as much as it did the intellectual ferment in, and historical reassessments of, Black American culture in the late 19th century

    Ⓒ as much as it had reflected, during the late 19th century, the intellectual ferment and historical reassessments of Black American culture

    Ⓓ as much as it was reflective and characteristic of the intellectual ferment and historical reassessments of late 19th century Black American culture

    Ⓔ as much as it does the intellectual ferment and historical reassessments of late 19th century Black American culture

41. Just as the various languages contributing to English broaden and enrich its expressive range with words as diverse as the Arabic *simoon,* the Greek *zephyr,* and the Native American *chinook,* <u>so the many musical traditions coexisting in U.S. culture create unlimited possibilities for the fusion of musical styles</u>.

    Ⓐ so the many musical traditions coexisting in U.S. culture create unlimited possibilities for the fusion of musical styles

    Ⓑ similarly, the coexistence of many musical traditions in U.S. culture create unlimited possibilities in the fusing of musical styles

    Ⓒ the many musical traditions coexisting in U.S. culture are creating unlimited possibilities in musical styles' fusion

    Ⓓ in the same way, possibilities for the fusion of musical styles are unlimited, owing to the many musical traditions that coexist in U.S. culture

    Ⓔ so it is in U.S. culture, where the many coexistent musical traditions make it possible that unlimited fusion of musical styles may be created

STOP
**IF YOU FINISH BEFORE TIME IS CALLED, YOU MAY CHECK YOUR WORK ON THIS SECTION ONLY.
DO NOT WORK ON ANY OTHER SECTION IN THE TEST.**

PRACTICE TEST
ANSWER KEY

Quantitative Section

1.	C		20.	D
2.	E		21.	B
3.	B		22.	D
4.	A		23.	E
5.	D		24.	B
6.	A		25.	E
7.	C		26.	C
8.	D		27.	E
9.	C		28.	D
10.	D		29.	E
11.	C		30.	B
12.	D		31.	B
13.	E		32.	A
14.	C		33.	B
15.	A		34.	B
16.	D		35.	E
17.	D		36.	A
18.	A		37.	D
19.	A			

Verbal Section

1.	C		22.	D
2.	E		23.	A
3.	C		24.	D
4.	B		25.	B
5.	D		26.	A
6.	B		27.	E
7.	C		28.	E
8.	D		29.	C
9.	D		30.	A
10.	A		31.	C
11.	C		32.	B
12.	C		33.	C
13.	A		34.	A
14.	A		35.	D
15.	D		36.	B
16.	C		37.	B
17.	E		38.	B
18.	D		39.	A
19.	E		40.	E
20.	C		41.	A
21.	E			

COMPUTE YOUR
GMAT PRACTICE TEST SCORE

The steps outlined in the pages that follow will allow you to calculate your GMAT Practice Test score. However, keep in mind that this score should not be taken too literally. Practice test conditions cannot precisely mirror real test conditions. Your actual GMAT scores will almost certainly vary from your practice test scores.

Step 1: Figure out your Quantitative raw score. Refer to your answer sheet for the number right and the number wrong on the Math sections. Multiply the total number of Math questions you got wrong by .25 and subtract the result from the total number of Math questions you got right. Round the result to the nearest whole number. This is your raw Quantitative score.

Total Number Right	Total Number Wrong	Math Raw Score
☐	$- \left(.25 \times \boxed{} \right) =$	☐ (rounded)

Step 2: Figure out your Verbal raw score. Refer to your answer sheet for the number right and the number wrong on the Verbal sections. Multiply the total number of Verbal questions you got wrong by .25 and subtract the result from the total number of Verbal questions you got right. Round the result to the nearest whole number. This is your raw Verbal score.

Total Number Right	Total Number Wrong	Verbal Raw Score
☐	$- \left(.25 \times \boxed{} \right) =$	☐ (rounded)

Step 3: Find your Quantitative scaled score and percentile ranking. Use the chart below to find the scaled score and percentile ranking corresponding to your raw Quantitative score.

Math Raw Score	Math Scaled Score	Math Percentile	Math Raw Score	Math Scaled Score	Math Percentile
<2	17	5	20	34	63
2	18	7	21	34	63
3	19	9	22	36	70
4	20	11	23	36	70
5	21	14	24	38	77
6	22	17	25	38	77
7	23	20	26	39	80
8	23	20	27	40	83
9	24	23	28	41	85
10	25	27	29	42	88
11	25	27	30	42	88
12	27	35	31	43	90
13	28	39	32	44	93
14	29	43	33	45	94
15	30	47	34	46	96
16	30	47	35	47	97
17	31	51	36	47	97
18	32	55	37	49	99
19	33	59			

Step 4: Find your Verbal scaled score and percentile ranking. Use the chart below to find the scaled score and percentile ranking corresponding to your raw Verbal score.

Verbal Raw Score	Verbal Scaled Score	Verbal Percentile	Verbal Raw Score	Verbal Scaled Score	Verbal Percentile
< or = 0	16	10	21	32	66
1	16	10	22	33	70
2	17	12	23	33	70
3	18	14	24	34	74
4	19	16	25	34	74
5	20	19	26	34	77
6	20	19	27	36	81
7	21	22	28	37	84
8	21	22	29	38	87
9	22	25	30	39	89
10	23	29	31	39	89
11	24	23	32	40	92
12	25	37	33	41	93
13	25	37	34	42	95
14	26	41	35	43	96
15	27	45	36	43	96
16	28	50	37	44	98
17	29	54	38	46	99
18	30	58	39	47	99
19	31	62	40	48	99
20	31	62	41	49	99

Step 5: Find your total scaled score and percentile ranking. Add your raw Quantitative score and your raw Verbal score from Step 1. This is your total raw score. Use the chart below to find the scaled score and percentile ranking corresponding to your total raw score.

Total Raw Score	Total Scaled Score	Total Percentile	Total Raw Score	Total Scaled Score	Total Percentile
0	200–230	<1	40	560	64
1	240	1	41	560	64
2	250	1	42	570	67
3	260	1	43	570	67
4	270	1	44	580	70
5	280	1	45	580	70
6	290	2	46	590	73
7	300	2	47	590	73
8	310	3	48	600	75
9	320	4	49	600	75
10	330	5	50	610	78
11	340	6	51	610	78
12	350	7	52	620	81
13	360	8	53	620	81
14	370	10	54	630	83
15	380	12	55	630	83
16	390	13	56	640	85
17	400	15	57	640	85
18	410	18	58	650	88
19	420	20	59	650	88
20	430	23	60	660	90
21	440	25	61	660	90
22	450	28	62	670	91
23	460	30	63	670	91
24	470	34	64	680	93
25	480	37	65	680	93
26	490	40	66	690	94
27	490	40	67	690	94
28	500	43	68	700	95
29	500	43	69	710	96
30	510	47	70	720	97
31	510	47	71	730	98
32	520	50	72	740	99
33	520	50	73	750	99
34	530	53	74	760	99
35	530	53	75	770	99
36	540	57	76	780	99
37	540	57	77	790	99
38	550	60	78	800	99
39	550	60			

Part Four

Practice Test Explanations

QUANTITATIVE SECTION EXPLANATIONS

1 **(C)** Here we have a percent problem with no numbers. One thing you know: *You can't simply subtract the percents to get "25% minus 20% equals a 5% increase,"* because the percents are of **different** wholes. The percent decrease is a percentage of the new, increased amount, not a percentage of the original amount. The best way to solve problems like this is to use a concrete number. *Since we're dealing with percents, the number to start with is 100.* (Don't worry about whether 100 is a "realistic" number in the context of the problem; we just need a convenient number to tell us how big the final amount is relative to the starting amount.) Say the price of copper starts at $100. 25% of $100 is $25, so if the price of copper increases by 25%, it rises by $25 to $125. Now the price decreases by 20%. 20% is just $\frac{1}{5}$, so the price drops by $\frac{125}{5}$ or $25. So the price drops to $100. That's the original price, so the answer is (C).

2 **(E)** This problem is just a matter of keeping the information straight. The easiest way to do this is to make a scratchwork chart, putting one person's initial above another when the first person is known to be taller. *The trick is to make sure you don't unwittingly imply a relationship in heights when none is stated; so draw your chart very carefully.* Sidney is known to be taller than Roger, so Sidney's initial goes above Roger's. Roger is taller than Vernon, so Vernon goes below Roger (and Sidney). Billy is taller than Roger, so he goes above Roger. But who is taller: Sidney or Billy? We have no way of knowing, so we'll put Billy next to Sidney. Billy is also taller than Felix, so we put Felix underneath Billy. However, we have no idea of Felix's height in relation to anyone else's, so we should put Felix off to the side. Your chart might look something like this:

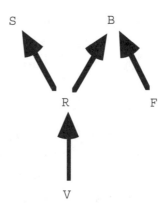

Now try the answer choices. As we just said, we only know Felix's height in relation to Billy, so (A) is out. (B) isn't necessarily true either: Both Sidney and Billy are taller than Roger, but we don't know which is taller than the other. (C) is out for the same reason as (A): Felix is a mystery man. That kills (D), too: Though Sidney and Billy are both taller than Roger, we can't conclude that Sidney is also taller than Felix simply because Billy is. (E) is left by process of elimination. Just to check, Billy is taller than Roger and Roger is taller than Vernon, so Billy does indeed have to be taller than Vernon.

3 **(B)** From the stem: It's a rate problem. We want the number of letter-size copies the machine makes per minute. This can be determined from any rate given for letter-size copies (e.g., number of copies per minute or per hour or per second). *You may have thought of the formula: work = rate x time.* Here we want to determine how much work (the number of copies) gets done in a certain amount of time (1 minute). We need the rate.

(1) INSUFFICIENT: We know that the rate for 11" × 17" copies is half that for letter-size copies, but we have no idea what either rate is. Eliminate (A) and (D).

(2) SUFFICIENT: Here we get a rate for the appropriate size copy. Since we know how many minutes it takes to make 100 copies, we could solve to find how many copies the machine makes in one minute. Choose (B).

4 **(A)** You can save yourself some time on this question if you recognize that you're only being asked to estimate here. You want the **least** number of televisions sold that will push the salesman over $200 in commission. So you don't need to know the **exact** dollar amount of commission that he'll make. He makes 25 percent commission, or $\frac{1}{4}$ of the price of every set he sells.

Each set costs $325; $\frac{325}{4}$ is a little more than $80. At about $80 commission per set, 2 sets give him $160, and 3 sets give him $240. So 3 sets will put him over $200. Estimating saves you the time and tedium of actually dividing $\frac{325}{4}$ and then actually finding multiples of 81.25.

5 **(D)** When you're faced with an inequality, make sure you understand what it means—don't deal with it by just manipulating symbols. Here, $xy > 0$ means xy is positive. This means that either x and y are both positive or they're both negative. They can't have different signs. Seeing the question in terms of positives and negatives can make it easy to answer. If x and y are both positive, (A) and (E) are true. If x and y are both negative, (B) and (C) are true. That leaves only (D), which must always be false. A fraction can only be negative if the numerator and denominator (x and y here) have **different** signs.

6 **(A)** The first thing you know when you see a problem like this is that it doesn't require advanced exponential computation. The GMAT folks aren't interested in difficult computation; they want to know if you understand the basic rules of manipulating exponents. Indeed, the point is to **eliminate** the need to work with exponential expressions. You can do that by converting the expressions on either side of the equation into exponents with the same base. Then the solution becomes a matter of comparing the two exponents. When you're dealing with exponential expressions and you see 27 and 9, you should always think 3^3 and 3^2. The equation can be rewritten: $(3^3)^{(a-3)} = (3^2)^{(2a+4)}$.

When you raise a power to an exponent, you **multiply** the exponents. Thus, $(3^3)^{(a-3)} = 3^{3(a-3)}$ and $(3^2)^{(2a+4)} = 3^{2(2a+4)}$. So the equation is just $3^{3(a-3)} = 3^{2(2a+4)}$. Since both sides of the equation have the same base, 3, we can set the two exponents equal: $3(a - 3) = 2(2a + 4)$. The rest is simple algebra.

7 **(C)** From the stem: In order to determine the standard deviation for a set of numbers, you need to know how the numbers are spread out within the set. Since the table (stem) gives us the averages and the number of students, we need information about how spread out the students are in Class A and Class B in order to solve.

(1) INSUFFICIENT: This statement gives you information about how spread out Class A is, but offers you no information about Class B.

(2) SUFFICIENT: This statement gives you information about how spread out Class B is, but offers you no information about Class A.

In combination: the statements are sufficient since statement (1) gives information about the standard deviation of Class A and (2) gives information about the standard deviation for Class B. Although you cannot determine the exact standard deviations of either class, you can see that Class B has a much narrower distribution of members than Class A and from this you could determine that Class A would have a greater standard deviation than Class B. Choice (C) is the correct answer.

8 **(D)** From the stem: You are given the number of consecutive integers in the set and are asked to find the greatest integer on the list. If you can determine the value and location in the sequence of a specific integer in the set, you can find the value of the greatest integer in the set.

(1) SUFFICIENT: You're given one variable and one equation for the smallest integer on the list. That means you could solve for the smallest integer and add 10 to find the largest term. The correct answer is either (A) or (D).

(2) SUFFICIENT: This one's pretty tricky. Remember that rather than overinvesting your time on a question like this, you could take a quick guess and move on.

You are given a new equation, but since there are even exponents involved, there may be more than one answer. In order to solve, start by rewriting the negative exponents: $\frac{16}{x^2} = \frac{1}{y^2}$. Then cross-multiply to get $16y^2 = x^2$. Since y is 11 terms ahead of x, you can substitute $y - 10$ for x in the equation. The equation then looks like this:

$$16y^2 = (y - 10)^2$$
$$16y^2 = y^2 - 20y + 100$$

Set this equal to zero and solve:

$$15y^2 + 20y + 100 = 0$$

Divide through by 5.

$$3y^2 + 4y - 20 = 0$$
$$(3y + 10)(y - 2) = 0$$
$$y = -\frac{10}{3}, y = 2$$

The only integer answer is 2, so statement (2) is sufficient. Keep in mind you could use trial and error or guess on a lengthy, complex problem such as this. Again, the correct answer is (D).

9 **(C)** We're told that the average of $3a + 4$ and another number, which we'll call x, is $2a$. That means $\frac{(3a+4)+x}{2} = 2a$. We can solve for x in terms of a : $(3a+4) + x = 4a$; $x = 4a - (3a + 4)$; $x = a - 4$. We're asked to find the average of x and a. That's just the average of $(a - 4)$ and a, which is $\frac{(a-4)+a}{2}$, or $\frac{2a-4}{2}$, or $a - 2$. The algebra here is simple; the difficult part is remembering what numbers you're taking the average of, and what number we're looking for. First, we're looking for x, but the answer is not x in terms of a; the answer is the average of x (expressed in terms of a) and a. You must also, of course, remember that you get the average of two numbers by adding them and dividing by two.

You could also have solved this by picking a number for a, say 2. Then, $3a + 4$ is 10, and the average of 10 and the unknown number x is $2a$, or 4. So $\frac{10+x}{2}$ $= 4$, $10 + x = 8$, and $x = -2$. The average of x and a, therefore, is just the average of -2 and 2, which is $\frac{2+(-2)}{2}$, or 0. So look at the answer choices for the ones that equal 0 when $a = 2$. The only one that fits is (C), $a - 2$.

10 **(D)** We're told to figure out when Jan will catch up with Tom. Jan reads at the rate of 40 pages per hour and Tom reads at the rate of 30 pages per hour. Tom starts reading 50 minutes ahead of Jan. Since 50 minutes is $\frac{5}{6}$ of an hour, by the time Jan starts reading at 5:20, Tom has already read $\frac{5}{6} \times 30 = 25$ pages. You might have saved yourself some work by noticing that Jan gains 10 pages an hour on Tom, since she reads 10 pages an hour faster. Since he's got a head start of 25 pages at 5:20, it should take her $\frac{25 (\text{pages})}{10 (\text{pages} / \text{hour})} = 2.5$ (hours) for her to catch him. You can also work out the problem algebraically. The number of pages Jan has read at any given time after 5:20 is $40x$, where x is the time in hours from 5:20. At 6:20 she's read 40 pages, at 7:20 she's read 80 pages, etcetera. The number of pages that Tom has read at any time after 5:20 is $25 + 30x$. We want to know when these quantities will be equal, that is, when $25 + 30x = 40x$. Solving for x we get $25 = 40x - 30x$, $25 = 10x$, $2\frac{1}{2} = x$. So it takes $2\frac{1}{2}$ hours for Jan to catch Tom. Since Jan started at 5:20, this means she will catch Tom at precisely 7:50.

11 **(C)** From the stem: This is an average problem where you are given the number of employees and are asked to find the average number of cups of coffee consumed per person. To find the average, you need the sum total which is the total number of *cups* of coffee consumed.

(1) INSUFFICIENT: This gives you the amount of coffee consumed, but not in cups. Instead you are given the total number of cans of coffee grounds consumed.

(2) INSUFFICIENT: No information is given regarding how much coffee was consumed last month.

In combination: the statements are sufficient since statement (1) gives us how much coffee was consumed in cans of grounds, and then statement (2) tells us how many cups are made by a one-pound can. Treating this like one long word problem, you can see that it can be solved, and choice (C) is the correct answer.

12 **(D)** The hardest part about this question is figuring out what we're being asked. A "divisor" is a number that evenly divides into another number; that is, a divisor is a factor. The number 12 is a divisor of the numbers 12, 24, 36, 48, etcetera. (A number is a divisor of itself.) So we're looking for the greatest number that is a factor of at least two different positive integers less than 144. Look through the answer choices for the largest number that has two multiples less than 144. Remember that one of the number's multiples will be the number itself (the number times one). (A) and (B) are easily

eliminated: 143 is a divisor of 143, but obviously has no other multiples less than 144. The same goes for 142. (C) is a little tricky: 72 is a divisor of 72 and 144, but we're looking for two positive integers **less than** 144. So the answer is (D), 71, which is a divisor of 71 and 142.

13 **(E)** From the question stem: All we know is that x is a prime number. We want enough information to determine which prime number x is. Our method, then, is to try to find more than one prime that fits with whatever information we're given. If we can, the information is insufficient; if we can't—if we can find only one prime that fits with the information—then the information is sufficient.

(1) INSUFFICIENT: If $x < 15$, x could be 2, 3, 5, 7, 11, or 13. Eliminate (A) and (D).

(2) INSUFFICIENT: If $(x - 2)$ is a multiple of five, then x is 2 more than a multiple of 5. So the question is: Can we find more than one prime number that is 2 more than a multiple of five? Yes. Multiples of 5 are 0, 5, 10, 15, 20, and so on. Two more than 5 is 7—a prime number. While 2 more than 10 is 12, which isn't a prime number, 2 more than 15 is 17, which is prime. Eliminate (B).

In combination: Statement 1 narrowed down the possible values of x to 2, 3, 5, 7, 11, and 13. Remember that 0 is a multiple of 5 as well. So both 2 and 7 are 2 more than a multiple of 5, so we cannot find a single answer to the question using both statements. Choose (E).

14 **(C)** This may have looked overwhelmingly complicated, but there's actually an intuitive approach that saves the day. Both people are traveling at *about* a floor per second. There are forty floors between them. So it would take one person about 40 seconds to traverse this distance, and it would take two people about 20 seconds when they are traveling towards each other. So each will travel for about 20 seconds. Now, let's plug that in and see just how far off we are. Twenty seconds is one-third of a minute; Steve travels 57 floors a minute; so in 20 seconds Steve travels $57 \times \frac{1}{3} = \frac{57}{3} = 19$ floors. Joyce would, in the same twenty

seconds, travel $63 \times \frac{1}{3} = \frac{63}{3} = 21$. Well, that makes exactly forty stories that the two would travel, which is exactly what we need. Steve moves up 19 stories and Joyce descends 21 stories.

If you find this method unclear, you could have solved this question by first adding the two rates. Steve travels at 57 floors per minute and Joyce at 63 floors per minute. So they are decreasing the number of floors between them at a rate of 57 + 63 or 120 floors per minute. This is 2 floors per second. Since they start out 40 floors apart, it'll take them $\frac{40}{2}$ or 20 seconds to meet. After 20 seconds, which is $\frac{1}{3}$ of

a minute, Steve will have moved $57 \times \frac{1}{3}$ or 19 floors and he will be on the 30th floor, the same floor Joyce will be on after 20 seconds.

Assuming you didn't see either of these, or were pressed for time, you could have estimated and guessed. Joyce is traveling faster, so she'll go farther. That means they can't have met at the halfway point (floor 31) or any of the floors closer to her. Eliminate (D) and (E). Since they are traveling at nearly the same rate, they would have to meet near the halfway point, floor 31. Eliminate (A). At this point, you can guess between (B) and (C).

15 **(A)** There's a sneaky way to solve this quickly. In 8 hours George will have copied 50 pages, and Sonya will have copied **more than** 50 pages (since she needs only 6 hours to do 50 pages). That means that in 8 hours the two of them together can copy more than 100 pages. But all the answer choices except (A) are longer than 8 hours, so (A) must be correct.

Not all rate problems work out so nicely, though, so let's look at the straight math approach, for future reference.

George takes 8 hours to do a 50-page manuscript, so each hour he copies $\frac{50}{8} = 6\frac{1}{4}$ pages. Each hour Sonya

KAPLAN

copies $\frac{50}{6}=8\frac{1}{3}$ pages. Working together, then, in one hour they would copy $6\frac{1}{4}+8\frac{1}{3}$ or $14\frac{7}{12}$ pages. Divide that number into 100 (the number of pages we want copied) and we'll have the number of hours needed. It's a nasty piece of calculation, but looking at the choices shows us that the only possible solution is $6\frac{6}{7}$.

16 **(D)** Solving this problem depends on understanding how to factor quadratic equations. First solve the equation in the question stem and then plug the possible values for x into the equations in the choices. If you can intuitively see the values for x in the equation $x^2 - 2x = 3$, all well and good. If not, you'll have to solve for x. If $x^2 - 2x = 3$, then $x^2 - 2x - 3 = 0$. The next step is to factor $x^2 - 2x - 3$ into two parenthetical expressions, which will be of the form $(x + ?)(x + ??)$, where ? and ?? are two numbers whose sum is -2 and whose product is -3. There are only two pairs of integers with a product of -3 (that is, -1 and 3, 1 and -3), and of these only 1 and -3 have a sum of -2. So the factored equation is $(x + 1)(x - 3) = 0$. If $(x + 1)(x - 3) = 0$ then $x = -1$ or $x = 3$. So you can plug those values in the choices and see which expression cannot equal 0. When $x = 3$, (A), (B), and (E) are all equal to 0. (C), however, equals 4, while (D) equals -6. So now we check (C) and (D) when $x = -1$. (C) equals 0, while (D) equals 14. So (D) cannot equal 0.

17 **(D)** The correct approach here is not to multiply out the numbers, but rather, to factor completely the large number, then compare its factors to 5^2 and 3^3. Any 5s or 3s that can't be factored out of $2^5 \times 6^2 \times 7^3$ will have to be factors of n. So, completing the prime factorization, we get: $n \times 2^5 \times 2^2 \times 3^2 \times 7^3$. We can combine the 2s: $n \times 2^7 \times 3^2 \times 7^3$. The only common factors so far, then, are two 3s. That means that the two 5s and the remaining 3 must all be factors of n, in order for the two 5s and three 3s to be factors of the entire product. The smallest number that has two 5s and one 3 as factors is $5 \times 5 \times 3$.

18 **(A)** From the stem: The formula for the area of a rectangle is: area = length × width. So here we have: area = $a \times b$. We need values for both a and b in order to solve for the area. Or do we? No, we don't. Since we are only asked for the rectangle's area, rather than its length and width, we can answer the question without actually determining a or b. All we really need is the **product** of a and b. (After all, a rectangle with area 6 could have sides of 3 and 2 or sides of 6 and 1. Either way, it has an area of 6.)

(1) SUFFICIENT: While we cannot solve the equation for either variable, we can find the product of the two variables. We multiply both sides by b. This gives us $2ab = 15$. Now we can divide both sides by 2 and get a value for ab. Eliminate (B), (C), and (E).

(2) INSUFFICIENT: We cannot solve this single equation for either variable, nor can we find the value of *ab* from it. Choose (A).

19 **(A)** From the stem: We want the total dollar value of the investor's stocks. Let's let *a* represent the value of a share of stock *A* and *b* represent the value of a share of stock *B*. The value of all the investor's *A* stock is the number of shares times the value of one share, and the value of all her *B* stock is the number of shares times the value of one share. Since we know the number of shares for each stock, we can set up the following equation: Total = 75*a* + 100*b*. All we need is the value of one share for each stock.

(1) SUFFICIENT: As in an earlier problem, we can find the value of an expression involving both of the variables without finding the value of either variable. We're told that 3*a* + 4*b* = 160. 3*a* + 4*b*, notice, is exactly one twenty-fifth of the investor's portfolio. (She has 75*a* + 100*b*.) So we can multiply both sides of the equation by 25. This will give us—on the left side of the equation—the investor's portfolio. And on the right side of the equation we'll get the dollar value of the investor's portfolio. Eliminate (B), (C), and (E).

(2) INSUFFICIENT: We get an equation with two variables in it. We can't solve for either variable, nor can we find the value of a fraction of the investor's portfolio. Choose (A).

20 **(D)** If you were surprised to get this wrong, you probably picked (A). It's a logic task that many people prefer to visualize, using dashes for desks. We'll just refer to the desks as 1, 2, 3, and 4, in that order, and we'll call the students *X* and *Y*. In order to keep at least one empty desk between the two, we have to keep either one or two empty desks between them. If we keep only one desk between the two, there are two ways the chairs can be occupied: *X* can be in 1 with *Y* in 3, or *X* can be in 2 with *Y* in 4. If, on the other hand, we keep two empty chairs between the students, then there's only one way to occupy the desks: *X* in 1 and *Y* in 4. So the answer is 3, right? Wrong. *X* and *Y* can be switched in all three of our orders. (Look on the bright side: This is the type of mistake that you only make once—better now than on Test Day.)

21 **(B)** From the stem: We need the ratio of men to women. The only thing to keep in mind is the difference between ratios and actual numbers.

(1) INSUFFICIENT: The phrase *3 less than* ruins it. Otherwise we'd have a 1:2 ratio of women to men, giving us a 2:1 ratio of men to women. But with the *3 less than* thrown in, we cannot derive a ratio. In math jargon, *ratios are comparisons by division or multiplication, using a common divisor or multiple; less than is a comparison by addition or subtraction. We can't get the former from the latter.* Dropping the

math jargon and picking numbers, if there are 9 people in the class, we get 8 men and 1 woman—an 8:1 ratio. But if there 12 people in the class, we get 10 men and 2 women—a 5:1 ratio. Eliminate (A) and (D).

(2) SUFFICIENT: $\frac{2}{5}$ is a comparison by division; it **is** a ratio. There are two women for every 5 men—a 5:2 ratio of men to women. Choose (B).

22 **(D)** Make sure you grasp the situation in the question stem. A warehouse has two kinds of coats in it: full-length and shorter coats. Initially 15 percent of the coats are full-length, but then a number of the short coats are removed. We're asked to calculate what percent of the **remaining** coats are full-length. The key to this question is first to calculate the **number** of full-length coats. At first there are 800 coats in the warehouse; if 15 percent of these are full-length, then $\frac{15}{100} \times 800 = 15 \times 8 = 120$ coats are full-length. Then 500 short coats are removed. So that makes 300 coats in total remaining. There are still 120 full-length coats in the warehouse. What percentage of 300 does 120 represent? $\frac{120}{300} = \frac{40}{100} =$ 40 percent.

23 **(E)** From the stem: we are dealing with three integers, q, r, and s. We need to determine either that they cannot be consecutive or must be consecutive. Anything else is insufficient.

(1) INSUFFICIENT: This tells you that q, r, and s are evenly spaced and that r is the middle term, but the terms could be 1, 2, 3; or 0, 5, 10; or a myriad of other options.

(2) INSUFFICIENT: Again, from this statement, all we can determine is that we are dealing with evenly spaced integers, but we do not know whether they are consecutive or spaced further apart.

In combination: Since each statement gave the same information about integers q, r, and s, the statements in combination are insufficient as well. Choice (E).

24 **(B)** From the stem: This is a typical word problem, begging to be set up as an equation. We'll use r for orchestra (we don't want the letter o, as it might get confused with the number 0), m for first mezzanine, and s for second mezzanine tickets. The total number of tickets sold is 2,350. Therefore: $r + m + s = 2,350$. We need to solve for r. Any information that allows us to solve for r will be sufficient, whether or not it allows us to solve for the other variables.

(1) INSUFFICIENT: This equation only relates m to s. We get $m = \frac{1}{2}s$. That tells us nothing about how many orchestra tickets were sold. Eliminate (A) and (D).

(2) SUFFICIENT: By giving us an equation relating r to the sum of the other tickets (the sum of m and s), this statement allows us to replace $m + s$ in the original equation with $1.5r$, leaving only one variable to solve for. We're told that $m + s = 1.5r$.

Thus, we can substitute $1.5r$ for $m + s$ and solve: $r + 1.5r = 2350$. Choose (B).

25 (E) To solve this, you need to know the formula for the area of a triangle, and you need to understand the basics of coordinate geometry. First, you should notice that point C is on the x-axis. That means C has a y-coordinate of 0, which allows you to eliminate (A) and (D). Even if you couldn't figure out how to do any more, this would considerably improve your odds of guessing.

In general, any time they tell you the area of a triangle, you should suspect that the formula for the area $\left(\frac{1}{2} base \times height = area \right)$ *will come into play.* Can we use this formula to find the x-coordinate of C? Well, notice that the segment AC is a base of the triangle. Since this segment lies entirely along the x-axis, and since A is at the origin (with an x-coordinate of 0), the length of the segment is exactly the x-coordinate of C. So if we find the length of the base AC, we'll have C's x-coordinate. Can we find the height of the triangle with AC as its base? The y-coordinate of the apex B is k, so the distance of B above the x-axis is k. Since the base lies along the x-axis, that means the height of the triangle is k. Now we have enough to fill in our equation: $\frac{1}{2} base \times height = area$. $\frac{1}{2} base \times k = 8$, where b, the base, is equal to the x-coordinate of C. We get:

$(b)(k) = 16; \; b = \frac{16}{k}$.

The coordinates of C are $\left(\frac{16}{k}, 0 \right)$.

26 (C) Use the probability formula:
$$\text{Probability} = \frac{\text{Desired}}{\text{Possible}}$$

First determine the number of possible outcomes of rain for City X over a 5 day period. There are two possibilities for each day—rain or no rain—so the total number of possible outcomes would be $2 \times 2 \times 2 \times 2 \times 2 = 32$.

Then to determine the desired outcomes, you're best approach is to list the ways in which you could get rain on exactly 3 days. They are as follows: RRRNN; RRNRN; RRNNR; RNRRN; RNRNR; RNNRR; NRRRN; NRRNR; NRNRR; NNRRR. There are 10 desired outcomes in all, and a systematic run-through of the possibilities should account for them all. So the probability is $\frac{10}{32} = \frac{5}{16}$, and choice (C) is the correct answer.

27 (E) The question asks for the gross profit: that's the cost of the soda minus the cost of the syrup used in making the soda. The cost of the syrup is km, the cost per liter times the number of liters of syrup. The cost of the soda is j (the price per liter) times the number of liters of soda. But the number of liters of soda is just the number of liters of syrup, m, plus the number of liters of water, which is mw, since the recipe requires w liters of water for every liter of soda. Therefore, the cost of the soda is $j(m + mw)$. That makes the gross profit $j(m + mw) - km$. The answer is not expressed in exactly this

KAPLAN

form; finding it depends on your ability to use the distributive law in algebraic expressions. Recognizing (E) as the answer is just a matter of seeing that $jm(1 + w) = j(m + mw)$.

If algebra daunts you, you might have preferred to do this question by picking numbers. The problem is that you still have to figure out how to do the substitution in order to get the right number for the gross profit. As always, pick small numbers for the variables. Say $w = 2$, $m = 4$, $j = 3$ and $k = 5$. Then we have 4 liters of syrup; that costs $4k = 20$ dollars. We have $4w = 8$ liters of water; that makes $8 + 4 = 12$ liters of soda. The total cost of the soda is $12j = 36$ dollars. So the profit is $36 - 20 = 16$ dollars. The correct answer choice should result in 16 if we plug in all the above values for w, m, j, and k. The only choice that works out is (E). *Sometimes when you pick numbers you'll find that more than one choice gives the right answer; in those cases you have to try to narrow it down again with a new set of values, and that can be time-consuming.*

28 **(D)** From the stem: We want the average. Using the average formula, which is $\frac{\text{sum of terms}}{\text{number of terms}}$, we can set up the expression for the average number of cars sold per salesperson, $\frac{11a + 16b}{a + b}$ where a is the number of salespeople at location A and b is the number of salespeople at location B. Any information that allows us to evaluate this expression will be sufficient.

(1) SUFFICIENT: Here we get an equation that allows us to express each of a and b in terms of the other. Since a is $3b$, we can substitute $3b$ for a in our original expression and solve for the average. Eliminate (B), (C), and (E).

(2) SUFFICIENT: Here we get the total number of cars sold at each of A and B. This allows us to determine the number of salespeople at each location, which we've symbolized as a and b. With values for a and b, we can find the value of the expression $\frac{11a + 16b}{a + b}$ and thus determine the average. Choose (D).

29 **(E)** If an "anglet" is one percent of a degree, then there are 100 anglets in each degree. Since there are 360 degrees in a circle, there are 100 × 360, or 36,000, anglets in a circle. Never let the introduction of a new term like "anglet" worry you; *questions that introduce new terms are usually easy, involving little more than a simple substitution.*

30 **(B)** From the stem: You know that 600 people were polled, and you know that they voted either in one of three categories: in favor, against, or undecided. In terms of equations and variables, we have 1 equation and 3 unknowns: $F + A + U = 600$.

(1) INSUFFICIENT: Gives you information about those who were in favor and those who were against, but since we are given no information on those undecided, the statement is insufficient.

(2) SUFFICIENT: Gives you the number undecided and an equation from which you can find the number against the bill. Once these two values are determined, you can find the number of those in favor. Choice (B) is the correct answer.

31 **(B)** We're looking for the cost of the bricks that were actually used to make the fireplace. In order to find that, we need to know how many bricks were used, and what each brick costs. Since $\frac{3}{4}$ of the bricks were used, $\frac{1}{4}$ of the bricks weren't used. That unused quarter of the total amounted to 190 bricks. That means that number of bricks that were used, $\frac{3}{4}$ of the total, amounted to 3×190, or 570 bricks. Each brick cost 40 cents, so the total cost of the bricks that were used must have been 40×570 = 228 dollars.

32 **(A)** This problem asks for the expression with the greatest **absolute** value, *so we have to remember to consider negative values; problems like this are often set up to trip up those who assume the answer must be a positive number.* The only way to solve this is to try each choice. *Since* x *can be any number from* −2 *to* 2 *inclusive, and we're looking for the greatest possible absolute value, it makes sense to plug these two extreme values of* x *into each choice.* For each choice, then, the largest possible absolute value

will result either from giving x the value of 2 or from giving x the value of −2.

In (A), $3x - 1$ is 5 when $x = 2$, and −7 when $x = -2$. In (B), $x^2 + 1$ is 5 when $x = 2$ and also when $x = -2$. In (C), $3 - x$ is 1 when $x = 2$, and 5 when $x = -2$. In (D), $x - 3$ is −1 when $x = 2$, and −5 when $x = -2$. In (E), $x^2 - x$ is 2 when $x = 2$, and 6 when $x = -2$. Out of these possible values for the expressions, −7 has the largest absolute value, so (A) is the answer.

33 **(B)** Don't make the mistake of multiplying out the parentheses—that would be the equivalent of beginning a race by shooting yourself in the foot. We're presented with two quantities that have a product of zero. As a good test taker, you realize that in order for this to be the case, at least one of the two quantities must have a value of zero. *So the question is really asking: What's the smallest value of* x *that will make one of these parenthetical expressions equal zero?*

You can save yourself further time by checking the second expression first (it probably looked easier to work with anyway). Suppose $x^2 - 4 = 0$. Then $x^2 = 4$, and x can be 2 or −2. That immediately narrows down the choices to (A) and (B), since −2 is already smaller than (C), (D), and (E). You can then check (A) directly by seeing whether $\frac{12}{x} + 36$ is 0 when x = −3: $\frac{12}{-3} + 36$ equals $(-4) + 36$, which equals 32,

KAPLAN

which is definitely not 0. So (A) can't be the answer and we're left with only (B). If you didn't see this testwise shortcut, you could have checked for any other possible values of x by setting $\frac{12}{x} + 36$ equal to 0, and solving: $\frac{12}{x} + 36 = 0$; $\frac{12}{x} = -36$; $-36x = 12$; $x = \frac{12}{-36}$; $x = -\frac{1}{3}$.

You'd still have discovered that -2 is the smallest value of x, but it's better to have known the GMAT well enough to sense the shortcut

34 **(B)** From the stem: We need b. There's nothing more to it than that.

(1) INSUFFICIENT: This is one equation with two variables. We cannot solve for either variable. Eliminate (A) and (D).

(2) SUFFICIENT: *The equation hasn't been simplified, and that should set off alarm bells.* It looks to be insoluble: one equation, two variables. Yet, the variable a occurs twice. When we simplify, by removing the parentheses, we get $a = b - 1 + a$. Subtracting a from each side, we have $0 = b - 1$. This can be solved for b. Choose (B).

35 **(E)** Solving this is just a matter of restating each answer choice as a simple number by multiplying out the powers of 10. *To multiply by a positive power of 10, simply move the decimal point to the right the same number of places as the exponent of 10.* So to simplify (A),

take 0.00001 and move the decimal point 8 places to the right. After 5 places we have 1.0; 3 more places gives us 1,000. We want a number greater than 1,000.01, so we move on. Moving the decimal 4 places to the right in (B) only gives us 101. (C) becomes 110. (D) converts to 1,000.01 exactly. Therefore we know (E) is right without figuring it out (as a matter of fact it converts to 1,000.1). If you know your exponents, this is simple. One final caution, though: On simple problems like this, don't get sloppy. It would be a shame to miss an easy question just because you got a little careless moving the decimal point over.

36 **(A)** From the stem: We want information about the values a and b or about the value of their sum. We keep in mind that neither a nor b is necessarily positive or an integer.

(1) SUFFICIENT: The numerator is *the difference of two squares*. This is a common expression on the GMAT and we know instantly that it factors into $(a + b)$ times $(a - b)$. Canceling the $(a - b)$ from both the numerator and denominator, we're left with the value of $a + b$. Eliminate (B), (C), and (E).

(2) INSUFFICIENT: There's a common GMAT trap here. You might have been inclined to remove the exponent from the left side of the equation in order to get a value for $a + b$. Can we find the value of $a + b$ knowing that $(a + b) = 36$? No. There are two numbers that, when squared, result in 36. So $a + b$ could equal 6 or -6. Choose (A).

37

(D) From the stem: As with the previous question, we want information about the sum of two variables. Unlike the previous question, though, we get useful information. If the two expressions are equal, and if the bases are equal, then the exponents have to be equal. (2 taken to some power can only equal 2 to that power.) So we start out knowing that $(2m + 1) = (n + 2)$. One equation, two variables.

(1) SUFFICIENT: Approached abstractly, we have another, different equation. Thus, we now have two equations and two variables. We can solve for the variables and add them. Approached less abstractly, this equation allows us to solve for the value of n (hint: 256 is 2^8). Substituting the value of n into the original equation, we can solve for m. Then it's just a matter of adding. Eliminate (B), (C), and (E).

(2) SUFFICIENT: Similar story here. It's a second, different equation with the same two variables found in the equation in the question stem, so we can solve for the values of the variables. Thus, we can determine their sum. Choose (D).

KAPLAN

Verbal Section Explanations

1 (C) In question 1 we're asked to strengthen the researchers' alarming conclusion that the misinformation they've discovered in journal advertisements could lead doctors into misprescribing drugs. This argument works only if we assume that doctors give credence to the ads. Since *the best way to strengthen an argument is to confirm the truth of an assumption*, we want a choice that says doctors are indeed influenced by the information in the ads. According to (C), doctors use the ads as a serious resource for information about new prescription drugs. So (C) is correct.

(A) indicates the ads are important to publishers as a source of revenue, but does nothing to show that the ads are important to doctors, let alone that they can affect doctors' prescriptions.

(B) and (D) support the notion that the ads are or can be misleading: (B) tells us that journal editors often can't tell whether an ad is deceptive; (D) tells us that ads are usually less accurate than articles evaluating the drugs. But we already know that the ads contain misleading information, so these choices add nothing. (E) weakens the argument by suggesting that a government agency is watching out for potentially harmful, misleading claims.

2 (E) Did you spot the incorrect verb in the original? The beginning of the underlined part should be "an index . . . that **is** called objective," not "an index . . . that **are** called objective." If you catch an obvious error like this, quickly scan the other choices for versions that repeat it. That knocks out (B). (Remember you don't need to reread (A); it's the same as the original, and we already know that's

wrong.) Now, how to pick between (C), (D), and (E)? The crucial difference here is between the wordy phrase *progress, such as what is made*—in (C) and (D)—and (E)'s *progress such as that.* (E)'s wording is preferable.

3 (C) Sometimes the GMAT requires you to recognize grammar you would never use in spoken English. That's true for the use of *and so* here. *And so, to do so,* and similar uses of the word *so* are often featured in GMAT English. Because they're infrequently used even in written English, they sound funny, and the test writers are hoping you'll think they're wrong. Here (C) is best because it replaces (A)'s awkward *it causes them to lose* with the much shorter *so lose.*

Passage 1—Women in the Labor Market

Topic and Scope: Participation of women in the labor market; specifically, the status of women in matters of pay and promotion.

Purpose and Main Idea: The author wants to identify and discuss two to three specific conditions that restrict job opportunities for women, particularly women with children. The main idea is summed up in the second sentence: The author agrees with what "analysts" say—"women comprise a secondary labor market where rates of pay and promotion prospects are inferior to those available to men."

Paragraph Structure: Paragraph 1 lays out the basic viewpoint, explaining that women are disadvantaged by "social values which require women to give priority to home and family over paid employment." Paragraph 2 adds evidence: In order to meet domestic responsibilities, many women work part time, a "precarious" form of employment. Paragraphs 3 and 4 discuss problems faced by women who leave the job market temporarily to have children. Many end up in low-status jobs, and even professional women fail to get promoted.

The Big Picture: The author's viewpoint and the paragraph structure are both clear-cut. And the topic itself is pretty familiar and accessible. So grab onto the small handful of key points, don't linger over the paragraphs, and move confidently to the questions.

The Questions

4 **(B)** This is the only choice that encompasses the clearly expressed topic, scope, and point of view.

(A) incorrectly broadens the scope to employers' practices in general, whereas the author is concerned only with pay and promotion. Besides, the author restricts himself to discussing the current state of affairs; he doesn't advocate anything.

(C) takes a detail in paragraphs 2 and 3 and wrongly blows it up into the author's primary concern.

(D) and (E) are completely off the topic, and, contrary to what (D) says, the author doesn't take issue with others' views.

- The correct answer to "global" questions has to cover the same topic and scope, and reflect the same tone, as the passage itself.

5 **(D)** Lines 34–36 say that "when the typical houseworker returns to the labor market she is unsure of herself in her new environment." Such women, in other words, experience anxiety.

Lines 23–25 suggest that it is up to working women themselves, not employers (A), to make child-care arrangements.

(B) is an *au contraire* choice. Paragraph 4 says that women in high-status positions, such as professionals, face problems advancing their careers while caring for their children.

The passage doesn't compare conditions for today's working mothers with those that existed twenty years ago (C). Although lines 18–23 imply that reasonably priced child care can be difficult to find (E), the passage doesn't go so far as to suggest that the expense of child care often makes it unprofitable for mothers to work.

6 **(B)** The gist of paragraph 4 is that even women of high ability and status—professionals—face career problems if they decide to have children.

(A) is an *au contraire* choice. The point of paragraph 4 is to explain that even the most able women may *not* be able to "overcome" the difficulties "of integrating career and motherhood."

Paragraph 4 does not address labor policies (C) or increasing female participation in the labor force (D). Moreover, the author doesn't ever "defend changes" or "modify a hypothesis."

KAPLAN

(E) is too vague. Paragraph 4 draws a definite link between career opportunities and children: It's not about a general lack of career opportunities for women.

- When you're asked about the *why* of a detail, pay careful attention to the context in which it appears.

7 **(C)** The second sentence of paragraph 1 says that rates of pay and promotion are worse for women than for men. The next sentence attributes this situation to the fact that women have responsibilities at home that interfere with their jobs.

The passage states that some women work part time (lines 30–32), not that women in general tend to get work in industries that rely on part-time labor (A).

Paragraph 4 indicates that professional women sometimes lack the technical skills of their male counterparts (B) but this isn't the reason the passage gives for their inferior pay and promotion rates.

According to lines 26–27, part-time women, not women in general (as choice (D) says), are likely to be laid off in an economic slowdown. Besides, this fact has nothing to do with inferior pay and promotion rates.

(E) is beyond the scope of the passage: The author doesn't discuss general workplace discrimination against women.

- Don't overthink. Go to the relevant portion of text and find the answer.

8 **(D)** The legislator in question 8 argues (here's the conclusion) that the state ban on casino gambling should be rescinded because (here's the evidence) one, it's inconsistent with other state policies; two, it's "impractical" because efforts to enforce it are hopeless; and three, legalizing gambling would reduce the crime rate. We're asked for the best weakener, and *in an argument that makes a proposal, we know to look for a choice that shows that the proposal won't achieve its goal (usually for a reason the author hasn't considered) or that it carries unacceptable side effects.* (D) says that legalizing gambling would attract criminals who habitually engage in illegal activities other than gambling. Although their gambling would now be legal, as the author argues, (D) strongly suggests that these hoods would bring other illegal activities to the state. This gravely weakens the legislator's claim that legalizing gambling would reduce crime.

The key to rejecting the incorrect choices lies in accurately remembering the legislator's argument; beware of choices that attack claims she didn't make or undermine a conclusion that she didn't draw. (A) implies that dropping the ban would reduce gambling and (C) implies that it may increase it. Yet the legislator's argument requires neither that gambling remain popular nor that it not become more popular. As for (B), the legislator never gave "significant savings" as a reason for revoking the ban, so the news that there won't be any such savings doesn't hurt her. It's not at all clear what effect, if any, (E) has on her proposal. That alone is good enough reason to discard it. *Remember, in GMAT Critical Reasoning you don't want to make an argument on behalf of an answer choice. If the connection between a choice and an argument is vague or tenuous, look elsewhere.*

9 **(D)** The Kaplan strategy of *looking at the question stem before tackling the stimulus* really pays off with question 9. We're given the conclusion—that the cat in question is acting out its dreams. We'll be looking for the researchers' evidence, and in order to answer the question, we'll be thinking along the lines of adding to this evidence so as to further support the conclusion. Realizing all of this, before we even read the stimulus, makes its story and our lives easier.

Before neuron removal, we're told, the dreaming cat's cortex fires messages but the cat doesn't respond. After neuron removal, the dreaming cat gets up and jumps around. We want to strengthen the conclusion that the cat is acting out its dreams. (D) establishes that the neurons prevented the cerebral cortex's messages from reaching the spinal cord during sleep. Therefore, the removal of the neurons allowed, for the first time, messages to reach the spinal cord while the cat slept. This makes it more plausible that when the cat rose and pounced, it was responding to those messages—acting out its dreams.

(A) is ambiguous and unhelpful. If the cat wasn't already dreaming when the neurons were removed, then their removal would presumably prevent the cat from dreaming (since they trigger the dream state); in that case, it couldn't have been acting out its dreams. If the cat was already in a dream state when the neurons were removed, then we have no idea about the effect of removing the neurons. (B) adds nothing to the information in the stimulus. We already know that the cerebral cortex is busy during sleep. And from the strategic point of view, (B) ignores the experiment with the neurons, and that's precisely what we're interested in; *always be wary of choices that ignore a critical part of the stimulus.* If (C)

were true, there would be no messages, therefore no dreams, coming from the cerebral cortex after the neurons were removed, so the cat couldn't be acting out its dreams. Be careful; *on strengthen/weaken questions, the test makers commonly present choices that have the opposite effect of the one they ask for.* (E) is irrelevant, although it might have been tempting to create an argument around it (don't do that!): "brain waves" (*a new term, be wary*) don't matter. We're interested in how brain messages (dreams) travel; specifically, what stops them, during the sleeping state, from being acted on.

10 **(A)** From a quick scan of the answers, you see the main difference is between choices that use *is* and choices that use *was*. Now, use logic. Pay attention to the time clue *recently*. The shepherd's body was only **recently** found, so it wouldn't make sense to put the discussion of "How long ago did he live?" in the past. *Is,* in (A) and (D), must be correct. It's also important to be able to recognize and quickly eliminate illogical choices like (D). (D)'s wording doesn't really make sense. What does it mean for a dead person to be "thought of as apparently living"?

11

(C) Pick up on clues. Here, the sentence practically hits you over the head with one. It begins *In contrast to,* so there **has** to be some kind of contrast. Problem is, the original version doesn't give you one. It uses the connector *and* to join the sentence halves. Scanning choices, we see that (B), (C), and (D) all end with *but.* This makes sense—American poetry is **not** distinct **but** an outgrowth. However, (D) uses the unnecessary *it was considered by.* Avoid the passive when you can. Finally, every time you see a connector like *not . . . but,* remember you need parallelism between the part of the sentence following *not* and the part following *but.* (C) gives it to you.

Passage 2—Freedom of Information Act

Topic and Scope: Freedom of Information Act; specifically, the amendments to the Act.

Purpose and Main Idea: The author's intent is to describe the positions and roles of the government's legislative, judicial, and executive branches in regard to the Freedom of Information Act's revision. Because the author's purpose is descriptive, not argumentative, the passage has no specific main idea.

Paragraph Structure: Paragraph 1 describes the Freedom of Information Act and provides the historical context for the revision process. Paragraph 2 outlines proposed House and Senate amendments. Paragraph 3 reveals that the executive branch was opposed to these amendments. Paragraph 4 adds more detail about the legislative amendments. Paragraph 5 indicates that the legislative and executive branches unsuccessfully sought compromise; the amendments were adopted despite an executive veto.

The Questions

12

(C) Lines 27–29 say that the Justice and Defense departments objected to revision as "costly, burdensome, and inflexible." They opposed revision, in other words, for administrative reasons.

According to lines 29–31 the Justice and Defense departments argued that changes "might actually hamper access to information." But they did not go so far as to suggest that the revision was an attempt to limit public access to information (A).

Although the Pentagon thought that revision might pose national security problems, it didn't argue that changes violated specific national security agreements (B).

(D) and (E) are beyond the scope: Neither the Justice nor the Defense department protested revision on the grounds that it would weaken either their power or presidential authority.

- The correct answer to an explicit detail question is always there in the text. Find and reread the relevant piece of text. Don't answer based on a hunch.

13

(A) The Pentagon voiced this argument, apparently concerned that the judiciary did not have the "departmental expertise" to determine which military records could be released without jeopardizing national security.

(B) and (C) speak of records in general, not military records in particular, so national security isn't necessarily at issue in these choices.

(D) says that some judges may be politically motivated, but that doesn't mean that they'll jeopardize national security.

(E) doesn't connect judicial review to national security. Does the President's approval have any necessary connection to national security? Nothing within the passage would imply this. You will never have to add information or make unwarranted assumptions to justify the correct answer. That kind of creativity isn't rewarded on the GMAT.

- Learn to spot and eliminate answer choices that are too broad in scope.

14 **(A)** Lines 43–46 indicate that Ford was opposed to the release of FBI records. He didn't want them to be open to public scrutiny.

(B) and (E)—*au contraire* choices—wrongly suggest that Ford was open to the idea of a release of FBI records.

Ford might have opposed a release of FBI records for administrative reasons (C), but the passage doesn't say for sure.

There is no hint in the passage that Ford believed it was more important to protect confidential sources than personal privacy or investigative secrecy (D). Paragraph 4 tells us that all three are protected by the Hart amendment, but no distinction like (D)'s is drawn.

- Don't go too far with inferences. The correct answer is usually a paraphrase of information in the passage.

15 **(D)** Here's a great example of how concision is rewarded on the GMAT. There's no need to use an awkward construction like "at least as much as a hundred and more" when (D) says the same thing simply and more concisely.

16 **(C)** In question 16 you're asked to compare two rival theories; this is a GMAT question type that crops up regularly. *The key is understanding exactly what is under dispute and exactly which theory you're concerned with.* The traditional theory says that Neanderthals were simply superseded by modern humans and there was virtually no interbreeding between the two groups. The new theory says that modern humans evolved from Neanderthals and from other early types of *Homo sapiens*, and are therefore descendants of Neanderthals. So the dispute is whether Neanderthals were supplanted by a rival group of unrelated humans, or by humans who were at least partly descended from them. We're asked to support the new theory. (C) does that by presenting a physical similarity between the early modern humans and the Neanderthals, both of whom lived in central Europe. So we have sort of a "missing link" between the two groups; this doesn't prove the new theory, but we are only asked for support. *On GMAT "strengthen the argument" questions, out and out proof isn't necessary.*

Keep track of the question and the different theories! (A) provides more support for the old theory than for the new one: If modern humans first appeared in Africa and then migrated to Europe, they can't have evolved from "the Neanderthals of Europe." (B) might seem tempting, but these similarities between Neanderthals and modern humans are only cultural; they don't imply a close physical relationship between the groups. (B) might have looked good at first, but you should have dropped it when you read (C). (D), like (B), compares the cultures of the two groups, but it points out differences. Since cultural similarities don't provide much support for the theory that the groups are biologically related, cultural differences certainly can't do the job. (E) refers to "unique physical traits" of Neanderthals, which is the opposite of what we want. We want something that suggests a biological link between Neanderthals and modern humans, whereas (E) sets Neanderthals apart.

17 (E) Whenever you see a sentence with the word *like*, remember that it must compare the same type of things, using language that is similar. Ingesting lead "was a significant health hazard **for** the ancient Romans," just as it "is **for** modern Americans." What's being compared is **the hazard for** Romans and Americans, not the hazard to Romans and Americans themselves.

18 (D) When an introductory phrase is set off by a comma, make sure it logically refers to what follows. It's not Nathanael West's first novel, or "when Nathanael West staying in Paris," that was "born Nathan Weinstein." It's Nathanael West himself, so (D)'s right.

19 (E) Reading the question stem first (always a fine idea) for question 19 warns you to be on the alert for something the author has overlooked. The author argues against the notion that fertility treatments are responsible for the increased incidence of twins by presenting an alternative explanation—that the increase has occurred because more women are having children later in life, and these older women are statistically more likely to bear twins. This sounds plausible, but remember *the key questions in GMAT causal arguments: Is the causality as simple as the author believes? Could another cause have been at work?* If women over 35 are much more likely to use fertility treatments that often result in

twin births, then it's possible that the twin births among older women are in fact due to fertility treatments. The problem (E) points out is not that the "alternative explanation" is illogical or impossible, but that it might be dependent on the very explanation it's supposed to replace.

(A) and (D) introduce irrelevant considerations. The author's argument is that fertility drugs aren't responsible for the increase in twins. It doesn't matter that, as (A) says, many of these older women aren't first time mothers. Nor does it matter that, as (D) says, these older women are no more likely to produce *identical* twins. As for (B), the author's point was simply that women over 35 are more likely to have twins than are younger women; her argument doesn't require that only women over 35 bear twins. (C) is dead wrong: since the author argues that the drugs are not responsible for the increased incidence of twins, she must believe, rather than overlook, the idea that any correlation between drugs and the increase of twin births is coincidental.

Passage 3—Predicting Earthquakes

Topic and Scope: Earthquake prediction; specifically, the passage outlines factors that contribute to earthquakes and that lend themselves to scientific measurement for prediction purposes.

Purpose and Main Idea: The author wants to show that scientists have several methods of monitoring quake-related activity and making predictions.

Paragraph Structure: Paragraph 1 explains that quakes result from identifiable, predictable phenomena. Quake prediction is based on "long- and short-range precursory phenomena." Paragraph 2 differentiates quake-prone regions along active faults near the Pacific from less quake-prone inland regions. Paragraph 3 is about the monitoring of quake-prone zones by networks of "base stations." Various types of precursors are mentioned. Paragraph 4 explains that different types of "short-term" precursors are still being identified.

The Big Picture: The topic and scope are clear from paragraph 1, but the passage goes into a lot of detail. *The way to handle details is to stay keyed to the paragraphs. In other words, don't let details distract you from bigger points.* For instance, paragraph 3 focuses on the use of base stations to monitor precursors— that's the gist there. The detailed facts about precursors should be skimmed. Don't worry about them until a question asks.

The Questions

20 **(C)** Paragraph 1 contrasts coastal regions, where crustal strains build rapidly, with inland regions, where strains build more slowly. (C) paraphrases that distinction.

(A) flatly contradicts the passage—the first paragraph states that crustal strain is great in coastal regions.

(B) contradicts the passage—quakes are less numerous in *inland* areas.

(D) also contradicts the passage—you can infer that in coastal areas, which experience frequent quakes, precursory phenomena must be common.

(E) contradicts the passage—paragraph 1 indicates that coastal regions confront thrusting sea floor plates.

21 **(E)** Choice (E) encompasses the passage's topic and scope, plus the content of all 4 paragraphs—the importance of precursors.

(A) is too narrow—the passage says little about earthquakes in inland areas.

(B) mentions introductory information in paragraph 1. It neglects the passage's topic—methods of earthquake prediction.

(C) has the same problem as (A)—it's too narrow. Coastal regions are only part of the picture in this passage.

(D) is also too narrow, and it's inconsistent with the passage. Precursory phenomena are key to earthquake prediction.

- Answers to "primary purpose" questions must be consistent with the information in every paragraph.

22 **(D)** This is the best choice. The focus of the paragraph is on "precursory phenomena," which seismologists study in order to predict quakes.

(A) is too narrow—the relationship between accumulated and critical strain only comes up at the end of the paragraph.

(B) is also too narrow—the need to space base stations at precise intervals is a minor point made at the beginning of the paragraph.

Inland and coastal areas are compared (C) in paragraphs 1 and 2, not in paragraph 3.

The paragraph never suggests "that critical strain is not spread evenly along most major fault lines," (E).

23 **(A)** Choice (A) is consistent with the concluding sentence of paragraph 3. Calculations based on an area's critical strain can help in predicting when a quake might occur.

There is nothing anywhere about calculating "the severity of an initial rupture" (B).

It's unclear what the term *seismic force* means, so (C) is no good.

(D) refers to an unrelated detail from the beginning of the paragraph.

E) is tempting, but (A) captures the idea more precisely. The passage is about earthquakes, not crustal movement in general.

24 **(D)** In question 24, the Federal government was kind enough to provide low-cost flood insurance to coastal property owners. Unfortunately, this caused a new problem—the resulting boom in coastal construction has led to dangerous land erosion. What's the best way to solve this problem? Well, in GMAT Critical Reasoning, *the first task in solving a problem is to correctly identify the cause of the problem.* The cause here is construction, both existing and expected construction. Since beachfront construction caused the erosion, a good solution would be to put an end to this construction. (D) would likely accomplish this. Not only does it discourage new construction by canceling flood insurance benefits, but it may well facilitate removal of some of the existing dwellings by compensating residents to relocate.

(A) may prevent the construction of property additions, but it wouldn't do anything to halt the boom in the construction of new buildings or to get rid of existing buildings. As for (B), we already know that the erosion rate is "dangerous"; that's why we're looking for a choice that suggests a solution. Recommending further study isn't a solution. (C) sounds like a good plan for preventing flood damage to new buildings. We are asked, however, to prevent erosion, and we're given no reason to think that elevating houses will do so. (E) makes the same mistake. (E) would protect the buildings from flood damage, but the problem we're to address is that of protecting the beaches from erosion.

25 **(B)** Think about what the sentence is telling you. The seam "is overcast . . . **in** a separate process." The seam is not "overcast . . . **instead of** a separate process."

26 **(A)** What is the author arguing? asks the question stem. Well, he says that conventional methods of measuring intelligence, such as IQ tests, classify people with Williams syndrome as retarded, on a par with Down's syndrome sufferers, because they're poor at math and can't tell left from right. He calls this label "misleading," pointing out that people with Williams syndrome are often gifted in other areas, such as language and music, whereas Down's syndrome sufferers have limited abilities in all areas. What could be his point in telling us this? Well, certainly he's saying that the conventional tests don't do a good job of evaluating the people with Williams syndrome, since they miss the gifts that these people have. That's (A): His argument is that conventional intelligence tests can't accurately measure people with disorders like Williams syndrome.

When you're asked for the author's point, be careful not to be misled by choices that simply restate a part of the author's argument. For instance, (B) may or may not be true (it's not stated by the author), but it's not the author's main point. He compares the two syndromes to make another point, about the failure of conventional intelligence tests. (C) is closer: the author seems to imply (C), but this isn't what he's trying to prove. It's merely a piece of his argument. It's something he implies on the way to making his point about the failure of intelligence tests to measure people with Williams syndrome. (D) discusses what might happen when people with Williams syndrome are diagnosed as mentally retarded, but the author's focus is on the mislabeling itself, not on its possible results. Like (C), (D) seems reasonably inferable from the argument, but isn't the point of the argument. As for (E), the author never suggests that the mathematical and spatial skills of people with Williams syndrome either can or should be developed.

27 **(E)** After reading the stem for question 27, we go to the stimulus with eyes peeled for Koch's counterargument. Koch, we learn, is unconvinced by von Pettenkoffer's dramatic demonstration. When, after drinking a bottle of bacteria, von Pettenkoffer doesn't develop cholera, he claims to have proved that the bacterium doesn't cause cholera. Koch disagrees, saying that von Pettenkoffer's stomach acid killed the bacteria before it could affect him. Be careful; we don't want to strengthen Koch's original argument—that the bacterium causes cholera, but rather his second argument—that von Pettenkoffer's stomach acid killed the bacteria. (E) says that when the cholera bacteria is ingested with bicarbonate of soda, a stomach acid

neutralizer, it's more likely that the person will develop the illness. (E), then, shows that acidity has an inhibiting effect on cholera bacteria, exactly as Koch argued.

(A) sounds intriguing, but according to Koch, the primary way of transmitting cholera can't be through ingestion. So, according to Koch, extra acid shouldn't mean fewer instances of cholera, and (A) can't support his argument. (B) would explain why von Pettenkoffer didn't catch cholera, and leave it possible that the bacterium is indeed cholera-producing, but we want evidence to support the argument that stomach acid prevented von Pettenkoffer from becoming ill. (B) weakens that argument by pointing to antibodies. If (C) is correct, and cholera is endemic in areas where the bacteria is found in the drinking water, then the disease probably is being transmitted by ingestion; this weakens the claim that stomach acid kills the bacteria. (D) is outside the scope of the passage. The existence of *E. coli* bacteria in the lower intestine cannot support Koch's argument that stomach acid kills cholera bacteria.

28 **(E)** GMAT sentences often introduce errors by separating parts of a sentence that must agree, hoping this separation will cause you to miss the fact that these parts don't. "Have" and "will continue to" are both parts of the verb here. Both must go with "perpetuate." But you can't say "they have . . . perpetuate," as (A) and (B) do. Neither can you say "it has . . . perpetuate," as (C) does. (D)'s "it has perpetuated and will continue perpetuating" is grammatical but too wordy and awkward. (E) says the same thing concisely using "it has continued to perpetuate."

29 **(C)** You can simplify long sentences like this one by zeroing in on what's being tested. The first thing to do is notice whether you see anything funny when you read the sentence. A key error is that "legislation" is singular, but *were,* its verb, is plural. So (A) can be crossed off. Scan the choices now. Don't worry about the rest of the sentence. How do the choices deal with this one error? (E) repeats it. (D)'s *has only mitigated* isn't parallel to its other verb, *abolishing.* (B)'s *has only mitigated* is not parallel to *abolishing* either. Choice (C), with *only mitigated, rather than abolished,* has two parallel verbs. *Rather than* is a connector that must link grammatically parallel terms.

30 **(A)** We need the choice that suggests most strongly that the judge was wrong to consolidate the cases. Remember, the judge agreed to consolidate the cases based on the precedent set by asbestos exposure cases. So the best way to cast doubt on the judge's decision is to break the link between the asbestos cases (his evidence) and these repetitive stress injury cases (his conclusion). (A) points out a significant difference between the two situations. In the asbestos cases the product in question was the same in each situation, while in the stress injury cases, the type and quality of office equipment is different in each case, suggesting that there may be differences in manufacturer liabilities. So there is less of a reason for combining the individual cases, and the asbestos cases make a poor precedent.

(B) is tricky. It might seem unfair that the judge's decision may benefit the defense by limiting the number of witnesses for the plaintiffs, but (B) doesn't attack the judge's reasoning, which was based on legal precedent. Instead, (B) weakens the author's argument that the decision will hurt the defense. (C) brings up a common cause of repetitive stress injuries, but doesn't tell us that it was actually the problem in these cases. More importantly, it does nothing to show that the judge was wrong to combine the cases. (D) points out a difference between asbestos exposure and repetitive stress injuries, but it's a difference in the severity of the injuries. This doesn't indicate that the judge was wrong to see a legal parallel between the two types of cases. As for (E), the judge's decision to combine the cases doesn't in any way preclude an investigation of the medical condition that the plaintiffs claim. The judge hasn't assigned responsibility or rendered a verdict, only decided on a method of proceeding with the cases.

31 **(C)** In questions like this, temporarily ignore words set off by dashes. Ignoring this material in each version should make it easier for you to "hear" what's wrong. In the original sentence, the actual subject is *each;* this singular noun doesn't agree with the plural verb *are.* (D) reverses the problem: the plural *novels* doesn't agree with the singular verb *is.* (E)'s *every one of the novels* makes the sentence a virtual run-on. (B) has subject/verb agreement but adds the awkward, wordy "each of them novels in William Kennedy's 'Albany Trilogy.' (C) is much less awkward and also features agreement between the plural *novels* and *are.*

32 **(B)** We're told that from 1977 to 1989 the percentage of their own income that the richest one percent of Americans paid to federal taxes decreased. At the same time, the proportion (or percentage) of all federal tax revenues that was paid by these same rich Americans increased. We're asked to clear up this apparent discrepancy: A lighter tax burden on the wealthy resulted in their carrying more of the overall tax load. If, as (B) has it, the richest one percent are making much more money than they once did, then the actual amount of money they pay in federal taxes can increase, even though the percentage of their own income that this amount represents decreases. This increased amount of taxes paid could represent an increased proportion of the total federal tax revenues.

(A) suggests that the IRS has increased its tax-collecting efficiency, but this is irrelevant to the question of how one percentage can increase while the other decreases. (C) could explain how taxes on the rich account for more of the total tax revenues (because more of their investments are taxable), but it doesn't explain why these increased taxes account for a smaller percentage of their incomes. (D) is an odd one: If we assume (which we can't) that the elimination of loopholes hurt the rich more than the tax cut helped them, we could see how they might pay more taxes despite the cut in the top tax rate. But that just presents us with the old problem: If they're paying more taxes, how can they be paying less of their income to taxes? On the other hand, if we assume (which we can't) that the tax cut in (D) means they're paying less in taxes, how can they be bearing more of the tax burden? *On a question asking for an explanation, avoid any choice that leaves you wondering.* (E) shows how the richest one percent account for a higher percentage of overall tax revenues. They've coughed up an additional 45 billion dollars while everyone else has only had to come up with an additional 5 billion—the 5 billion left from the 50 billion after subtracting the 45 billion that the very rich paid. However, this leaves out the other part of the dilemma—it doesn't show how they can be paying less of their income.

Passage 4—Food Contamination

Topic and Scope: Food contamination; specifically, the various hazards that can contaminate food and lead to human illness.

Purpose and Main Idea: The author's purpose is describe, not argue. The passage doesn't have a specific main idea or thesis. Instead, their authors are content to describe and discuss, rather than argue or advocate.

Paragraph Structure: Paragraph 1 is about the definition of food contamination and the three major hazards, and the reminder that it's still important to be on guard against contamination. Paragraph 2 focuses on the hazards; specifically, the most serious risk, biological. It contains a good deal of detail; note it, but it is unnecessary to memorize or even understand it all. Paragraph 3 does more of the same; continuation of biological discussion—more definitions and examples, but nothing that changes the overall idea that we must be on our guard against contamination.

The Questions

33 **(C)** Choice (C) is the only one that effectively captures the main idea of the entire passage rather than one specific aspect or detail of the passage.

(A) uses some wording from paragraph 1, but leaves out the issue of contamination altogether, and specifically the idea that knowledge of contamination is what's necessary. (B) focuses on a mere detail of paragraph 2—that biological hazards are the most serious. But that's certainly not the main point. (D) and (E) are also statements that may be true, but don't encompass the whole passage. *Wrong choices in global questions will often be true statements that nonetheless don't rise to level of Main Idea. Here, only (C) is broad enough to cover the passage's topic, scope, and purpose.*

34 **(A)** Not every inference ventures far from the main point or basic gist of the author's argument. (A) fits the bill nicely. Note how closely related this is to the author's overall point.

(B) is a distortion. Although the sources of contamination seem varied and complex, there is nothing here to suggest that a diligent food service manager will be restricted in the amount she can know about contamination.

(C) misses the scope of the passage by focusing on the decision to *hire* a manager. Even if we infer that a manager's understanding of these issues must be a consideration in hiring, since it's so important, we still can't say it's the *primary* consideration. (D) uses the extreme word "exclusively," and consequently is too extreme. In fact, the author states that prevention is only part of the battle—knowledge is also necessary so that a manager knows what to do "in the event that a . . . crisis does arise."

(E)'s pessimism is reminiscent of (B). A clear understanding of the author's purpose and tone allows us to eliminate choices like these that don't jibe with either.

The first few words of (E) are on the right track; in fact, "vitally important" is synonymous with (A)'s "crucial." But the whole choice needs to fit, and the rest of (E) misses the point.

35 **(D)** The striking term "pathogenic organisms" that appears in the question stem is relatively easy to locate in paragraph 2. Correct choice (D) comes right out of lines 23–27, with the keywords "such as" acting as the link between pathogenic microorganisms and bacteria and parasites. Even in a passage with lots of unfamiliar terms, it all boils down to good critical reading. Let's look at the wrong choices. In (A), the passage doesn't tell us what the most common form is. Nothing in paragraph 2 suggests (B), but paragraph 3 actually suggests the opposite—some microorganisms can cause disease even after being killed. A careful reading of the sentence in which "pathogenic organisms" appears shows that choice (C) distorts the meaning of the sentence. Toxins are not the same as pathogenic microorganisms. (E): How hard it is to detect pathogenic organisms is outside the scope—never mentioned or implied.

36 **(B)** It's not the new technology that's "employing the system of binomial nomenclature." Only people can do that. You need the choice that has a group of people as its subject, and that's (B) with "taxonomists." Don't be thrown by technical language. You don't have to understand anything about taxonomy or "binomial nomenclature" to see that the underlined part of this sentence should feature a subject that can be logically modified by the preceding phrase.

37 **(B)** GMAT English is precise. In everyday speech, you can get away with "I have a lot of pressure at work," when you mean "I am **under** pressure." On the GMAT you can't. You have to use the correct idiomatic phrase, which is "**under pressure to** show high profits." Choices (C) and (D) both use "showing;" always be wary of "–ing" verbs. (E) adds needless verbiage.

38 **(B)** Question 38's stimulus describes how two regions of a country were affected differently by the same crisis. Although demand for both the tropical crops of Region A and the basic food-stuffs of Region B was only slightly affected by the drop in income levels after 1929, Region A was much more affected by the decrease in demand. The author gives us a hint when she says that Region B "could adjust the supply of its crops." *Whenever we get a hint on an "explanation" question, we take it.* So what we look for when we go to the choices is the reason why Region B was able to survive the decrease in demand by adjusting the supply of its crops, while Region A could not make these adjustments. The best reason is provided by (B): Since annual crops are renewed each year, the supply can easily be adjusted for the following year. Perennial crops, however, live longer than one year, so adjusting the supply isn't easy. What you plant one year has an impact on the supply of crops for a long time; small, quick adjustments can't be easily made. So (B) provides information, consistent with the clue we found in the stimulus, that explains why Region A's farmers couldn't follow the example of their colleagues in Region B. Even if you were confused by annual versus perennial, (B) explicitly tackles the question of why Region B's crops were more easily adjusted. That's a tip-off that (B) is correct.

Now you might have wondered exactly why all of this was so. You might have tried to understand what economic forces were at play here. If you did, that was a mistake. *Like Reading Comprehension, Critical Reasoning isn't about understanding every background detail. It's about understanding what the author is interested in telling you.* Here that's the information in the last two sentences.

(A) tells us that Region A's crops cost more than Region B's crops, but we've already been told that demand for Region A's crops hasn't dropped much, so we can't take this to mean that the Depression made Region A's crops unaffordable. In general, one would expect the higher prices for Region A's crops to make its economy stronger. (C) says that Region A's tropical goods are less prone to drops in demand. Again, that's not bad news for A's farmers, so it doesn't explain the disaster that befell them; besides, the stimulus already told us that demand for the two regions' crops dropped about the same. (D) tells us about the competition that Region B faced; clearly that doesn't help to explain its success, or Region A's failure. (E) just expands on information we already have. We knew that demand for region B's crops only declined a bit—now we know why. The problem is that demand also dropped only a bit for Region A, so (E) does nothing to explain the differing fortunes of the two regions' economies.

39 **(A)** In a complicated sentence like this, it's probably best to focus on eliminating wrong answers. There are some wrong phrases that are obvious, for instance, the awkward, unidiomatic "such a number of Astronomy majors in a given year as there are today," in (D). There's also the confusing "a number of Astronomy majors such as there are today," in (C). It's unclear what that phrase means, and (C) also begins with the illogical "while." Looking at the other choices, you see that (B) is both awkward and confusing. The meaning of "as many . . . as there are in a given year today" is unclear, and (B) also makes Mitchell a "founding professor," whatever that is. (E) has the bizarre locution "a number . . . just as large . . . as the number that is there today." This is both awkward and ungrammatical; "the number that **are** there" would at least be correct.

Notice how much text is underlined in this sentence. There will only be a few such questions in each section, and they're good ones to take a quick guess on if you're pressed for time.

40 **(E)** You need to be precise and logical to get a question like this right, but you don't need to be a grammar expert. Think about what the sentence is trying to tell you. Chesnutt's fiction reflects the "interests of his contemporary 'local colorists,'" and it also reflects "the intellectual ferment" of the time. In short, his fiction reflects one thing **as much as it does** another. The word "does" is critical; it's what makes the phrase idiomatic. Choice (E) is correct because it alone contains this logical and idiomatic form of comparison. (E)'s "does" is also the only verb that correctly parallels the verb "reflects" in the first part of the sentence. Choices (B), (C), and (D) all contain verbs—"did," "had," and "was"—that aren't consistent with the present-tense "reflects;" they all add awkwardly wordy phrasing, too.

41 **(A)** Be familiar with idioms likely to appear on the GMAT. The correct idiomatic construction is "just as . . . , so . . ." Knowing this, you can narrow the choices down to (A) and (E) here. What follows "just as" must parallel what follows "so." That's why (E) can't be right: "Just as the various **languages**" isn't parallel to "so **it is** in U.S. culture." In (A), "the various languages" correctly parallels "the many musical traditions."

Part Five

Getting Into Business School

CHAPTER FOURTEEN

Where to Apply

HIGHLIGHTS

- Find the right kind of school for you
- Review the key criteria for selecting a program
- Assess your chances of getting in

The question of where you should apply is usually a two-part question. First: Which business schools should you consider, regardless of your chances? And second: Which of these schools can you actually get into?

What Schools Should You Consider?

Once you've made the decision to pursue graduate business management studies, the decision about where to go to school shouldn't be taken lightly. It will have a major influence over your daily life for the next several years and will influence your academic and career paths for years to come. Many students allow themselves to be influenced by a professor or mentor or rankings in popular magazines, then find that they're unhappy in a certain program because of its location, workload, cost, or some unforeseen factor. With all those scary things said, remember: This is for your own good! Some hard work today will help to ensure that you'll be happy in your choice tomorrow. Let's take a look at some of the factors that you'll need to consider when choosing a school.

Overall Reputation

Each year, several publications release rankings of business schools. You should start with reviewing these rankings because they will provide you with a frame of reference for how different schools are regarded in the marketplace.

Kaplan Business School Forums

Kaplan Educational Centers offers Business School Forums and seminars every year in several cities. Forum attendees will meet representatives from individual business schools and listen to panelists discuss how an M.B.A. has enhanced their career. Topics covered include the secrets of the GMAT, how to get into business school, and women and M.B.A.'s. Visit www.kaplan.com or call (800) KAP-TEST for more details.

Although you should not place too much stock in the rankings, you should consider a program's overall reputation. The higher your school is regarded in the marketplace, the better your job prospects are likely to be upon graduation. You will notice that there is a general correlation between schools' rankings and starting salaries.

You should find out which programs are highly regarded in the areas that interest you. Which schools are viewed as responsive to students' changing needs, and which schools are seen as less responsive? What schools are "hot"? How have they earned that designation?

Teaching Methods

Business school professors teach using the case method, lectures, or, in most cases, a combination of both. Everyone learns differently, so select a school with a teaching environment that allows you to thrive.

A lecture-based classroom is, in all likelihood, what you experienced as an undergraduate. The professor provides information, and interaction between the students and the professor, or between the students, is controlled and generally limited. In a case-method environment, on the other hand, the professor doesn't lecture but rather facilitates an open dialogue with the students by asking probing questions and giving students most of the "air time."

Each class revolves around actual business situations, and students are cast in the role of decision maker. For example, you're given the facts about a struggling business, and you're placed in charge and must develop a plan to improve the performance of the business. The case method is particularly popular at programs that specialize in teaching general management. Harvard Business School and Virginia's Darden School are two of the better-known schools that use the case method as their principal teaching tool.

Is one teaching method inherently better than the other? That depends on you. Some students prefer the more controlled, structured environment of traditional lectures. Others thrive on the case method, in which a less formal, no-holds-barred, open forum encourages many viewpoints but provides no single answer.

Some students feel that the case method is better suited to some subjects than others. A marketing case on new product introductions, for example, may lead to a riveting class discussion. But the case method can be a ponderous way to learn accounting principles.

Case Method

Many business schools use the case method—a teaching method that uses real-life business cases for analysis and requires each student to participate actively in classroom discussions. If you think that you might not thrive in this type of environment, you should consider schools that use a more traditional, lecture-based approach.

Another issue to keep in mind is that in a case-method classroom, as much as half of your grade will be based on class participation. If you are someone who needs no encouragement to air your views, you'll have no problem. If, however, you think you'd be less than eager to participate in this type of forum, you should seriously consider whether it would be the right environment for you.

Most programs enhance the value of your educational experience by exposing you to real-world situations where possible. For example, many schools will encourage students to undertake a field study in their second year. Business simulations, computer-based programs that enable you to test your decision-making skills, are also a popular teaching tool.

Computers

In an ongoing effort to adapt to technological change, most business schools have completely integrated personal computers into their programs. Many schools will require you to have your own laptop computer. The degree to which you'll be expected to use the computer will vary by program, but you should make an effort to have at least a minimum comfort level with computers before starting school.

School Location

The two key questions that you should consider regarding a school's location are: How will it affect the overall quality of your business school experience, and how will it affect your employability? Some students prefer an urban setting. Others prefer a more rustic environment. Some want their business school to be part of the overall university campus; others would like a separate campus.

Geography may be an important criterion for you. Perhaps you're constrained by a spouse's job. Or perhaps you know where you want to live after graduation. You won't be limited in where you can find a job if you graduate from a school that has a national reputation, but if you attend a school with more of a regional name, be sure that it is highly regarded in that area.

For some students, two years of trying out an unfamiliar part of the country may be a terrific experience, regardless of where they head after graduating. For others, who, for example, hate cold weather, there may be little gained by going to school in a cold weather state.

Computer Tip

Most B-schools require the use of a computer, particularly for spreadsheet analysis. You should at least be comfortable using a computer before classes begin.

Curriculum

To maximize the value of your business school experience, be sure that a school's curriculum matches up with your own interests. If your primary interest is general management, then seek out those programs whose strengths include general management.

The top-tier schools tend to be strong in all areas, but even the elite programs are viewed as having particular specialties. For example, Kellogg is thought to be especially strong for marketing, Wharton for finance, and Harvard for general management. Of course, many Harvard M.B.A.'s pursue finance careers; Wharton grads, marketing; and Kellogg grads, general management. You should, nevertheless, familiarize yourself with the general marketplace perceptions about the programs you're considering. It will help you think more clearly about the selection process.

Remember, there's no right or wrong way to learn about business. Find an environment that works best for you. Don't put yourself in a situation in which you don't have access to the courses or training you're seeking. It's your education. Your time. Your energy. Your investment in your future. By being proactive, you can help guarantee that you maximize your B-school experience.

Faculty

The quality of a school's faculty is important and is reflected in each program's reputation. An important question to ask, though, is will you get to take classes with a school's marquee professors? With the proliferation of executive education programs, top teachers at many highly ranked schools are sometimes assigned to teach executive education students instead of M.B.A.'s. If one of your prime motivations in attending a certain program is to take classes from specific professors, make sure that you will have that opportunity.

Competitiveness

By its nature, and by the nature of the students it attracts, business school also fosters a competitive environment. Programs are filled with students who are bright, talented, and ambitious. But business is also about cooperation—working together towards a common goal. Many schools have addressed this by introducing team-based learning into their curricula.

Some schools have reputations for fostering an intense environment, whereas others are considered more supportive. Try not to base your perceptions about the academic environment at various schools on the schools' reputations alone. Sit in on first-year classes to assess the dynamics. Ask yourself: Do the students work well together? Do they support each other? Do they treat each other with respect, even when they disagree? Does the professor facilitate a positive learning atmosphere?

You should also determine what kind of learning environment you prefer. Then take a look at how different programs strike the balance between competition and cooperation. Find out about each school's grading system. When a program grades on a forced curve, some students feel motivated and others feel unwanted pressure. How do you think you'd react to it?

When you visit a school, talk to students to learn how they feel about the environment. You'll probably get a variety of viewpoints, but there's no better way to get a feel for what a school is like, what the students are like, and how you will fit in there.

Placement

When you get right down to it, the main purpose of attending business school is to enhance your career prospects, both short- and long-term. Look into each school's placement records to find out:

- How many companies recruit on campus?

- What kinds of companies recruit on campus?

- Are these companies that you might have an interest in?

- What percentage of the class has job offers by graduation?

- What is the breakdown of jobs by industry?

- What is the average starting salary?

Try not to overemphasize the significance of average starting salary when you evaluate programs. Although there is a correlation between the top-ranked schools and starting salaries, keep in mind that there are a number of factors that will determine your starting salary and your overall attractiveness to prospective employers. For example, some recruiters will place a high value on your pre–business school experience. To other companies, your B-school academic record will be most important.

Also, some industries, notably management consulting and investment banking, pay at the high end of the spectrum. So the salary statistics of schools that send a high percentage of students into these fields are skewed upward.

If you enroll in a traditional two-year program, learn about summer job opportunities between your first and second year. For one thing, the

Job Placement

You should look closely at the placement data of the B-schools that you are considering applying to. Make sure that their graduates have a reasonable success rate in finding good jobs.

money will be helpful. For another, your summer position can give you first-hand experience in a new job or industry that you can leverage when you graduate. Many summer jobs ultimately lead to full-time offers. Plus, a substantive summer experience will make you a more attractive job candidate for prospective employers.

Finally, don't just look at the first jobs that a school's graduates take. Where are they in 5, 10, and even 25 years? Your career is more like a marathon than a sprint. So take the long view. A strong indicator of a school's strength is the accomplishments of its alumni.

Class Profile

Because much of your learning will come from your classmates, especially in case-method classes, consider the make-up of your class. A school with a geographically, professionally, and ethnically diverse student body will expose you to far more viewpoints than will a school with a more homogeneous group.

To get a feel for the class profile of a particular school, take a look at these readily available statistics:

- Undergraduate areas of study
- Percentage of international students
- Percentage of women
- Percentage of minorities
- Percentage of married students
- Average years of work experience
- Types of companies for which students worked
- Average age and age range of entering students

Let's take a closer look at average age. Over the past few decades, students attending business school have been getting older. Currently, the average age of the entering student is approximately 27 at many of the top schools. But the average is a little misleading because it consists of many 26 year-olds and significantly fewer 30-, 40-, and 50-year-olds who skew the average age upward.

So, if you're an older applicant, ask yourself how you will fit in with a predominantly younger group of students. For many, the fit is terrific. For others, the transition is tougher. The answer depends on you, but it's something to consider.

Class and Section Size

Class size and structure are two factors that will have a significant impact on your business school experience. Some students prefer the intimacy of a smaller class and the opportunity to get to know everyone. Others prefer the energy of a larger class and the increased resources and facilities that it can support.

Many programs divide the class into sections, also known as *cohorts,* and have students take all or most of their first-year classes with that same group. In fact, at some schools, section members actually stay in the same classroom and the professors rotate among rooms.

There are several advantages to the section concept. By working with the same classmates day after day, you build a camaraderie borne out of a shared, often intense, first-year experience. You get to know each other in a way that is not possible in a more traditional classroom structure. More likely than not, you'll forge lasting relationships with your section mates. The downside of the section system is that you have less exposure to classmates who are not in your section. Organized club activities, however, enable you to meet other students outside the classroom who share your interests.

Networking

Forging relationships—with your section mates, your classmates, and, in a larger sense, all the alumni—is a big part of the business school experience. One of the things that you'll take with you when you graduate, aside from an education, a diploma, and debt, is that network. And whether you thrive on networking or consider it a four-letter word, it's a necessity. At some point it may help you advance your career, land a piece of business, or perhaps even finance a new venture.

Many programs have large, organized networks that you can access. This is a strong selling point for those schools. Like any other single factor, don't make networking potential your sole criterion, but keep it in mind as you evaluate programs.

Workload

Think about how hard you are prepared to work. It's generally true that the more effort you put in the more you'll gain, but some programs really pile it on first-year students. That can limit the amount of time and energy that you'll have left to devote to outside activities.

For students with families, the first year of B-school requires not just a sacrifice of income but of time that you can spend with your spouse or children. Don't underestimate how all-encompassing your first year will be. At some point this can be a strain on even the strongest relationships. Fortunately, the second year tends to be more manageable.

B-School Tip

Don't be reluctant to ask admissions officers, professors, or students about the nature and volume of the work that is expected of students at their school.

If you enroll in a part-time program, the time constraints may be even more severe because you have to handle the rigors of your course load on top of your job.

Quality of Life

Your business school experience will extend far beyond your classroom learning, particularly for full-time students. That's why it's so important to find out as much as you can about the schools that interest you. For example, what activities would you like to take part in? Perhaps convenient recreational facilities or an intramural sports program is appealing. If you'd like to be involved in community activities, perhaps there's a school volunteer organization. Regardless of your interests, your ability to maintain balance in your life in the face of a rigorous academic challenge will help you keep a healthy outlook.

Housing is another quality-of-life issue to consider. Is campus housing available? Is off-campus housing convenient? Is it affordable? Where do most of the students live?

Quality of life is also an important consideration for spouses and significant others, especially if school requires a move to a new city. When the first year takes over your life, your spouse may feel left out. Find out what kind of groups and activities there are for partners. For example, are there any services to help your spouse find employment?

Full Time versus Part Time

In a full-time program, you can focus your energy on your studies to maximize your learning. You're also likely to meet more people and forge closer relationships with your classmates. Many programs are oriented toward the full-time student and that many top-tier programs don't offer part-time programs. A part-time schedule may also make it difficult for you to take classes with the best professors.

There are, however, many compelling reasons attending part time may make sense for you. It may just not be economically feasible for you to attend full time. Or perhaps your employer is willing to subsidize part or all of the cost if you continue working. You also may not want to abandon the career track that you're on.

Although some prospective employers may place more value on an M.B.A. earned full time, others recognize and respect the commitment required to complete an M.B.A. part time. If you decide to attend business school part time, the good news is that there are many fine programs from which to choose.

Free Time

During your B-school career, you will have a life outside of the classroom (though it may not feel that way at first). Make sure the activities that interest you are readily available at the schools you're considering.

Full Time

Attending B-school full time, when possible, is usually the best option. It allows you to focus on your studies, build relationships with your classmates, and take courses with the best professors.

KAPLAN

M.B.A. versus Executive Education

For most applicants with two, three, or four years of work experience, executive education is not a feasible option because they don't have enough experience. But if you are a middle manager or a small-business owner with a need for functional training, executive education programs may be worth exploring.

Executive education programs, a growing area for many business schools, essentially bring together individuals with similar educational needs and provide a focused, intensive learning experience. For example, middle managers with 10 to 15 years experience may attend a 12-week, full-time program to study such core subjects as marketing, finance, operations, and management accounting. It's sort of a mini-M.B.A.

If the M.B.A. is important for you as a credential, be aware that executive education programs generally do not award M.B.A.'s. If your organization will be sponsoring you and you plan to stay there, this may be an invaluable career opportunity that you don't want to pass up.

If you are looking for training in very specific areas, then perhaps much of an M.B.A. program's curriculum would not be of interest to you, and executive education would make more sense. So although executive education is not a substitute for an M.B.A., you may find it worth considering.

Where Can I Get In?

Now that you've developed a list of schools that meet your needs, you should take an objective look at your chances of getting into them.

Assessing Your Chances

An important first step is to take a hard look at yourself. A good way to get a sense of how business schools will perceive you is to make up a fact sheet with your GMAT scores (or projected scores), your grade point average (GPA), and your work experience. Outside activities will contribute to the overall "score" that admissions officers will use to evaluate you, but let's stick with the raw data for now.

The next step is to find a current source of information about B-school programs. There are several guides published every year that provide data about acceptance rates for given years, median GPA, and GMAT scores; check out, for example, Kaplan/*Newsweek's* annual careers guide. The

Part Time

Attending B-school part time may be right for you if your employer agrees to pay for your education or if you want to stay on your career track.

Executive Education

Executive education may be the ticket for you if you're a middle manager or small-business owner who needs training in core business subjects.

Application Tips

Put your GMAT score and GPA alongside the median numbers of the schools that interest you. The comparison will give you a general idea of where you stand, but remember that schools don't just look at their applicants' numbers.

Safety Schools

You should apply to at least one school that is virtually certain to accept you. Make sure that it's a school that you would actually attend.

Dream Schools

Apply to one or two very competitive schools. You might be pleasantly surprised. Again, apply only to schools that you would actually attend.

school of your dreams may not care very much about your GPA, but it might be very interested in your GMAT score. Make sure you find out what your target school prioritizes in its search for worthy applicants.

One of the best ways to gauge whether you're in contention for a certain program is to compare your numbers to theirs. And remember that you needn't hit the nail on the head. Median means average, so some applicants do better or worse than the GMAT score or GPA cited. And, remember all those other factors, most importantly your work experience, that add up to make you a desirable applicant. Comparing numbers is merely a good way to get a preliminary estimate of your compatibility with the schools of your choice.

"Safe" Schools

Now that you have some idea of where you fall in the applicant pool, you can begin to make decisions about your application strategy. Some students waste their time and money with a scatter-gun approach, shooting off applications to a host of schools.

No matter what your circumstances, it's wise to choose at least one school that is likely to accept you. Make sure it's one that fits your academic goals and your economic circumstances. If your GMAT scores and GPA are well above a school's median scores, and you don't anticipate any problems with other parts of your record or application, you've probably found a safe school.

"Wishful Thinking" Schools

Reach high and apply to one or two very competitive programs. You may be surprised! Some people underestimate their potential and apply only to "sure thing" schools. This can often lead to disappointment when they end up at one of these schools and discover that it doesn't provide the rigorous training that they want. This doesn't mean that everyone should apply to the top one or two schools. Your "wishful thinking" school may be a less competitive school.

CHAPTER FIFTEEN

When to Apply

- Learn how to set up an application schedule
- Keep track of important deadlines

With business school applications on the rise again, the issue of when to apply for admission has become very important. There are perfect times to begin and end the application process. You should begin a year before you plan to enter school. Find out the following essential dates as early as possible and incorporate them into your own personal application schedule:

- Standardized test registration deadlines
- Transcript deadlines (some schools send out transcripts only on particular dates)
- Letters of recommendation
- Application deadlines (submit your application as early as possible to ensure that you get a fair and comprehensive review)
- Financial aid forms (federal/state programs, universities, and independent sources of aid all have definite deadlines)

Setting Up an Application Schedule

The following "seasonal" schedule is organized to help you understand how to proceed through the admissions process.

Summer

- Request applications from schools. If they're not available yet, ask for last year's so you can get a feel for the questions you'll have to answer.

Mark Your Calendar

Keep track of the deadlines for the GMAT, admissions applications, financial aid forms, and other materials. Submit everything on time; missing a deadline may be fatal to your admissions chances.

GMAT Registration at a Glance

- GMAT, Distribution & Receiving Center, 225 Phillips Boulevard, Ewing, NJ 06828-7435
- E-mail: gmat@ets.org
- Phone (800) GMATNOW or (609) 771-7330
- Fax (609) 883-4349
- The *GMAT Information Bulletin* has details about registering for the GMAT. It is available from ETS by mail. You can also find it at most Kaplan Centers and colleges and universities.
- Check ETS's Website at www.gmat.org for complete information about registering for the GMAT.
- Register early to secure the time you want at the test center of your choice.
- Cost at press time: $190.00 (USD) worldwide.

- Write drafts for your essays and talk them over with others.
- Browse through business school catalogs and collect information on different grants and loans. Create your own B-school library.
- Consider registering for the GMAT in the fall. This will give you plenty of time to submit your scores with your application.
- Research your options for test preparation. Take the test included in this book to give you a good idea of where you stand with regard to the GMAT.

Early Fall

- Ask for recommendations. Make sure that your recommenders know enough about you to write a meaningful letter. Once your recommenders have agreed to write a recommendation, let them know when deadlines will be, so you can avoid any timing conflicts.

Late Fall

- Take the GMAT.
- Request applications from schools, if you haven't already done so.
- Request institutional, state, and federal financial aid materials from school aid offices.
- Request information on independent grants and loans.
- Order transcripts from your undergraduate (and any graduate) institution(s).

Winter

- Fill out applications. Mail them as early as possible.
- Fill out financial aid applications. Mail these early as well.
- Make sure your recommendation writers have the appropriate forms and directions for mailing. Remind them of deadline dates.

Spring

- Sit back and relax (if you can). Most schools indicate how long they will take to inform you of their decision. This is also a crucial time to solidify your financial plans as you begin to receive offers of aid (with any luck).

The timing described here is rough, and you needn't follow it exactly. The most important thing for you to do is make yourself aware of strict deadlines well in advance, so that you'll be able to give your application plenty of quality time.

CHAPTER SIXTEEN

How to Apply

···

- Find out what B-schools look for
- Learn how to assemble a winning application
- Ace your application essay and interview

···

Your first step is to order the application forms from the various schools that you've selected. You can do it by mail, but the quickest way is to call the admissions offices around July and have them put you on their mailing lists. Once the applications begin arriving you'll notice one thing quickly: No two applications are exactly alike. Some ask you to write one essay or personal statement, and others may ask for three or more. Some have very detailed forms requiring extensive background information; others are satisfied with your name and address and little else.

Despite these differences, most applications follow a general pattern with variations on the same kinds of questions. So read this section with the understanding that, although not all of it is relevant to every application, these guidelines will be valuable for just about any business school application that you'll encounter.

How Do Schools Evaluate Applicants?

Each business school has its own admissions policies and practices, but all programs evaluate your application on a range of objective and subjective criteria. Regardless of which schools you are pursuing, understanding how admissions officers judge your candidacy can give you a leg up on the competition.

Kaplan Admissions Consulting

Kaplan Admissions Consulting provides personal, one-to-one admissions advice. We help you:

- Select appropriate schools and programs
- Develop polished applications
- Brainstorm and create winning essays
- Master the art of interviewing
- Deal with special circumstances

For more information about Admissions Consulting, call (800) KAP-TEST or E-mail us at admissions@kaplan.com.

Academic Record

In reviewing your academic record, admissions officers will look at:

- Your GPA
- The reputation of your undergraduate school
- The difficulty of your courses
- Your performance in quantitative courses

Generally, all admissions officers use the application process to measure your intellectual abilities, management skills, and personal characteristics. When you submit your application, admissions officers will evaluate the total package. Most admissions officers look for reasons to admit candidates, not for reasons to reject them. Your challenge, therefore, is to distinguish yourself positively from the other candidates.

Intellectual Ability

To assess your intellectual ability, admissions officers look at two key factors: your academic record and your GMAT score.

Academic Record

Your grade point average (GPA) is important, but it's just part of the picture. Admissions officers will consider the reputation of your undergraduate institution and the difficulty of your courses. Admissions officers are well aware that comparing GPAs from different schools and even different majors from the same school is like comparing apples and oranges. So they'll look closely at your transcript. Do your grades show an upward trend? How did you perform in your major? How did you fare in calculus and other quantitative courses?

Admissions officers focus primarily on your undergraduate performance, but they will consider graduate studies and nondegree coursework that you have completed. Be sure to submit those transcripts.

If you have a poor academic record, it will be tougher to get into a top school, but by no means impossible. Your challenge is to find other ways to demonstrate your intellectual horsepower. A high GMAT score, intelligently written essays, and recommendations that highlight your analytical abilities will help. If your record does not show any evidence of quantitative skills, you should consider taking courses in accounting and statistics to demonstrate your aptitude.

GMAT

An integral part of the admissions process at virtually all schools, the GMAT measures general verbal and quantitative skills and is designed to predict academic success in the first year of a graduate business school program.

When admissions officers review your GMAT score, they'll look primarily at your overall score. However, they'll also look at your quantitative and verbal subscores, particularly if they have any questions about your abilities in either area. If you've taken the GMAT more than once, schools will generally credit you with your highest score, though some may average the scores or take the most recent.

Used by itself, the GMAT may not be a great predictor of academic performance, but it is the single best one available. The GMAT does not measure your intelligence, nor does it measure the likelihood of your success in business. As with any standardized test, by preparing properly for the GMAT, you can boost your score significantly.

The GMAT contains two essay sections, dubbed the "Analytical Writing Assessment" (AWA). The essays you type into the computer are graded on a 1 to 6 scale and sent to the schools you designate along with your traditional 200–800 score. The AWA is designed to provide schools with information about your communications skills that is not otherwise captured in the GMAT.

Essentially, the AWA is another tool that schools can use to evaluate you. Although it won't reduce the importance of the essays on your applications, it may alter the number of essays a school asks you to write. Business schools have recognized that the AWA provides you with an opportunity to demonstrate your ability to think critically and communicate complex ideas in a very limited time period. For that reason, admissions officers may be as interested in reading your writing samples as they are in relying solely on your GMAT score.

Even though the AWA is scored separately from the multiple-choice sections, you should prepare for it with the same intensity that you put into preparing for the rest of the GMAT. Outstanding writing samples can help you stand out from the crowd. Conversely, seriously flawed essays can reduce your admissions chances.

Management Skills

To evaluate your management skills, admissions officers look at work experience and other relevant activities. That does not mean that you need to have managed people to be an impressive candidate. Perhaps you've managed projects, resources, or portfolios. Each of these can provide an excellent forum for you to demonstrate evidence of your management aptitude.

You can communicate some of your management abilities through the straightforward "data" part of your application. Be sure to describe your job responsibilities. Don't list your title and assume that an admissions offi-

Note

Scoring high on the GMAT will help you get into the B-school of your choice. Preparation is the key to GMAT success.

Management Skills

To measure an applicant's management potential, admissions officers look at a person's work experience. Whether you've managed people, projects, resources, or portfolios, you should use that experience as a springboard to demonstrate your management aptitude.

cer knows what you do or the level of your responsibilities. This is especially important if your job is nontraditional for an aspiring M.B.A.

Admissions officers will look at your overall career record. How have you progressed? Have you been an outstanding performer? What do your recommendation writers say about your performance? Have you progressed to increasingly higher levels of responsibility? If you have limited work experience, you will not be expected to match the accomplishments of an applicant with ten years experience, but you will be expected to demonstrate your abilities.

The essays also provide an opportunity to demonstrate your management aptitude. Many essay questions specifically ask you to discuss your professional experiences and how you handled different situations. With thoughtful, well-written essays you can highlight your management strengths for admissions officers.

Extracurricular activities and community involvement also present opportunities for you to highlight your skills. For younger applicants, college activities play a more significant role than for more seasoned applicants. Your activities say a lot about who you are and what's important to you. Were you a campus leader? Did your activities require discipline and commitment? Did you work with a team? What did you learn from your involvement?

Personal Characteristics

Most admissions officers look for applicants who show leadership, maturity, integrity, responsibility, and teamwork.

Active community involvement provides a way for you to demonstrate your management skills and to impress admissions officers with your personal character. In fact, many applications ask directly about community activities. If you are contemplating getting involved in your community, here's a chance to do something worthwhile and enhance your application in the process.

Personal Characteristics

The third, and most subjective, criterion on which schools evaluate you is your personal characteristics. Admissions officers judge you in this area primarily through your essays, recommendations, and personal interview (if applicable). Although different schools emphasize different qualities, most seek candidates who demonstrate leadership, maturity, integrity, responsibility, and teamwork.

The more competitive schools place special emphasis on these criteria because they have many qualified applicants for each available spot in the class. In fact, the top-tier programs generally require numerous essays so that they can get a complete feeling for each applicant's personal qualities.

KAPLAN

Who Reviews Your Application?

At most schools, the board includes professional admissions officers. And at some schools, second year students and/or alumni play a role in reviewing applications and interviewing candidates.

Admissions officers are not always representative of the group of students they admit. Many boards contain a high percentage of women and minorities. Board members recognize the importance of diversity in the classroom and in many cases have a mandate to increase it. Although some admissions officers have had management training and business experience, many have not. They tend to be people-oriented and have strong interpersonal skills. They want to get to "know" you through your application, and they are partial to well-written essays.

What Decisions Do They Make?

Upon reviewing your application, the admissions board may make any number of decisions, including:

- **Admit:** Congratulations, you're in. But read the letter carefully. The board may recommend or, in some cases, require you to do some preparatory coursework to ensure that your quantitative or language skills are up to speed.

- **Reject:** At the top schools, there are far more qualified applicants than there are spaces in the class. Even though you were rejected, you can reapply at a later date. However, if you are considering reapplying, you need to understand why you were rejected and whether you have a reasonable chance of being admitted the next time around. Some schools will speak with you about your application, but they often wait for the end of the admissions season, by which time you may have accepted another offer.

- **Deferred admit:** This decision is reserved for when the admissions board considers you a strong candidate, but believes you would benefit from an additional year or two of work experience before attending. Because most applicants now have at least two years experience before applying to school, deferred admission is not as common now as it once was.

- **Reject with encouragement to reapply:** This isn't just a polite rejection. One step down from a deferred admit, it's a way for a school to say, "we like you, and we think with more experience you'd be a strong candidate."

- **Hold over until the next decision period:** Sometimes the admissions board isn't comfortable making a decision by the scheduled reply

Application Tip

Admissions officers want to get to know you through your application. Make it easy for them.

Admissions Decisions at a Glance

Here's a rundown of the types of decisions that admissions boards make:

- Admit
- Reject
- Deferred admit
- Reject with encouragement to reapply
- Hold over until the next decision period
- Waiting list
- Request for an interview

date. Perhaps you're right on the borderline, and the board wants to see how you stack up against the next group of applicants. In this case, all you can do is wait, but frequently the result is positive.

- **Waiting list:** Schools use the waiting list—the educational equivalent of purgatory—to manage class size. The good news is that you wouldn't be on the list if you weren't considered a strong candidate. The bad news is there is no way to know with certainty whether you'll be accepted. Be aware, though, that schools do tend to look kindly upon wait-listed candidates who reapply in a subsequent year.

- **Request for an interview:** Schools at which an interview is not required may request that you interview prior to making their final decision. Your application may have raised some specific issues that you can address in an interview, or perhaps the board feels your essays did not give them a complete enough picture to render a decision. Look at this as a positive opportunity to strengthen your case.

Preparing Your Application

A key part of getting into the business school of your choice is to develop a basic application strategy so you can present yourself in the best light.

Your Application as a Marketing Tool

When it comes to applying to business school, you are the product. Your application is your marketing document. Marketing yourself doesn't mean that you should lie or even embellish; it just means that you need to make a tight presentation of the facts. Everything in your application should add up to a coherent whole and underscore the fact that you are not only qualified to be in the class but that you should be in it.

Many application forms have a certain tone, one that's comforting and accepting. Why would you like to come to our school, they seem to be asking. They do want an answer to that question, but what's even more important—the subtext for the whole application process—is a bigger question: Why should we accept you? This is the question that your application will answer. And with some effective marketing strategies, your answer will be clear, concise, coherent, and strong.

So how do you portray an image? First of all, it should fit; it should be natural. Don't bother to try to sell yourself as something you're not: It'll be uncomfortable to you, and it probably won't work.

Application Tip

Devise a plan to present yourself that will stick in the minds of admissions officers. Remember to:

- Present facts concisely
- Double-check to make sure that information doesn't conflict
- Exclude any useless, unnecessary information

Besides, part of what readers do when they evaluate your application is form an image of you from the various parts of your application. Your job is to help them, not hinder them.

Maximizing the Various Parts of Your Application

Let's take a close look at how you should approach the specific parts of your application.

Essays

Your essays are a critical part of your application. The situations you choose to write about and the manner in which you present them can have a major bearing on the strength of your candidacy.

Writing effective essays requires serious self-examination and sound strategic planning. What are the major personal and professional events that have shaped you? What accomplishments best demonstrate your management abilities? Remember, admissions officers are interested in getting to know you as a complete person. What you choose to write about sends clear signals about what's important to you and what your values are.

Common Essay Questions

Every application is unique, but most will include essay questions that fall into one of several basic types. Here are the kinds of questions you can expect to see:

1. Describe (one, two, or three) significant accomplishments, and discuss why you view them as such.

Here, the admissions board is looking to get a sense of what you consider important. Throughout the application review process, the board will be gauging not only your management aptitude but also the kind of person you are. The events you choose to write about say a lot about you, as do the reasons you consider them significant.

2. Why are you pursuing an M.B.A.? Where do you hope to be five years from now? ten years?

Admissions officers want to see that you've thought through the reasons for going to business school, that you're committed to it, and that you have a clear understanding of what the experience is all about. Although they don't expect you to necessarily map out your entire career path, they will look for you to demonstrate forward thinking.

Essay Tip

Application essays are an opportunity for you to show admissions officers what you're really made of.

Teacher Tip

For the application, I remind them that the personal statement is the only place in this whole ordeal they they actually get to be a person. They should not waste that by drawing attention to the bad stuff. Accentuate the positive.
—Fran Longo
   Boston, MA

Application Tip

Business schools want you to tell them why they should accept you into their program. Taken together, the elements of your application should answer that question.

3. What are your strengths and weaknesses?
Answer truthfully. Don't settle for "pat" responses. When discussing your strengths, you may want to include a brief example of an experience that highlights your strengths, if length permits.

Writing about weaknesses can be tricky. The board is looking for evidence of self-awareness and maturity, but be careful about raising red flags. For example, if you apply to a case method school that requires classroom participation and you write that you're uncomfortable speaking in front of a group, the board will question whether you can thrive in that environment. Of course, you should be asking yourself the same question, anyway. Describing a weakness that's really a strength; "I'm so honest that . . . " or "I'm so committed to my employees that . . . " is a common, safe approach, but it doesn't provide much insight and it may turn off some admissions officers.

4. Describe an ethical dilemma you've faced, and discuss how you handled it.
With this question, admissions officers will evaluate not just your ethical "compass," but also your thoughtfulness, maturity, and integrity. They want to see how you think through situations in which there are no easy solutions. What's most important is that you demonstrate your ability to exercise responsible judgment and learn from difficult personal circumstances.

5. Is there anything else you would like the admissions board to know about you?
This question is your opportunity to discuss anything you haven't yet had the chance to present. For example, if your undergraduate performance is the weak link of your application, you can use this space to explain it. Or if there's a gap in your employment record that is likely to raise a red flag, now is the time to discuss it. But don't be defensive about it. Many applicants have had to overcome weak grades, unpleasant professional experiences, or difficult personal circumstances. Discussing the hardships you've faced in a straightforward, nondefensive manner and demonstrating how you've grown from the experience can help you turn a potential pitfall into a strength on your application.

6. Describe a setback or failure and discuss what you learned from it.
Regardless of the event you choose to discuss, here is an opportunity to demonstrate your thoughtfulness and maturity, as well as your capacity for growth and change.

7. If you could effect one change at your current job, what would it be?
Admissions officers recognize that many (especially younger) applicants

have not yet reached levels to make fundamental changes at work. This question lets you flex your brain power in talking about changes you'd like to see. It reveals how knowledgeable you are about business in general and your business in particular. It also provides clues about how you think. For example, do you think about big picture issues, or do you focus on the details?

8. Describe a situation in which you demonstrated . . . (teamwork, leadership, responsibility).
A question like this will give you insight into the personal qualities that a school considers especially important in its students. Be sure to discuss the specifics of the situation you present. If the question is about a leadership situation, answer such questions as: How did you demonstrate it? Did you have group meetings? Individual meetings? How did you motivate people? What was the end result? By discussing the details, you'll provide the admissions board with valuable insight into your management style and aptitude.

General Essay Tips
Once you've determined what you plan to write for each essay, keep the following tips in mind:

- **Length:** Schools are pretty specific about how long they want your essays to be. Adhere to their guidelines. If you feel you need to write an extra sentence or two, fine. But don't write three pages when an essay asks for one. If thousands of other applicants can limit their responses to one page, so can you.

- **Spelling/typos/grammar:** Remember, your application is your marketing document. What would you think of a product that's promoted with sloppy materials containing typos, spelling errors, and grammatical mistakes?

- **Write in the active voice:** Candidates who write well have an advantage in the application process because they can state their case in a concise, compelling manner. Less effective writers commonly write "passively." For example:

> Passive voice: *The essays were written by me.*
> Active voice: *I wrote the essays.*

Strong writing will not compensate for a lack of substance, but poor writing can torpedo an otherwise impressive candidate.

- **Tone:** On the one hand, you want to tout your achievements and present yourself as a poised, self-confident applicant. On the other

Essay Tip

1. Don't dwell on your weak points.
2. Don't employ dull chronological histories.
3. Don't disregard length limitations.
4. Don't lie in your essays—or in any part of your application.

Essay Tip

In the admissions world, creativity is risky. Essays that try too hard to be unique encounter a wide range of responses: amusement, boredom, confusion, and irritation, to name a few.

hand, arrogance and self-importance do not go over well with admissions officers. Before you submit your application, be sure that you're comfortable with the tone as well as the content.

- **Creative approaches:** If you choose to submit a humorous or creative application, you are employing a high risk, high reward strategy. If you're confident you can pull it off, go for it. Be aware, though, that what may work for one admissions officer may fall flat with another. Admissions officers who review thousands of essays every year may consider your approach gimmicky or simply find it distracting. Remember, your challenge is to stand out in the applicant pool in a positive way. Don't let your creativity obscure the substance of your application.

Making Your Essay Distinctive

Depending on the amount of time you have and the amount of effort you're willing to put in, you can write an essay that will stand out from the crowd. One of the first mistakes that some applicants make is in thinking that "thorough" and "comprehensive" are sufficient qualities for their essays. They try to include as much information as possible, without regard for length limitations or strategic intent. Application readers dread reading these bloated essays. So how do you decide what to include? There are usually clear length guidelines, and admissions officers prefer that you adhere to them. So, get rid of the idea of "comprehensive" and focus more on "distinctive."

Unless they ask for it, don't dwell on your weak points. A strong essay, for example, about how much you learned in your current position and how the experience and knowledge you've gained inspired you to apply to business school will give readers what they want—a quick image of who you are, how you got that way, and why you want to go to their school. One of the best ways to be distinctive is to sell your image briefly and accurately, including real-life examples to back up your points.

"Distinctive" means that your essay should answer the questions that admissions officers think about while reading essays: What's different about this applicant? Why should we pick this applicant over others? Authentic enthusiasm can be a plus, and writing about parts of your life or career that are interesting and relevant help grab a reader's attention.

The Interview

Because communication skills are such an integral part of effective management, many B-schools include personal interviews as part of the admissions process.

- **Review your application.** If you've submitted your application prior to the interview, your interviewer is likely to use it as a guide and may ask specific questions about it. Be sure you remember what you wrote.

- **Be ready to provide examples and specifics.** Professionally trained interviewers are more likely to ask you about specific situations than they are to ask broad open-ended questions. They can learn more by asking what you've done in situations than by asking what you think you'd do. Here are a few situations an interviewer may ask you to discuss: "Tell me about a recent accomplishment." "Discuss a recent situation in which you demonstrated leadership." "Give me an example of a situation where you overcame difficult circumstances." As you think about these situations, be prepared to discuss specifics—what you did and why you did it that way. You do not need to "script" or over-rehearse your responses, but you should go into the interview confident that you can field any question.

- **Be open and honest.** Don't struggle to think of "right" answers. The only right answers are those that are right for you. By responding openly and honestly, you'll find the interview less stressful, and you'll come across as a more genuine, attractive candidate.

- **Ask questions.** The interview is as much an opportunity for you to learn about the school as for the school to learn about you. Good questions demonstrate your knowledge about a particular program and your thoughtfulness about the entire process.

- **Follow proper business decorum.** Be on time, dress appropriately, and follow-up with thank you letters. Treat the process as you would a job interview, which in many respects it is.

- **Watch your nonverbal cues.** Nonverbal communication is much more important than people realize. Maintain eye contact, keep good posture, sustain positive energy, and avoid nervous fidgeting. It will help you come across as confident, poised, and mature.

- **Be courteous to the administrative staff.** These people are colleagues of the board members, and how you treat them can have an impact, either positive or negative.

- **Relax and have fun.** Interviews are naturally stressful. But by being well prepared, you can enhance your prospects for admission, learn about the school, and enjoy yourself in the process.

The Application Essay at a Glance

- Create a quick image of who you are and why you want to go to business school.
- Sell your image briefly and accurately.
- Include real-life examples to support your points.
- Make sure your enthusiasm shines through.

Interviews at a Glance

- Practice with friends beforehand.
- Dress appropriately.
- Be prepared to discuss the details in your application.
- Use the interview to flesh out your application and to impress the interviewer.

Recommendations at a Glance

Actions that you should take to help your recommenders:

- Tell them about deadline dates early.
- Arrange a meeting to discuss your background and goals.
- Give them materials to help them write their recommendation.
- Clue them in on the marketing image you're using.

Recommendation Tip

As a rule, you should waive your right to read letters of recommendation. Admissions officers place greater trust in recommendations written in confidence.

Recommendations

Whether a school requires one, two, or three recommendations, they will generally look to them as supporting documents that will confirm the substance of your other application materials. Choose recommenders who can write meaningfully about your strengths. One of the more common mistakes is to sacrifice an insightful recommendation from someone who knows you well for a generic recommendation from a celebrity or an alumnus/a. Admissions officers are not impressed by famous names. So unless that individual knows you and can write convincingly on your behalf, it's not a strategy worth pursuing. Good choices for recommenders include current and past supervisors, professors, academic and nonacademic advisers, and people you work with in community activities.

If a school requests an academic recommendation, but you are not able to provide one, try to identify someone who can discuss your intellectual attributes, particularly if your academic record is not your strength. Similarly, if requesting a recommendation from your employer would create an awkward situation, look for someone else who can comment on your management skills. Your recommendations are not likely to make or break your application, but they will confirm your strengths and in some cases help you overcome perceived weaknesses in your application.

If you wish to submit an extra recommendation, it's generally not a problem. Most schools will include the letter in your file, and those that don't will not penalize you for it. You should, however, send a note explaining why you have requested an additional recommendation so it does not appear that you can't follow instructions.

Asking for Recommendations

There are two fundamental rules of requesting recommendations: ask early and ask nicely. As soon as you decide to go to business school, you should start sizing up potential recommendation writers and let them know that you may ask them for a recommendation. This will give them plenty of time to think about what to say. Once they've agreed, let them know about deadlines well in advance to avoid potential scheduling conflicts. The more time they have, the better the job they'll do recommending you. As for asking nicely, you should let the person know you think highly of their opinion and you'd be happy and honored if they would consider writing you a letter of recommendation.

Wait! Before You Submit Your Application . . .

When you've completed your essays and you're ready to submit your application, take two more steps to ensure that your application is as strong as it can be.

- **Be sure to read your essays in the context of your entire application.** Does the total package make sense? Does it represent you favorably? Is everything consistent? Have you demonstrated your intellectual ability, management skills, and personal characteristics? Most importantly, do you feel good about the application? After all, you don't want to be rejected with an application that you don't believe represents the real you.

- **Have someone you trust and respect review your application.** Someone who has not been involved in writing the application may pick up spelling or grammatical errors that you've overlooked. In addition, because your application is an intensely personal document that requires significant self-examination, you may not be able to remain objective. Someone who knows you and can be frank will tell you whether your application has "captured" you most favorably.

Some schools prohibit you from using any outside help on your application. A last minute once-over from a friend or family member is probably within reason, but you may want to ask the school directly what is permissible.

Putting It All Together

There are no magic formulas that automatically admit you to, or reject you from, the school of your choice. Rather, your application is like a jigsaw puzzle. Each component—GPA, GMAT score, professional experience, school activities, recommendations—is a different piece of the puzzle.

Outstanding work experience and personal characteristics may enable you to overcome a mediocre academic record. Conversely, outstanding academic credentials will not ensure your admission to a top-tier school if you do not demonstrate strong management skills and solid personal character. Your challenge in preparing your application is to convince the admissions board that all of the pieces in your background fit together to form a substantial and unique puzzle.

Application Tip

Once you've finished your application, get someone else you trust to read it and make corrections and suggestions. Type your final draft and proofread it carefully. Make sure the application is perfect—that means no typos!

Application Tip

Make sure your application conveys:

- Who you are
- Why you want to go to business school
- Why the school you're applying to should accept you

Notes

Notes

Notes

Notes

How Did We Do? Grade Us.

Thank you for choosing a Kaplan book. Your comments and suggestions are very useful to us. Please answer the following questions to assist us in our continued development of high-quality resources to meet your needs.

The title of the Kaplan book I read was: _____

My name is: _____

My address is: _____

_____

My e-mail address is: _____

What overall grade would you give this book?   Ⓐ   Ⓑ   Ⓒ   Ⓓ   Ⓕ

How relevant was the information to your goals?   Ⓐ   Ⓑ   Ⓒ   Ⓓ   Ⓕ

How comprehensive was the information in this book? Ⓐ   Ⓑ   Ⓒ   Ⓓ   Ⓕ

How accurate was the information in this book?   Ⓐ   Ⓑ   Ⓒ   Ⓓ   Ⓕ

How easy was the book to use?   Ⓐ   Ⓑ   Ⓒ   Ⓓ   Ⓕ

How appealing was the book's design?   Ⓐ   Ⓑ   Ⓒ   Ⓓ   Ⓕ

What were the book's strong points? _____

How could this book be improved? _____

Is there anything that we left out that you wanted to know more about?

Would you recommend this book to others?   ☐ YES   ☐ NO

Other comments: _____

_____

_____

Do we have permission to quote you?   ☐ YES   ☐ NO

Thank you for your help.
Please tear out this page and mail it to:

Managing Editor
Kaplan, Inc.
888 Seventh Avenue
New York, NY 10106

KAPLAN

Thanks!

Plan Ahead!

When you return this form to Kaplan, you will receive a copy of Kaplan's free Financial Aid Handbook. Then, we'll send you your Federal Stafford loan application.

It's Easy!

Yes! **Please send me a Free Financial Aid Handbook, as well as an educational loan kit with an application for the Federal Stafford loan.**

Last Name _____ **First Name** _____

Permanent Address (where your applications will be mailed) _____

City _____ **State** _____ **Zip Code** _____

Phone (Daytime) _____ **Phone** (Evening) _____ **Email Address** _____

Undergraduate GPA (if applicable) _____

City _____ **State** _____ **Zip Code** _____

Top School Choice (s) _____

Earliest Start Date (month/year) _____

Please return this form to Kaplan.

You may fax it toll free any time to 1-800-844-7458, or mail to:
Att: KapLoan, 888 Seventh Avenue 22nd Floor, New York, NY 10106

kaptest.com

Educational
Loans

1-888-527-5626

KAP–34

About Kaplan

KAPLAN TEST PREPARATION & ADMISSIONS

Kaplan's nationally recognized test prep and admissions courses cover more than 30 standardized tests, including secondary school, college and graduate school entrance exams, foreign language, and medical and professional licensing exams. In addition, Kaplan offers a college admissions seminar course, one-on-one college admissions counseling, private tutoring and a variety of free information and services for students applying to college and graduate programs. Kaplan offers its services at centers worldwide and online at **www.kaptest.com**. Kaplan Learning Services partners with schools and districts to increase student success on a broad range of standardized assessments including state-wide tests and college admissions.

SCORE! LEARNING, INC.

SCORE! Educational Centers help K-10 students build confidence along with academic skills in a motivating, sports-oriented environment. ***SCORE!* Prep** provides in-home, one-on-one tutoring for high school academic subjects and standardized tests. **eScore.com** is the first educational services Web site to offer parents and kids newborn to age 8 personalized child development and educational resources online.

THE KAPLAN COLLEGES

The Kaplan Colleges system (**www.kaplancollege.com**) is a collection of institutions offering an extensive array of online and traditional educational programs for working professionals who want to advance their careers. Learners will find programs leading to professional, bachelor and associates degrees, certificates and diplomas in fields such as business, IT, paralegal studies, legal nurse consulting, criminal justice and law. The Kaplan Colleges system also includes Concord Law School (**www.concordlawschool.com**), the nation's first online law school, offering J.D. and Executive J.D.™ degrees for working professionals, family caretakers, students in rural communities, and others whose circumstances prevent them from attending a fixed facility law school.

QUEST EDUCATION

Kaplan's Quest Education unit (**www.questeducation.com**) is a leading provider of post-secondary education. Quest offers bachelor and associate degrees and diploma programs primarily in the fields of healthcare, business, information technology, fashion and design.

KAPLAN PUBLISHING

Kaplan Publishing (**kaplan.simonsays.com**) produces retail books and software. Kaplan Books, published by Simon & Schuster, includes titles in test preparation, admissions, education, career development, and life skills; Kaplan and Newsweek jointly publish guides on getting into college, finding the right career, and helping children succeed in school.

KAPLAN INTERNATIONAL

Kaplan International (**kaptest.com**) serves students and professionals, providing intensive English instruction, university preparation, test preparation programs, and housing and activities at three campuses and eight city centers in the U.S. and one center in London. Kaplan also has a strong presence overseas, with 34 centers in 16 countries outside of North America.

KAPLAN COMMUNITY OUTREACH

Kaplan provides educational career resources to thousands of financially disadvantaged students annually, working closely with educational institutions, not-for-profit groups, government agencies and grass roots organizations on a variety of national and local support programs. These programs profiled at **www.kaplan.com** help students from a variety of backgrounds achieve their educational and career goals.

KAPLAN PROFESSIONAL

Kaplan Professional provides licensing and continuing education training, certification, and professional development courses for securities, insurance, financial services, legal, IT, and real estate professionals and corporations. In addition, Kaplan Professional provides solutions to businesses to meet the demanding needs of professional education, tracking and regulatory compliance. The portal to all services is **www.kaplanprofessional.com.**

Self Test Software is a world leader in exam simulation software and preparation for technical certifications including Microsoft, Novell, Oracle, Lotus, Cisco and A+ and Network+, serving businesses and individuals.

Perfect Access Speer is the leading provider of software training and consulting to the legal market in North America.

The Schweser Study Program is the largest worldwide provider of training tools for the Chartered Financial Analyst (CFA®) examination.

Dearborn is a leading provider of licensing and continuing education training and certification for securities, insurance and financial services professionals as well as corporations, independent schools and colleges, and conducts classes in more than 160 locations throughout the U.S. and abroad (**www.dearborn.com**).

Dearborn Trade publishes more than 250 titles specializing in finance, business management and real estate, plus well-read consumer real estate books to help home buyers, sellers and real estate investors make informed decisions.

Real Estate Education Company is the nation's most comprehensive source of real estate materials for pre-and post licensing, continuing education and professional development, with training materials available in print, software, CD-ROM, and through **RECampus.com**, its online real estate campus.

Want more information about our services, products or the nearest Kaplan center?

1 **Call our nationwide toll-free numbers:**

1-800-KAP-TEST for information on our test prep courses, private tutoring and admissions consulting

1-800-KAP-ITEM for information on our books and software

1-888-KAP-LOAN* for information on student loans

2 **Connect with us online:**

On the web, go to:
www.kaptest.com
Via email:
info@kaplan.com

3 **Write to:**

Kaplan
888 Seventh Avenue
New York, NY 10106

*Kaplan is not a lender and does not participate in determination of loan eligibility.

CD-ROM Installation and Technical Support

Congratulations! You've purchased the best test prep software on the market, the software that's more fun than an abacus and more educational than an overhead projector. Our CD-ROM is the most comprehensive, instructive, and entertaining software product in the field of test prep to arrive since . . . well, since the dawn of humankind!

In this software, you get:

- Interactive Lessons detailing the famed Kaplan approaches to each question type
- Full-length and practice tests, so that you can try out your new skills as you move through the sessions;
- A plan detailing your own personalized study plan based on your needs;
- A Math review section, for reviewing mathematical concepts;
- Math and grammar flashcards;
- Fast-action games that help you review for the GMAT;
- Invaluable admissions information—and more!

The CD-ROM provides the tools that will help you devise your own personal test-taking plan. Each test you take is closely analyzed, with detailed feedback on your strategic performance, including answers to these questions:

- Do you know when you've found the right answer?
- If you have second thoughts, should you change your answer?
- Can you recognize wrong answers?
- Are you spending too much time on questions? Naturally, every question comes with a complete explanation. And our detailed scoring charts will track your progress on every type of question. Only this CD-ROM offers this range of features essential for successful test performance.

Installation Instructions

Windows™ CD-ROM:

If your CD-ROM has ID# 126201-04X:

1. Start Microsoft Windows 3.1 or later version
2. Insert the CD-ROM.
3. If you are using Windows 3.1 or 3.11, then from Program Manager, choose Run from the File menu and type d:\setup.exe (where d: is your CD-ROM drive). If you are using Windows 95 or higher, from the Start menu, choose Run and then d:\setup.exe (where d: is your CD-ROM drive.)
4. Press OK and follow the prompts

If your CD-ROM has ID# 126201-04:

1. Start Microsoft Windows 95 or higher.
2. Insert the Higher Score CD-ROM.
3. From the Start Menu, choose RUN and choose d:\setup.exe where d: is your CD-ROM drive.

Macintosh® CD-ROM:

1. Insert the CD-ROM into the drive.
2. Double-click the Install icon.
3. You will be presented with a dialog box that will let you choose Easy Install or Custom Install. If you choose Easy Install, the program will automatically install and update your files if necessary. If you choose Custom Install, you can choose where to install the different components of the program and whether to overwrite existing versions of files.
4. When installation is complete, click the icon to begin the program.

Tech Support

If you have any questions or problems that don't seem to be covered in this manual, call our tech support line at (503) 968-4058. You can speak to a tech support rep between the hours of 9 A.M. and 8 P.M. EST Monday through Friday, and between 9 A.M. and 8 P.M. EST Saturday and Sunday, or you can leave a message and a representative will get back to you the following business day. When you call, please refer to the ID number printed on the CD-ROM.

Copyright and Permission Notices

Reading passages in the tests on the *Higher Score on the GMAT* CD-ROM, as on the actual GMAT, are condensed and adapted from published material. The ideas contained in them do not necessarily represent the opinions of Kaplan Educational Centers. To make the text suitable for testing purposes, we might in some cases have altered the style or emphases of the original.

Kaplan, Inc. wishes to thank the following for permission to reprint excerpts from published material used with test questions appearing in this book and on the *Higher Score on the GMAT* CD-ROM:

"The Multisectoral Framework for the Analysis of Labor Mobility and Development in LDCs: An Application to Post-War Puerto Rico," by Carlos E. Santiago and Erik Thornbeke, *Economic Development and Cultural Change*, Vol. 37, No. 1, October 1988. Copyright © 1988 by the University of Chicago Press. Reprinted by permission of the authors and the University of Chicago Press.

"Hot Gas in the Universe," by Roger A. Chevalier and Craig L. Sarazin, *American Scientist*, November-December 1987, Vol. 75, p. 609.

Nan Elizabeth Woodruff's review of Barbara Jeanne Field's *Slavery and Freedom in the Middle Ground in Journal of Social History*, Vol. 20, Summer 1987, pp. 807–809.

"The Profit Motive in Medicine," by Dan W. Brock and Allen E. Buchanan, *Journal of Medicine and Philosophy*, Vol. 12, 1987. Copyright © by The Journal of Medicine and Philosophy, Inc. Reprinted by permission.

"Sharing the Burden of the International Debt Crisis," by Stanley Fischer, *American Economic Review*, Vol. 77, May 1977. Reprinted by permission of *American Economic Review*.

"When Are Interests Interesting? The Problem of Political Representation of Women," by Virginia Sapiro, *American Political Science Review*, Vol. 75, 1981. Reprinted by permission of *American Political Science Review*.

"Towards a Typology of Female Entrepreneurs," by Stanley Cromie and John Hayes. *Sociological Review*, Vol. 36, No. 1.

Sound effects on the CD-ROM provided courtesy of Dominion Entertainment, Inc.

Photo Credits:
© Archive Photos/Edwin Levick/PNI
© Hulton Deutsch/PNI
© Culver Pictures/PNI
© Magnum/Chris Steele-Perkins/PNI

Minimum System Requirements

For CD-ROMs with the ID number 126201-04X:

	Windows	Macintosh
Operating System:	Windows 3.1, Win95	System 7.0 or higher
CPU Type and Speed:	486SX, 50 MHz	68040 or higher
Hard Drive Space:	16.5 MB	16.5 MB
Memory:	8 MB	8 MB
Graphics:	640 x 480 x 256	640 x 480 x 256
CD-ROM Speed:	2X	2X
Audio:	16-bit	16-bit
Other:	Mouse, Modem	Mouse, Modem

Note: Internet connection required for Web features

For CD-ROMs with the ID number 126201-04:

	Windows	Macintosh
Operating System:	Windows 95 or higher	System 7.5.5 or higher
CPU Type and Speed:	486SX or higher (Pentium recommended)	Power PC
Hard Drive Space:	15 MB	18 MB
Memory:	16 MB	24 MB (more RAM is required to run with Internet browser or Virtual Memory must be enabled)
Graphics:	640 x 480 x 256 (thousands/millions recommended)	640 x 480 x 256 (thousands/millions recommended)
CD-ROM Speed:	2X	2X
Audio:	16-bit	16-bit
Other:	Mouse, Modem	Mouse, Modem

Note: Internet connection required for Web features

Software License/Disclaimer of Warranties

KAPLAN